More Praise for *Push Back*

'This important new volume is essential reading for those wishing to understand the decades-long conflict in Sri Lanka, the quest for accountability, and the challenges of building peace in the wake of conflict.'

Chandra Lekha Sriram, University of East London

'A brilliant exposition of the end game in the Sri Lankan civil war. This book is essential background reading for anyone interested in how civil wars end and the role of different actors in these processes.'

Kevin Clements, University of Otago

About the author

Judith Large is a senior research fellow at the Conflict Analysis Research Centre, University of Kent. She has over twenty-five years' experience in international conflict analysis, mediation and peacebuilding, ranging from work with civic groups and national governments to UN agencies, including the UNHCR, UNDP, BCPR and WHO.

PUSH BACK

SRI LANKA'S DANCE WITH GLOBAL GOVERNANCE

JUDITH LARGE

ZED
Zed Books
London

Push Back: Sri Lanka's Dance with Global Governance was first published in 2016 by Zed Books Ltd, The Foundry, 17 Oval Way, London SE11 5RR, UK.

www.zedbooks.net

Copyright © Judith Large 2016.

The right of Judith Large to be identified as the author of this work has been asserted by her in accordance with the Copyright, Designs and Patents Act 1988.

Typeset in Sabon by Swales & Willis Ltd, Exeter, Devon
Printed and bound by CPI Group (UK) Ltd, Croydon, CR0 4YY
Index by Ed Emery
Cover design by Kika Sroka-Miller
Cover photo © Chris Stowers/Panos

All rights reserved. No part of this publication may be reproduced, stored in a retrieval system or transmitted in any form or by any means, electronic, mechanical, photocopying or otherwise, without the prior permission of Zed Books Ltd.

A catalogue record for this book is available from the British Library.

ISBN 978-1-78360-655-9 hb
ISBN 978-1-78360-654-2 pb
ISBN 978-1-78360-656-6 pdf
ISBN 978-1-78360-657-3 epub
ISBN 978-1-78360-658-0 mobi

CONTENTS

Acknowledgements	*ix*
Abbreviations	*xiii*
Timeline of Sri Lankan history	*xv*
Foreword	*xxi*
Map of Sri Lanka	*xxiii*
Introduction: reflections on 'optics' – Sri Lanka and dilemmas in the study of violence and global governance	1
1 War's end and competing models for recovery	22
2 Executive presidency and the unitary state	47
3 Non-interference Sri Lankan style	70
4 The outsiders	94
5 Majoritarianism or divide and rule	122
6 Home-grown solutions and the quest for accountability	146
7 Small state in a large system	173
Notes	*198*
Bibliography	*231*
Index	*261*

ACKNOWLEDGEMENTS

This book was inspired by the work and engagement of particular individuals, both in and outside Sri Lanka, notably Kishali Pinto Jayawardena, Chandra Jayaratne, Paikiasothy Saravanamuttu, Asanga Welikala, Faaiz Ameer, Sreen Saroor, Ruki Fernando, Bhavani Fonseka, Suthaharan Nadarajah, Madurika Rasaratnam and David Whaley. Particular thanks go to Malcolm Rodgers for his thoughtful insights and useful, structured conversations along the way; to Swarna Rajagopalan for her patient explaining of the intricacies of South Asian conceptions of sovereignty and nationhood; to Visaka Dharmadasa and Fred Carver for their individual sharing and permissions to use the diagrams in Chapter 6; to Sherine Xavier for special conversations; and to Miriam Young for her quiet encouragement. Alan Keenan of the International Crisis Group writes acute informative updates and briefings and has been approachable for deliberations on ways of understanding national and international developments, as have Peter Bowling, Richard Reoch and Yolanda Foster, who shared their country experience. The Centre for Policy Alternatives (CPA) and International Centre for Ethnic Studies (ICES) in Colombo both produce excellent study resources and have been welcoming in Colombo, even at short notice. Appreciation is also extended to the Social Architects, and to the many interviewees and contacts in Kandy, Mannar, Jaffna, Kilinochchi, Trincomalee, Batticaloa and Sampur who gave of their time and trust. Feargal Cochrane at the Conflict Analysis Research Centre (CARC), University of Kent, offered a collegial base in the UK, and warm thanks go to Sakuntala Kadirgamar for her long-term friendship and to Saro Kadirgamar for her generosity and special hospitality. Gillian Evans provided technical support, and continual moral support came from Martin Large and the family. Kenneth Bush, who was generous and passionate in his reflections and memories of extensive experience in Sri Lanka, died suddenly before the draft manuscript was completed. His loss will touch many.

Useful in-depth learning, critical considerations and reflections were prompted by participation in an ICES conference on 'Ethical Futures: Dialogues on State, Society and Ethical Existence', held in Colombo from 30 May to 1 June 2013. Early observations also shaping this study came from working visits to Sri Lanka under the auspices of the Non-official Group of Friends of Sri Lanka led by Ambassador Richard Armitage, whose connection to the island dates back to an official mission in 1983. Particularly noteworthy for the inquiry was a sobering visit to Jaffna in 2010 with Dr Louisa Chan-Boegli and the former President of Mauritius, Cassam Uteem, and subsequent wider travel through the North and East with Ms Kara Bue. My thanks go to Zed Books and to Judith Forshaw. Any oversights or mistakes within these pages are entirely my own.

Much contested, and evident through institutional architecture with organising principles geared towards specific issue areas, global governance is not a fixed point or finite structural configuration but a system of relationships and transactions, beliefs, sanctions and incentives for behaviours. This book does not claim new theoretical breakthroughs. Rather, it seeks to tell the story of a particular ten-year period in the life of the Sri Lankan polity, its people and related interest groups. At its heart is a crisis of the state, and the question of how a ruling party sought to both court and refute international opinion. As such, it probes necessarily into the deep structures and contextual conditions that provided a basis for chosen positioning, messaging and actions from 2005 to 2015 by the Rajapaksa government.

The inquiry has been driven by the pressing challenge to understand both historical needs for and blockages to social justice in this particular South Asian context. More than that, its analytical lens suggests that we are all interconnected in terms of our varying respective networks, states, governments and shared transnational social movements; our actions or non-action with respect to norms of global governance. The Sri Lankan conflict is a macrocosm for its inhabitants and all those affected, including the diaspora. It is also a case study that provides a mirror on wider trends and dynamics, offering learning on war-to-peace transitions, social mobilisation, power and leadership, human rights advocacy, securitisation, protection, inclusion and accountability. The thought attributed to Gramsci, 'Pessimism of the intellect, optimism of the will', runs through this examination of one decade in an ongoing story. This book, a modest outsider view, is dedicated to the many talented and caring people actively working for a better future in Sri Lanka.

Judith Large, September 2016

ABBREVIATIONS

ACF	Action Contre la Faim
ADB	Asian Development Bank
ASEAN	Association of Southeast Asian Nations
BBS	Bodu Bala Sena (Buddhist Power Force)
BJP	Bharatiya Janata Party
BRICS	Brazil, Russia, India, China, and South Africa
CHOGM	Commonwealth Heads of Government Meeting
CID	Criminal Investigation Department
CPA	Centre for Policy Alternatives
CSO	civil society organisation
EPRLF	Eelam People's Revolutionary Liberation Front
FARA	Foreign Agents Registration Act
GDP	gross domestic product
GoSL	Government of Sri Lanka
GSP	General System of Preferences (EU)
ICCPR	International Covenant on Civil and Political Rights
ICES	International Centre for Ethnic Studies
ICG	International Crisis Group
ICJ	International Commission of Jurists
ICRC	International Committee of the Red Cross
IDP	internally displaced person
IFI	international financial institution
IIGEP	International Independent Group of Eminent Persons
IMF	International Monetary Fund

INGO	international non-governmental organization
JHU	Jathika Hela Urumaya (National Sinhala Heritage Party)
JVP	Janatha Vimukthi Peramuna (People's Liberation Front)
LLRC	Lessons Learnt and Reconciliation Commission
LTTE	Liberation Tigers of Tamil Eelam
MP	member of parliament
NAM	Non-Aligned Movement
NGO	non-governmental organisation
OECD	Organisation for Economic Co-operation and Development
OHCHR	Office of the United Nations High Commissioner for Human Rights
OIC	Organization of Islamic Cooperation
OISL	OHCHR Investigation on Sri Lanka
ONUR	Office of National Unity and Reconciliation
PLOTE	People's Liberation Organisation of Tamil Eelam
PR	public relations
PSC	parliamentary select committee
PTA	Prevention of Terrorism Act
R2P	responsibility to protect
SFM	Sri Lankan Secretariat for Muslims
SLA	Sri Lankan Army
SLMC	Sri Lanka Muslim Congress
SLMM	Sri Lanka Monitoring Mission
TELO	Tamil Eelam Liberation Organization
TGTE	Transitional Government of Tamil Eelam
TID	Terrorism Investigation Division
TMVP	Tamil Makkal Viduthalai Pulikal
TNA	Tamil National Alliance
TULF	Tamil United Liberation Front
UNDP	United Nations Development Programme
UNESCO	United Nations Educational, Scientific and Cultural Organization
UNHCR	United Nations High Commissioner for Refugees
UNHRC	United Nations Human Rights Council
UNOPS	United Nations Office for Project Services
UNP	United National Party
UPFA	United People's Freedom Alliance
UTHR (J)	University Teachers for Human Rights (Jaffna)

TIMELINE OF SRI LANKAN HISTORY

A distinctive, complex multi-centric civilisation can be traced back to the sixth century BC. Portuguese and Dutch occupation of coastal areas took place between 1505 and the late eighteenth century, followed by a British colonial period. After the fall of Singapore in World War II, the British moved their naval base to Ceylon and the island suffered Japanese bombing of military installations as a result.

1946 New constitution agreed. United National Party (UNP) founded.
1947 Elections see in new coalition government composed of Sinhala Maha Sabha Party, UNP and Tamil Congress.
1948 Ceylon granted dominion status and full autonomy within the Commonwealth of Nations.
1949 Parliamentary Elections Act amended to disenfranchise Indian Tamil plantation workers as well as many citizens with Indian or Pakistani ancestry.
1955 Ceylon becomes member state of the United Nations (UN).
1956 Sinhala-only language policy introduced. Widespread violence and Tamil deaths during ensuing protests.
1958 Anti-Tamil pogrom, attacks and counter-attacks, with victims from both communities.
1971 Janatha Vimukthi Peramuna (JVP) launches first uprising.

1972 Ceylon changes name to Democratic Socialist Republic of Sri Lanka as an independent republic. Buddhism made official religion. Vellupillai Prabakaran forms the Tamil New Tigers.

1976 Vaddukodai Resolution passed by Tamil politicians pledges the founding of an independent Tamil state. Liberation Tigers of Tamil Eelam (LTTE) formed, overtaking or doing away with other Tamil armed groups.

1978 New (second) constitution brings in new presidential system, a powerful executive with six-year terms and new powers, and a proportional representation electoral system.

1979 Prevention of Terrorism Act (PTA) brought in. Beginning of mass arrests of Tamil youth.

1981 Burning of Jaffna library, a regional centre of Tamil culture and learning.

1983 Mass anti-Tamil pogrom (Black July) following the ambush and killing of thirteen soldiers. More than 100,000 Tamils flee to India and more further abroad, in what is generally regarded as the beginning of open civil war (First Eelam War).

1985 Talks between the Government of Sri Lanka (GoSL) and LTTE in Butan. Attack on Anuradhapura (ancient capital and Buddhist sacred city) by Tamil militants kills over 140 Sinhalese civilians.

1986 Attack on Air Lanka plane in Colombo itself.

1987 Escalation of LTTE attacks followed by government Operation Liberation leading to an estimated 1,000 deaths and 2,000 arrests. Indo-Lankan Peace Accord signed. Some 50,000 Indian peacekeepers arrive in Jaffna to disarm LTTE and oversee implementation of the agreement, but this breaks down completely and they find themselves in open combat with the LTTE, who recapture Jaffna. Launch of second JVP uprising.

1990 India withdraws. Civil war resumes in full with LTTE forcibly evicting over 70,000 Muslims from northern areas (Black October). Beginning of Second Eelam War.

1991	LTTE suicide bomber blamed for assassination of Rajiv Ghandi.
1993	President Premadasa killed by LTTE suicide bomber.
1995	Government of Chandrika Kumaratunge and LTTE agree to talks which break down after an attack blowing up two navy vessels. Jaffna won back through Sri Lankan Army (SLA) attack.
1996	Suicide bombing at Central Bank building in Colombo kills more than 100 and injures an estimated 1,400. LTTE attacks army camp in Mullaitivu, killing over 1,000 troops.
1999	Attempted LTTE assassination of President Chandrika Kumaratunge, who survives.
2001	Suicide attack on Colombo international airport.
2002	Norwegian-brokered ceasefire agreement signed. GoSL and LTTE agree to talks.
2003	LTTE withdraws from talks. Ceasefire still in place.
2004	LTTE Colonel Karuna defects, creating split in the movement. Tsunami of 26 December kills some 30,000 and devastates coastal regions.
2005	Foreign Minister Lakshman Kadirgamar killed by suspected LTTE attackers in Colombo. LTTE resumes claymore and grenade attacks in Jaffna peninsula. Prime Minister Mahinda Rajapaksa wins presidential elections in November.
2006	GoSL responds to suicide attack on military compound in Colombo with air strikes in Tamil-controlled areas. European Union (EU) lists LTTE as a terrorist organisation and LTTE responds with the demand that European Sri Lanka Monitoring Mission (SLMM) members withdraw.
2007	Non-resident Tamils forced to leave Colombo, but expulsions stopped by Supreme Court ruling in response to a Centre for Policy Alternatives (CPA) petition. SLA begins to recapture Tamil areas.
2008	GoSL pulls out of ceasefire agreement formally. Full-scale offensive under way. International Independent Group of Experts (brought in by government to monitor human rights) leaves Sri Lanka citing interference with their work.
2009	President Rajapaksa takes over media ministry, Kilinochchi

falls to SLA, a private television station is attacked in Colombo, and Sinhalese editor Lasantha Wickremetunga is assassinated after writing a letter predicting his death by government forces. 'No fire zones' announced but plight of civilians trapped in the northern battle zone draws increasing international attention. Colonel Karuna is made Minister for National Integration and Reconciliation. UN High Commissioner for Human Rights accuses both sides of war crimes. UN food convoys stopped. Norway officially dropped as peace facilitator. In May, victory is declared over the LTTE and Prabhakaran killed when attempting to flee. Ban Ki-moon visits Colombo and secures joint statement with Rajapaksa about post-war recovery. Permanent People's Tribunal Dublin proceedings find that war crimes were committed.

2010 Presidential mandate secured through elections. Rajapaksa brought back with 57 per cent of the vote to opponent Fonseka's 40 per cent. Fonseka arrested and put on trial. Ruling coalition secures landslide win in parliamentary elections. Eighteenth amendment abolishes limit on number of terms for the Executive Presidency. UN Secretary-General appoints Panel of Experts on Sri Lanka. Rajapaksa announces Lessons Learnt and Reconciliation Commission (LLRC). Inaugural sessions of provisional Transitional Government of Tamil Eelam (TGTE) held in Philadelphia, USA. EU suspends GSP plus (General System of Preferences).

2011 Panel of Experts issues report calling for investigation into evidence of war crimes at end of war. LLRC issues its own report. Rajapaksa welcomed to Commonwealth Heads of Government Meeting (CHOGM) held in Perth.

2012 UN Human Rights Council (UNHRC) Resolution 19/2 calls for LLRC recommendations to be implemented and calls for action plan and for UN Human Rights Commissioner to work with GoSL on seeing through proposals.

2013 UNHRC Resolution 22/1 calls upon Sri Lanka to conduct independent investigation into alleged violations of international human rights law and international humanitarian law.

Tamil National Alliance (TNA) wins first elections to Northern Provincial Council with 78 per cent of the vote. CHOGM meeting hosted by Sri Lanka. Chief Justice impeached and replaced by presidential appointee. High Commissioner for Human Rights Navi Pillay visits Sri Lanka.

2014 UNHRC Resolution 25/1 calls on Office of the United Nations High Commissioner for Human Rights (OHCHR) to undertake a comprehensive investigation into alleged serious violations and abuses of human rights and related crimes, due to report back in March 2015. Permanent People's Tribunal Bremen finds evidence of war crimes. Rajapaksa says UN investigating team will not be allowed entry.

2015 Sirisena defeats Rajapaksa in January elections. Global Tamil Forum (GTF) speaks out in favour of new administration with hope for reform measures. Northern Provincial Council passes resolution on genocide, declaring no confidence in government-led efforts to investigate war crimes. OHCHR report delayed to September when UNHRC Resolution 30/1 outlines recommendations on reconciliation, accountability and human rights and requests GoSL to cooperate with special mandate holders and international assistance on these steps. Civil society invited by new government to join in measures for reconciliation and constitutional reform.

2016 June UNHRC oral report delivered by the High Commissioner for Human Rights Zeid Ra'ad Al Hussein, who cites mixed progress on 30/1 recommendations, notes that PTA still in place, and that there is ongoing need for consultations on missing persons. In Sri Lanka, the potential role of foreign judges in any criminal proceedings remains contested, refuted by government. July sees celebrations of sixty years of diplomatic relations between Sri Lanka and China and sixty-five years since the Rubber–Rice pact.

2017 High Commissioner due to issue final report on implementation of 2015 resolution.

FOREWORD

There is a widespread impression that all is well in Sri Lanka, and that it is a trouble-free and pristine tourist destination. News from the small island nation is continually defused by reports of desperate conditions of conflict, displacement, suffering and despair from other regions. This book explores the conduct of the Rajapaksa government in its ten years of power and examines how it contributed to past and ongoing tensions between counterterrorism and human rights compliance. As these tensions came in sharp focus within the country, international diplomacy failed in upholding basic rules of war and a new global consensus emerged in which the defeat of terrorism justified the means.

The author draws on encounters with Sri Lankans from many walks of life, asking them questions about the kind of society they want and the relationship of their country to a wider world community. The country's patchy human rights record, with its litany of enforced disappearances and extra-judicial executions, provides an unsettling backdrop to these conversations. This book examines the history and context within which an abuse of state power occurs, by interrogating the foundations of a particular government's entrenchment, including the majoritarian unitary state, the role of the executive, the justifications for increased military spending and the prominence of the military accompanied by the need for visibility. There is equally a recognition of the areas of reform and the acute need to bring in meaningful peace.

The Sirisena government faces new and old challenges. There is a shift in gear, yet the long-standing need to allow representation and inclusion has not been comprehensively addressed. Real peacebuilding requires the transformation of structures, interests, power and relationships. This cannot be achieved if archaic and authoritarian structures of state power are still in place or reinforced by new pieces of legislation. The new government promised to do away with the oppressive structures of the past. This book is a reminder why it needs to live up to its promise.

Charu Lata Hogg
Michael D. Palm fellow, Williams Institute, UCLA Law
Associate fellow, Chatham House

MAP OF SRI LANKA

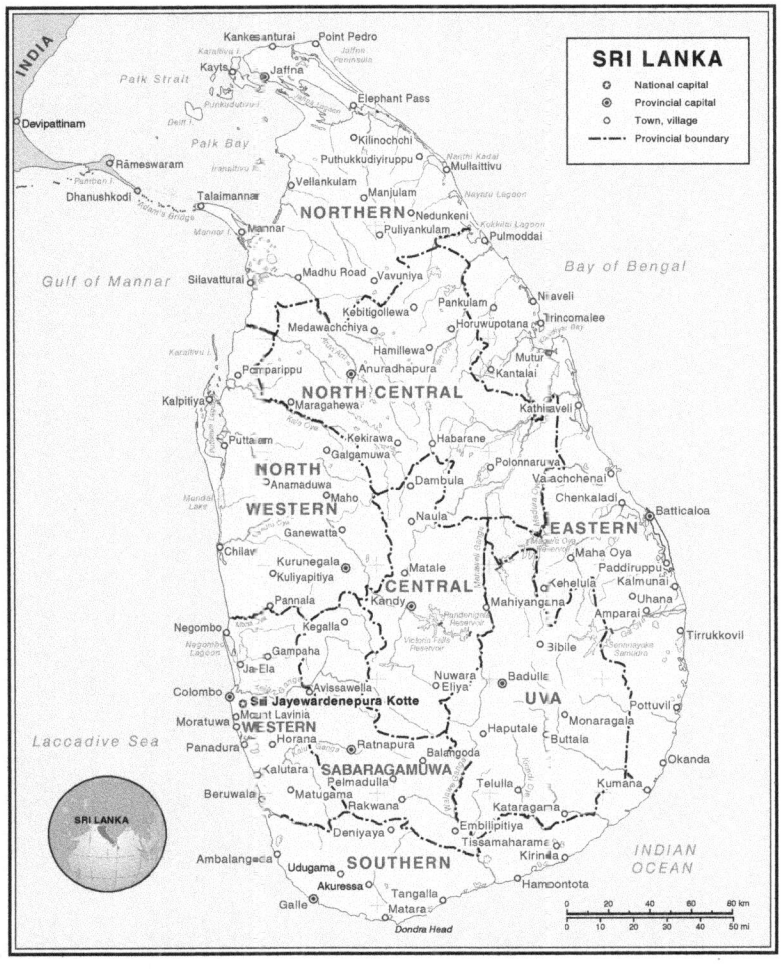

INTRODUCTION

Reflections on 'optics': Sri Lanka and dilemmas in the study of violence and global governance

In January 2015, a government fell in Sri Lanka, with elections ousting President Mahinda Rajapaksa in what many saw as a 'shock defeat' (BBC 2015). The enormity of the election outcome was greeted with surprise and relief by many observers who had feared that a third term for Mr Rajapaksa would have robbed Sri Lanka's democracy of whatever little vigour was left in it (Uyangoda 2015). In spite of an astrologer's prediction and perhaps an overreliance on believing that the state security apparatus would come to his aid to overturn an unfavourable result, Rajapaksa was out and a former colleague was in. The new President Sirisena chose as his Prime Minister a man who had been associated with ill-fated peace attempts in a civil war that ended in military victory (and mass atrocity) instead.[1] With parliamentary elections the following summer confirming a narrow majority, the country was set on some kind of new trajectory, scarred by war and unfinished political business in terms of majority/minority relations that has been unresolved for decades.

For a country characterised by peaceful, incremental political transition from colonial to independent status, Sri Lanka's (then Ceylon's) postcolonial experience entailed considerable internal violence and bitter socio-political cleavages. An anti-state uprising took place in 1953; race riots in 1958; the first Janathā Vimukthi Peramuṇa (People's Liberation Front, the JVP) insurgency in 1971.[2]

State repression was experienced both in the South, against the JVP, and in the North and East against the Liberation Tamil Tigers of Elam (LTTE), aided by the use of extraordinary laws such as the Public Security Ordinance and the Prevention of Terrorism Act. While the 1983 killings of Tamils marked 'one of the most horrendous incidents' in post-independence history,[3] the upsurge in violence against both Sinhalese and Tamils by government forces by the late 1980s resulted in such high numbers of deaths and disappearances that at that time Sri Lanka registered the second-highest number of cases of involuntary disappearances in the world, next only to Iraq (Pinto-Jayawardena 2015). The JVP had struck at the heart of the state, targeting state employees, officials, their families, even opposition figures who would not follow the call to take up arms. Formal and informal counter-insurgency methods were developed during both the JVP and Tamil uprisings. Sri Lankan security forces were given almost unlimited powers to combat both, which included shooting suspects on sight and disposing of bodies without an inquest. These were civil wars known for 'taking no prisoners'. The JVP insurgency, the LTTE insurgency and the United National Party (UNP) government's counter-insurgency war were all defining events that remain deeply embedded in the collective memory and experience of violence. Into this must be factored three decades of civil war that 'provided the space, as well as contexts, for multiple agents of terror, violence and death to practice their vocation freely and to chilling effect'.[4]

At the same time, the Sri Lankan polity has distinguished itself, seemingly out of proportion to its size as an island entity, as an actor in international relations and in the development of systems that came to be known as part of institutional global governance. Since independence in 1948, Sri Lanka has contributed to the United Nations (UN) system in multiple ways, including its norm-setting process. Present in San Francisco at the Japan peace conference in 1951, Sri Lankan delegates pleaded that Japan should be integrated into the world community with dignity, with J. R. Jayawardene (Finance Minister at the time) arguing against crippling reparations and for supported full recovery. Sri Lanka has produced important UN professionals, including three Under-Secretary-Generals and a Vice President of the International Court of Justice, to name a few. These and other high-level officials have played a strong role in international development by influencing global policy through leadership in diverse areas, ranging from the law of the sea to disarmament, children in armed conflict, and climate change. Jayantha Dhanapala was appointed by UN Secretary-General Kofi Annan to take on the role of Under-Secretary-General and re-establish the Department of Disarmament after the UN reforms of 1997. Radhika Coomaraswamy served in distinguished capacities, including as Special Rapporteur on Violence against Women and Under-Secretary-General for Children in Armed Conflict. Thousands of Sri Lankan citizens have served in UN peacekeeping efforts around the world. At the time of writing, over 1,000 troops are deployed to missions in Haiti, South Sudan and the Central African Republic (Nandy 2015).

This book looks primarily at one ten-year period (2005–15) of political machinations on the part of a particular government in power during and following a bitter civil war – a decade chosen for several reasons. Among these are the residual resonance of the post-2009 so-called 'Sri Lankan model' throughout the region, if not more widely; the shifting normative and power balances on the international stage that provide its backdrop; the resounding rejection of an already declining 'liberal peace' international interventionist mode; and the realisation that the military solution undertaken has not meant the demise of a minority's aspirations or needs amid what is actually a long-running crisis of the postcolonial state. It is precisely this intersection of local and global levels of agency and influence that will inform the choices and the pathways that Sri Lankans take in their own way. The central theme of the book may be articulated in three questions:

- What was the trajectory of the Rajapaksa government in winning the war against the LTTE and seeking to establish a renewed unitary state?
- How did the government deal with international actors and norms, as well as internal opposition to the nature of the military defeat and the illiberal measures chosen for post-war recovery?

- What, if any, mitigating circumstances and conditions can be identified that are relevant to notions of 'global governance' that have had an impact on Sri Lankan politics and society?

It will assist exploration of the questions above if we first expand on requisite 'optics' to the themes of both global governance and illiberal peacebuilding.

Global governance: contested frameworks of understanding

Globalisation and global governance are not the same thing, but they are closely interlinked in terms of process and theory. Hofferberth (2015) notes that the report of the 1995 Commission on Global Governance echoed and reinforced the notion of globalisation by referring to a 'global neighbourhood'.[5] With regard to globalisation, Vaughan (2011) offers a graphic picture:

> Contemporary world politics is shaped by centripetal and centrifugal forces. At the same time that globalisation is pulling many of the planet's inhabitants together, fragmenting processes are pushing people apart. The world is simultaneously becoming more cosmopolitan and more parochial. Powerful non-state actors now vie with sovereign states. Intricate patterns of transnational exchange compete with emotional ties of national identity. Nation-states are enmeshing with complex networks of transnational governance that include corporations, banks, and intergovernmental and non-governmental organisations. In sum, the world today is being shaped by forces that challenge the Westphalian state-centric view of international politics.

Global governance has been defined very simply as '[e]fforts to bring more orderly and reliable responses to social and political issues that go beyond the capacity of states to address individually' (Gordenker and Weiss cited in Dingwerth and Pattberg 2006). According to this view, global governance is seen as functioning through transnational institutions and interests that carry authoritative weight for decision making and actions by actors more or less beyond the full control of individual state governments. The machinations of Rajapaksa then reflect a classic tension between a claim of state sovereignty versus transnational demands and pulls. It is a mode of influence that may be exercised through state cooperation and through public sector actors, but also through non-state actors, be they civil or market-driven, in the form of deregulated economic penetration. Pascal Lamy observes that global governance grew through international cooperation over the past century and a half, underpinned by the treaties and agreements through which state entities have gradually agreed to renounce portions of their sovereignty. Comprising both formal institutions such as the UN system and Bretton Woods Institutions, and informal structures including the G5, G7, G8 and now G20, global governance emerges as a discernible system that has taken a 'few small steps away from state sovereignty and the "security blanket" of the Westphalian system' (Lamy 2015). He also acknowledges that the ideological infrastructure of global governance, while not exclusively derived from the Washington Consensus, was produced in the West and reflects the development of globalised market capitalism and a political system of liberal democracies.[6]

Some see the peak of globalisation as having been in the late 1990s and early 2000s, a time period that would encompass the beginnings of Sri Lanka's short-lived but heavily internationalised 'peace process'. Abdelal and Katz (2014: 133) look over the past few decades as a transition from deteriorating international unipolarity[7] to emergent multipolarity, with accompanying ideational challenges and political backlashes. This is in keeping with the notion of a 'neo-Westphalian' world, a condition of renewed importance for both sovereignty and religion, with a decline or rollback of universal norms about human rights (Hopgood 2013: 166).[8] Sri Lanka's rolling back of a once promising democracy and the persistent rise of militant political Buddhism provide a compelling case study in this light. It remains the case, however, that throughout the previous long years of conflict the Sri Lankan government remained an active member of the international community and is a signatory of numerous international charters, conventions and protocols, such as the International Convention on Civil and Political Rights (Crawley et al. 2015: 9), under which there are commitments and obligations. To all intents and purposes, Sri Lanka may be seen as having been an active participant in systems of global governance. The broad meaning of the term can be taken from the many-layered definition below (Thakur et al. 2014: 1–2) and further refined accordingly:

> Global governance entails multilevel and networked relations and interactions for managing and facilitating linkages across policy levels and domains. It consists of formal and informal arrangements that provide more order and stability for a world in constant and rapid flux than would occur naturally – the range of international cooperation without a world government. Intensifying global interdependence, growing recognition of problems that defy solutions by a single state or organization, and increasing numbers and importance of nonstate actors have all contributed to the growth of global governance as an analytical framework ...
>
> The content of global governance embraces the totality of laws, norms, policies, and institutions that define, constitute, and mediate relations between citizens, societies, markets, and states in the international system – the wielders and objects of the exercise of international public power. The architecture of global governance is made up of formal international organizations with the UN system as the core of the organized multilateral order, formal regional and subregional organizations, and informal general-purpose groupings. The most visible example of the latter in recent times is the Group of 20 (G20) heads of state or government, but these groupings also include the old Group of 7 (G7) and the new Brazil, Russia, India, China, and South Africa (BRICS) groupings of the industrialized and emerging market economies, and even informal but functionally specific and single-problem-oriented institutions like the Proliferation Security Initiative and the Nuclear Security Summits, as well as transnational networks of civil society and market actors.

Led by interests and values, based on elements of international law and the UN charter, global governance encompasses an active web of networked formal and informal relationships: multilevel relations and networks that link policy levels and states. Critics of the emphasis on international cooperation and regulation point to the need to understand power and control mechanisms, illustrated in analytical developments over the past decade of work on 'governmentality'. Lo Schiavo suggests that the Foucauldian concept of governmentality contributed to the development of a critical approach in studies on governance, one that 'unveils' the *spirit in the machine* of governance arrangements:

> The concept of governmentality is defined by Foucault in these terms: 'the ensemble formed by institutions, procedures, analyses and reflections, the calculations and tactics that allow the exercise of this very specific albeit complex form of power, which has as its target population, as its principal form of knowledge political economy, and as its essential technical means apparatuses of security.' (Foucault 1991: 102, quoted in Lo Schiavo 2014: 187)

This study of the Rajapaksa decade and Sri Lanka's emergent confrontation with its recent past is thus centred along the lines of the informing conditions for national government per se: historical precedent, structures and dominant ethos; cognitive and technical elements in the 'mentality' of the regime; the practices of social and repressive control employed; and the cross-currents of connections between internal and external actors. Many of those who resisted the regime looked to international norms and institutions for widening support and leveraging influence. They sought transactional power, or *possibility*, through the ability to bypass the state centre and bring influence to bear from external sources. In the sphere of mobilisation, then, global governance was taken as 'something more practical: the collective effort by sovereign states, international organizations, and other non-state actors to address common challenges and seize opportunities that transcend national frontiers' (Stewart 2014). In the same year as the Government of Sri Lanka (GoSL) victory over the LTTE, Hongying Wang and James Rosenau (2009: 6) wrote on 'China and global governance', noting the following:

> Global governance, as it is commonly understood today, has three distinctive features. First, the term highlights the global scale of many of the world's pressing issues, such as economic interdependence, migration, financial crises, drug trafficking, environmental degradation, and various health pandemics. Second, it emphasizes that while governments continue to perform important functions, non-state entities have become significant actors in making demands, issuing directives, and pursuing policies, thus shaping how the world is governed. Third, it presumes a number of norms of 'good governance' rooted in Western experience, such as market competition, human rights, democracy, transparency, accountability and rule of law.

This book is geared in particular to the second and third points above. Moreover, it is situated clearly in a multi-polarising world period in which those norms of governance are being challenged in processes in which previously understood Western-driven neoliberal hegemony is in decline. In a post-post-Cold War era, the behaviours of the Rajapaksa regime demonstrate and are representative of international fluctuations, although it will be seen that the official Sri Lankan justifications for military action were couched in familiar language such as self-defence, humanitarian action, and counter-terrorism. Increasingly, the role and legitimacy of the UN and the efficacy of the Universal Declaration on Human Rights, the Geneva Conventions and international humanitarian law are contested openly and at times brazenly.[9] While it is evident that power has not passed from nation-states to international organisations and global institutions, Sri Lanka is compelling because of the interplay between government and international authority, while at the same time there is a marked attempt at counterbalancing power relations 'from below' through Sri Lankan social movements and civil actors, often in alliance with their counterparts in other states.

Illiberal peacebuilding

In his own penetrating study of global governance, Duffield located strategic complexes within the liberal project, 'nodes of authority' enmeshing international non-governmental organisations (NGOs), governments, militaries, international financial institutions (IFIs), private security companies and businesses in the pursuit of global security (Duffield 2014 [2001]: 12). He particularly stressed the reinvention of development policy, with conflict resolution central to its radicalisation – a radicalisation made all the more striking through its almost all-encompassing endorsement by an expanding network of global governance.

> Comprised of NGOs, agencies, military coalitions, international financing institutions, and donor governments, the goal of the network of global governance ... was the establishment of 'liberal peace': one that resolves conflict, reconstructs societies, and establishes functioning market economies as a way of avoiding future war. (Harmer 2014)

It could be argued that the Rajapaksa government turned the table on systemic leanings towards stabilisation of the borderlands,[10] instrumentalising aid and setting terms and conditions for Western agency work in Sri Lanka. The theme ceased to be liberal peace and became illiberal conquest.

From the end of the war with the LTTE through military defeat in May 2009, the Sri Lankan government rejected the norms of liberal peace, vehemently refusing offers of UN good offices and claiming frequently to be turning Eastward rather than relying on previous allies and alliances in the West. Sri Lanka under Rajapaksa's rule is not the first country to engage in what has been 'illiberal peacebuilding', described by Soares de Oliveira (2011) as:

> a process of post-war reconstruction managed by local elites in defiance of liberal peace precepts on civil liberties, the rule of law, the expansion of economic freedoms and poverty alleviation, with a view to constructing a hegemonic order and an elite stranglehold over the political economy.[11]

Rwanda and Eritrea are often cited in this respect; Soares de Oliveira's study is of Angola, and he also refers to Rafik Hariri's Lebanon rebuilding under Syrian influence. But post-war Sri Lanka seemed Janus-like, simultaneously straddling both its own proud internal imposition of victorious Sinhala Buddhist hegemony and a craving for recognition and acceptance from the Western powers and interests it claimed to eschew. Anything the 'international community' wanted in terms of recovery or reconciliation, the GoSL would do in its own way, *sans* assistance. If technical or humanitarian aid were to be accepted, it would be on the government's terms. Symbolic forms and language to do with justice, devolution and inclusion resonated inside as well as outside the country, but were issued in a climate of repression and centralised control. Internal mechanisms were designed to the letter in instrumentalist legal formations, but failed to deliver as part of what one observer privately called 'Sri Lanka's "rich and lurid history" of national commissions of enquiry'. And yet the question arose as to whether replication, diffusion, and even political theatre might be rehearsals for the real thing. This would be the challenge to the post-Rajapaksa era.

It should be noted that alongside scholarship on liberal and illiberal peace there has also been a vocal analysis of 'hybrid' peace, which gives credence to the blend of indigenous process and form with liberal tenets and assumptions: democratisation, human rights, rule of law, market economy and neoliberal incorporation. Höglund and Orjuela (2012) examine both hybrid peace governance and illiberal peacebuilding in the Sri Lankan context with particular reference to social and political divides. They describe the Colombo anti-UN demonstrations of 1 May 2011, when effigies of the Secretary-General were burned and placards showing the leaders of Cuba, Venezuela, Libya, Russia and China were paraded under the banner 'For New World Order'. There is, they acknowledge, 'no clear-cut mix of international liberal and local illiberal' (ibid.: 90). In a more recent analysis, Nadarajah and Rampton (2015) point to the limits of hybridity, arguing cogently that social and political justice cannot be programmed from above but must emerge through agency and localised struggle.

Sri Lanka and global governance

The Rajapaksa pursuit of military victory at all costs – what some have deemed Sri Lankan exceptionalism (DeVotta 2015: 211) – also raises questions about the agency of small states in the wider and changing system. David Lewis (2010: 660) points to the shifting nature of norms and the promotion of counter-narratives, the fact that norms are not fixed or static but highly contested:

> Although this process of contestation reflects shifting power relations, and the increasing influence of China, Russia and other 'Rising Powers', it does not mean that small states are simply the passive recipients of norms created and contested by others. In fact, Sri Lankan diplomats have been active norm entrepreneurs in their own right, making significant efforts to develop alternative norms of conflict management, linking for example Chechnya and Sri Lanka in a discourse of state-centric peace enforcement.

There is evidence that some in the leadership saw things in this way,[12] and the question warrants further exploration. Deftly drawing on a statement of support from the 118-member Non-Aligned Movement (NAM) in early 2010, Permanent Representative to the UN Palitha Kohona declared that Sri Lanka was resisting external pressure in the management of its internal affairs (objecting to the Secretary-General's Panel of Experts) and that the perception of Sri Lanka being singled out for harsh treatment must be avoided (IPS 2010). Defence seminars held in Colombo after the war presented Sri Lanka as a world leader in counter-insurgency and conflict termination.

For the five years following the end of war, Sri Lanka appeared to be a state clearly still at odds with a significant portion of its population (both domestically and in relation to a politically sophisticated diaspora) while also in conflict with Western states and international norms. The country's trajectory revealed a marked difference between state building and peacebuilding and was indicative of the residual relevance of geo-politics, the potential strength of small states in the face of 'global governance', and the resilience of alternative international networks for reciprocity, reinforcement and exchange. The GoSL could turn away from the US and EU to China, India, Iran and Pakistan for affirmation and resources.

The Rajapaksa government seemed to want to be inside the international community and at the same time totally outside it and unencumbered by it. There are certain contradictions in its position, which warrant scrutiny. Firstly, the enterprise of the LTTE arose from a wellspring of Tamil grievances that were themselves based on constitutional rights and (originally) notions of inclusion in the Sri Lankan state, which then led to demands for a separate state. The very grounds for grievance seemed to be airbrushed away after the war under the rubric of the defeat of terrorism. In this sense, human rights were not an imposed Western agenda, but a need, a claim and a rationale for Sri Lankans. Secondly, it is not only 'liberal peace' paradigms that call for conciliation or the demonstration of mercy after war. Nigeria after the Biafran War is a case in point where the political refrain of 'No Victor, No Vanquished' informed outreach to and inclusion of the Igbo people who had also fought on a platform of self-determination.[13] This was due to Nigerian leadership, with no reference to the UN or to external authorities or norms. Thirdly, the religion of Buddhism (in Sri Lanka, Theravada Buddhism is the state religion) is often understood as having central tenets that include compassion (Tambiah 1992; E. J. Harris 2005; Bhikkhu 1999). But then major world religions, when linked to state power, seem to prove amenable to mobilisation and multiple interpretations.

Contemporary wars and zones of political violence are frequently characterised by postcolonial state crisis, competing claims of minorities, interventionist interests, counter-insurgency measures, elite power bids and regional dynamics. In the aftermath of the Cold War, the doctrines and practice of global governance have been closely intertwined with political and economic neoliberal reform agendas, privileging certain actors, ideas, values and interest groups over others. Sri Lanka's political trajectory was informed by the strains of such reform measures, and their effects on the contestation of the state. While this book will show how a particular government style under the Rajapaksas sought to reject international normative interference, there were also formal and informal systems at work inside and outside Sri Lanka that in turn actively opposed him in his project. As Cochrane, Duffy and Selby argued in their seminal work *Global Governance, Conflict and Resistance* (2003), the characterisation of global governance and resistance as binary opposites is problematic; they may be viewed as inextricably interlinked forces that, through their synthesis, form a process, or overlapping and intertwined processes, to do with sites of power.

This tension acts in several intersecting ways that are relevant to Sri Lanka's trajectory, not only during its civil war but also in light of constitutional and economic reform measures set against a particular postcolonial experience. The frequent tendency to limit the internal lens of examination only to 'unitary state versus LTTE' reifies two particular nationalisms and denies the complexities of actors, social groups and dynamics within the polity, and their disparate but dynamic quest for a social contract. In our context of a globalised world, it is noteworthy that, in the aftermath of the defeat of the LTTE in 2009, there arose a Transnational Government of Tamil Eelam – not a government in exile as per historical precedents, but a functioning virtual body with international membership and representation.[14] Over the past two decades, the world system has undergone fundamental shifts in power relations between states and the reorientation of 'North' and 'South' through the rise of India, Brazil, China and others, with an attendant pursuit (through BRICS summits) of systemic legitimacy for a new global order. Emerging powers have leveraged market capitalism and new communications technology to achieve economic and social development at high speeds and levels, while they are less inclined to accept a cosmopolitan political or normative space, much less any erosion of often hard-won sovereignty. At the same time, in both North and South, there is no reduction in inequality, and financial crisis lends itself to new forms of instability. The very location of Sri Lanka has rendered it a prime crossroads for related influence and change: an axis of East–West geo-political pulls vis-à-vis China and the US.

We can also turn to the personal, the individual level, when considering global governance and Sri Lanka. Jani de Silva (2005) conducted a detailed investigation of a case during the JVP uprising in which schoolboys were abducted and found murdered in a small village in southern Sri Lanka. The victims were neither insurgents nor suspected insurgents, but it was thought that they had been taken by the Sri Lankan military. Amnesty International highlighted the disappearances in October 1991, leading to questions being raised in parliament and a denial from the UNP government that the boys had ever been held in custody. The parents' group, however, was summoned to the Presidential Secretariat and told that there would be an investigation. This was not immediately forthcoming, but in a communication to the UN Working Group on Enforced and Involuntary Disappearances in 1992, the UNP government exonerated all the schoolboys of any involvement with the JVP. At that stage, Sri Lankan government cooperation with an institution of global governance, a UN body, related directly to the individual parents involved.[15] Between its 1980 establishment and 2006, the UN Working Group on Enforced and Involuntary Disappearances transmitted 12,319 cases to the Sri Lankan government.[16] Field missions were undertaken in 1991, 1992 and 1999. In 6,570 cases the fate of the missing was established due to cooperation between government, NGOs and other relevant intergovernmental organisations in the field, as well as assisted searches by family and workers visiting from the UN.

It was also the case that elements of global governance later worked to Rajapaksa's favour. In May 2006, when he was newly elected, the Council of the EU listed LTTE as a terrorist organisation, leading to blanket restrictive measures and bans on travel and financial transfers. The Council's statement indicated that by such an action they hoped to push the LTTE back to negotiations. The GoSL was also urged to clamp down on the use of violence and address a culture of impunity. While this EU measure had a marked effect on LTTE fundraising capacity, the 'terrorist' label also offered the incoming Rajapaksa government a justification to start a fully fledged war against the LTTE. 'For terrorists, in the post 9/11 meaning of the term, are people … with whom you do not negotiate' and 'who need to be flushed out of their holes'; in the discursive context of the 'war on terror, labeling an organization as terrorist in order to push it to the negotiation table is, at best, paradoxical' (Demmers 2012: 126).

Chapter outlines

The first chapter revisits the nature of the war's end in Sri Lanka, its co-option of war on terror discourse and official vehement denials of civilian casualties, and then contrasts competing models for post-war recovery. It interrogates why, with a dominant interest in economic regeneration and 'take-off' as the 'Wonder of Asia', the Rajapaksa government was so concerned to forestall and block opinion and visiting missions from the UN that it designed its own approach to reconciliation through a government mechanism. Chapter 1 also explores the application and ramifications of the 'Sri Lankan model'; the extent of unfinished business internally; and the potential and limits of stabilisation approaches to post-war recovery.

Chapter 2 begins to unpack the prevailing conditions for postwar decision making, directives and political trajectory through the unitary state and executive presidency; and the extent to which structures and mechanisms were ingrained in Sri Lankan history and how they were used to counter demand for a settlement to the national question. In Chapter 3, the notion and practice of non-interference, Sri Lankan style, is explored. This involved planning for both blockage and counter-hegemonic diplomacy in Geneva and New York, support from non-Western allies and considerable investment in opinion shaping and public relations. Internally, dissident voices were silenced or made targets as threats to the integrity of the state, while limits were placed on the ultimate degree of control given to transnational networks and international links. Chapter 4 seeks to understand the dynamics between government and external actors: 'the outsiders', which includes both internationals working in-country and donor agendas preceding and during the abortive ceasefire and the return to war. It asks what role international aid architecture played in shaping attitudes, as well as why Sri Lankan

NGOs themselves became targets in fraught confrontations over political futures. The relative failures of UN structures – and the subsequent interrogation of those failures – are relevant in this exploration.

Chapter 5 questions whether and how Sri Lankan majoritarianism has been understood as a counterforce to inclusive reform, examining the instrumentalisation of identity politics, threat and mobilisation. This is linked with often recognised 'divide and rule' measures in party politics, social relations, and the demographic military, socio-economic and cultural occupation of the North and East. In Chapter 6, the call for 'home-grown solutions' is interrogated, insofar as dispersed communities and the diaspora also saw Sri Lanka as 'home'; regional interests and attention from global institutions were brought to bear on key problems and needs, as articulated by war survivors, political activists and human rights actors. Particular scrutiny is given to whether the Human Rights Council in Geneva became a vehicle for activating internal 'regime change', or at least for raising the game on moves towards political settlement. Lastly, Chapter 7 rounds off with Sri Lanka as a small state in a large system, highlighting patterns of action, reaction and change over the past decade, the role of international actors and the geo-politics of US/China/India relations. It looks at the implications from the Sri Lankan experience for developing understandings of the dynamics of global governance and for querying networks of pressure, legitimacy and action in a changing international system.

Some caveats

Sunil Bastian is one scholar whose work connects the post-1977 era in Sri Lanka to a new, liberalised phase of globalised capitalist developments:

> These processes have external and internal dimensions. The intensification of the global linkages and the influence of institutions of global governance in Sri Lankan affairs are two external dimensions ... since the external and internal

are intricately linked it is difficult to understand Sri Lankan social processes without taking into account the globalised context. (Bastian 2003: 14)

Bastian warns against the ideological myopia of liberalism, which can mean always viewing the historical evolution of developing societies through the prism of Western capitalist societies, and highlights the need to examine what the French social scientist Bayart called the 'distinct historicity of societies'. Both these reminders are echoed here when exploring the linkage of civil war experience and its aftermath to global governance. There are particular caveats to such a focus. The first is respect for all those on the receiving end of violence in Sri Lanka, and the limitations of external enquiry in relation to internal lived experience. In short, 'all sides' have suffered loss. This means a degree of humility in recognising and honouring less than visible meanings and intimacies of the severe collective violence that has been part of Sri Lankan modern society, and the multiplicity of personal legacies and often unresolved experiences in this regard. Just as Paul Richards deconstructed the outsider view of a 'new barbarism' on the part of youth in Sierra Leone during the 1990s, and as Kalyvas documented in his monumental study on *The Logic of Violence in Civil War*, violence has long spilled beyond political agendas to kill individuals and destroy communities (Richards 1997; Kalyvas 2006; Volkan 1997). For outside observers and human rights activists, this violence has had a cruel, a vicious, even a vindictive nature. In her acute interrogation of the interplay of culture, history and personal dynamics as mentioned above, de Silva (2005) brought insights to a particular case of abduction and torture, refuting the notion of 'meaningless' or 'irrational' violence. As her story of abducted and tortured schoolboys reveals, both the anti-government and anti-JVP struggles were also used as cover for settling personal disputes. 'Terror tactics' fuelled their own replication in an atmosphere of social breakdown. 'Such acts remain transgressive,' she acknowledges, but they are frequently fraught with powerful and symbolic meanings, which need to be carefully extricated and made intelligible. Only then can we comprehend what was taking place in society (ibid.: 10).[17] It has been estimated that over 40,000 lives were lost during the war between the state and the JVP armed revolutionary organisation (Samavarayake 2008: 282).

This takes us to the second caveat: many of the political actions and positions that feature between 2005 and 2015 have clear antecedents in Sri Lankan experience and need to be referenced or drawn in where possible as context – the 'then' that informs the 'now'. Take, for example, the insistence on Sinhalese dominance, from 'Sinhala only' policies that sparked Tamil disaffection to the persona projected by Mahinda Rajapaksa, hinting that he was the reincarnation of an ancient, legendary king. De Silva discerns acute influences from more than one wave of 'globalisation', which has both disrupted and shaped island society. Globalisation (which Appadurai calls a term for a world of disjunctive flows) produces problems that manifest themselves in intensely local forms but have contexts that are anything but local.

And across the centuries, Sinhala society has always been open to influences from without. The global has been a constant factor. Sri Lanka was often occupied by foreign invaders, remnants of whose armies stayed behind. 'Sinhalaness' has always been enriched by heteroglossia. Heteroglossia creates hybridities ... All invading groups stamp upon the native peoples not only their cultural forms, but biological traits and characteristics through their progeny who were often a product of mixed cohabitations. (Appadurai 2001: 6)

But it was precisely in the face of such provocative hybridizations that internal consolidation was most provoked. It was the 'old' globalisation – or the West-European incursions – which were culturally and racially of such a radically different kind, that finally spurred on the defensive cultural renaissance of the late 19th century. Thus early Nationalists ... also articulated the anxieties of cultural obliteration which plague many members of the Sinhala-speaking intelligentsia today, in almost identical terms. (De Silva 2005: 234)

If we look to history, we can also find examples of tolerance and Hindu–Buddhist accommodation in the earlier polity of the Kandyan Kingdom in an altogether different system, one that coexisted with Tamil-speaking Vanni chieftaincies of the North; there are also other ancient precedents (M. Roberts 2012; Wijeyeratne 2013: 69; Tambiah 1986; Stewart and Strachern 2002: 140–4).[18] The topic of non-Westphalian models of the state will figure later in this book with reference to contemporary debates on political futures. For our immediate focus, more recent modern historical precedent is relevant. There is rich contemporary material in the public domain in the form of histories and film archives: for example, the June 1987 Granada TV documentary *Island at War*.[19] This features an in-depth discussion of a reprisal attack on Tamil civilians (massacres of Sinhala citizens took place near Trincomalee in April 1987, killing 126, and in May in Colombo with an estimated 200 casualties). The occasion was 'Operation Liberation', an offensive launched to recapture a strip of land – the area of Vadamarachchi in the Jaffna peninsula – from the LTTE. Recorded interviews with the affected population on the ground have a familiar resonance: the army had dropped leaflets instructing civilians to seek safe shelter in a temple that was then bombed; there are accusations that firebombs were used, barrels filled with petrol but also mixed with a chemical that caused severe burns. Film shows women, children and elderly victims and it is reported that 'perhaps 300 innocent civilians' were killed. The government spokesperson counters with the position that only military targets were attacked. Leaflets were dropped in 2009 urging civilians to seek safety in a no-fire zone; subsequently, despite glaring evidence to the contrary, there was an official denial of civilian casualties.

The old film clip is resonant with aspects of modern globalisation. People at village level are interviewed and filmed about their version of an incident within the state carried out by state forces; this is presented to government representatives for comment; and in turn it is broadcast thousands of miles away to an external audience and with additional inputs from the groups who are contesting central government, namely EROS (Eelam Revolutionary Organisation of Students) and the LTTE.

Thirty years later the country would still be trying to come to terms with the manner in which the war ended, the declaration of 'no-fire zones' which were in turn fired upon, the full-frontal assault on LTTE forces and on humanitarian law, in the presence of internationals, on the screens of internationals, and spoken of in the corridors of power in the UN itself. These are dilemmas that will haunt many for years to come, and created a situation that prompted Palitha Kohona, the then Sri Lankan Permanent Representative to the UN, to state in 2009 that: 'Winners are never tried for war crimes.' He went on: 'If you look at the history of war crimes there isn't one instance where a winner of a war has ever been tried before a tribunal.' He spoke against a turbulent background in world affairs. International headlines in the winter of 2008–09 highlighted Israel's war in Gaza; war and social fragmentation continued in the Democratic Republic of Congo; and concern for conflict management mounted in the aftermath of Russia's dispute with Georgia over Ossetia and the campaigns of the Chechen War. The need for civilian protection during internal war was highlighted particularly with reference to Gaza, finding resonance in humanitarian circles and for campaigns to resolve disputes fuelled by identity needs and territorial claims (Kretzmer 2009). International media attention was given to the plight of civilians in Afghanistan and Iraq Body Count entered its sixth year of documenting an ongoing death toll in Iraq.

Maithripala Sirisena emerged as the 'common candidate' in opposition to the Rajapaksa regime seemingly out of nowhere as a relative unknown in the high politics of Sri Lanka in late 2014. He campaigned vigorously against corruption, but also on platforms appealing mainly to the three-quarters Sinhalese majority on the island. His message clearly opposed any federal devolution of powers and maintained that the military presence in the North should continue. He also stated that he would not allow the Rajapaksas or military personnel to be put on trial internationally. One of his first actions on taking office was to request a six-month deferral of a forthcoming UN report on atrocities committed during and after the war, from 2002 to 2011. International Crisis Group analyst Alan Keenan noted that the climate of fear had altered dramatically, and that people could now openly voice views and opinions, and also that the President had moved quickly to pass a budget which addressed cost of living concerns. With diplomatic damage limitation under way, there was an almost audible sigh of relief in many Western capitals. It remained to be seen what political issues of substance inherited from the previous decade would be dealt with, and whether minority aspirations would remain of international interest and concern. It is this intersection of the local with the other, the national and international, that lends itself to the central theme of this book: namely, the relationship of Sri Lanka to global governance with regard to the legacy of a bitter war. In conclusion, this book is as much about local actors, the would-be interveners and the norm-carriers as about the Rajapaksa regime.

CHAPTER 1

War's end and competing models for recovery

Peace without unity, unity without reconciliation, and reconciliation without accountability. (Paikiasothy Saravanamuttu)

The way the war ended cast a legacy on its aftermath, and two models of recovery were advocated by those in power as a means to peace: namely, the Singapore model of economic development to make Sri Lanka the Wonder of Asia, and notions of reconciliation, as defined in government circles. The residual dilemma was the clash between these dominant approaches and the actual underlying causes of the war.

War to peace transitions may be understood through the prisms of resistance, accountability and that elusive term 'governance'. Resistance because civil war and its ending entail the reconfiguration of power relations and friction among and between societal actors; accountability because a population and its leaders need to come to terms in some way with the effects of violence and construct a viable narrative on which to begin again; and 'governance' in the sense of levels of norms and mechanisms to enable the renewed functioning of a given society. The Liberation Tigers of Tamil Eelam fought for over three decades in Sri Lanka, a bitter armed struggle in which ceasefires failed to hold and a degree of territorial control was achieved and then lost. This civil war arose from historical grievances over language rights, issues of land, higher education, employment and the socio-political status of the minority Tamil community.

War's end

In the aftershock of the military defeat of the LTTE in May 2009, a mixture of euphoria, anxiety and profound uncertainty seemed to grip the capital Colombo. The city was a grey and concrete labyrinth of military fortification: watchtowers, roadblocks, checkpoints, razor wire, enforced curfew and armed patrols. International media had reported for months about the northern assault: a frantic situation in the Vanni including entrapment and deprivation and attacks on thousands of civilians. In February, an interview with Defence Secretary Gotabaya Rajapaksa[1] aired on BBC appeared to condone attacks on hospitals if they were outside the official no-fire zone (Crawford 2009). Satellite imagery abounded of the full pincer effect of the assault, as well as rumours of additional satellite imagery held by US intelligence. What had been fever-pitch activity in embassy and mission corridors to find a ceasefire or halt to hostilities gave way to diplomatic numbness, while citizens were encouraged to celebrate a final victory over terrorism.[2]

For over a quarter of a century, the veracity of the Tamil–Sinhala conflict had attracted considerable international attention and intervention attempts, from the Government of India (at considerable cost, with the related assassination of Rajiv Ghandi) to numerous relief and development NGOs dedicated to peace making, a process of Norwegian-brokered talks and the international donor community backing economic incentive packages, particularly in the wake of the 2004 tsunami. As the Petrie report would later observe, the UN's political engagement in Sri Lanka during the period from 2007 to the end of the conflict in May 2009 was consistently secondary to the efforts of other external actors (UN 2012). These included countries in the region, primarily India and China. Norway sponsored the Ceasefire Agreement, with the EU, Japan and the US joining a Co-Chair Group of States to coordinate financial contributions to Sri Lanka in support of the peace process. The UN was not invited to be a member of the Co-Chair Group.

The final determined government offensive of the war was launched in late 2008. International agencies were forced by official directive to relocate from the Vanni in September 2008, a time when hundreds of thousands were being displaced within this increasingly dangerous conflict zone (IDMC 2009). By January 2009, an editorial in *The Economist* was asking 'Where have all the people gone?' in reference to the deserted streets and destroyed buildings in Kilinochchi, once the showcase de facto capital city of the declared Tamil Eelam (*The Economist* 2009). The LTTE had lost the city, with thousands of families displaced into the district around Mullaitivu. A final offensive was under way under the rubric of counter-terrorism with a rejection of perceived halfway measures and compromise as per the Norwegian brokered (aborted) peace initiative. There was a total rejection of calls for a ceasefire as the final battle loomed in 2009. Rajapaksa was quoted as saying: 'They are trying to preach to us about civilians. I tell them to go and see what they are doing in Iraq and Afghanistan' (Revise 2009). It was widely reported that a quarter of a million civilians were trapped in a shrinking area of land, caught in the crossfire and suffering casualties as well. Rumours flew of a massacre of people who were not themselves combatants and had no exit possibility, later confirmed in the wake of the final battle (Weiss 2012).[3]

In fact, Norwegian facilitation (Sorbo et al. 2011) had been accepted and tried not long after the advent of the US-led narrative on 'the war on terror', described in detail by Kleinfeld in 2003. Kleinfeld documents how both the People's Alliance Government and the Tamil Tigers of Tamil Eelam used the '9/11' lexicon 'associated with the U.S. attacks and early global response to brand their adversary as terrorist, to recode political and conflict narratives in September eleventh terms, and to indicate the appropriate scale and scope of the war' (Kleinfeld 2003). The future Defence Secretary Gotabaya Rajapaksa, a US citizen, was living in California at the time of the Bush administration measures that echoed 'with us or against us' as an uncompromising stance (Montlake 2009). His official governmental website invoked geo-political analogies when referring to subsequent United Nations Human Rights Council (UNHRC) war crimes investigations, stating that the:

> Sri Lankan government should closely study the Iraq case. It should be a priority. The Iraq case presents an excellent

opportunity to highlight the double standards adopted by those threatening to haul Sri Lanka up before an international war crimes tribunal on the basis that the local process lacked credibility. (MoD Sri Lanka 2014)

It was Gotabaya who warned ambassadors, news agencies and international NGOs of dire consequences if they were 'partisan' in their concern for the LTTE or made comments in support of their cause during the military ground offensive. As he singled out BBC journalists and the Swiss and German ambassadors for particular criticism, a joint statement was issued by five leading Sri Lankan bishops calling on both sides at war in the Vanni to keep civilians safe from the line of fire and calling on the government to invite the International Committee of the Red Cross (ICRC), the United Nations High Commissioner for Refugees (UNHCR) and independent Tamil leaders to monitor and manage relief in the war zone.[4] When the President met with Manmohan Singh in New Delhi in November 2008, the Indian Premier also called for restraint and presented a copy of a unanimous resolution passed by the Tamil Nadu state legislative assembly that called for an immediate ceasefire and resumption of negotiations (transCurrents 2008; Kelegama 2013).

Just seven years earlier it had been suggested that Sri Lanka had come 'to serve as a laboratory and showcase for liberal peacebuilding' (Höglund and Orjuela 2012: 94) when the country embarked on a path of third party facilitation to resolve the long-standing conflict with the LTTE. Now the picture changed to one of triumphant military victory, as video footage released on 18 May 2009 showed the bloodied body of the LTTE leader, Velupillai Prabhakaran, after a violent all-out attack by the Sri Lankan military under the presidency of Mahinda Rajapaksa (Saddlesmania 2009). Public statements from Colombo rejected notions from Western governments at the time that clemency should have been shown; moreover, civilian deaths were denied and Western interference decried, as a 'Look East' policy was revived with pride and defiance. According to UN documentation, approximately 40,000 civilians had been killed in the first five months of 2009, with an estimated 300,000 displaced in the Northern Province (UN 2011a). Most internally displaced persons (IDPs) were held at the Manik Farm, the government IDP centre located between Vavuniya and Mannar districts. It was not long before 'credible allegations' associated with the final stages of the war surfaced in a way that would only loom and grow for the next five years. The Panel of Experts mandated by the Secretary-General reported that 'between September 2008 and 19 May 2009, the Sri Lanka Army advanced its military campaign into the Vanni using large-scale and widespread shelling, causing large numbers of civilian deaths. This campaign constituted persecution of the population of the Vanni' (UN 2011b). This was in stark contrast to the government's framing of operations as a humanitarian rescue operation. Sri Lanka is party to the 1949 Geneva Conventions (but not to additional protocols) and saw accession to the International Covenant on Civil and Political Rights (ICCPR) in 1997. But Mahinda Rajapaksa signalled that this 'small island state, 270 miles long and 150 wide as the crow flies' (Tambiah 1986), once a newly independent democracy with pride in a democratic constitution and parliamentary system, would stand up to liberal global norms[5] and that his government alone knew what was best for its people – for *all* its people. At least its ruling elite did so, defiant in triumphalism, rejecting any question of means and ends and being particularly angered by press reports of diaspora Tamil protests across the world during the final days of what the UN Independent Review Panel would later refer to as 'carnage'.[6] The same panel found that the LTTE was also guilty of severe human rights violations against civilians in the course of combat.

War's end, while a relief for many citizens, particularly in the South (where people had suffered decades of uncertainty and fear), left many minority communities in an initial state of shock. Its coverage was fraught with competing narratives and depictions. Was it heroic triumph or brutal bloodbath? 'We have liberated the whole country from LTTE terrorism,' Rajapaksa declared, addressing parliament in the Tamil language and stressing that the war 'was not waged against the Tamil people' (Weaver and Chamberlain 2009). To general Sinhalese euphoria in the South, a national holiday was proclaimed and the victory celebrations began. Meanwhile, a chasm of desperate proportions loomed between southern experience and what was happening in the North and East of the country. Overseas Tamil diaspora groups mourned and in many cases protested,[7] as in London, where frantic demonstrations led to violence outside the Houses of Parliament. Speculation resumed on 'what next' for post-war recovery.

An article in the *Indian Defence Review* concluded that in the final analysis the Rajapaksa model was based on a military precept and not a political one: 'terrorism has to be wiped out militarily and cannot be tackled politically. That's the basic premise of the Rajapakse Model.' The writer went further to argue that the first principle in the Rajapaksa model was political will and 'the second principle of Rajapakse's "how to fight a war and win it" is telling the international community to go to hell', as the British and French foreign ministers, David Miliband and Bernard Kouchner, found out during their visit. They were cold-shouldered for suggesting that Sri Lanka should halt the war and negotiate with the LTTE (Shashikumar 2009). As late as five years later Mohammad Ali Babakhel was widely quoted from an article published in a national Pakistani newspaper saying that Sri Lankan forces' all-out onslaught against the Tamil Tigers can be replicated in Pakistan against the Islamist rebels. 'The Sri Lankan strategy shows that with military might and popular support the state can defeat insurgents,' Babakhel said in his opinion piece. 'If the [Sri Lankan] model cannot be replicated, at least it can be a source of inspiration [for Pakistan]' (*Daily Mirror* 2014). Chinese Foreign Minister Yang Jiechi commended Sri Lanka on its success in defeating terrorism and reiterated China's support for maintaining Sri Lankan independence, territorial integrity and sovereignty – and also for supporting 'One China' with regard to Taiwan and Tibet (*Asian Tribune* 2009).

Winning the war and winning the peace: constitutional reform and devolution

There was, however, some residual hope for the political following the military, and the stated national agenda in the immediate post-war period seemed promising. For many observers, 'the defeat of the LTTE secessionist insurgency in 2009 provided the government with an unprecedented opportunity to move in the direction of ethnic reconciliation, constitutional reform for greater democratization, and enhanced regional autonomy for ethnic minorities' (Uyangoda 2011a). The President stated: 'Our intention was to save the Tamil people from the cruel grip of the LTTE. We all must now live as equals in this free country ... we must find a homegrown solution to this conflict. That solution should be acceptable to all the communities' (Weaver and Chamberlain 2009). There was some hope that, at a minimum, a demoralised Tamil population would be offered something in the form of a '13th plus', a reference to a constitutional amendment intended to devolve power to provincial councils. This measure was introduced to create provincial councils as a follow-up action to the Indo–Sri Lanka Agreement of 1987 in order to devolve powers to the Tamil majority North and East (Senadhira 2013).

Now Indian Prime Minister Manmohan Singh emphasized the acute need to address the resettlement of IDPs, and urged the government to undertake speedy rehabilitation and reconstruction efforts in northern and eastern Sri Lanka. Singh underlined the need for meaningful devolution, based on the thirteenth amendment that would create the necessary conditions for lasting political settlement.[8] It was widely reported that Sri Lanka had given assurances to India during talks between Rajapaksa and Manmohan Singh (and subsequently to UN Secretary-General Ban Ki-moon) that the government would go beyond the thirteenth amendment to devolve substantial powers to Tamil majority areas. Rajapaksa announced that his government was committed to a political solution. The Tamil National Alliance (TNA), as the largest political group representing the Sri Lankan Tamil community, dropped its demand for a separate state and advocated for dialogue and meaningful federal solutions. Supporters of the government encouraged it to take steps towards reconciliation and the rebuilding of trust between Sri Lanka's three major ethnic communities: Sinhalese, Tamils and Muslims. There were also calls for the government to investigate the allegations of serious violations of international humanitarian and human rights law by both sides in the final stages of the war and to establish at least some degree of accountability.

In the course of the thirty-year protracted war, a negotiated settlement had been continuously pursued and pushed by interlocutors and the donor community. 'Reconciliation' became a loaded term, just as the word 'federalism' was so highly charged that it became almost taboo. The resumption of the war had 'made reconciliation synonymous with defeatism in the majority psyche, and an elusive goal for the minority' (Thaheer et al. 2013). Post-victory, the Sri Lankan government would regard reconciliation as almost synonymous with reconstruction and the maintenance of stability. And the first priority was to consolidate the regime. Rajapaksa called for presidential elections in November 2009, some two years ahead of schedule, in order to secure an indisputable majority and capitalise on his post-war popularity. Ironically, his main challenger was former colleague and General Sarath Fonseka, who campaigned on a platform of restoration of democratic rights, polling well among Tamil and Muslim voters.[9] Rumours flew when presidential candidate Fonseka was routed in his attempts at political opposition in 2010, then imprisoned after claims that he held evidence of war crimes and was prepared to go public. It was increasingly clear that the President would not look backwards but instead would focus on a march forwards that was to have no detractors. His emphasis was on reconstruction and infrastructure development as the path to the future for an economically vibrant Sri Lanka, an 'Emerging Wonder of Asia'. Then, in an interview for Indian television, Defence Secretary Gotabaya resoundingly refuted any prospect of a political solution:

> Mr. Gotabaya Rajapaksa's comments, made in the course of an interview to Headlines Today television, reveal a troubling contempt for the Tamil minority. He has trashed 'the political solution talk,' asserting, among other things, that it was 'simply irrelevant' because 'we have ended this terrorism in Sri Lanka, making the egregious assertion that when the 13th Amendment was being drafted, 'the government of Sri Lanka was not involved.' (*The Hindu* 2011)

The Singapore model

In his ambitious and visionary manifesto, the *Mahinda Chintana*, President Rajapaksa outlined specific goals encompassing multiple aspects of Sri Lanka's economy and society, including 'a land of plenty', clean water, electricity and houses for all, a law-abiding society, 'a clean, green environment' and future prosperity. The *Mahinda Chintana* also stated that the new era would 'break the fundamentalist concepts of a traditional homeland and a separate state and empower the citizens of this country to arrive at a peaceful political solution which would devolve power to all its citizens' (Department of National Planning 2010: 52). President Rajapaksa said that his main target was to develop the economy. The peace and prosperity agenda was a high-profile one for the GoSL, and the language of 'regional empowerment' was also used. The CIA's *World Factbook* of 2010 lists Sri Lanka's public debt at an estimated 82.9 per cent of gross domestic product (GDP) for 2009. But government spokesmen boasted of Chinese loans at 2 per cent interest only, and of growing outward trade with the East, while hoping for better relations with the West as well (DeVotta 2007). Per capita income had reportedly doubled from just over $1,000 to $2,000 'during the last four years when we were at war and we will double it again in the next five years' (Godbole 2015).[10] Singapore and Malaysia were put forth as role models. The President's vision for recovery rested solely on economic prosperity, and the aim of increasing Sri Lankans' average annual income from $2,100 to $4,000 in the next few years; to follow a 'Singapore model' and become a regional hub for trade, shipping and communications. In charting this course he drew on contested policy already strongly rooted in the politics of postcolonial Sri Lanka. Economic policy and subsequent dislocation are seen by some critics as contributing to the crisis of the state that underlies modern Sri Lankan levels of violence.[11] The trend for looking to Singapore may be traced back to President J. R. Jayawardene (Krishna 1996)[12] and later R. Premadasa, who sought the introduction of a Lee Kwan Yew-style system to the country. Both of these men were great admirers of Lee and openly followed an ideological position of what they called the 'Singapore model' for Sri Lanka. They sought effective, centrally directed policies for economic expansion, bringing in the 1978 Constitution with a new basis for state power and economic reform.

Vision of a regional hub

In Rajapaksa's words:

> [the] next massive leap forward is to transform Sri Lanka into a strategically important economic centre of the world ... to transform Sri Lanka to be the pearl of the Asian silk route once again, in modern terms. Using our strategic geographical location effectively, I will develop our motherland as a naval, aviation, commercial, energy and knowledge hub, serving as a key link between the East and the West.

These words are from the *Mahinda Chintana* document, which presents a fairy linear graph with improved per capita income to one side and the following benchmarks for progress:

- 2005: hampered by terrorism;
- 2009: peace and development;
- 2016: technologically advanced, knowledge-based and self-sufficient economy.[13]

The 'Five Hubs plus Tourism' outline was showcased in 2010. Sri Lanka would become a centre for the Asian region, a vibrant, advanced intersecting point for shipping lanes, air routes and telecommunications. It would achieve excellence in the five hubs, which in turn would bring prosperity to the nation. The hubs would look something like this:

- The naval hub: Sri Lanka would reclaim what had been a vibrant position on the Indian Ocean silk route. A new port would be constructed at Hambantota, container handling capacity would be doubled at the Port of Colombo, and new port developments would be sited at Oluvil, Kankesanthurai and Trincomalee.

- The aviation hub: with its key strategic capability, Sri Lanka would take a lead in the skies through the modernisation of Bandaranaike International Airport and the construction of a new airport at Hambantota.
- The commercial hub: Sri Lanka would forge ahead to develop along the same lines as Hong Kong, Singapore and Dubai as one of Asia's foremost jurisdictions in the fields of commercial services, international banking and investment.
- The energy hub: energy resources would be developed, from oil and gas to renewable sources, as well as providing greater thermal energy capacity. New oil refineries were planned in Hambantota and Sapugaskanda, and work would be undertaken to see that mineral sand resources could be used to generate nuclear power.
- The knowledge hub: in ancient times, Sri Lanka's Buddhist monasteries were recognised seats of learning, from which the teaching of the Buddha spread out to the rest of Asia. Sri Lanka would attract national experts who have excelled internationally to return to the country. The education system would be reformed and ICT training developed to attract both foreign and domestic students, equipping Sri Lanka for success in a modern economy.

Basically the 'Emerging Wonder of Asia' would be based on the design and implementation of expansive infrastructure-centred mega-development projects: for example, the total redevelopment of Hambantota and the Sampur coal-fired power plant and industrial park as well as the creation of new, specialised economic zones and luxury tourism enclaves (Law and Society Trust 2014; Buthpitiya 2013; Sirimane 2014).

The 'Singapore model' had its own particular resonance in Sri Lanka; in Sinhala, it was known as *singappooruwak* (implying a concept of being Singapore-like) and was seen as derivative of '*Jayawardena mathaya*', J. R. Jayawardena's vision that aimed to make Sri Lanka a new industrialised nation by the year 2000. In the words of one minister: 'The law and democratic principles sometimes hamper development but a pinch of dictatorship can expedite the expected target at the expected time as witnessed in many Asian Tiger countries.' He went on to argue that: 'It is no doubt that people have to undergo hardship when large scale development projects are implemented either by the state or the private sector. But they will have to bear it for the larger interest of the country' (Jayasekera 2011).[14] He possibly meant cases such as Sampur's special economic zone, some 5,000 acres of land from which hundreds of families were evicted and forced to relinquish their hereditary ownership, hence losing their farms and livelihoods as well. Not everyone agreed with this approach. An editorial by Shanie in 2011 lamented the redevelopment of Colombo:

> on the Singapore model and the eviction of the urban poor who have been long-time residents of the city [which] is in keeping with that plan. The human element gets lost in such plans. What is even more appalling is that both civil society and the media have been intimidated into silence. This perhaps also follows the Singapore model where the opposition have to undergo much harassment. (Shanie 2011)

The Singapore model thus had its critics. There was concern that the city state had suffered its own political purges and had a less than vibrant democracy and that there was state control of the press. Then there were named contradictions as well. For example, the 2010 decision that the Sri Lankan national anthem would be sung only in Sinhala (salt in the old wound of the 'Sinhala only' policy of 1956, which sparked riots and division) ran counter to important elements of Singapore state policy: whereas the majority community in Singapore is Chinese, the national anthem is sung in Malay, the mother tongue of the minority. English, Chinese and Malay are all recognised as official languages. Another theme that provoked discussion was the issue of corruption. One critic noted in 2010 that as late as the 1980s Singapore was considered a 'corrupt state':

> Last year, Transparency International ranked Singapore as among the three least corrupt countries in the world. It is widely acknowledged that the critical factor that helped Singapore

achieve this status is strong political will, something that is sadly lacking in many developing countries. Like Singapore, Sri Lanka has the legal and institutional mechanisms to fight bribery and corruption ... There is the Independent Commission to Investigate Allegations of Bribery or Corruption (it ended its term last month without a new committee being appointed), an independent judiciary, the Auditor-General, the Attorney General, Parliamentary Committees, such as the Public Accounts Committee (PAC) and the Committee on Public Enterprises (COPE), the Public Services Commission, the Police Commission, the code of conduct for government officials, the declaration of assets for certain grades of public officers, the public procurement procedure, and so on.

Sri Lanka is also a signatory to the United Nations Convention Against Corruption. In fact, retired Supreme Court Judge, Saleem Marzoof PC, once remarked that Sri Lanka can legitimately boast of the best anti-corruption laws in the entire Third World. We have the laws, but we haven't been able to check bribery and corruption, which is rampant in Sri Lanka. Last year, Transparency International ranked Sri Lanka in 97th place on its corruption perception index ... Inadequate legal provisions cannot be the reason for this sorry state of affairs.[15]

By February 2011, on celebrating its sixty-third year of independence, Sri Lanka would nonetheless claim to be one of South Asia's fastest-growing economies. Social indicators, with the exception of those in the North and East, were the best in the region, and its strategic location gleaned investment from both Asian giants: China and India. The growth rate was up to around 8 per cent, the stock market was doing well, and tourists had returned for beach holidays thanks to the island's scenic beauty. Moreover, the International Monetary Fund (IMF) congratulated the GoSL as it released a standby agreement loan tranche despite the high ratio of public debt to GDP. Celebrations took place in a still militarised capital city, alongside protest demonstrations by the UNP and by citizens against authoritarian rule, attacks on (plus disappearances of) media personnel and human rights defenders, and a boycott of the event by Tamil political leaders in protest at the government's failure to share power.

In five years following the end of the war, Sri Lanka would receive some $4 billion from China in the form of aid, soft loans and grants, with nearly 70 per cent of infrastructure funded by Chinese banks and institutions and built by Chinese companies, often with their own labour brought in and housed on site. Major projects included: Hambantota Port; the A9 Highway, which linked central Sri Lanka to the previous war zone; the Southern Expressway, to speed up transit times along the southern coast; the Colombo Port terminal expansion; the Norochcholai coal-fired power plant, intended to provide over a third of the country's power; and the first phase of the Southern Railway (Barta 2014). But at the same time as it was expanding its infrastructure, the 'Emerging Wonder of Asia' was basing its economy more and more on military penetration through access to land, business franchises including tourist resorts and construction, and significant continual recruitment in spite of the post-war status of the country. Twenty per cent of GDP in the budget was for defence expenditure; a country of 21 million boasted 2.1 million army personnel. Urban development, waterways, and the registration of NGOs were now under the control of the Department of Defence.

Goodhand would observe that the government flagship 'Eastern Awakening' (*Nagenahira Navodaya*), launched in the wake of the 2007 conquest of the East, which combined counter-insurgency with economic development planning, constituted a dress rehearsal for the campaign that followed in the North (Goodhand 2010). In the North, the number of military personnel stationed there increased, particularly in Jaffna.

High security zones surrounded by razor wire and cement blocks encompassed former village sites and fields that had once been agricultural land. Checkpoints and roadblocks took hold as the processing of IDPs began. The first work on housing construction was to provide homes for the military. In both Jaffna and Batticaloa, police registration of travelling Tamils began in 2011. Tamils travelling to Sinhalese areas were routinely required to register with the police, while no such requirement was in place for Sinhalese citizens. In March 2012, a report from the International Crisis Group (ICG) outlined the extent of military control of northern Sri Lanka (ICG 2012a). Along with registration requirements on Tamils (including interviews about family members and ID photo records), the ICG documented intimidation from government-controlled Tamil militias and the violent suppression of dissent. The report argues that the Sri Lankan military has 'become an army of occupation physically and psychologically'.

If the Singapore model was given strong promotion, critics now raised the question of whether the economy was in fact following more closely the former Indonesian (Suharto-led) 'military business' paradigm. The air force operated private flights to Jaffna. Rajasingham-Senanayake observed that, along the A9 road to Jaffna, the military ran tea shops, competing with recently returned impoverished IDPs:

> In the war-ravaged North and East, [the military] has acquired extensive public and private lands under the banner of providing 'security', and it is setting up large farms to grow vegetables and fruits in the Mannar district. The ramifications of this, however, have left Tamil and Muslim farmers landless, as some of their lands, now occupied by the military, have been earmarked for business ventures, including a coal-fired power plant, tourism projects and agro industries. (Rajasingham-Senanayake 2011)

There was no question that the war-ravaged North and much of the East were in sore need of reconstruction. The districts of Mullaitivu and Kilinochchi had suffered the devastation of practically their entire infrastructure and whole-scale population displacement. Massive programming was scheduled in two phases: first, a 180-day concerted effort at de-mining, resettlement of IDPs, provision of an energy grid and telecommunication reconstruction. The second phase would look at wider infrastructure development, electricity, transport, water supply, health, education and livelihoods. The Governor of the Northern Province was a Major General; of the Eastern, a Rear

Admiral (ICG 2011a). Sri Lanka planned for development hubs in areas of maritime capability, aviation, commerce and trade, power and energy, and for the knowledge-based economy, and, with the help of the IMF and foreign donors, to dedicate $1.5 billion to $2 billion a year on road and rail development, power production, port facilities, and water and sanitation. But many asked whether this was sufficient to heal a society still fractured by past injustice and shared loss in violent conflict. Where exactly was reconciliation positioned in the post-war agenda?

Reconciliation

Writing in August 2010, noted political analyst Paikiasothy Saravanamuttu observed that Sri Lanka faced the challenge of moving from being a post-war to a post-conflict nation. His suggestion was clear. 'The priorities should be: peace via a political settlement reconciliation through aiding the plight of internally displaced persons, the reversal of the culture of impunity over human rights violations and promoting unity by resisting majority domination' (Saravanamuttu 2010).[16] The *Mahinda Chintana* outlined reconciliation measures for the North and the East ranging from elections for the Northern Provincial Council and dedicated funds for resettlement and reconstruction, to the rolling back of high security zones from private agricultural land in Jaffna. Taken at face value these would sound like potential steps to reconcile after the extreme suffering and loss of way, in keeping with mainstream understandings of the term. Kaufman refers to the ideal definition of reconciliation as 'characterised by mutual recognition and acceptance, invested interests and goals in developing peaceful relations, as well as fully normalised, cooperative political, economic and cultural relations' (Kaufman 2006: 207).[17]

In practice under Rajapaksa, however, the 'spirit' did not always match the 'words' in Sri Lankan politics, where the discourse and practice of reconciliation became enmeshed with resistance to interference from the UN and Western governments. Ban Ki-moon's personal intervention to seek reassurances on accountability for possible human rights violations at the end of the war met with no visible response or institutional inquiry mechanisms. He reacted to this with a proposal for a UN advisory panel on Sri Lanka (mentioned above) with the task of advising him on appropriate measures. Views and definitions of reconciliation diverged sharply, with the Sri Lankan government proceeding to use the term seemingly to mean rehabilitation. To reconcile meant to bring back into the fold, and to correct deviant behaviours, hearts and minds. They did, however, establish a Lessons Learned and Reconciliation Commission (LLRC) in the country. This was initially to be a seven-member commission dealing with the period from 2002 to 2009, and in particular with 'incidents', with no mention of root causes or underlying grievances. In September 2010, Rajapaksa addressed the UN with the following message on the LLRC:

> This independent Commission, comprising eight Sri Lankans of eminence and stature, has already begun its work. Recently, the Commission handed over to me an interim communication recommending certain administrative steps that may need to be taken in the reconciliation process.
>
> We believe that for the rebuilding and healing of our nation to succeed, the process must evolve from within. If history has taught us one thing, it is that imposed external solutions breed resentment and ultimately fail. Ours, by contrast, is a home grown process, which reflects the culture and traditions of our people. (*Asian Tribune* 2010)

The LLRC proved to be a classic example of Sri Lankan 'push-back' at international standards and at the UN in particular. An editorial in India minced no words: 'the real motive of LLRC was to bail out the government from being brought under the scanner of an international commission of enquiry that would have meant big trouble for Sri Lankan President Mahinda Rajapaksa' (Newman 2012). There were concerns over impartiality, given that the incumbent Attorney General was chosen to chair, with members including an individual who had served with the UN ad hoc Committee on Measures to Eliminate International Terrorism, and another who had served as Sri Lanka's Permanent Representative to the UN during the final stages of the war. All members were personally chosen by the President, with a standing tenure of nearly eighteen months of which less than a month was spent outside Colombo and only six days in the war zone of the Vanni itself. Additional issues arose over language. Many people needed to give testimony in Tamil and were not sure that they were understood; gender sensitivity was lacking in terms of any means for private expressions about sexual violence. There was no witness protection, and a lack of transparency for the Commission's approach and plans. Amnesty International (2011) issued a statement: 'Sri Lanka's LLRC is not a credible accountability mechanism. Its mandate is seriously flawed and in practice it falls far short of international standards on national commissions of inquiry.' Doubts were voiced by Sri Lankan civil society, by many in the diaspora and by international human rights organisations. Amnesty International sent a submission to the LLRC in August 2010 highlighting what it called systematic failures of domestic mechanisms to bring about justice, truth and reparations for victims.

In October 2010, Amnesty International, Human Rights Watch and the ICG declined an invitation to testify before the LLRC, noting its severe shortcomings, including the Commission's 'inadequate mandate, insufficient guarantees of independence, and lack of witness protection'. The UN Secretary-General's Independent Panel expressed the view that the LLRC could not satisfy the commitment on accountability given by the President of Sri Lanka and the Secretary-General of the UN (Ratwatte 2012). They found that the Sri Lankan justice system was incapable of providing accountability. The independence of the Attorney General had been eroded and the continuation of emergency regulations and the Prevention of Terrorism Act at that time precluded the judiciary from holding the government to account.

The LLRC released its report on 16 December 2011. Its impact and proceedings will be further examined in Chapter 6. An analytical study of 105 recommendations in the report categorised them into eight issue areas that had been listed by the UN Human Rights Council: 1) credible investigations of allegations of extrajudicial killings and enforced disappearances; 2) demilitarising the North;

3) implementing impartial land dispute resolution mechanisms; 4) re-evaluating detention policies; 5) strengthening formerly independent civil institutions; 6) reaching a political settlement on devolution of power to the provinces; 7) promoting and protecting the right of freedom of expression for all; and 8) enacting rule of law reforms (Verité Research 2012).

In a speech delivered at the Platform for Freedom meeting convened in May 2012, Saravanamuttu hailed the LLRC report as one of the most important documents in the history of the country since the end of the war and since independence. He recognised that it highlighted the challenges facing the country in terms of human rights, for reconciliation and for governance itself (Vikalpa Sri Lanka 2012). This talk was given following the passing of a resolution by the Human Rights Council in Geneva calling on the Sri Lankan government to fulfil its legal obligations towards justice and accountability, and to 'expeditiously provide a comprehensive action plan to implement the recommendations of its Lessons Learnt and Reconciliation Commission and also to address alleged violations of international law' (Human Rights Watch 2012). Saravanamuttu pointed to the fact that the LLRC report was still available only in English and not in either national language, stating that it was a matter of priority for it to be translated and made available immediately in all public libraries. The very essence of democracy, he argued, was the ability of citizens to make informed choices, and to do so they need information. A national debate was needed to identify the priority substantive recommendations of the LLRC that needed to be implemented in order to make a real difference and contribution to reconciliation. Priorities defined by civil society and implementation monitored by civil society would include: demilitarisation of the north-east; a decrease in the military presence, which currently was one solder to eight civilians; the reduction of the military's role in economic and civic or political life; and information about and access to LTTE detainees. (Promises had been made since 2010 to the TNA with no demonstrable progress.) A public listing and database of detainees was needed, as lack of knowledge of the whereabouts of family members continued to cause much personal suffering and resulted in great public tension and mistrust, undermining any possibility of wider reconciliation. A related outstanding concern was provision for legislation regarding the right to information. Reconciliation required a political framework, and it was the GoSL's responsibility to act for a political settlement by responding to TNA proposals, re-establishing bilateral talks, and – only after demonstrable progress had been achieved on these – establishing a parliamentary select committee to agree to the recommendations in a short timeframe. This vision called for a particular blend of accountability and responsive governance for healing and social renewal in Sri Lanka.

In the short term, there was little visible change, and many people inside Sri Lanka had simply never heard of the LLRC. In official statements, infrastructure and economics were continually given precedence over politics and governance reform, as though economic development would blunt political aspirations and grievances. Development planning itself was centralised, with all decisions going through the Ministry for Economic Development, as per Basil Rajapaksa's *Uthuru Wasanthaya* or 'Northern Awakening' programme and the Presidential Task Force. The GoSL had also drafted a National Human Rights Action Plan in 2009, something to present to the UN Universal Periodic Review that year, and there was a Presidential Adviser on Reconciliation who prepared a draft reconciliation policy. It was claimed that the government was in 'talks' with the TNA leadership, but the latter despaired of delays and lack of substance.

Meanwhile, in the North, people were banned from public grieving, no memorials to fallen Tamils were allowed, graveyards were razed by bulldozers, and Hindu shrines destroyed to make way for Buddhist sites. In March 2012, Ambika Satkunanathan described how she had asked Tamils across the North whether they felt that a public ceremony to mark the end of the war and to commemorate those killed was desirable, and whether they had thought about convening such an event.

The immediate response from every person interviewed was that since they felt they couldn't even speak of issues relating to the ethnic conflict, they couldn't imagine holding public events to remember the dead. This is evidence not only of the severe restrictions placed upon the freedom of expression and assembly amongst the Tamil communities, but also the alienation this population feels from the state and the majority Sinhalese community. (Satkunanathan 2012)

Both grieving and grievance as legitimate dimensions of experience for the defeated Tamils were to be eclipsed by a dominant narrative in which a deviant terrorist threat had been and was still being cleansed from the country. The Ministry for Rehabilitation and Prison Reform produced films and numerous press releases on its work with former fighters and child soldiers – now to be called 'beneficiaries' and 'our children'. On the positive side, education was offered very rapidly in showcase programmes to young former LTTE cadres, and the programmes rolled out their exam successes: for example, two fortunates would go on to medical school. But the Ministry was top heavy in its messages, although the social engineering was possibly well intentioned: for example, the 'Peace Village' in Vavuniya with its mass marriage of 53 couples who were given plots of land to farm for the 'inculcation of family values'. A polished presentation given to members of parliament and the diplomatic community stressed 'distorted morals and social values' as a cause of the LTTE-led war. The very smooth PowerPoint presentation included a classic iceberg image with a tip of 'armed conflict'. Under the waterline were causal markers including 'distorted history', 'brainwashed psychology' and 'remnants of unresolved issues from colonialization'. Underlying the war were 'imbalances: conceptual, moral and physical', plus 'distorted morals and social values'. No root causes in terms of grievance over language or opportunity were identified whatsoever.[18]

If the new narrative insisted on deeming Tamil grievances as pathological rather than rooted in historical experience and political validity, the impact of well-intentioned reintegration policies had to be doubted. The gap in social understanding and experience between South and North was stark – both were victims with their own experience of suffering, yet intelligent (and no doubt compassionate) businessmen in the South now believed that 'the North and East is where the Land and opportunity are' – as though the land was not previously inhabited or claimed. It existed in such a southern mind as an open (empty) frontier, ripe for exploitation.[19]

In his 2013 critique of the political economy of post-war Sri Lanka, Bastian examined this type of economic penetration and the policies of the Rajapaksa regime in relation to global capitalism. He is clear that the post-war ideological debates on managing state–society relations were dominated by the notions of development and reconciliation, and that these were posed as an alternative to the fundamental reforms of the state that would be necessary to meet Tamil demands for self-governance. 'It wants to forget the war, how it ended and the implication of these events especially on the nature of the state ... It ignores creeping authoritarianism' and assumed a post-conflict phase for Sri Lanka, when in fact it was post-war and still profoundly conflicted (Bastian 2013).

TNA spokesmen privately voiced the view that their government counterparts did not take 'dialogue' seriously: meetings were continually cancelled or delayed, any encounter was kept to a minimum of time, and nothing of substance was ever voiced, much less put on the table. They could not endorse a parliamentary select committee with no meaningful or agreed agenda. By 2012, however, they had – along with the Sri Lanka Muslim Congress (SLMC) – for the first time contested provincial council elections in the Eastern Province, expressing a hope that their combined support would outdo the government majority. There were discussions on forming a coalition for provincial government. No party was able to command an absolute majority in the thirty-seven-member council. In the event, the TNA won eleven seats; the SLMC seven; and the main opposition UNP secured four seats. The ruling United People's Freedom Alliance (UPFA) finished with fifteen seats, and then pressured the SLMC to join it in forming the council. Pollsters concluded that 63.7 per cent of the votes were anti-government. Respected sources reported that five elected TNA councillors from the Eastern Province fled to Colombo and were in hiding after intimidation (and offers of houses or money) to join the ruling party. Senior TNA leader Sampanthan issued a statement to the press indicating his disquiet at post-electoral developments. On 18

September 2012, the ruling coalition's Najeeb Abdul Majeed was sworn in as the Chief Minister in the Eastern Province. Locally, the TNA was pressured and intimidated to give way, and it appeared that the SLMC was also put under pressure. The first provincial council elections in the North would not be held until 2013.

The actions of the government belied any claim of offering meaningful representation in the Eastern Province, just as no political reform was under discussion with TNA leaders. Rajapaksa had opted for a recovery model based on 'hardware' over 'software'. He had prioritised a grand vision of development, shifted away from Western aid and partners to largely Chinese backing, and had rewritten the story of the war and its aftermath. But his approach was in danger of losing sight of the post-war needs shared by all communities. Colombo was basking in redevelopment and beautification but the displaced urban poor could not simply be rendered invisible, and numerous rural villages were still in need of poverty alleviation. 'The benefits of infrastructure remain elusive to people, the sharp sense of marginalization, the dichotomy of macro-level development and micro-level grievances of people … *per contra*, the aspirations and unresolved grievances of people lie buried under paved roads and grand structures' (Thaheer et al. 2013: 156).[20]

Visaka Dharmadasa, the Kandy-based founder of the national Association of Parents of Missing Soldiers (which she established in 1998, as the mother of a missing soldier), travelled to Vavuniya to speak with mothers of the Tamil dead and missing, and was met initially with suspicion. Allaying their personal fears of herself as a person, talking about the chain of military command that sends fighters on any side to their deaths, and gaining their trust, she found that some 500 families came forward needing to search for lost loved ones. There was no national mechanism, no official recognition of this dimension of unfinished business after the war. In the words of Laksiri Fernando, the government had 'an ideological or policy disorientation that precludes its move towards reconciliation … the belief that after the defeat of the LTTE, there is nothing left to reconcile and the Tamil people might slowly adjust to the new reality'.[21]

In the aftermath of a vanquished LTTE, and in post-war Sri Lanka, who then were 'the Tamil people'? A remarkably diverse and differentiated population, as evidenced by the list below of attendees who travelled to a privately organised forum in Switzerland in November 2009: Tamil United Liberation Front, Up-Country Peoples Front, Eelam People's Democratic Party, Sri Lanka Muslim Congress, All Ceylon Muslim Congress, Democratic People's Front, Tamil Eelam Liberation Organisation, Eelam Revolutionary Organisation of Students, All Ceylon Tamil Congress, Tamil National Alliance, Tamil Makkal Viduthalai Pulikal, Tamil Arasu Kadchi, People's Liberation Organisation of Tamil Eelam, and the Ceylon Workers Congress. Some of these individuals had not spoken to each other for years, or had found themselves in oppositional positions during the cut and thrust of war-induced division. They debated, pondered and came up with a joint statement that was circulated in Sri Lanka on their return:

Joint Statement: 25 November 2009

We, the representatives of the political parties of the Tamil-speaking peoples unanimously:

Affirm the historic meeting enabling an exchange of views initiating, and express a full commitment to, a common forum among representatives of all Tamil-speaking peoples;
  Recognise 'Tamil-speaking peoples' comprise three distinct peoples: Tamils, Muslims, and Tamils of Indian origin;
  Respect the distinct and separate identities, interests and positions of the parties;
  Recognise and affirm the need for unity and consensus among the Tamil-speaking peoples while acknowledging differences with regard to some issues and the paths to pursue them;
  Commit to the engagement by all segments of society towards a just and durable political solution through a dignified, respectful and peaceful process;
  Agree and commit to continuing our dialogue.

The statement above arose from deliberations by representatives from within Sri Lanka, many of whom had to reconcile between and among themselves after years of often bitter division and a not always cohesive struggle. Meanwhile, internationally, other discussions were taking place on the development of the Transitional Government of Tamil Eelam (TGTE 2010). Global human rights institutions were not forgetting the way the war had ended, and internal soul searching was under way within UN circles. Resistance to Rajapaksa's post-war agenda was not going to disappear; the issues of accountability and governance reform would find additional momentum on an international stage.

CHAPTER 2

Executive presidency and the unitary state

Democracies have citizens. Kings need subjects. Absolutist monarchs need absolutely servile subjects. (Tisaranee Gunasekara)

The thrust of Mahinda Rajapaksa's particular brand of presidentialism may be understood through consideration of his personal political trajectory, as well as of the context and constitutional ethos in which he emerged to take power. Both the executive presidency and the unitary state had prior foundations, which Rajapaksa built on in an agile fashion. Both were intrinsically linked to political economy, from which he would additionally benefit. The prevailing message of the unitary state was not only directed at conflicted Sinhalese/Tamil/Muslim relations but also intended to transcend a very particular tension characterised as 'between neoliberalism and populism' and seen in the disparity between the newer urban middle classes and increasingly impoverished small farmers in the periphery. Gunawardena points to the paradox represented by the Rajapaksa brothers, Mahinda and Gotabaya, the former Defence Secretary. As president, Mahinda exuded the image of the villager, the populist voice rallying against any external threat to the common people. Gotabaya, on the other hand, took on the beautification of Colombo as a modernised city exemplifying privatisation, outsourcing and the world of international finance (Gunawardena 2015). Executive powers invested in the former enabled the latter pursuit, through the transfer of urban development affairs to the Department of Defence.[1]

As understood in political theory, presidential and parliamentary systems of government differ in the relationship between the executive and the legislature. In a parliamentary system, the executive is composed of sitting members of the legislature, including the prime minister and cabinet, whereas in a presidential system the executive is headed by a directly elected president, meaning greater separation of powers between the executive and legislature. Key considerations in practice, then, are oversight and the balance of powers; hence the notion of 'checks and balances' (Guruparan 2015a: 429).[2]

In Sri Lanka, within a year of the 2009 military victory, the following could be observed:

> Mr Rajapaksa himself, besides being president, is minister of defence, finance and planning, ports and aviation, and highways. In all, he is directly responsible for 78 institutions. One, the defence ministry, is a condominium with his brother, Gotabaya, the defence secretary. Besides control of the armed forces, police and coast guard, it has expanded its remit to take in immigration and emigration, as well as, curiously, the Urban Development Authority and the Land Reclamation and Development Corporation.
>
> Another Rajapaksa brother, Basil, is economic-development minister and senior presidential adviser, with oversight, among other things, of wildlife conservation and the boards of both investment- and tourism-promotion. He also runs a presidential task force set up to develop the war-ravaged north and east.
>
> A fourth brother, the eldest, Chamal, has forsaken his former cabinet seat. All is not lost, however. He has been elected unopposed as speaker of parliament. (*The Economist* 2010)

This extraordinary ascendancy was assumed by a man who once marched in protest at human rights abuses in his country. He was also an active campaigner for trade union and labour rights and served as chairman of the Sri Lanka Committee for Solidarity with Palestine for thirty years (Al Jazeera 2010). Here was a man who had not only studied law and human rights, but had himself been detained as an activist when leaving for Geneva in 1992 to take part in the thirty-first session of the Working Group on Enforced or Involuntary Disappearances. His detention was challenged in court,[3] and yet under his own tenure the judiciary was undermined and dissident voices advocating for reform were threatened or even silenced. While there is a record of his own one-time opposition to the executive presidency in Sri Lanka (Jabbar 2014; Sri Lanka Liberal Democrats 2009),[4] it was on his watch that privilege and dispensation were taken to new levels.

A lawyer by profession, Rajapaksa carefully cultivated the image of being a southern son of the soil. He wore traditional national dress and was hardly ever seen without his trademark maroon shawl; this was adopted from an uncle, a state counsel, who wore a reddish brown shawl to symbolise the particular red lentil cultivated by farmers in his home region. Admirers noted that the President 'keeps a cow in his garden', even when in high office. Although attired in country garb as a badge of the common man's honour, President Rajapaksa would effectively be anointed 'king' and deemed a reincarnation of Sinhalese King Dutugemunu, who reigned from 161 BC to 137 BC – a legendary or mythical figure known for having defeated an invading Tamil army (Liyanage 2013).

When the UPFA won a small majority in the 2004 parliamentary elections, Rajapaksa became Sri Lanka's thirteenth Prime Minister. The following March (2005) saw him visiting Northern Ireland, hosted by the Ulster-based International Conflict Research Institute (INCORE). According to the INCORE website:

> During this visit, the Prime Minister was briefed about varied peace and conflict related activity ongoing across the University; the current state of the peace process in Northern Ireland with a particular focus on strategies for breaking political stalemate and deadlock; and the post-conflict social, economic and physical regeneration of the region. (INCORE 2005)

That same year he challenged Ranil Wickremesinghe in the presidential elections. Ranil was strongly identified with the Norwegian intervention (by then in serious difficulty) and international attempts to deliver a liberal peace in Sri Lanka. In stark contrast to this, Rajapaksa campaigned on a platform of Sinhalese nationalism in alliance with hard-line parties such as the JVP, the

Jathika Hela Urumaya (JHU, a political party of Buddhist clergy) and Mahajana Eksath Peramuna (MEP), all of whom were distinct advocates of the unitary state. As early as 2006 a huge cardboard placard appeared at Maradhana junction in Colombo proclaiming him to be 'next to Dutugemunu'.

The stage was set for post-war Sri Lanka to be distinguished by a cult of personality that included the hailing of Mahinda Rajapaksa as the 'High King of Sri Lanka', an infallible hero. This began soon after military victory through a consistent narrative that constructed a mythical pedigree for the Rajapaksas, connecting them to this ancient warrior King Dutugemunu and also to the Buddha. Rajapaksa was hailed as the 'Lion in the Lion Flag', 'Father of the Nation', 'Wonder of the World and the Universe', 'Golden Sword which Defends the Nation', 'Golden Thread which Unites Sundered Hearts', 'Leader who Conquered the World' and 'The Sun and the Moon to a Country which Defeated Terror'. He was even proclaimed by the Sangha as the 'Universally Renowned Lord of the Three Sinhala Lands' (Gunasekara 2014a). In fact, there was official endorsement of the association between the President and Dutugemunu, the Sinhala King who had defeated 'invading Tamils' more than 2,000 years before. 'It took 13 years for Dutugemunu to regain lost territory and establish total sovereignty over Sri Lanka. But it took less than three years for Mr Rajapaksa to achieve the same goal,' Sri Lanka's Ministry of Defence posted on its website, adding rather ruefully that kings were 'not restrained by issues of human rights' (Harrison 2013).

Constitutional history: background to the executive presidency and the unitary state

On independence in 1948, Sri Lanka had an impressive international reputation; it was known as a country with strong democratic traditions and high levels in literacy and health indicators, with its own welfare state provisions offering free education and food security for all its citizens. Venugopal (2015) describes the historical dilemma thus: by the mid-1940s, the government had initiated a range of transformative social welfare schemes such as subsidised food, free education and free public health, which changed life for the better for the large majority who had hitherto been deprived. Thus, by the early 1960s, Sri Lanka was seen widely as an unusual and precocious development miracle.

> Between 1946 and 1963 the infant mortality rate dropped from 141 per 1000 to 56 per 1000, while life expectancy increased from 43 to 63 years. The adult literacy rate, which was already comparatively high in 1946 at 58%, rose quickly to 72% by 1963. But these improvements also occurred in the absence of anything near a commensurate increase in economic growth, so that Sri Lanka had, in terms of social welfare indicators, burst into the league of countries that were a factor of between five and 10 times wealthier in terms of income. (Venugopal 2015: 672)

Venugopal argues persuasively that Sri Lanka's executive presidency was born out of an elite impulse to create a more stable, centralised and authoritarian political structure that would overcome and reverse the negative economic effects of a populist electoral democracy. It was argued that powers were needed in a strong central leadership that could direct liberalising reforms which a populist parliament would most likely oppose. The public were unlikely to support either market reform or fiscal austerity, deemed by modernisers as critical to lifting Sri Lanka from its agrarian base.

The privileged role of Buddhism, Sinhala as the official language, the nature of public service and the executive's power over the lower judiciary all derive from the 1972 Constitution, which affirmed the unitary state in its second article. The opening and ending of the document invoke the Buddhist ideal in Pali vernacular: *Devo vassatu kaalena/sassasampatti hetu ca/phito bhavatu loko ca/raja bhavatu dhammiko* – that is: 'May the rains fall in time/May the harvest be bountiful/May the people be contented/May the king be righteous' (Rajagopalan 1997: 8). Here was an evocative cultural claim, in keeping with departure from the less colourful British-imposed Soulbury Constitution that had prevailed since 1946. More a charter for government reform than a formal constitution giving identity to a state, the Soulbury Constitution outlined administrative provisions including the prohibition of parliamentary interference in both religious practice and the privileging of one religion above another.

The only part of the 1972 Constitution that dealt with smaller units than the unitary state was its description of electoral units. This was the first constitution of the Republic,[5] which removed the notion of an independent civil service and paved the way for the politicisation of the bureaucracy. The independence of the judiciary was weakened by several provisions that tilted the balance of power firmly towards the legislature, and the safeguards for minorities provided under the previous Independence Constitution were abolished. The 1972 Constitution, which was enacted 'on the tenth day of the waxing moon, in the month of Vesak in the year two thousand five hundred and fifteen of the Buddhist era', changed the name of the country from Ceylon and proclaimed that the 'Republic of Sri Lanka shall give to Buddhism the foremost place' and that 'it shall be the duty of the State to protect and foster Buddhism' (Tamilnation.org n.d.). These origins lend themselves to a description of Sri Lanka as an ethnocracy, as explored by Welikala in his comparative work on state and constitutional history. He offers the following definition, quoting Yiftachel:

> Ethnocracy denotes a type of regime that facilitates and promotes the process of ethnicisation, that is, expansion and control. It surfaces in disputed territories, where one ethnonational group is able to appropriate the state apparatus and mobilise its legal, economic, and military resources to further its territorial, economic, cultural, and political interests. The struggles over the process of ethnic expansion become the central axis along which social and political relations evolve.[6] (Yiftachel 2006)

Welikala (2008) cites the *vamsa* tradition of Sinhala–Buddhist historiography, meaning that Sri Lanka was not only the *Sihaladeepa* (the island of the Sinhalese), but also the *Dhammadeepa* (the island of the *dharma*). In modern terms, this means that the unitary state is the natural form of centralised government that is required to defend the Sinhala–Buddhist patrimony, especially against the historic 'other', the Tamils (Welikala 2008; Nadarajah and Vimalarajah 2008). It is noteworthy that, during trips to the North in 2010 and 2011, one still heard frequently in private conversation the phrase 'two nations', such was the bitter reality after the loss and destruction of the LTTE administration (which functioned alongside Sri Lankan state public service provision), territorial control and long-standing, socialised aspirations. Welikala (2015c) points to a state in which the constitutional order is substantially at odds with the ethno-cultural diversity of its polity, and consistently incapable of accommodating its multinational character. 'Beneath the stiff carapace of ethnocratic state sovereignty, therefore, lurks a fundamental crisis of legitimacy and chronic instability.'[7]

This leads to his second characterisation: that the unitary state also presents in constitutional reform debates in ways that are opposed to Sinhala–Buddhist chauvinism, and, moreover, that are grounded in modern political theory and civic nationalism with strong overtones of state sovereignty, non-intervention in the domestic affairs of states, and 'Third World' solidarity. This he describes as a 'Jacobin' position because of its view of the republican nation-state: nation and state in a unitary discourse of national identity and institutional form, inclusive of managed commitments to devolution. Welikala reminds us that this vision of the nation-state accommodates pluralism so long as minority claims do not seriously challenge the overarching unitary nature of state, nation and sovereignty. Its accommodation does not extend to the recognition of any sub-state *national* claims, and the use of force is seen as justified in suppressing sub-state national movements should they threaten unitary order, as consistent with the sovereign state.

Subsequently, the 1978 Constitution changed the electoral system to proportional representation, with an unintended consequence of weakening the relationship between the MP and the voter. This was because MPs no longer represented a specific electorate but were elected to an electoral district often containing numerous traditional electorates. It can be argued that, because candidates were now compelled to campaign throughout an electoral district with a number of diverse constituencies, election campaigns under the proportional representation system became more costly. There were negative consequences: candidates with the wealth and means to finance expensive campaigns had a better chance of winning; and there was greater likelihood of candidates needing to depend on patrons, benefactors or rich businessmen, thereby making corruption an integral dimension of electioneering. Apart from the fact that proportional representation is often viewed outside Sri Lanka as a panacea for the shortcomings of 'first past the post' systems, it is important to note electoral processes in particular relation to Sri Lanka. The 1978 Constitution did not specifically affirm the principle of parliamentary sovereignty in the same manner as the 1972 version, but nonetheless 'seemed implicitly to perpetuate some of the theoretical assumptions about the ultimate supremacy of Parliament'. It would seem that structural constraints on elections themselves and how parliament functions will play into the hands of a strong executive (Anketell and Welikala 2013).

By then the government was shifting away from the previous 'dirigisme' or state-controlled economic policies that had characterised the post-independence period, shaping industry and trade: high tariffs for the protection of domestic industry, price and exchange controls, and restrictive policies aimed at the private sector in favour of high welfare spending. The economy would be liberalised to enhance the private sector and to take an export orientation geared to a new positioning in global markets. And then, in the 1978 Constitution, Article 30 proclaimed that there would be a President of the Republic. There were robust debates at the time. Dudley Senanayake, the leader of the UNP, warned in a statement made outside the Constituent Assembly that a presidential system would spell disaster for Sri Lanka:

> The presidential system has worked in the United States where it was the result of a special historic situation. It worked in France for similar reasons. But for Ceylon it would be disastrous. It would create a tradition of Caesarism. It would concentrate power in a leader and undermine parliament and the structure of the political parties. In America and France it has worked but generally it is a system for a Nkrumah or a Nasser, not for a free democracy.[8]

Immunity provisions for the President were also enacted under the 1978 Constitution, as was the conferral of immunity for state officials under emergency laws. In Sri Lanka, the President is given immunity for actions taken during his or her term under the constitution (ICJ 2012). Amendments to the constitution since 1978 have frequently augmented presidential powers, with the exception of the seventeenth, which was passed in 2001 when Chandrika Kumaratunga held the presidency. This actually reined in presidential power by making it mandatory for a Constitutional Council to approve the appointment of all Supreme Court judges, the Auditor General, Attorney General and heads of independent commissions.

Rajapaksa's executive presidency

The seventeenth was overruled subsequently by the eighteenth under Rajapaksa. His eighteenth amendment infamously abolished limits on how often a president could seek re-election and hold office. It replaced the ten-member Constitutional Council with a five-member Parliamentary Council with power to 'observe' rather than approve or veto appointments, and brought 'independent' commissions under the control of the President. Or, to quote an observer from Delhi at the time: 'In short, it is all about arming the President with absolute power'(ICJ 2012). An editorial in the *Sunday Leader* was scathing:

> This is a classic example of Rajapaksa governance – the Independent Commissions will not be abolished; they will merely be rendered utterly meaningless ... Another proposed amendment will enable the President to sit in parliament and take part in parliamentary proceedings. This amendment too will be touted as a 'democratising' measure which reduces the power of the President by making him accountable to parliament. In reality, it will enable the President to attend parliament at will, interfere in its work, and most importantly, to keep government parliamentarians on a very short leash.

The Rajapaksas would know that an impeachment motion or a radical power shift in parliament, though not highly likely, is not impossible. Chamal Rajapaksa was made the Speaker precisely to prevent such a mishap. With the new amendment, the President himself will be able to play the 'Big Brother' to UPFA parliamentarians. This amendment, which violates the principle of separation of powers, will further empower the President under the guise of restraining him.[9] (Gunasekara 2010)

Rajapaksa could now appoint his own choices (loyalists or cronies?) to all so-called independent commissions, thus paving the way for the total politicisation of every previously democratic institution in the country. The text of the eighteenth amendment was not made available to the public or even to parliamentarians until it was presented on the floor for a vote. It was sent to the Supreme Court as an 'urgent' bill. The ICG (2010c) called it a de facto constitutional coup which indicated that the 'many decades old democracy is hanging by a thread'. It was passed by a two-thirds majority in a move that did not inspire confidence in due process:

> Inefficiency, and unfairness results if jobs are handed out as political patronage. TUC secretary Saman Rathnapriya said the end of the 17th amendment will mean a politicised and corrupt public service. Navarthne Bandara, president of the Postal Officers Union, said that under the new arrangements 'power to appoint officials to the public service will be vested with ministry secretaries who are appointed by ministers under whose whims and fancies they will function. This will surely have the public service eating out of the politician's hand'. The pressure group CPA (the Centre for Policy Alternatives) says the 17th amendment did not work because of 'intransigence and contempt for constitutional provisions on the part of successive presidents, rather than any fatal structural flaw that made it inherently unworkable.'[10] (Colman 2010)

There were indeed systemic deficits in operating to constitutional provisions, working to legal frameworks and standards of procedure. One observer pointed to 'executive meddling' as having long politicised and corrupted Sri Lanka's courts system. 'Telephone justice', whereby the Attorney General's or President's office called judges and directed them how to rule in particular cases, was rumoured to be common right up to the Supreme Court (DeVotta 2013).

In terms of expanding central powers, Rajapaksa infuriated many by advocating a strong centre that connected to the grass-roots or village level, bypassing regional devolution in the classic sense both through a *Grama Rajya* or village community concept (Gunasekara 2011)[11] and through budget control via the Divinegume ('Improving Lives') plan for a new government agency that would amalgamate development budget allocations under the authority of the Minister of Economic Development, namely his brother Basil. In essence, the Divinegume bill was to shift an additional $600 million to Basil Rajapaksa for development and poverty alleviation, with little if any oversight[12] and a secrecy clause forbidding Divinegume personnel from divulging any information about the working of the programme. As it happened, in this case the Supreme Court, led by Chief Justice Shirani Bandaranayake, ruled against the government:

> The president's reaction was to summarily sign the order removing Mrs. Bandaranayake, even as pro-government thugs brandishing poles gathered outside her official residence to celebrate the presidential ruling and intimidate her – lest she refused to give up her post. Their actions were consistent with recent attacks against those associated with the judiciary, including an assault on the Judiciary Service Commission secretary after he complained about executive interference in the courts; members of Sri Lanka's Bar Association being issued death threats; and prominent lawyers who protested vocally against the Chief Justice's impeachment receiving threatening letters from a secret group identifying itself as the Patriotic Front. (DeVotta 2013)

The very public impeachment and its unabashed show of an abuse of executive power brought vehement reactions both internally and externally. Opposition parliamentarians rejected the nominal select committee report endorsing the Act; the Bar Association protested in full; lawyers took to the streets in protest; and a broad range of civil society groups registered their objections (Rezwan 2013). The International Commission of Jurists issued an outright condemnation of the impeachment, as did numerous Western governments. In November 2012, UN Special Rapporteur Gabriela Knaul called on the Sri Lankan government to reconsider the impeachment and ensure that any hearing complied with principles of due process and fair trial (UN 2012); UN High Commissioner for Human Rights Navi Pillay expressed concern that the action would set back agendas for accountability and reconciliation; and from the EU came a statement by High Representative Catherine Ashton about the impeachment process, stating that 'the independence of the judicial branch cannot be made subject to actions by any other branch of government' (EU 2013).

While the Commonwealth Secretariat had issued several statements, the *Colombo Telegraph* (2012) reported that at least one of two independent eminent jurists (whose opinion had been sought within the Secretariat) had found the impeachment flawed and in violation of Commonwealth values and that the Commonwealth Secretary-General had withheld these findings. There began a state of limbo with the newly appointed Chief Justice simply not being recognised by numerous leading legal figures in Sri Lanka. But the President did not back down.

Unitary or unipolar state

Rajapaksa was on his way to heading one of the biggest governments in the world, with more than 100 ministers and deputy ministers in office. On closer scrutiny this looked more like a vast networked structure of patronage and control – politicians would thrive only if inside the ruling circle. The real government was much smaller, being concentrated around the three Rajapaksa brothers who managed nearly 70 per cent of the state budget between them. 'The family had captured the country's economy, administration as well as the management of the ruling Political party' (Mckenzie 2014). While the eighteenth amendment demonstrably enhanced presidential powers – allowing the direct appointment of members of all independent commissions and the judiciary, and removing presidential term limits, paving the way for stronger and longer time in office – there were other changes in store. Oversight of all NGOs was put under the remit of the Department of Defence, with subsequent new regulations requiring NGOs to report the sources of all funding and account directly for spending. In July 2010, NGOs working in the northern district were put under new restrictions, allowing no 'soft' projects (trauma work and empowerment or psycho-social programmes). In November of the same year, the International Committee of the Red Cross (ICRC) was asked to close all offices in northern Sri Lanka and operate exclusively from Colombo, the government arguing that the country's needs had changed since the end of the war. The ICG suggested that the message being sent to Tamils in Sri Lanka and in the million-strong diaspora was a humiliating one that undermined the chances for political reconciliation (ICG 2010b). There would be direct central control of post-war recovery in the North.

The centralisation of power and the personalisation of decision making meant that the unitary state was beginning to look like a unipolar one, relying on a type of command development, in that political and military personnel were utilised to oversee recovery measures in the North while also participating in massive infrastructure projects being directed countrywide from the centre. There were historical precedents for central control of development in Sri Lanka: for example, in the realm of agriculture and the installation of primarily Sinhalese farmers through large settlement schemes and mass irrigation designed, built and overseen by central government. Notable among these is the Accelerated Mahaweli Development Programme, which irrigated over 85,000 hectares of land and resettled some 78,000 families; it was overseen by a government authority with little transparency and high degrees of control over the construction of five dams, rural infrastructure and roads, and associated business enterprises. The Mahaweli Authority, established in 1979, was privileged in its purview and not known for its accountability.

Unipolar command development

Post-war command development with regard to the North was initially the means of responding to huge humanitarian challenges: the resettlement of IDPs, de-mining activities, and provision for the basic needs of civilians. All decisions relating to recovery in the North were taken by the Presidential Task Force (which had no Tamil members), which had neither consultative processes nor the involvement of local people or voices from ground level. Task force guidelines were not made public, its members were appointed directly by the President, and it was chaired by his brother Basil Rajapaksa, Minister of Economic Development. Its remit extended from overseeing resettlement of IDPs to discretionary powers over access concerning national NGOs and international agencies, and top-down, centralised implementation strategies that contributed to 'consolidating the regime in the Northern Process' (Saparamadu and Lall 2014: 16).

On a visit by the author to Jaffna and the surrounding area in early 2010, local people who had been 'resettled' privately expressed severe levels of insecurity, in that land could be claimed and encroached upon with little or no notice, ruined houses destroyed rather than rebuilt, and general morale lowered by the presence of intimidating gangs. This was despite a consistently high ratio of soldiers to civilians. 'So much military, so little security,' was a common lament. At least back in the day of the LTTE, locals observed, you could leave your daughters at home and feel they were safe. It is important to note here the direct line from government to paramilitaries such as the LTTE breakaway Karuna group and Eelam People's Democratic Party (EPDP), which had helped the GoSL fight the LTTE in arrangements predating Rajapaksa. Conditions of service changed, however, to a reportedly free rein for extortion and kidnap for ransom as income generation. There was a known, practical agreement with the army to look the other way or just not be present – gangs would tip off the military in advance so that their operations would not be hindered so as to turn a blind eye in a systematic fashion.[13]

New communication systems for internet and mobile access had been prioritised, while fishermen in ancient wooden boats hoped that undersea mines had been cleared sufficiently for them to resume fishing. Bulldozers would appear on a previously claimed site in the middle of the night, the newcomer claiming it for their own use. Major new military bases required the seizure of large amounts of public and private land and the continued displacement of tens of thousands of people, while previous settlements disappeared into the high security zones. The growing involvement of the military in agricultural and commercial activities presented further obstacles, if not total blockages, to economic recovery for northern farmers and businesses. When challenged through public protest, the military demonstrated no inhibition in physically attacking demonstrators, and it was 'credibly accused of involvement in enforced disappearances and other extrajudicial punishments'.[14] Although the northern region was enjoying some sort of revival, attention was focused on identifying economic potential that was not always in keeping with local skills or the transitional sectors of small-scale agriculture, fisheries and animal husbandry, among other areas.

> [The] Rajapaksa regime wanted to keep each and every development activities under the command of itself. Because of this very reason the post-war development model and its supplementary activities [were] glued to 'Mahindha Chinthana' political propaganda ... In other words the development process that needed to be decentralized became highly centralized under this extremely politicized act ... as the eventual result of politicization of development ... [The] Rajapaksa regime used this ... to manage their political power in the post-war context and to legitimize its name in the nationalistic politics against both nationally and internationally confronted pressure groups. (Rajapaksha 2013)[15]

In February 2014, researcher Aftab Lall would blog about his encounters with the ever-present long arm of the Presidential Task Force:

> I remember getting increasingly anxious. We knew of the sensitivities around issues of displacement and the evictions that have taken place due to the establishment of high security zones (HSZs) all over the North of Sri Lanka, both during and after the war. We were also well aware of the omnipresence of the military, often in plain clothing – keeping a close eye on visitors. My colleague, familiar with government actors, managed to extract us from further interrogation (what are you doing here? how did you hear about these people? etc.). Our interviews and conversations with civil servants in the northern administration revealed a strong control over information around the resettlement process. We were told that information on the resettlement process could only be shared after getting approval from the Presidential Task Force (PTF). (Lall 2014)

A less than united unipolar unitary state

Behind the formal constitutional principle, beneath the rhetoric of a rosy Singapore-style successful future for all Sri Lankans, lay depths of complicating factors. 'We must unite,' Rajapaksa said, addressing minority Tamils in a public rally in the former war zone of Mullaitivu in 2014. 'Forget the past and let us build this country together' (*The Hindu* 2014). He was campaigning before the election in which he would finally be defeated. As his successor formed a government and moved to firm up political alliances, the old hurts and unfinished business raised their head. Tamil critics pointed out that minorities had not voted for the new president so much as against the old one:

> Sirisena also signed an agreement with the ultra-nationalist Jathika Hela Urumaya (JHU), *promising not to tamper with the unitary character of the constitution*, even though most Tamils

are close to unanimous in their view that a solution cannot be found within a unitary state. A unitary state centralises power in the centre. In a majoritarian democracy like Sri Lanka, this implies exclusive control of state power by the dominant community – the Sinhalese. For more than 60 years now, Tamils in Sri Lanka have been demanding self-determination against such a system, either through autonomous arrangements or a separate state. (Guruparan 2015b)

The depth of Tamil feeling, the uneasy accommodation in the East between 'Tamil-speaking' Muslims and others, the countrywide webs of patronage, rural and urban power formations, and intricacies of family lines and caste shape a force field at the heart of the so-called Sri Lankan democracy.[16] Sri Lankan elections are conducted regularly, even frequently, in a multiparty system. The electoral system operates at three levels: the national, subnational and local. Presidential and parliamentary elections are held nationally. Elections to provincial councils are held subnationally, while elections to municipal councils, urban councils and *Pradeshiya Sabhas* are conducted at the local level. As early as 2008, a *State of Democracy* report on Sri Lanka noted that the conduct of free and fair elections had become complicated, not least because the electoral commission had difficulty demonstrating independence, given presidential discretion on appointments and its very composition (International IDEA 2008).[17]

On 18 December 2009, the 'National Policy on Local Government' aspiration was published in the official *Gazette of the Democratic Socialist Republic of Sri Lanka*, claiming it was 'peoples' desire for all local units of human habitat to "emerge as microcentres of growth on modern lines"'. Therefore, the government would 'establish an efficient, effective and people's friendly local governance in Sri Lanka through the active participation of all civil society partners, community organizations and promoting a grass root level governing organization of "Jana Sabha" for a prosperous village government'. It is a rosy message referencing a friendly governance environment and participatory democracy.[18] Political commentators were not impressed with subsequent developments.

Tisaranee Gunasekara (2011) commented that the new *Jana Sabha* system of government looked set 'to gut the powers of local-level state structures in Sri Lanka, strengthening the hands of the Colombo regime'.[19] It had emerged that Sri Lanka's *Jana Sabhas* would be appointed, not elected institutions, and that they would be given most of the powers generally allocated to provincial councils and local government authorities. They would have the power to draw up their own budgets and development plans and to receive financial allocations from central government: that is, they would have control over the development budget disbursed to MPs, including expenditure and monitoring. *Jana Sabhas* were slow to take off and were defunct by 2015, according to local sources. By the time that Rajapaksa was defeated electorally, there were sixty *Jana Sabhas* established in his home district of Hambantota and twelve in another municipal area, Kurunegala.

But pressure for devolution based on the thirteenth amendment would not go away. While elections had been held for the Eastern Provincial Council in May 2008, the Northern Provincial Council remained under governor administration until September 2013 when elections were finally conducted, a shift attributed in a CPA policy paper to the context of Geneva as well as the impending Commonwealth Heads of Government Meeting (CHOGM) to be hosted by Sri Lanka in November that year (Ganeshathasan and Mendis 2015: 5). Some of Rajapaksa's confidence may have been dented by India's vote at the UNHRC in March 2012, when it criticised continuing human rights violations in the country, followed by the 2013 call for war crimes investigations. Moreover, word was that at village level in the North, few people had heard of the LLRC but 'everyone knows about Geneva'. Six months after taking office, the newly elected Chief Minister in the North stated in an interview that the change hoped for by people at the election, from a centrally oriented administration to a provincial administration, was not happening. They were trying to establish democratic governance in a province (in his own words) overwhelmed by an occupying military force, which systematically sought to subjugate the populace, change the demography, destabilise the economy, impose an alien culture and stultify legitimate democratic aspirations, while continuing with grave human rights abuses:

> Despite numerous promises we still have a Chief Secretary, appointed in contravention of the law, functioning in collaboration with the Governor, who was the former Army Commander of the Northern Province, to establish a parallel administrative structure. Apart from the legality of the structure, from a practical perspective how can one expect to carry out governance democratically, effectively or efficiently, when you have a parallel structure in place, backed by an ominous and omnipresent military? To make matters still worse, we have the bogey of the Tiger being resurrected to justify further militarisation. However, this was not unexpected. We knew the inadequacy of the 13th Amendment and did expect some interference, though the scale of interference from the military despite being in the spotlight of the world is worrisome for what it portends, not only for the North-East but for the rest of the country. (Srinivasan 2014)

The impression was that all sectors of public life were now in a degree of turmoil. Universities and doctors were on strike; the unions were restless; lawyers and judges had called for protests over interference in the judicial process; United Bhikku Front, an organisation of Buddhist monks affiliated with Sri Lanka's main opposition party, the UNP, was calling via a ten-point plan for the executive presidency to be done away with; and continual power cuts were blamed in part on substandard work on a Chinese-built power plant. The Securities Exchange Commission lost its second head in the space of less than a year, amid speculation about corruption and allegations of 'pump and dump' misuse of the stock market. A breakaway from the JHU, the Bodu Bala Sena (Buddhist Power Force or BBS) was increasingly visible from 2012, violently attacking churches and mosques, agitating against halal food and even the dress code of the veil, and conducting a campaign of intimidation against Muslim and Christian minority groups.

Executive overreach and the unitary state under fire

Sri Lanka faced international condemnation for domestic policies from two very different quarters. The Jeddah-based Organisation of Islamic Cooperation (OIC), an intergovernmental body with fifty-seven member countries, pointedly expressed its concerns over the escalating ethnic tensions in Sri Lanka that were damaging and affecting the island's Muslim community and its businesses sector. The OIC (formerly known as the Organisation of the Islamic Conference) is the second largest intergovernmental organisation after the UN, with a membership spread over four continents (Rasooldeen 2013). It is the collective voice of the Muslim world and strives to safeguard and protect the interests of Muslims in the spirit of promoting international peace and harmony among various peoples of the world.

The OIC was responding via effective lobbying by the Sri Lankan Secretariat for Muslims (SFM), a civil society organisation dedicated to working for the social inclusion of the Sri Lankan Muslim community, through advocacy efforts, capacity-building programmes on research methods, information gathering and documentation, as well as skills training to advocate for minority rights. The SFM highlighted concern over a mass rally attended by 15,000 in Maharagama and the vilification of Muslim dress, custom and mosques. They documented racist posters and handbills in public places, the harassment of people in Muslim dress, death threats directed at Muslim businessmen, desecration of mosques and Muslim businesses, and various public insults towards Muslim beliefs – and the fact that the government had not called a halt to the BBS's activities.[20]

At the same time, the decision to hold the 2013 CHOGM in Sri Lanka was mired in controversy. In April, the Commonwealth Law Conference meeting in Cape Town urged Sri Lanka's suspension from the councils of the Commonwealth on the grounds of serious breaches of the rule of law and judicial independence, noting the impeachment of the Chief Justice. It was also asserted that staging the CHOGM in Sri Lanka would tarnish the reputation of the Commonwealth. A resolution to this effect was ratified by the

Commonwealth Lawyers Association, the Commonwealth Legal Education Association and the Commonwealth Magistrates' and Judges' Association. While the Foreign Secretary of Bangladesh reassured President Rajapaksa that his country would 'stand by our Sri Lankan brothers on the issue of human rights', protests and demonstrations were growing in Tamil Nadu, Canada and the UK. The President pushed on relentlessly with public relations overtures in Commonwealth states, and observers noted how important the CHOGM was to his image and to the image of Sri Lanka. Four years after defeating the LTTE he wanted to:

> show the world that Sri Lanka has left its troubles behind. He was already on the case at the last CHOGM, held in Perth in 2011, when he strained to conjure up the sense of a paradise regained. Sri Lanka, he observed, had 'famous beaches' and 'lofty mountains', with 'an amazing variety of flora and fauna and safari parks teeming with wildlife'. Having seen off 'thirty years of violent terrorism unleashed by the world's most ruthless terrorist organisation', it was now a place 'full of promise, with an economy poised to take off' ... However, a Commonwealth Charter was in place to bring together 'the values and aspirations which unite the Commonwealth – democracy, human rights and the rule of law'. The document goes on to list no fewer than 16 'core values and principles', among them tolerance, respect and understanding, freedom of expression, the separation of powers and good governance, which the Commonwealth's 53 member states are all now pledged to uphold ... The problem is that Rajapaksa, for all his eagerness to seize the Commonwealth's helm, has spent years undermining those values and principles. Though democratically elected, he has relied on his popular mandate to sidestep or get rid of all the safeguards that ordinarily stop democrats from turning into demagogues.[21]

The CHOGM went ahead in Colombo, minus heads of state from India, Canada and Mauritius, conducted in purpose-built summit venues via lucrative commercial deals with China worth $1.5

billion. Much of the infrastructure for the CHOGM was funded by China, including a $292 million highway connecting the capital's international airport to the main city. Xinhua news agency reported that sites for the opening ceremony and the main sessions were also built or refurbished by funds from China (Firstpost.com 2013). If the impeachment and the way it was conducted against Bandaranayake boded ill for good governance and for Sri Lanka, some claimed that Secretary-General Sharma and the Commonwealth Secretariat were themselves bruised by this particular CHOGM and came out the worse for wear. Rajapaksa's action was in violation of the core values of the Commonwealth of Nations, notably the 2003 'Latimer House Principles on the Three Branches of Government'. The Latimer House Principles require the state to uphold the rule of law by protecting judicial independence and maintaining mutual respect and cooperation between parliament and the judiciary (Fernandez 2013).

In the wake of the CHOGM, the Venerable Maduluwawe Sobitha, convener of the National Movement for Social Justice, issued a public statement saying that it was time for the presidential system to be abolished, claiming that it had taken the country to new depths of corruption and lawlessness:

> The daily expenses of the Executive President is close to Rs. 23,400,000 [approximately $160,000] – it's a financial burden, which the country cannot afford. Moreover, it is also influencing and interfering with every segment of the country's administration as reflected by the rampant favouritism and nepotism within the foreign service where even military men who have committed cold blooded murders in Rathupaswala and Katunayake have been given diplomatic postings. (*Colombo Telegraph* 2014a)

He went on to state that the prevalent system was one in which drug lords and thugs – rather than ordinary, law-abiding citizens – could survive and thrive due to the heavy financial costs involved, and to express concern over widespread corruption, particularly within the judicial system but also through arbitrary donations. He also observed that the plight of small farmers had become so severe that those unable to grapple with their deteriorating financial situation were resorting to suicide by poison.[22]

In its seventh annual report on Islamophobia, the OIC reiterated its concern over intimidation and lack of protection for Muslim communities in Sri Lanka, also raising questions over the Sri Lankan government's unofficial patronage of extremist Buddhist group BBS (*Colombo Telegraph* 2014b). From Geneva, UN High Commissioner for Human Rights Navi Pillay also expressed her deep alarm at intercommunal violence, a year on from her visit to Sri Lanka and subsequent report to the UNHRC (UN 2014). This came in the midst of the rising tide of international calls for an investigation into war crimes, and must have seemed like maximum interference in internal affairs for the Executive President, increasingly accused of overreaching his powers and with wider and wider cracks showing in his version of the unitary state. Pushing back against international interference became a major effort in its own right.

CHAPTER 3

Non-interference Sri Lankan style

> Non-interference in the internal affairs of States, as clearly reflected in the UN Charter and the principles of NAM, must remain an abiding principle to be followed in spirit and letter. (President Mahinda Rajapaksa, address to the sixteenth Non-aligned Movement summit, Tehran, 30 August 2012)

The Rajapaksas in power embodied a particular elite preference for carefully choreographed responses to international criticism; to notions of global governance, human rights and humanitarian principles. Sri Lanka has a long history of international engagement; was a founding member of the South Asian Association for Regional Cooperation (SAARC); a member of the Commonwealth of Nations, the UN, the G77 and the Non-Aligned Movement (NAM). The region has a long-standing preference for non-interference as a principle, with strong articulations of sovereignty, particularly in Thailand, India and China.[1] From the frantic diplomatic attempts to avoid a bloodbath at the end of the war, to the report of Ban Ki-moon's Panel of Experts, to three contested resolutions at the UNHRC in Geneva (and three subsequent High Commissioner's reports), through to the 2014 Office of the UN High Commissioner for Human Rights (OHCHR) investigation interrogating war crimes in Sri Lanka, the government was under scrutiny for over five years. This scrutiny was actively resisted and countered by the government, which cultivated its own positional defiance of normative stances regarding civilian casualties incurred during their military defeat of the LTTE.

Two important observations may be noted regarding concerns expressed from the days of the final offensive to the post-victory period. The first is that the significant loss of life after the final military assault was not something that suddenly happened as a tragic blunder; rather, it was a clear destination towards which the military was headed, that some in the international community (and within Sri Lanka) thought could be avoided for the sake of saving civilian lives (TamilNet 2009).[2]

Secondly, theirs was not the first military victory in contemporary civil wars under the rubric of counterterror. In Peru, for example, the government defeated the Shining Path in 1992, subsequently also capturing its leaders in 1999. But in this case the wider civil society was given a role in shaping the new social contract; establishing a truth commission, designing policy for prosecution of those who had committed severe human rights violations during the conflict, and contributing to criteria for reparations. Former President Fujimori, who oversaw the military victory of the Shining Path, was himself convicted in 2008 for killings and disappearances undertaken by the state during the civil war. National debates encompassed a broad interrogation of what underlying grievances and disparities would fuel such a war.

This chapter will begin with an examination of the 'push back' undertaken within UN proceedings, and will then look at the emphasis the government put on image management abroad. Finally, it will outline how the Tamil diaspora was perceived as a serious threat, with measures taken to combat the risk of their anticipated interference.

Defensive posturing

As demonstrated in earlier chapters, in Sri Lanka the official approach to reconciliation stepped back from any political agenda of grievance or aspirations on the part of the Tamil minority and promoted a picture of the LTTE as terrorists by definition. Rajapaksa and his circles fully expected to proceed with 'business as usual' in their national project of the state. The response to international opinion deemed as 'interference' took several forms between 2005 and 2015. The public was told that conditionalities and offers of assistance from former allies in the West would be rejected. UN officials James Elder of UNICEF and Peter Mackay of the UN Office for Project Services (UNOPS) were expelled from the country when they dealt with information in ways not deemed appropriate, and visas were controlled accordingly to keep other people out. The government took on UN measures by pushing back through formal, institutional mechanisms and procedures, as well as occasional bouts of intimidation and threat. It played off the humanitarian actors present in the country through strict control and securitisation, and it invested financially in professional image management abroad. Lastly, the GoSL orchestrated internal mechanisms to demonstrate self-sufficiency in legal competence, while at the same time limiting freedom of expression in the country and maintaining a climate of fear. It was a carefully choreographed approach to steering its own agenda for state consolidation and control.

Already in war's aftermath there were sceptical views in country with regard to turning East rather than West for the sake of non-interference:

> The country appears to be turning away from its traditional western donors in favour of regional allies whose assistance comes without the same unpalatable demands. According to government officials, money from these Asian and Middle Eastern countries, including Libya, Iran and Myanmar, does not have strings attached. That, however, remains to be seen. No aid, not even from your own backyard, comes without concessions, even if not explicit. When the Iranians offered credit support to Sri Lanka two years ago, Iranian firms were subsequently offered a project in the country ... Since being elected three years ago, Mr Rajapaksa has warded off 'interference' from the West on issues such as human rights and International Monetary Fund aid with strings attached. However, earlier this year, the IMF offered a US$1.9 billion standby credit facility to the government to offset the impact of the global slowdown. (Samath 2009)

In fact, the IMF had closed its office in Sri Lanka in February 2007 after a period of sustained criticism from government quarters, when finance officials repeatedly asserted that Sri Lanka was not in need of IMF assistance. When a balance of payments crisis required it to seek urgent assistance, however, the government was quick to reposition and fully embrace the IMF, including its conditionalities, in 2008–09. Thus, there is a certain irony in the observations of Feizal Samath quoted above.

Pushing back

Sri Lanka claimed a propaganda victory when the UNHRC passed a resolution praising its defeat of the Tamil Tigers and condemning the rebels for using civilians as human shields in May 2009. This Sri Lankan-proposed resolution, which described the conflict as a domestic matter that 'doesn't warrant outside interference', gained backing from twenty-nine countries including China, India, Egypt and Cuba. In fact, it was a countermove by Colombo against an EU initiative to garner support for Sri Lankan accountability. A commentator noted of the Sri Lankan success: 'The seasoned poker player has tabled a counter resolution titled "Assistance to Sri Lanka in the Promotion and Protection of Human Rights"' (Bhadrakumar 2009).

Experienced diplomat Dayan Jayatilleka makes it clear how another kind of battle was fought in Geneva, one he came to call 'strategic counter-hegemonic resistance':

> The backdrop of the special session of the UN Human Rights Council in 2009 on Sri Lanka was this: The thirty year-long Sri Lankan war was reaching its endgame and we were going to win; the Tigers were going to lose. There was a lot of pressure not only from the Tamil Diaspora communities from the émigrés but also the liberal humanitarian view that there would be a blood bath which had to be stopped by a humanitarian intervention by the formula of a 'humanitarian pause'. Lakhdar Brahimi and Chris Patten had written a piece in the *New York Times* about the imminent 'bloodbath on the beach'. The EU Parliament was pushing a resolution for a 'humanitarian pause' and the resumption of negotiations with

the Tigers. This was the template for the EU resolution that was planned for the Human Rights Council.

A Special Session of the sort that was held years later on Libya and Syria in the Human Rights Council was sought to be held on Sri Lanka. This required 16 signatures. The Sri Lankan team and its allies in the Non-Aligned Movement (NAM) and in the South Asian Association for Regional Cooperation (SAARC) managed to hold it back while the war was on. As Sri Lanka's Permanent Representative to the UN in Geneva at the time, I was fully conscious of what we were doing in fighting hard to hold back the 16 signatures from being obtained so that a special session could not be moved in which there could have been a UN mandated call for a 'pause' on what would be the final attack on the Tigers. Personally driven by David Miliband and Bernard Kouchner, 'led from behind' (as the Wikileaks cable of May 9th 2009 proves) by US Secretary of State Hillary Clinton, and carried on the wave of mass demonstrations in almost every Western capital by the Tamil Diaspora (including a self-immolation in front of the Palais de Nations), there was no possibility of preventing the issue coming up later, though delay it we did, buying precious time until the war was fought to a victorious finish by our armed forces. (Jayatilleka 2015)

Jayatilleka is clear that he had assembled a 'side', networked successfully so that negotiations between Sri Lanka and the EU-led West were conducted by neighbours India and Pakistan, and the then current and incoming chairs of the NAM, Cuba and Egypt, together with Sri Lanka. No compromise was possible because the EU and its allies were 'dogmatically insistent' that any reference to 'sovereignty' should be deleted from the text, that the UN High Commissioner for Human Rights should engage in a fact-finding mission to the war zone and report to the council within six months, and that an international accountability mechanism was imperative. In his words, as Sri Lanka's then Permanent Representative, he 'rejected such a sellout of the Sri Lankan armed forces and citizens, our hard fought and finally won victory over secessionist terrorism, and the long-standing principles of the NAM' (Jayatilleka 2015).

In the course of the next year, pressure would mount on the Sri Lankan government. It came from within, when former General Fonseka went public on his willingness to testify in any international war crimes investigation. He was arrested within hours of this statement and accused of plotting against the government. Envoys from Brussels who had urged for an improvement in human rights in keeping with the General System of Preferences (GSP) trade agreement confirmed that their deadline for compliance was genuine – concessions would be withdrawn if no improvement were documented. The rolling out of the LLRC was met with doubt by domestic critics and human rights bodies internationally due to its limited mandate and the fact that those appointed to it lacked independence. Minister of External Affairs G. L. Peiris went on a highly publicised visit to present the LLRC plan to Secretary of State Hillary Clinton, who also urged the government to give the commission powers for probing war crime allegations. UN High Commissioner for Human Rights Navi Pillay called publicly for an international dimension to the examination of war crimes' allegations. G. L. Peiris responded by accusing her of 'pursuing Sri Lanka' in a way that was repugnant to the basic values and principles that are enshrined in the UN system, stating that 'any foreign intervention is not only unwarranted but will also be a source of hindrance, a detriment to the work of the commission as it gets underway' (Haviland 2010).[3] The President's visit to Delhi, while it would result in the signing of a joint agreement, was met with protests and angry demonstrations on his arrival.[4] The release of WikiLeaks cables in which an American ambassador linked Rajapaksa to war crimes came in tandem with the President having to cancel an address in Oxford due to protests (Borger 2010).[5]

In May 2011, a book called *The Cage* was published by former UN spokesperson in Sri Lanka Gordon Weiss, detailing events in the final stages of the war as witnessed by UN staff members. UK television's Channel 4 documentary *The Killing Fields* was in circulation, depicting horrific scenes of atrocities during the later days of the war. Sri Lanka and the Panel of Experts report (to which it had still not officially responded) were mentioned several times in the Security Council debate on the protection of civilians in armed conflict on 10 May. The High Commissioner said in her opening statement of the UNHRC that the report contained important new information. Soon after, the new Special Rapporteur on Extrajudicial Executions issued a statement saying that Channel 4's execution videos[6] had been found to be authentic by several experts. At the beginning of June, Amnesty International and Human Rights Watch, together with Channel 4, aired a one-hour documentary during a side event at the council meetings, detailing executions, alleged government attacks on hospitals and scenes of the dead.

The same day as the film showing, Sri Lanka organised a side event and continued with a narrative of progress in its post-war recovery. Severe criticisms of the UN panel report were raised, and there was both an audience for this and a degree of support from 'like-minded' countries. Russia, China, Pakistan and others came out in defence of Sri Lanka. The following year, however, they were defeated in the March 2012 sessions when a clear majority of the council's members backed an American-led proposal calling on the Sri Lankan government to account for the high number of civilian fatalities at the end of its long and brutal civil war. In spite of what *The Economist* termed 'exhaustive, sometimes aggressive' Sri Lankan lobbying against this initiative, the Geneva-based council's forty-seven members voted, by twenty-four to fifteen, for a resolution urging the government to implement the recommendations of its own LLRC and to start a credible investigation into allegations of widespread human rights abuses. Eight of the member countries abstained (*The Economist* 2012). The headline at this particular vote was the shift in India's position, moving to a vote for the resolution and against Sri Lanka.[7]

During the previous months, embassies and missions had received phone calls lobbying for the government position; demonstrations were organised in Geneva and Colombo; and human rights activists were harangued and intimidated. February saw a wave of anti-UN protests across over a hundred cities in Sri Lanka, while in Colombo an estimated 3,000 people marched on the US embassy, carrying signs (which were often in English) calling on the US to stop supporting terrorism. On exiting Bandaranaike Airport in Colombo, visitors were met with a sign stating: 'We strongly protest against hypocritical foreign intervention against the Sri Lankan Government. Immigration and Emigration Dept. Authorized Officers Union.'[8] A government minister began a hunger strike in front of the UN building in Colombo, such was the evident pro-government feeling unleashed in the capital. Privately, the word on the street was that the going rate for payments to demonstrators made it worthwhile for many, although no doubt volunteers were out in force as well. On a large banner behind the fasting minister, Wimal Weerawansa, was a message in English and Sinhala: 'Abolish UN Special Advisory Panel.' The demonstrations grew to the point of trapping staff inside the building and temporarily closing the offices. The Friday Forum, a gathering of business, diplomatic and civic leaders based in Colombo, issued a statement of concern:

> It is unfortunate that the public is constantly being told that the resolution represents an unwarranted external interference by the international community in the affairs of the country. The international community is therefore presented as a distinct entity which is alien to Sri Lanka. The Friday Forum wishes to point out that raising issues concerning the situation on human rights in the UNHRC is legitimate because Sri Lanka is a member of the international community and a State bound by the UN Charter and international treaties ratified over a period of time. The UN Charter and these treaties bind all States that are parties to these documents. The idea of State sovereignty cannot therefore be misrepresented to suggest that there can be no scrutiny of events in Sri Lanka. By accepting the UN Charter and these treaties Sri Lanka has voluntarily made itself accountable to a progress review on implementation of the human rights standards set by them and this process of scrutiny cannot be avoided. None of this is seen as interference in our internal affairs or a violation of our sovereignty ...

Much of the aggressiveness that we have seen in relation to the events of the past few weeks indicates that despite the end of the armed conflict there is a constant obsession with achieving victory and a dominant concern with not being defeated. This is manifested in many of the statements even in the media on the adoption of the resolution, such as 'we have achieved victory in defeat' and 'we have only lost the resolution by one vote.' This is hardly the path to achieving peace and reconciliation. The words of the *Dhammapada* that 'victory breeds hatred, the defeated live in pain, happily the wise live giving up the idea of victory and defeat' have special relevance for all Sri Lankans at this time.[9]

Nonetheless, in the popular nationalist media message, any resolution for Sri Lankan accountability was also a vote for the LTTE. At a March sub-summit meeting in Geneva, pro-government supporters (not nominally part of the official delegation) causing disturbances were brought under control by the UN police after what was deemed threatening behaviour. On this occasion, NGOs, human rights organisations, representatives of Tamil organisations (including the diaspora) and the High Commissioner Navaneethan Pillay took part and testimony was given by Sandhya Ekneligoda, whose husband had been abducted in 2010 and remained missing.[10] It took courage to appear before such proceedings, where she was 'intimidated, abused and ridiculed'.[11] A lead article in the Sri Lankan *Daily Mirror* (2012) reported that:

> At the same time in Sri Lanka itself, newspapers, news websites and TV and radio stations have since January been running a continuous campaign of vilification, including naming and in many cases picturing activists, describing them as an 'NGO gang' and repeatedly accusing them of treason, mercenary activities and association with terrorism.[12]

These reports had included 'barely veiled' incitement, threats of retaliation, and readers' comments that called for the burning down of the houses of named civil society activists, with at least one such comment calling openly for them to be killed.

The vehement and defensive stance was in reaction to the previous year's publication of the over 200-page *Report of the Secretary-General's Panel of Experts on Accountability in Sri Lanka* (UN 2011a). It examined the final period of the war between September

2008 and May 2009, documenting a wide range of alleged serious violations of international humanitarian and human rights law that had been committed by both the government and the LTTE, some of which amounted to war crimes and crimes against humanity. On the report's publication on 25 April, the UN also issued a statement saying that it had been shared in its entirety with the GoSL on 12 April; an invitation to respond was issued at the same time as publication, but no reply was forthcoming (UN 2011).

On 12 September 2011, Secretary-General Ban Ki-moon sent the report of his delegated Panel of Experts to the Human Rights Council. It encompassed credible allegations of serious violations committed by the government, the killing of civilians through widespread shelling, and the denial of humanitarian assistance. Credible allegations regarding the LTTE included using civilians as human shields and killing civilians attempting to flee LTTE control. The panel – chaired by Marzuki Darusman of Indonesia and comprising Yasmin Sooka of South Africa and Steven Ratner of the United States – recommended that the government respond to the allegations by initiating an effective accountability process beginning with genuine investigations. The report was rejected by the Sri Lankan government on the basis of it being personally commissioned by the Secretary-General rather than by a formal body such as the Security Council. Thereafter, they would refer to it only as the 'Darusman Report' (UN Regional Information Centre for Western Europe 2011).

Specifically, the panel found that in stark contrast to any humanitarian rescue undertaking, the conduct of the war represented a 'grave assault on the entire regime of international law designed to protect individual dignity during both war and peace'; the military advance into the Vanni between September 2008 and 19 May 2009 had constituted persecution of the population, and around 330,000 civilians had been trapped in an ever decreasing area fleeing shelling but kept hostage by the LTTE. The government had shelled three 'no fire zones', the UN hub, hospitals and food distribution lines, and near the ICRC ships coming to evacuate the wounded. The LTTE was found to have used the civilian zone as a buffer, refusing to let people leave and forcing them to dig trenches and work in such a way as to blur the distinction between civilian and military, firing artillery close to IDPs and shooting point blank at those who tried to flee. The immediate aftermath of the war was also examined, and accountability called for from both parties as a duty under domestic and international law. Very importantly, the panel stated that it 'did not advocate a "one-size-fits-all" formula or the importation of foreign models for accountability; rather it recognizes the need for accountability processes to be defined based on national assessments, involving broad citizen participation, needs and aspirations' (UN 2011b: iv).

The first full-length Sri Lankan official statement concerning the last phase of the war was a 160-page document entitled *Humanitarian Operation: Factual analysis* published in July 2011; it pointedly did not reference the UN panel report, and states in its opening paragraph that 'at each stage in the operation Sri Lanka took extraordinary steps to respect and protect the lives of civilians' (Ministry of Defence 2011). By claiming the discourse of humanitarian intervention, Sri Lanka elevated its actions to identify precisely with steps taken internationally by other actors. They had utilised the rubric earlier with regard to such actions as the 2003 US and UK invasion and occupation of Iraq, labelled 'humanitarian intervention' by UK Prime Minister Tony Blair.[13] Now it was being used in a bid for legitimacy on the part of Sri Lanka. Frank Furedi's 1994 work on the 'moral rehabilitation of imperialism' put forth a scenario in which 'for all intents and purposes there are today two types of nation: the ones that have the legitimate right to interfere in the life of others, and the ones that have no intrinsic moral authority to run their own affairs' (Furedi 1994). Furedi claimed that the very legitimacy and moral integrity of less developed societies also implicitly question their right to exist, and as such directly invite intervention. He pointed to an absence of serious criticism of Western intervention in Panama, Iraq, Somalia and Bosnia as suggesting that new conventions relating to the management of international affairs have already been accepted. This point of view has seemingly been internalised by a section of Sri Lankan elites in power, as shown in the 2009 opinion expressed concerning possible UN mediation below:

The GoSL would never accept such interference, and this is further complicated by great power dominance and intrusive measures such as the Responsibility to Protect ... This principle gives not just the right but a supposed duty to intervene – but gives it to a select and powerful few. It goes beyond the UN Charter and gives a new imperative to powerful countries so that they can (for instance) 'walk in to Iraq' or anywhere. It is an emotive rationalization for arbitrary decisions without defined principles. Sri Lanka both objects and rejects this.[14]

When President Rajapaksa addressed the UN General Assembly on 23 September 2011, he advocated the need for 'dialogue, deliberation and consensus' in resolving disputes, reiterating the worldwide threat of terrorism, and maintained that there was economic progress in the North of Sri Lanka. But his speech carried another dimension for his international audience, warning of the dangers of powerful countries interfering in smaller ones:

It is important to remind ourselves that every country cherishes the values and traditions, and deeply held religious convictions it has nurtured over the centuries. These cannot be diluted or distorted under the guise of human rights, by the imposition of attitudes or approaches which are characteristics of alien cultures.

In the given Sri Lankan state narrative, those who interfered (i.e. Norway, the co-chairs and the 'international community') would have neutralised Sri Lanka's strength and denied a victory over terror. External interference must be resisted.

The principle of non-interference as enshrined in Association of Southeast Asian Nations (ASEAN) principles and generally articulated regional norms lends credence to Rajapaksa's claims, as Indian and Chinese governments also resist external third-party involvement in their internal conflict zones. Foreign Minister Yang reiterated in 2009 that China strictly adhered to the cardinal principle of non-interference in internal affairs of sovereign states (*Asian Tribune* 2009), and that, stemming from this principle,

China has supported Sri Lanka on issues pertaining to human rights in multilateral forums. The GoSL boycotted the 2010 Nobel Prize ceremony for China's jailed dissident Liu Xiaobo. In early 2014, Chinese Foreign Ministry spokesperson Hua Chunying was quoted as saying: 'We believe that people in Sri Lanka have the wisdom and capacity to manage their internal affairs, and oppose some countries' interference in Sri Lanka's domestic affairs under the pretext of the human rights issue.' She added: 'We oppose politicizing and imposing double standards on the issue of human rights' (Ondaatjie 2014).

Sri Lanka was not a party to the Geneva Protocols I and II that were additional to the 1949 Geneva Conventions; these dealt respectively with international and non-international armed conflict. Nor had it subscribed to the 1998 Rome Statue of the International Criminal Court. Concerns that Tamil citizens who had sought refuge in the 'no fire zones' had been shelled (severely harmed or killed) were dismissed by the government as a disinformation campaign by the LTTE in the diaspora.

However, Sri Lanka is a state party to the UNHRC in Geneva, as argued stirringly in 2014 by Chandra Kumarage, Convenor of Sri Lankan Lawyers for Democracy:

> It is universally accepted that the UN Charter which came into force on 14 October, 1945 signifies that rights of human beings were a matter of international law since a stated purpose of the founding of the UN was to achieve international cooperation in promoting and encouraging respect for human rights and fundamental freedoms for all without distinction to race, sex, language, or religion. Despite its many shortcomings the UN Charter recognized formally that human rights have an international dimension and are no longer solely a matter falling within the exclusive jurisdiction of a state ...
>
> Sri Lanka is a state party to the Human Rights Council which is a UN Charter based important institution and it has been actively participating in its activities. When several resolutions were moved against Sri Lanka on the alleged human rights violations and war crimes allegations it never denounced

them stating that those resolutions were outside the mandate of the UN Human Rights Council. Once Sri Lanka was even able to turn [the] tables against one of those resolutions and make it a resolution in its favour. It spent millions of rupees of Sri Lankan people's money to campaign and lobby against the UNHRC Resolution. Now that the UNHRC is going to implement the duly adopted resolution the government is taking up various objections, including questioning of the legality and the Council's power to adopt such resolutions. What if the government was able to defeat the resolution? Obviously no country or international body will accept this duplicitous attitude of the Sri Lankan state vis a vis its international legal obligations and international relations. (Kumarage 2014)

Image management: the public relations campaign

The EU decided in July 2010 to withdraw Sri Lanka's preferential trade access to EU markets, claiming contractual non-compliance with terms of agreement regarding human rights. Within months, the Sri Lankan government was paying a top British PR firm about £3 million ($4.7 million) a year to try to enhance the country's post-war image. The BBC's Sinhala service reported that the Bell Pottinger Group was hired to lobby UK, UN and EU officials. Bell Pottinger, whose motto on its website is 'Better reputations, better results', was believed to be lobbying on Sri Lanka's behalf, particularly in Brussels. A. N. Cabraal, Governor of the Central Bank, was quoted as saying: 'So many people are spending huge sums of money to tarnish our country's image. We will do everything possible to boost that image and I believe it is our duty' (Pathirana 2010).

In the UK, the group's main focus was said to be countering what the Sri Lankan government called propaganda by pro-Tamil Tiger groups in the influential Tamil diaspora. The firm helped to promote the UK visit of Sri Lankan Foreign Minister Professor G. L. Peiris, who gave a keynote speech at London's International Institute of Strategic Studies (IISS). Image promotion or not, there were protestors outside the IISS before, during and after the talk. Such was their influence that Bell Pottinger claimed at the end of the year to have written Rajapaksa's speech to the UN, mentioned above.

A picture of the money spent under the Rajapaksa regime on international image management and public relations came to light in early 2015, at the onset of the new administration of President Sirisena. Foreign Affairs Deputy Minister A. P. Perera was responding to a question raised in parliament when he stated that that during the previous five years four US companies had been contracted to build a positive image of Sri Lanka abroad. The Minister mentioned American lobbying firms such as Patton Boggs LLP, Cranford Johnson Robinson PR, Steve Hedges and Majority Group LLC. Patton Boggs had been sought out to cultivate allies in Congress, prevent bills or resolutions against Sri Lanka in Congress, assist with the removal of Sri Lanka from the Watchlist on Trafficking in Persons, help the travel warning for Sri Lanka to be lifted, and organise a US business delegation to Sri Lanka. Cranford Johnson Robinson PR was tasked with handling media work for Sri Lanka and conducting image-building campaigns with the US press. The services of Steve Hedges' company had been obtained to research and give publicity to the GoSL's initiatives of rehabilitation and reconciliation work, to respond to inquiries about Sri Lanka in the media and from others, and to oversee media aspects during visits of foreign dignitaries. Majority Group was assigned to obtain assistance in blocking or getting rid of negative resolutions, to organise congressional delegations to Sri Lanka, to plan fundraisers for congressmen, and to organise Capitol Hill member meetings (Gamage 2015).

Sri Lanka's *The Sunday Times* had earlier reported that its own investigations had prompted a review of mandatory information forwarded to the US Department of Justice by public relations and lobbying firms contracted by Sri Lanka using 'vast sums of public money'. The FARA (Foreign Agents Registration Act) Unit of the US Justice Department announced that it would conduct a re-examination in accordance with regulatory requirements. Discrepancies between registered information on addresses and contracting parties from Sri Lanka had been identified; under the terms of the FARA, any person who wilfully violates provisions in any registration statement is liable, when proved, for a fine of not more than $10,000 or imprisonment for more than five years. For some offences, the punishment is not more than $5,000 or imprisonment of not more than six months, or both.

The report also detailed the amounts spent on public relations overseas. While the actual fee to be charged by Beltway and Nelson Mullins was not then known, the total amount due to the other PR and lobbying agencies worked out at $1,380,000, or more than 179.4 million rupees, for one year. This amount did not include the payment from the Central Bank of Sri Lanka, which had signed on the Liberty International Group LLC from August 2014 for one year. The agency would receive an annual fee of $760,000 (or over 99 million rupees) from the bank. The grand total that Sri Lanka would pay PR and lobbying firms in the US would thus be a staggering $2,140,000 or over 278.2 million rupees (*The Sunday Times* 2014d).

The Central Bank of Sri Lanka confirmed that it had hired Liberty International after it had ended its contract with Thompson Advisory Group, to which it paid millions. Its statement underlined the need for

> a robust Communication Programme in the USA ... fashioned to create and maintain a conducive political and economic environment in the USA to enhance Sri Lanka's long-term political and economic aspirations, and to develop a comprehensive information platform where decision makers in the USA would receive clear and accurate information about conditions in Sri Lanka so that it would serve to attract a higher volume of private sector investments. (*The Sunday Times* 2014d)

The Sunday Times and other critics were not impressed, questioning the efficacy of diplomacy for a start, and warning of the dangers of having a government within a government. But its critique went further.

The saga of the PR/lobbying firms and how they are hired willy nilly by powerful persons in the UPFA Government ostensibly to win over the Obama Administration and change (or 're-calibrate') its policies towards Sri Lanka raises more questions than it answers. Matters are made worse when some maintain a stoic silence whilst others are engaged in laughable semantics better explained by the Sinhala adage *koheda yanney, malley pol* or 'Where are you headed? There's coconut in the bag'. (*The Sunday Times* 2014d)

Megan Wilson reported from Washington DC in late October 2014 that the GoSL had hired its eighth Washington firm, in anticipation of the results of the UN human rights investigation into alleged war crimes. The firm Levick was subcontracting through Liberty International Group (owned by former Republican Senator Connie Mack) to represent the semi-autonomous Central Bank of Sri Lanka. Mark Irion, President of Levick, was quoted as saying that its mission was to utilise 'communications supported advocacy to tell Sri Lanka's amazing story of recovery after a decades long civil war against a brutal terrorist organization, as well as to assist the Central Bank in communicating opportunities for trade and investment between our two nations'. Contract documents stated that representation was needed because 'the current international media focus on Sri Lanka [was] unbalanced', according to disclosures by Liberty International Group to the Justice Department under FARA (Wilson 2014).

To take on the media war, the Sri Lankan government also sponsored production of a film in 2011 to counter the influential Channel 4 documentary on the 'no fire zones'. The production, *Lies Agreed Upon*, was screened in London for parliamentarians in an event organised by the Sri Lankan High Commission; at the US Congress at a gathering sponsored by the Congressional Congress on Sri Lanka and Sri Lankan Americans; in New Zealand; and in the Dag Hammarskjöld Auditorium at the UN. The latter, on 28 September 2011, was hailed as a particular press coup, as noted in the following statement from the Colombo paper *The Sunday Observer*: 'The screening of "Lies Agreed Upon" at the UN Headquarters is seen as a diplomatic victory for Sri Lanka, because LTTE lobbyists and sections of the Tamil diaspora supportive of the terror group could not get "Killing Fields" screened in the UN itself despite their best efforts.'[15]

Reception of the film was mixed, as it either confirmed a point of view or was seen as making no difference to the opposite viewpoint due to an already deeply polarised and emotive debate. The ICG commented on the documentary, saying that there was nothing in the programme that disproved or even directly challenged the many specific credible allegations – including those in the report of the UN Secretary-General's Panel of Experts. But it also noted that:

> The government's film makes clear that so long as campaigners for justice and peace in the Tamil diaspora do not clearly recognise the crimes of the LTTE and clearly repudiate their violent forms of militant struggle, and the damage it did to all communities in Sri Lanka, their efforts towards justice will remain weak. (ICG 2011b)

In general, the justice system did not look in good shape in Sri Lanka, as executive authority was increasingly brought to bear on it. The unseemly impeachment proceedings against Chief Justice Dr Shirani Bandaranayake began (see above) when she oversaw rulings against the government, particularly when she opposed a bill introduced in parliament by the Economic Development Minister, Basil Rajapaksa. The Supreme Court ruled that the bill, which would empower the central government to control a $614 million development budget, violated the constitution. The court added that it had to be approved first by nine provincial councils. Despite the Supreme Court ruling that impeachment proceedings were unconstitutional, she was removed from office by the President in a case that attracted international concern and the strongest of protests from lawyers and judges within Sri Lanka. The following March, Sri Lankan diplomatic bravado – if not hubris – was evident again in Geneva, when the government sponsored a resolution in the UNHRC entitled 'Integrity of the Judicial System'. It expressed the conviction that 'the integrity of the judicial system, together with independence and impartiality, is an essential prerequisite for the protection of human rights and fundamental freedoms, for upholding the rule of law and democracy'. Stressing that the integrity of the judiciary must be observed at all times, the resolution was co-sponsored by states including Belarus, China, Cuba, the Democratic Republic of Korea, Tajikistan and the Russian Federation (Jayawickrama 2015: 222).

Internally there was little confidence in the protection of human rights or the integrity of the justice system.[16] Sri Lanka had acceded to the ICCPR's First Optional Protocol in October 1997. From the 2000s onwards, as documented by Pinto-Jayawardena (2015), the right to lodge individual communications to the UNHRC was invoked frequently by Sri Lankans. This was primarily due to political interference with the Supreme Court from 1999 onwards, and a general conviction that justice was not being rendered by the domestic courts. Pinto-Jayawardena observes that many people therefore appealed to the UN committee, and the fact that not all the covenant rights had been guaranteed in Sri Lanka's constitution made resorting to the individual communications remedy particularly interesting.

> By late 2008 the UN Human Rights Committee had declared violations of ICCPR rights in eleven Communications of considerable importance. In some cases, the rights recognized as violated were also rights incorporated in Sri Lanka's Constitution, such as ICCPR Article 19, the right to freedom of expression, and ICCPR Article 7, the right to freedom from torture. In other instances, the Committee affirmed a number of rights that were not explicitly secured in the domestic constitutional structure. These included an expanded right to liberty and security, the right to be tried without undue delay and the principle that no one shall be compelled to testify against himself or confess guilt. The Government of Sri Lanka, before and after the one decade of Rajapaksa rule, declined to give effect to these recommendations. (Pinto-Jayawardena 2015)

Now diplomatic pushback at UN human rights mechanisms was sophisticated and at times brazen, messaging outwards as defence against inward interference.

The Tamil diaspora

If you were part of any official delegation to speak with the President or his brothers in the immediate aftermath of the war, there was a strong chance that you would hear from them that a high risk of interference and threat to Sri Lankan stability was to be found in the overseas Tamils; European countries would be requested to keep those under their jurisdiction under their watch and control. Put simply, they were labelled as LTTE sympathisers and potential terrorists.

The Tamil diaspora as a global phenomenon is a subject for in-depth study in its own right, and there is no doubt that for many there were deeply embedded sympathies for and/or structural connections (through sophisticated voluntary and coercive fundraising) to the LTTE over the years. The LTTE had become the lead contender for winning Tamil rights; it fought for righting political wrongs and offered a vision of self-determination as a departure from past, state-led repression. It is estimated that, between 1980 and 2007, Tamils from Sri Lanka claimed asylum or refugee status in thirty-one countries, with Canada, Germany, the UK, Switzerland and France being favourite destinations outside India (Vimalarajah and Cheran 2010). Canada hosts the largest Tamil diaspora at an estimated quarter of a million, and estimates for the UK range between 100,000 and 200,000. ICG analyst Alan Keenan observed in 2010 that the mood in the diaspora was a mixed one of anger, depression and denial, insofar as the LTTE had stood up for them, fought for them, and suffered a desperate end with the wiping out of key leaders. It was a humiliating defeat, compounded by the enormous death toll in the final months of the war and the internment of more than a quarter of a million Tamils. While many felt betrayed by the West and were demanding justice (or, in some cases, revenge), a minority may have felt relieved that they were no longer intimidated by the long distance project. For Vimalarajah and Cheran (2010), this dramatic turn of events following decades of ethno-political violence meant a re-articulation of demands for equality, justice and sovereignty, with the Tamil diaspora a key player in framing the post-war political trajectory. They also pointed to generational changes, new social media and technological means of transnational influence.

Still anticipating the worst in terms of militant resurgence, the GoSL conducted continual surveillance, internet interception and intelligence gathering on the diaspora, leading to the early arrest of 'KP' Kumaran Pathmanathan in Malaysia – he had succeeded Prabhakaran as LTTE leader. When several suspected cadres were arrested in Malaysia as late as 2014, Sri Lankan national news coverage gave credit to both the Terrorism Investigation Division (TID) and the state intelligence establishment.[17] In another development from the near neighbourhood, following the BJP election victory in India and on the occasion of a BJP representative attending a function in Colombo, *The Hindu* noted:

> Colombo's biggest but latent insecurity emanates from the 65 million Tamils, a mere 19 kilometres across the Palk Strait. Sri Lankans keep an inventory of Tamils worldwide. Dr. Swamy, who is the darling of policy-crafters and the military in Colombo, is a frequently heard and quoted voice touching the right chords, like making light of Tamil Nadu's politicians, stressing the centrality of national interest over narrow provincial political pressures. He suggested that the Indian policy of non-interference makes devolution Colombo's business, with police powers being devolved over time.[18]

And yet during the intervening five years, the diaspora had undergone a considerable transformation in organisation and strategy, adopting a conscious transnational positioning. Elections in 2010 for the Transnational Government of Tamil Eelam (TGTE) took place simultaneously in eleven countries; major Tamil civil society organisations overseas came together to form a Global Tamil Forum (GTF), with constituent meetings in Paris and London including representation from Australia, Canada, Malaysia, the US and European countries. New sites of confrontation began to look something like this: Major General Shavendra Silva, as acting permanent representative of Sri Lanka to the UN, wrote an assertive letter in January 2011 rejecting unequivocally any mandate or terms of reference of the Secretary-General's Panel of Experts, and reserving the right of sovereign Sri Lanka to conduct its own LLRC without interference. By the following September, a civil law suit had been filed against him in a New York court on charges of war crimes under his leadership of the infamous 58th Brigade.[19] Although charges were eventually dropped on the grounds of diplomatic immunity, it was a time-consuming and high-profile disruption to the carefully cultivated government-desired image of Sri Lanka. Just months earlier, a US court had issued a summons to President Rajapaksa himself when a $30 million civil law suit was filed under the Torture Victims Protection Act on behalf of one of the families related to a victim of the Trincomalee killings and the Action Contre la Faim (ACF) deaths of 2006.[20] Major General Jagath Dias was recalled from his post as Deputy Ambassador to Germany, Switzerland and the Vatican on allegations of war crimes. And, in February 2011, Tamils Against Genocide and the Swiss Council of Eelam Tamils submitted a file to the International Criminal Court requesting the launch of an investigation and the issue of an arrest warrant against Australian citizen Palitha Kohona, Sri Lanka's permanent representative to the UN in New York.

According to a cable dated 9 June 2010 released by WikiLeaks, South Africa's State Security Agency replied to GoSL concerns that a suspected LTTE military training camp was operating within its borders; that LTTE fundraising was still ongoing; and that the LTTE was in touch with former members of the South African military. Each instance was refuted, with the statement that 'LTTE does not have any offices or known representatives in South Africa'.[21] This had little influence on subsequent Sri Lankan official statements and surveillance actions, as reported by Natarajan (2012), who documented press interference, the blocking of Tamil websites and denial of service interruptions.

Reflections

Resolution A/HRC/25/1 was adopted in Geneva in March 2014: 'Promoting reconciliation, accountability and human rights in

Sri Lanka'. Through this, the UNHRC requested the UN High Commissioner for Human Rights to:

> undertake a comprehensive investigation into alleged serious violations and abuses of human rights and related crimes by both parties in Sri Lanka during the period covered by the Lessons Learnt and Reconciliation Commission (LLRC), and to establish the facts and circumstances of such alleged violations and of the crimes perpetrated with a view to avoiding impunity and ensuring accountability, with assistance from relevant experts and special procedures mandate holders.[22]

Rajapaksa responded immediately, accusing Western countries of being pushed by the Tamil diaspora to take the UNHCR resolution forward, saying that 'Sri Lanka will not tolerate foreign interference'.[23]

Within Sri Lanka there seemed to be an upsurge in media messaging on the dangers of a resurgent LTTE, without obvious evidence or clear trends indicating this to be the case. Possibly to prove a point on the internal threat, or as a response to the Geneva development, there were a number of arrests made in April that purported to counter a renaissance in the LTTE. An official government circular was issued citing (and looking remarkably like) UN document references – notably, 'Act No. 45 of 1968' – and specifically invoking 'paragraph 4(2) of the United Nations Regulations No. 1 of 2012'. This formidably official presentation (signed by the Secretary for Defence and Urban Development Gotabaya Rajapaksa) listed sixteen organisations and over 400 individuals for alleged links to terrorist activities. In the course of western and southern provincial council elections in the same month, President Rajapaksa used the UNHRC process and threat of 'international intervention' in campaigning, and also sharply criticised the TNA for its support of the Geneva resolution. The following month a counter-list was published online by the self-proclaimed TGTE, naming members of the government as war criminals.[24]

In terms of the enforcement and implementation of such measures, it is the state that can act; indeed, even under the successor government of Sirisena in 2016, many in the diaspora remained fearful of trying to return for fear of detention on the basis of being listed. But as a moral form of checkmate, it was an interesting stand-off.

During the five years following the military defeat of the LTTE, when the Rajapaksa government continued its strident theme of non-intervention, Burma/Myanmar undertook major democratic reforms and adjusted its external relations to normalise contacts with Western nations; the Philippines undertook a lengthy process of negotiation with the Moro Islamic Liberation Front, which included the good offices of Malaysia and an international contact group (established in 2009) that was composed of delegates from Japan, the UK, Turkey, Saudi Arabia and four international NGOs; and Thailand entered a tentative arrangement of talks facilitated by Malaysia to address its long-running southern conflict. While the Sri Lankan President did move from his initial position of 'no civilian casualties' at war's end, he nonetheless held fast to his conviction with regard to external opinion:

> It is not for outsiders to impose their values or their judgments on Sri Lanka. It is the same Sri Lankans who suffered from the ravages of LTTE terrorism for thirty years and who are now reaping the rewards of peace that will find solutions to our national issues – not outsiders. (*Shillong Times* 2011)

Rajapaksa's continual offensive against external interference and internal association with internationals did not happen suddenly or in a reactive vacuum. It needs to be understood through an examination of how internal reactions and conditions developed over time. This means also questioning the earlier influx of foreigners representing the 'international community' and its governance and humanitarian norms; how they were perceived and how they had their own influence on developing trends. This will be the theme of the following chapter.

CHAPTER 4

The outsiders

> It's all happened before and will happen again
> And we the onlookers
> But now I'm in it
> It's happened to me
> At last history has meaning
> > (Jean Arasanayagam)

Jean Arasanayagam[1] is a renowned Sri Lankan poet who refers to herself as an outsider and as such uses her work in the spirit of the possibility that sometimes those outside are the best witnesses. She was born into a Dutch Burgher family, descended from colonial arrivals from the Netherlands in the seventeenth century. The Dutch Burghers are the descendants of intermarriages between Dutchmen and women of Ceylon's indigenous communities, and Arasanayagam herself went on to marry into a Tamil family. The notion of the 'outsider' is a fluid one, and in situations of protracted conflict it is often used liberally; to apply to someone who was away from the site of attack when others in a community experienced it, to those who moved into a region from another locality, belong to a different caste, have a family lineage that differs from that of the dominant clan or patronage group. It can apply to someone who has lived abroad; to anyone who identifies externally through work or faith affiliation. In fact, Vimalarajah and Cheran (2010) argue that the dichotomy of 'insider–outside' seldom exists in the self-conception of the diaspora, and that a compelling differentiation of 'hostland' and 'homeland' is valid for thousands in the Tamil diaspora, all the more so after 2009. Many retain a sense of roots and belonging to something aspirational or longed for, unlike foreigners who come from abroad. In practice and experience this may vary or be open to interpretation. This chapter, however, will take as its chief focus the positions of staff working for international NGOs, relief and development agencies and diplomatic channels during the decade of the Rajapaksa period in government. As such, it will seek to interrogate their roles as social actors, as well as that of targeted, assumed trouble-makers that the regime sought to control. For background, it will also refer to the history of international assistance and NGOs on the island; to the recent evolving context of international aid architecture; and to the conflicted role of UN agencies up to and following the end of the war.

Under Rajapaksa, 'outsider' became a blanket term that was instrumentalised, even reified, as threat or obstacle. For a robust and radical rebuttal of the international community, foreigners and NGOs were a front-line target, just as civil society actors who spoke out or testified abroad were labelled traitors. A special parliamentary select committee on 'Investigating the Operations of Non-governmental Organisations and their Impact' presented its report to parliament in December 2008. Transparency International, one of the agencies summoned to testify before the committee, later issued a response in its own defence[2] following negative allegations regarding its work. Already that year, Rama Mani, head of the International Centre for Ethnic Studies, had been publicly vilified and had lost her visa; Norbert Ropers of the Berghof Foundation had been made to leave the island; and numerous national and international NGO staff were subject to threats and intimidation.[3] The German ambassador was criticised by the government for both his presence and his public remarks at the funeral of Lasantha Wickrematunge, and, in April 2009, a Swedish foreign minister was denied entry as part of a European diplomatic mission (possibly in anticipation of encouragement to push for a truce). At the end of May 2009, the head of FORUT, a Norwegian development NGO, was expelled with 48 hours' notice, ostensibly because FORUT staff were not allowed to hoist the Sri Lankan flag in triumph at the end of the war and take the decreed celebratory day off. In March 2010, Amnesty International and Human Rights Watch issued a note of grave concern over what they called a 'witch hunt' against journalists and NGO activists, citing the discovery of a list of thirty individuals to be targeted. Subsequently, in its annual report on Sri Lanka, Freedom House stated that among the most serious problems in the country was the government's hostility towards NGOs and the media:

> The government views any independent NGO as a threat and has been developing a set of laws to more closely control such groups. All NGOs are required to register with the government, and as of July 2009, 969 domestic and 309 international NGOs were registered. Current law allows the government to review the activities of NGOs and requires them to report their expenditures and sources of income. (Oberst 2010)

Aspects of the clampdown included the assumed association of NGOs with perceived international agendas, including federalism or democratic reform;[4] others may have stemmed from difficulties that had beset the tsunami response some years earlier (Mampilly 2009).[5] Gowrinathan and Mampilly (2009: 3) point out that in exerting strong control over foreign aid organisations, the government claimed to be correcting the mistakes it had made in managing the NGO sector after the tsunami:

> In addition to imposing regulations on INGO [international non-governmental organisation] activities, it has embarked on a campaign against groups perceived as 'terrorist sympathizers'. The heads of international aid organizations have been brought before parliament to account for relief operations in the conflict zone. Instead of building the capacity of local civil society organizations operating in the north-east, the government has harassed and threatened them.[6]

They cite the example of a YMCA group from Trincomalee attempting to deliver clothes and essentials to a local hospital being stopped, refused entry and interrogated on their connections to the injured. Clearly, the humanitarian was identified and perceived as partisan. Parliamentary select committee chair and JVP MP Vititha Herath went public in late 2008 stating that some leading INGOs and NGOs were a threat to national security, propagating federalism and aiding the LTTE, even alleging that such groups as MSF and Doctors of the World were a threat to state policies. His strongest criticism was reserved for NGOs working on conflict resolution and conflict studies.

Some background on international assistance and NGO development

INGOs and Western aid donors were active in Sri Lanka from independence onwards; an Asian Development Bank (ADB) study on civil society in Sri Lanka documents early ecumenical organisations arriving from abroad and the growth of locally owned initiatives, particularly in rural development and women's rights (ADB 2003). Sri Lanka became popular among international aid workers who found it a congenial place to work; a safe family station with natural beauty, great beaches and friendly people. It was seen as a safe setting in which to carry out aid work as the parties to the conflict had never endangered or threatened international organisation staff, unlike in some other situations in long-term low-intensity conflicts where aid workers had been kidnapped or killed. There was a widespread use of English, and an educated and socialised elite that was often seen to welcome development assistance. Donors worked around conflictual trends: for example, they did not directly address the politics of armed violence or the clash between government and Tamil representation. They sought to provide development models and poverty alleviation, particularly in the days of the Cold War rivalries with the old Soviet Union, which also gave aid and sponsored infrastructure projects. Kusal Perera (2014) observes that the first ever non-governmental initiative in Sri Lanka to work on racial justice and equality in society was the locally founded Movement for Inter-Racial Justice and Equality, popularly known as the MIRJE, which was started in 1979 as a proactive response to the critical problem of race riots.[7] Initially this was a membership movement, which drew on numerous social organisations and personalities including the political left and trade union activists. In Perera's view, the later influx of external organisations and grant aid funding was detrimental to genuine activism.

Amid the growing crisis, however, local activists sought and needed international counterparts. For example, in the wake of Black July's 1983 exodus of Tamils to India and further afield, there was a rising awareness in Europe, the US and Canada of human rights violations and conflict in Sri Lanka. Frerks and Van Leeuwn (2000: 70) document Dutch government concern to improve rights and living conditions in Sri Lanka (particularly in Tamil areas, at the request of the GoSL), partly in response to the acute refugee influx in the Netherlands. The Netherlands Institute of Human Rights in Utrecht hosted a 1984 conference on ethnic violence that considered the cases of Sri Lanka, Uganda and the Balkans. Out of this developed the Standing International Forum on Ethnic Conflict, Development and Human Rights (SIFEC), and subsequently, under the leadership of Martin Ennals, the founding of International Alert in the UK. With international public interest in Sri Lanka on the rise in the mid-1980s, critical developments in the country resulted in the GoSL asking for increased international humanitarian assistance. In the wake of Indian intervention and the attack on Jaffna by the Indian Peacekeeping Force in 1987, a new exodus of Tamil refugees in their thousands began, in particular across the Palk Strait to Tamil Nadu. UNHCR signed a memorandum of understanding with the GoSL in 1987. The same year saw donor pledges of $493 million to UN Development Programme (UNDP) programming for emergency reconstruction and rehabilitation in the north-east. The UN Commission on Human Rights and its sub-commission on the prevention of discrimination and protection of minorities passed a resolution calling on all parties to respect humanitarian law and invited the GoSL to cooperate with the ICRC. The government, meanwhile, was engaged in a brutal war with the JVP in the South at the same time.

For many Sri Lankan rights activists and NGO development agencies, the advocacy platform shifted to include the need to address political inequality and the underlying factors fuelling violence. By 1989, President Premadasa had his own commission to investigate civil society groups with political agendas. In an era when the island was known as the killing fields of South Asia, between 1990 and 1995 alone some 3.7 million Sri Lankan applications for asylum were submitted in Europe and North America (UNHCR 1997). It was in this context that the Norwegian approach was accepted, and outsiders allowed to facilitate within the country between the LTTE and the GoSL. Despite the subsequent breakdown of the ceasefire agreement and mixed sentiments about external involvement, as late as September 2006 Rajapaksa himself had agreed to an international commission to investigate disappearances and extrajudicial killings, in response to domestic pressures and the then field presence of the OHCHR. This commitment changed into a domestic mechanism or commission of inquiry, known as the Udalagama Commission, which was mandated to examine sixteen particular cases. It was intended that an international group would assist through observation and monitoring: the International Independent Group of Eminent Persons or IIGEP. However, the IIGEP withdrew in 2008 stating specific concerns on shortcomings in the process and failures to comply with international standards (Fonseka and Ganeshathathasan 2016).[8]

Meanwhile, smaller agencies were involved in trying to mediate informally on the ground and influence an end to the GoSL war with Tamil armed groups, as had been attempted at early British Quaker meetings in the 1980s with 'separatist Tamil leaders and government representatives, carrying messages between them in an effort to de-escalate the conflict' (Quakers in the World n.d.). In the late 1980s, British Quakers published a training manual on mediation for use in Sri Lanka (in the English language and targeted to rural audiences). Peace Brigades International (PBI) were present from 1989, and International Alert began programming in the early 1990s.

Development assistance: a shift in emphasis

Following the demise of the Soviet Union, and with the subsequent growth of Western overseas aid, there was a growing awareness of the implications of aid in conflict settings. The concept of peacebuilding was articulated by Boutros Boutros-Ghali in the early 1990s and became enshrined in UN practice. With the violent disintegration on Europe's doorstep through the war of old Yugoslavia and then the devastating genocide in Rwanda in the mid-1990s, there was renewed questioning on how to deliver aid effectively. Peter Uvin's seminal work *Aiding Violence*, published in 1998, critically examined the direct and indirect support (through externally funded development programming) to socio-political exclusion and grievance in Rwanda; Mary Anderson's 'Do No Harm' message was picked up by numerous Western governments and agencies at the end of the same decade (Uvin 1998).[9] Donors took seriously the idea that they could use their programming to do good.[10]

There was another factor behind the rising tide of international interest: during the early years of the new millennium, the possibility of taking credit for achieving peace in Sri Lanka, and demonstrating such an achievement as a model for others to follow, began to appear attractive to donors. Donor staff and academic conflict resolution consultants were attracted to Sri Lanka as a potentially successful experiment in liberal peacebuilding. Jeffrey Lunstead, former US Ambassador to Sri Lanka (2003–06), was candid in his view that Sri Lanka was popular with donors due to their belief in a peace process engagement which, if successful, would resolve a conflict marked by terrorism through peaceful political means – assisted by the international community:

> This would be a model for the region and indeed for the world. It would show that a seemingly intractable problem could be solved peacefully when internal actors were willing, and the international community could play a major role in assisting them. (Lunstead 2007: 5)

As the trend grew for donors to focus on peacebuilding and what was deemed 'conflict sensitive' practice, Sri Lanka came to be seen as a model or showcase of sorts. The war had economic and humanitarian impacts, which justified international assistance; diplomatic overtures had been accepted by a friendly government in 2002. The signing of the ceasefire agreement was widely and internationally endorsed; UN Secretary-General Kofi Annan hailed it as a step in the right direction and congratulated the parties for their courage and determination. The US and the EU welcomed the agreement and ensured their support. The major donors and politically significant international actors formed a group of co-chairs to support the peace process, bringing together the EU, the US, Japan and Norway. To provide an incentive and to encourage the parties to move forward with the peace process, the co-chairs hosted the Tokyo Donor Conference on Reconstruction and Development of Sri Lanka in June 2003, at which over $4.5 billion in financial assistance was pledged in addition to technical support for four years. The money was in principle conditional upon progress in the peace process, but critics later observed that there was no mechanism in place that allowed donors to reward parties for progress or to penalise failure: that is, the co-chairs had carrots but no stick (Holt 2011: 165). Human rights concerns were met with war on terror discourse.[11]

It became a coordination goal to support the supposed peace process in Sri Lanka.[12] Leaving aside the relative merits, problems or efficacy of the Norwegian approach to brokering an agreement, a situation emerged in which the conflict was seen by many as three-pronged: the GoSL, the LTTE and the international community. Walton and Saravanamuttu (2011) observe that Sri Lankan civil society[13] was severely polarised at the time between liberal-cosmopolitan and patriotic-nationalist tendencies, and suggest that during the ceasefire period donor policies had the effect of rendering civil society peace work apolitical and technical in approach. This in turn privileged a consensual rather than a politically engaged role for civil society actors, and saw the building of a Colombo elite of internationals who themselves attempted to take a lead on providing authority, group work and federal models.

The distinctive actor triangulation was formalised after the devastating Indian Ocean tsunami of late December 2004, with a three-way partnership for reconstruction through the Tsunami Affected Areas Program. Over half the damage was in the north-east, with deaths estimated at over 22,000 and displaced over 500,000. An early consortium saw LTTE representatives (who ran a parallel structure of local government in designated areas, in tandem with state-appointed government agents), government officials and INGOs begin collaborative planning. The Post-Tsunami Operational Management Structure, designed to bring the GoSL and the LTTE together for the coordination of relief efforts, failed when it was seized on by press-fuelled popular controversy and was successfully challenged by the JVP and JHU in the courts.[14] Elections brought a change of government and new pressures including restrictions on programming, which might in any case have run counter to military approaches for ending the war with the LTTE. Rajapaksa successfully rallied nationalist parties to the view that INGO involvement was neo-colonial (Gowrinathan and Mampilly 2009: 3). From 2005 onwards, there were increasing regulations to control NGOs, and it was clear by the end of the year that war and violent retaliation were again the order of the day. A situation had developed in which Sri Lankan organisations funded by and associated with Western donors were seen as tainted in ways that made them vulnerable to accusations of being anti-state.

What have the LTTE's NGO/INGO friends been doing in Sri Lanka?

Shenali Waduge, 30 December 2010

Sri Lanka's NGO/INGO sector number 3500 (7 per every square mile). Many of those who question the actions of these 'humanitarian aid workers' base their argument on the type of 'work' that has been done by them, why they are unmonitored & why they lack transparency and impartiality. As the Sri Lankan armed forces march to liberate the North of LTTE hegemony what these NGOs/INGOs have been doing can be finally unearthed (pun intended) & expose who actually benefitted from their 'humanitarian' kindness.

Many of the NGOs/INGOs present in Sri Lanka have benefitted by the continuing conflict in the country – the conflict being the very reason why they continue to remain. The 2004 tsunami was another reason for a further influx of NGOs into Sri Lanka & four years on it seems the tsunami

> victims are still without homes though less than 125,000 were displaced & the number of NGOs entering Sri Lanka is ever increasing.
>
> The NGOs/INGOs have enjoyed camouflaging their reason d'etre behind a crusade to depict Governments as being unconcerned for its citizens most of all the minorities. Sri Lanka's case has been no different.
>
> Presently we have a chorus of NGOs/INGOs denouncing the decision by the Government to relocate (local & foreign staff) from Kilinochchi to Vavuniya. The Government has gone the length by even offering to continue what they have been doing, if a list of all their activities is given to the Government.
>
> There are many who would opine that Sri Lanka is ungrateful to the UN/the INGOs & other NGOs presently involved in various development & humanitarian programs in Sri Lanka. As a developing nation, saddled with a conflict that has drawn on for over 25 years due to lack of proper leadership, we naturally must be grateful to the hand outs of aid etc that have been given. But realistically much of this aid has never really been free – whatever financial assistance we get from the World Bank or the IMF have necessitated that we align to their Structural Adjustment Programs (SAP) which means we must fall in line with any privatization programs to pay back all loans with plenty of interest ...[15]

Disjuncture and degrees of confusion

There arose severe anomalies in approaches taken by international agencies regarding positioning: for example, the designation of projects as 'post-conflict'. The experience described in the poem at the beginning of this chapter is not unlike that described by Ian Quick (2015) when reflecting on Trincomalee in 2007.[16] He had arrived in Sri Lanka to find a 'panoply of development agencies' with satellite offices along the 'forward defence lines' separating the LTTE and the Sri Lankan army, and the Scandinavian monitoring mission. His base was the UNICEF office in Vavuniya; the objective was 'peacebuilding', 'stabilisation' or 'early recovery'. He and his team helped people who had been displaced by fighting to return to and rebuild their homes and communities. But now he was himself in the war; his evacuation was pending, and the day had been marked by persistent anti-aircraft fire and the sounds of thudding artillery:

> What the hell happened? What have I been doing for the last two years?
> I'd arrived in 2005 with bold ambitions and impossible optimism. The job was coordinating post-conflict programmes with the United Nations ...
> Before long, however, the tit-for-tat incidents started. Concealed claymore mines scattered policemen's bodies across the dusty roads that I biked to work. Government thugs abducted suspected Tiger supporters in unmarked vans and 'disappeared' the bodies, the screaming of families two or three doors down waking me in the night. Over the course of five or six months, this escalated into open battle. There was increasingly frequent infiltration and artillery fire across the forward defence lines. A colossal truck bomb slaughtered nearly 100 sailors at one stroke, the town of Habarana going temporarily insane around me while I pleaded for radio guidance from our security advisers. Afterwards I was transferred between offices repeatedly, sometimes running away from the violence and sometimes towards it ...

Over the next few months there was an increase in general 'insecurity for civilians in Vavuniya but also the threats to humanitarian workers in particular' (CPA 2009: 26). Extrajudicial killings continued, particularly of young men and boys, with families frightened into silence through threats of repercussions; two local staff members of the Swiss Foundation for Mine Action were abducted, their burnt bodies found in February 2008.

In retrospect, it is striking that UN projects in Sri Lanka would be described as 'post-conflict' in 2005. A ceasefire – and only a ceasefire, not a negotiated agreement or solution – had been brokered in February 2002. At sessions in Norway the following December, there was provisional agreement on power sharing between the GoSL and the LTTE, but by April 2003 the LTTE had pulled out of talks after six rounds of negotiations. The next year saw a dramatic split within the LTTE with the departure of Vinayagamurthi Muralitharan (alias Karuna) followed by high-level assassinations on both sides. Burke and Mulakala (2005) note that donor response following the ceasefire was in many ways remarkable, given the absence of any significant political settlement; a no-war, no-peace environment was treated as though it were a post-conflict setting. Following the ceasefire, most donors and projects immediately adopted a post-conflict approach, with an assumption that war-affected areas needed recovery measures and that a peace dividend would underpin the transition from ceasefire to peace agreement. Thus, 2002–05 donor strategies reflected the hope and assumed trajectory of the ceasefire agreement, and commitment was seen as necessary to support any peace process (Chapman et al. 2009: 22). There was an additional synergy and incentive to assist, in that the new government's economic policy of promoting rapid reform through liberalisation, with a greater role for the free market and reduced state intervention, was for the majority of donors a policy portfolio very close to the prescriptions they themselves would offer. Then came the election of April 2004, the defeat of Ranil Wickremesinghe's ruling party, the UNP, and the appointment of Mahinda Rajapaksa by President Chandrika Kumaratunga. Later that year the country was hit by the devastating tsunami.

Kenneth Bush[17] first went to South Asia in his late teen years and to Sri Lanka 'before the Jaffna Library burning, before the Tamil United Liberation Front (TULF) were thrown out of parliament in 1981–82 for refusing to take an oath to the unitary state'. He recalls the 1987–90 period when the JVP was killing thousands of people, and the experience of working in the spring of 1990 with families in the South who had suffered loss, intimidation and bereavement. There was, he noted, no Sinhalese word for reconciliation in the deep South of Sri Lanka. Moreover, he returned in 2002 to Colombo and observed a new encroachment of INGOs. At a meeting of Colombo-based heads of agencies, almost everyone seemed to be new. 'Does anybody,' he asked, 'know where we were three years ago?' He also asked at the time how it was possible that the World Bank poverty alleviation plan made no reference to the fact that there was a war going on. He was appalled by the influx of new agencies (not always appropriate ones) after the tsunami and the mismanagement of resources.

Bush (2003a) later wrote extensively on intra-group dynamics in the war, and designed the influential Peace and Conflict Impact Analysis tool (Bush 1998; Bush 2003b). He was frustrated that newcomers could arrive with programming plans that seemed to be totally unrelated to the bitter violence, which was a constant in the North and East. Where was the situation analysis? Where was the real plan? The situation he and others found themselves in was the product of the very particular Sri Lankan experience with non-governmental and 'civil society' development, as well as wider global developments in international aid architecture. Moreover, the situation would be replicated with dire consequence in 2008, when the Common Humanitarian Action Plan (CHAP), which put forward the objectives, strategy and approach of the relief system, again took a business-as-usual position, with a focus on the displaced due to renewed war in the East and with no reference to anticipating increased violence or the need for additional preparedness in the Vanni (Niland et al. 2014: 5).

International donors began asking themselves what had gone wrong. A study commissioned by the UK's Department for International Development (DFID) outlined some of the key factors detracting from the aid effectiveness of bilateral donors engaging in Sri Lanka in 2005 (S. Harris 2005). These included continual government blockages to aid harmonisation for a coherent development agenda, the predominance of Japan and the banks in overall development assistance, and the failure of tsunami assistance to factor in the conflict context. As outlined in the report, the influx of humanitarian assistance through tsunami relief channels effectively dwarfed and deemed insignificant donors' earlier efforts to create a conditional economic incentive for the GoSL and the LTTE to see through the peace process to a successful conclusion. Secondly, bitter divisions developed around the questions of tsunami assistance delivery and the nature of its focus. This spilled over into antagonism towards international donors and aid agencies. Finally, assistance from the IMF, World Bank, the ADB and Japan, as well as the support of other non-Western donors, could be available in accordance with government policies, and through frameworks unrelated to political or conflict-related conditionalities, thereby strengthening the government's hand in ignoring pressure from other external actors.

Impending crisis

Before the tsunami, from 2002 to 2008, there were repeated warnings by UN human rights actors about violations, including alleged disappearances by state actors and the killing of civilians by government, the LTTE and the TMVP, as well as concerns over child recruitment by the LTTE and the TMVP. Despite recommendations by the International Human Rights Adviser to the Peace Process, Ian Martin, appointed with the agreement of the government and the LTTE, that an independent human rights operation be established this was not achieved. David Whaley, who worked with the UN there at the time, recalls that in the early days of the Sri Lanka Monitoring Mission (SLMM) (2003) both government and the LTTE agreed in principle to international human rights observers joining the monitoring mission, but the proposal that this be overseen by the UN was discouraged by the then Resident Coordinator.[18] At the time, relations between the UN and the GoSL were cordial; there was potential for agreement on independent international monitors. But at a critical juncture, the UN response was that human rights monitoring under UN auspices would make it harder for them to take an effective lead on development cooperation and humanitarian assistance. In retrospect, an effective human rights role was sacrificed in order to maintain a close relationship for development and access. Yet if independent monitors had been on the ground it would have been more difficult for the LTTE and government to utilize illegitimate behaviours of their own.[19]

Subsequently the UN Country Team were told repeatedly from 2007 onwards that there could be no guarantee of staff safety within the conflict zone, with particular reference to the Vanni after September 2008. Within three weeks, the UN withdrew all international staff, effectively ending UN assistance operations in the Vanni. The UN also tried to withdraw national staff, but the LTTE prevented staff dependants from leaving, which meant that many national staff chose to stay.

The increasing desperation in Tamil areas as the government pursued its repression of international agencies was courageously recorded and documented by Jaffna-based University Teachers for Human Rights (UTHR (J)). Their work confirms that when INGOs were ordered to quit the Vanni there was no longer any independent presence to oversee or monitor aid or need; the government had 'practically decapitated' humanitarian capability in the Vanni, rendering the suffering of the people an area open to propaganda and manipulation:

> As for the real reasons for not wanting expatriate staff in the Vanni, we might judge from the Mutur experience. From May 2006, the Government through paramilitary agents mounted pressure on international agencies in Mutur to quit. On a Sunday afternoon grenades were thrown at the offices of three INGOs and an employee of the Non-Violent Peace Force was injured. Three weeks later the office of the Emergency Architects was robbed and two foreigners there were threatened. Threatening letters were sent to others including ACF. Circumstantial factors point to the involvement of Military Intelligence with the complicity of the Police hierarchy ... ACF too pulled out, but later sent local staff back to Mutur a short while before the tragedy ...
>
> In early August 2006 when the LTTE took over Mutur after the start of hostilities, there were no expatriates. The Army retook the town after indiscriminate shelling in which about 50 civilians were killed. Shells struck the Hospital and places of refuge such as Arabic College. When there was a lull on 4th August the civilians vacated en masse. We could thus judge what is in store for the civilians in the Vanni from experience and the Human Rights Minister's inapt remark that they could

'pressure civilians to quit the LTTE-held area'. From 2006, there have been no guarantees for civilians. Schools, hospitals and places of worship have been hit.

It becomes much harder to give meaningful assurances to civilians in Vanni after removing international staff. Their presence would be the strongest deterrence against the LTTE provoking the Army from near places of refuge. (UTHR (J) 2008)

The same comprehensive report describes the way in which the government cowed international agencies: for example, in June 2007, two members of the Red Cross working in Batticaloa were abducted in a white van at Fort railway station. Their bodies were dumped near Ratnapura. The following month the humanitarian community organised a vigil for the victims at the railway station, but UN and INGO heads were reprimanded for allowing their staff to take part in 'political' activity. Personal intimidation, threat and slander were the order of the day.

The question was how to stand up to such government tactics and intimidation. Niland argues that the relief system response to accelerated warfare in 2008 was passive; that the biggest threat to civilians was clearly military strategy and it was obvious how political dynamics were driving the increased threat and a life-threatening crisis. But the network of agencies stuck to a response model that failed to address this, in that such situations are 'political' (Niland et al. 2014: 7). When the final offensive in the North came, when the reality of an all-out onslaught with no genuine humanitarian corridor was obvious, neither the ICRC nor the UNHCR suspended operations or approached the Security Council. In the words of an international aid worker present at the time (who prefers to be anonymous):

> Very few international organizations are willing to jeopardize their presence in-country. Presence is Protection, or so goes the argument. Everyone knew. WFP, SCF, Oxfam, UNHCR, UNOPS all had email, satellite links, daily reports from doctors

on site. What does it take to trigger intervention? Sri Lanka was the exception that should have proved the rule, but did not.

The belated 'big ask' was a humanitarian corridor for the evacuation of civilians. It was not to be. The ICRC evacuated some 14,000 civilian casualties within the first thirty-five days of the so-called declared 'no fire zone' amid what was deemed indiscriminate use of force; a UN convoy managed to bring out over 200 wounded civilians who had been trapped in the fighting in late January, with reports that the evacuation was followed by a promise from the government to give safe passage to all those still confined behind the front line (Senguptajan 2009). Aware of an estimated 250,000 civilians hemmed in by heavy fighting with dwindling food supplies, urgent international debates were conducted on a viable rescue response. Discussions took place in the corridors of the UN in New York, in Delhi, and in Washington DC (Nayar 2009). US Pacific Command (PACOM) sent an exploratory mission to sound out the viability of a sea mission to bring out civilians; its findings indicated that there was no permissible environment (Haniffa 2009). There were sensitivities anyway in Delhi, where the reaction to US Marines being involved in response to the tsunami emergency was something close to consternation (Agence France-Presse 2005);[20] and Tamil diaspora organisations in the US asserted loudly that such a mission would be complicit with ethnic cleansing in the region (TamilNet 2009).[21] Eric Solheim subsequently revealed that as a lead Norwegian negotiator he was instrumental in trying to formulate an international intervention:

> to send a ship with UN officials and representatives of the international community to the northern and eastern parts of the country. These officials would carry out a census in the war zone, including LTTE members and civilians and register them with their respective photographs. All these people were taken back to Colombo, and then they were to hand over their arms to the Lankan army. Except for the LTTE leader, Prabhakaran, and Pottu Amman, all the others were released under a general pardon. This was our plan.

If they accepted our proposal, thousands of people, including the LTTE killed in the war, would be alive today. The LTTE International wing leader, Kumaran Pathmanathan, was scheduled to visit Oslo to take a final decision in this regard. However, at the last moment Prabhakaran stopped him. Our security officials visited Kollampur to provide security for Pathmanathan. Later, we were informed the proposal was unacceptable.[22] (Solheim, cited in Jeyaraj 2012)

Stung by international failures to prevent what is now accepted as having been a mass atrocity – that is, the entrapment and killing of civilians culminating in military defeat – internal reviews and evaluations began in earnest, together with an acknowledgement of systemic institutional problems within the UN itself. When the Secretary-General's Panel of Experts presented its findings in April 2011, they included a memorandum stating its considered view that although many UN staff had distinguished themselves during the final stages of the conflict, some agencies and individuals had failed in their protection mandates, had under-reported government violations, and had suppressed reporting efforts by their field staff. The memorandum found that the UN had not adequately invoked principles of human rights, which are the very foundation of the UN. Rather, the tendency had been to do what was necessary to avoid confrontation with the government.

Subsequently, the Secretary-General's Internal Review Panel on United Nations Action in Sri Lanka of 2012 (also known as the Petrie Report or Internal Review Panel on Sri Lanka) produced a 128-page report (UN 2012) with a carefully drawn acknowledgement of failures, the reasons for them, and recommendations for the UN system. The Petrie Report is detailed in its account of individual attempts to influence the direction of the war: for example, the UN Secretary-General phoned Rajapaksa personally in February 2009, while reports were compiled and attempts made to draw government attention to the high level of civilian casualties and lives at stake. A tense standoff developed over whether casualties were being caused by the government at all, with the GoSL challenging UN data collection; eventually, the UN backed down in that it accepted that its figures might not be reliable.

Throughout the final, messy stages of the conflict, member states did not hold a single formal meeting on Sri Lanka – not at the Security Council, the Human Rights Council, nor the General Assembly. With no agreement on listing Sri Lanka as an agenda item, the Security Council held several informal 'dialogue' meetings, for which no written records were kept and no formal outcomes ensued. According to the Petrie Report findings, these sessions focused largely on the humanitarian situation; they did not emphasise the responsibilities of the government, nor did they clearly explain the link between government and LTTE action and the continual obstacles to humanitarian assistance. The report acknowledges the personal courage of some UN staff on the ground who continued at high risk to organise convoys and attempt measures for rescue and humanitarian response. But critically and simply it also points out that, at the leadership level, the UN did not confront the government directly with the fact that obstructing assistance was counter to its responsibilities under international law. In the words of Charles Petrie in a subsequent reflection:

> The main finding of the Internal Review Panel on the UN's actions in Sri Lanka, which I chaired, was the systemic failure of the organisation. This systemic failure was defined by poor institutional reflexes and timidity, stemming from the organisation's unwillingness to reveal the full extent of the horrors being perpetrated in the country in the hope of gaining greater physical access (which was not, in the end, forthcoming), and the secretariat's hesitation in raising Sri Lanka with a Security Council that it knew to be unwilling to take on the issue. Ultimately, it came down to a lack of ownership of the problem, by the system as a whole and at the highest levels. In such a context, the UN Humanitarian and Resident Coordinator and a number of his colleagues tried valiantly to do their best, but it was not good enough.
>
> It has been argued that, even were the UN to have performed better, or been more forthright in stating the information it

had, this would potentially have made little difference to what ultimately unfolded in Sri Lanka. It is of course impossible to know and easy with hindsight to say it would have (or not). But that was not the issue. The point is that the system did not use to the fullest extent its moral force. Even the most aggressive governments have been seen to change their behaviour when confronted by evidence of violations of international humanitarian law. And even if a stronger stance on Sri Lanka would not have altered the outcome, it would have demonstrated the UN's willingness to stand up for its principles, rather than allow them to be eroded, to the detriment of its future leverage in other situations. (Petrie 2014)

UN organisational morale had been hit very badly by the killing of three international staff members in a militia attack at Atambua in West Timor in 2001, and again in 2003 with the bombing of its Baghdad headquarters with casualties including Special Representative Sérgio Vieira de Mello. A decade later, in the wake of the Sri Lankan experience, the Secretary-General issued a message to all staff accepting the characterisation of 'systemic failure'; this was followed with a major follow-up plan of action to the Petrie Report, *Rights Up Front: A plan of action to strengthen the UN's role in protecting people in crisis*. *Rights Up Front* details specific actions to be taken by the UN in order to act on lessons from the past.[23]

Much has been written about the failure of the international community, of the 'outsiders', to rescue non-combatants trapped in the Vanni, and subsequently to stand up to President Rajapaksa when he stated clearly that the 'President wants reconstruction on his terms'. Individual aid workers have undergone considerable soul searching and whistle blowing over what they saw as inept or inadequate decision making and management (Chapman et al. 2009).[24] WikiLeaks cables indicate the standoff over standards and access that led to the eventual compromise by UN agencies in exchange for any presence or access whatsoever to the North (Aftenposten 2011). There has been less examination of the enabling conditions that were the backdrop to such an impasse.

International aid regimes and global governance norms

Studies of international aid, globalisation and global governance represent enormous fields of inquiry in their own right. What follows is an attempt to interrogate the wider milieu and dynamics that hindered – and to an extent paralysed – intervention attempts in Sri Lanka following the breakdown of the ceasefire, and, indeed, from 2009 onwards while the Rajapaksa government held power. Two fierce opponents, the LTTE and the GoSL, held the 'outsiders' at bay, forged ahead in their own fight to the death, and perpetuated the de facto non-resolution of long-standing Tamil grievances. They did this at a time when 'protection' was an articulated norm in the UN. It will be suggested that the formulation of donor policy was closely related to UN and US policies; and that, in the two decades from 1990 onwards, the aid industry effectively forged somewhat contradictory trajectories in its objectives and emphasis, first coupling development with 'peace', or conflict resolution, and then advocating both counter-terrorism and protection. Agency mandates and individual staff members were influenced and hampered in their operational ethos as a result.

Aid has always been both ideological and instrumental. Long before its current economic success and ability to shape overseas development, China was generous with technical assistance and aid to recipient countries in an outreach approach shaped by communist solidarity and the cultivation of client relationships to build allies and influence. The same may be said of American and Soviet overseas aid during the Cold War, as mentioned above. Japan took a striking leading role in humanitarian assistance, which has given it moral and diplomatic credibility in many circles. The Delhi-based Institute of Peace and Conflict Studies issued a report in 2011 identifying Iran as the largest lender and aid donor to Sri Lanka (Walker 2011).[25] Thomas Wheeler (2012) of Saferworld, however, put China ahead as the largest financer again, committing $760 million in loans by mid-2011, ahead of Japan's $413 million and $105 million from the World Bank. Net development aid to Sri Lanka for 2011 from the Organisation for Economic Co-operation and Development (OECD) was $611 million.[26] That said, the failures at the end of the war were put at the door of those from the institutionalised aid communities – those related to the UN and OECD – which may be considered 'front stage' in terms of any international norm regime. Backstage and less visible are the forces propelling decision making and interests.

Lai-Ha Chan (2011: 47) defines global governance as a 'system of rule' for established world order. He observes the importance to China and many in the region of state-centric values and the centrality of sovereignty. For many in the West, following the end of the Cold War, international shifts including the collapse of Yugoslavia and the rise of the EU meant a gradual norm shift in which self-determination and minority rights were viewed more favourably; witness the referendum and subsequent independence of Timor-Leste, the establishment of the state of Kosovo, and the tortuous pathway to nationhood for South Sudan. The readiness with which the EU and the UN supported these changes must have been anathema to many in South Asia. If the Sri Lankan 'peace process', or at least the ceasefire, was reliant on external donors and the received wisdom of the time that introducing resources could be an incentive to laying down arms, it was misjudged. Development in itself was a panacea; state sovereignty was not up for negotiation, and this was a case where one party would (it seemed) settle for nothing less than secession, and other (unlike Indonesia) would not move towards letting go or the sharing of power.

Historically, in order to deal with the TULF and other traditional Tamil elites, Velupillai Prabhakaran had built a professionalised military organisation dedicated to its own statehood, fashioning dedication through being prepared to die for the cause (whether by suicide bombing or by taking cyanide pills in case of capture), oaths of allegiance, taxation of Tamil and Sinhalese residents, illegal trade, and financial support systematically collected from the diaspora. His proto-state was in operation, the foundation for a Tamil Eelam that caught the imagination, hopes and aspirations of many and caused dread, fear and loathing in others:

> In order to deal with the EPRLF, the PLOTE and the TELO he developed a passionate commitment to secession and

Tamil independence, rejecting all other options as inherently treacherous and deserving of being dealt with in the most violent way possible.[27] (Biziouras 2014: 180)

In a mirroring of ethnic outbidding, Rajapaksa overrode liberal democratic thinking on federal reform and strove to achieve political success through messages of unity and Sinhalese Buddhist entitlement and dominance. No 'norms' of self-determination, intervention or other people's responsibility to protect would prevail in his state. In the same year as the military defeat of the LTTE, Russian forces completed their own brutal counter-insurgency war on Chechen rebels and declared Russian territorial integrity intact. For Western conflict resolution discourse at the beginning of the decade, underdevelopment was construed as a major factor in the perceived continuum from grievance to war, even as the global war on terror (referenced by both Sri Lanka and Russia in their internal wars) was being waged in Afghanistan and Iraq and promoted by the US government and its allies. Duffield's work on global governance captures the prevailing mood, when much discussion was on the inherent dangers of failing states and fragile contexts. In his words:

> The commitment to conflict resolution and the reconstruction of societies in such a way as to avoid future wars represents a marked radicalisation of the politics of development. Societies must be changed so that past problems do not arise, as happened with development in the past; moreover, this process of transformation cannot be left to chance but requires direct and concerted action ... Development resources must now be used to shift the balance of power between groups and even to change attitudes and beliefs. The radicalisation of development in this way is closely associated with the reproblematization of security. Conventional views on the causes of the new wars usually hinge upon their arising from a developmental malaise. (Duffield 2014 [2001]: 2)

In March 2005, ninety-one ministers of developed and developing countries taking responsibility for promoting international development, along with the heads of multilateral and bilateral development institutions, signed the Paris Declaration on Aid Effectiveness. This document is a collective endorsement of values including 'ownership, harmonization, alignment, results and mutual accountability'. The declaration notes 'increasing alignment of aid with partner countries' priorities, systems and procedures', and encourages decentralised donor decision making, which is meant to enable programmes to be flexible and responsive to fragile or conflict settings. There is mention of the need to reduce and counter corruption, and to build institutions for effective governance and equitable service delivery, and the encouragement of participation. Donors are encouraged to align behind governments in fragile states, and to avoid bypassing national budgets. When noting the tsunami disaster, it stresses that in such crises international humanitarian and development assistance should be harmonised within the growth and poverty reduction agendas of partner countries. The potential for aid to fuel ownership controversy due to the channels through which it is delivered is not addressed, nor are scenarios in which aid can reinforce divisive agendas. Thus the problems of non-fragile contexts in which the state itself is a party to violent conflict are not addressed.

Three years later, high-level representatives of donor and governmental agencies came together to review the Paris Declaration. Even as the UN and NGOs were being cleared from the Vanni, collective international commitment to the Paris Declaration was being reaffirmed in the Accra Agenda for Action; this included provisions endorsing analysis and the application of conflict sensitivity, measures such as a commitment to increasing recipient government accountability to citizens, allowing local and regional firms to compete for contracts, and commitments to corporate social responsibility. It called for donors to conduct joint assessments of governance and capacity and to examine the causes of conflict, fragility and insecurity.[28] Donor discourse, then, seemed to reflect the growing prominence of non-Western or 'non-traditional' donors operating in contexts such as Sri Lanka, many of whom do not question the role of the state, hold strong principles of non-intervention and national sovereignty, respect elites, and are distrustful of imported agendas in the name of democratisation or participation. A Sri Lankan country study undertaken by Kelegama and de Mel (2007: 32) maintained nevertheless that the Paris Declaration template could have been used to allay the fears of government, but also utilised in negotiations to include wider recipient and beneficiary voices.

Relief agencies adopted a different stance towards conflict dynamics. The code of conduct of the International Federation of the Red Cross and Red Crescent Societies (IFRC), for example, signed by some 446 agencies, differs markedly from the Paris Declaration, Accra Agenda for Action, and the OECD's guidelines and principles.[29] These guiding principles stress that the humanitarian imperative comes first; aid is given regardless of the race, creed or nationality of the recipients and without adverse distinction of any kind. Aid priorities are calculated on the basis of need alone; aid will not be used to further a particular political or religious standpoint. They also state that it is important to endeavour not to act as instruments of government foreign policy. The main difference is the IFRC code of conduct's emphasis on the primacy of citizens' and victims' needs, rather than government policy, for determining what assistance should be provided. Another important point is the requirement of neutrality relating to political or religious causes, and foreign policy. The code of conduct thus seeks to steer clear of strengthening the position of any particular conflict actor. The challenge in implementing these guidelines also brings out a central dilemma: how to alleviate the suffering of the most vulnerable in a way in which humanitarian aid is not a partisan or political act and should not be viewed as such. In Sri Lanka, development and relief agencies were expected to answer to, and take instructions from, a strong government.

While some civil society voices, Western donors and diplomatic representation operated on the premise that the conflict – the 'national question' – should not be settled militarily, sufficient funds bolstered the government coffers both to wage war and to gain in confidence over clamping down on dissent. As mentioned above, the inflow of assistance through tsunami relief channels effectively overwhelmed and rendered insignificant earlier donor efforts to create economic conditionalities or incentives for the GoSL and the LTTE to conclude the peace process successfully. Whereas in Aceh, the tsunami's aftermath opened up a space for previously bitter adversaries to decide to settle peacefully, and in Myanmar Cyclone Nargis brought about new opportunities for outsiders, relief assistance and the involvement of local populations, tsunami relief impacted in a totally different way on conflict dynamics in Sri Lanka (Hyndman 2009).

A major evaluation study of donor-supported activity in Sri Lanka was published in late 2009 and seriously considered the application of the OECD Development Assistance Committee (DAC) guidance in the years leading up to the end of the war (Chapman et al. 2009). A later summary account presented a breakdown of key findings:[30]

- Many strategies promoted 'peace', and some provided support for the peace process. Only a few explicitly addressed the root causes of the conflict.
- Few strategies were based on in-depth or recurring conflict analysis.
- The terms 'peacebuilding' and 'peace dividend' were used liberally. But there was no serious consideration of whether a 'peace dividend' could change the attitudes of hardliners.
- Most focus was on the 'costs' and not the 'causes' of conflict. So less attention was paid to power sharing, the political system and problems of injustice and impunity.
- Little recognition was given to political risks (such as delivering aid through a party to the conflict or supporting the agenda of a government that represented only a portion of the political spectrum and was vulnerable to electoral defeat).
- There was an overemphasis on the extent to which civil society and citizens could bring about transformation and peacebuilding.
- The 'whole of government' approach was an important strategic approach, but difficult to evaluate.
- The approach to conflict sensitivity was weak in early strategies, but this aspect was more explicit in later strategies.

For outsiders, the key learning was that it is the political actors who drive the process; the notion that aid in itself could act as a significant lever to promote peace in Sri Lanka was unrealistic. Linking aid to well-intended goals of reform or 'peace' was not effective as there was no strong domestic constituency for such goals. Burke and Mulakala (2005: 166) suggest that the only area in Sri Lanka in which the major donors stuck to a reform agenda was progress towards a liberal economic model. They point out that 'aid is the cart and not the horse':

> While political actors have used aid as a lever for their own political interests, donors should not mistake this manipulation for influence.[31] (Burke and Mulakala 2005)

Goodhand wrote that donors had 'probably never had so limited leverage in relation to government policy on humanitarian action, development or peacebuilding' (Goodhand 2010: S357). In order to join in post-war relief and recovery efforts and assistance, UN agencies were asked by the Rajapaksa government to sign up to official directives and approaches falling well short of recognised international standards. Moreover, they were required to undertake in writing not to speak or communicate with each other about their individual agreements with the government. These measures were divisive and indicative of the degree of control to be exercised in the wake of victory. From the end of the war to late 2012, UNHCR undertook a monthly compilation of government statistics to determine current numbers of IDPs and figures for those who had returned since April 2009. This was stopped because of the increasing difficulty in gathering data from local authorities (Raheem 2013: 27–8). Surveys of pre-2008 IDPs begun by UNHCR, UNOPS and the government in August 2011 were also abandoned in December 2012 because the Presidential Task Force for Resettlement, Development and Security in the Northern Province obstructed them (Glatz 2014). Concern grew about the lack of independent and verifiable data as well as deteriorating conditions for both localised security and human rights.

Indeed, Rajapaksa was resolute in his line on the outsiders and their domestic partners and counterparts. Post-war reconstruction was carefully controlled; human rights missions were denied entry;

international inputs limited to technical issues such as de-mining, housing and construction; record keeping relating to IDPs was limited so that government statistics could rarely be challenged. In July 2014, it was announced that NGOs would no longer be allowed to hold press conferences, issue press releases or conduct training.[32] This time, the GoSL was in much wider company worldwide, as during the previous three years more than sixty countries had tightened up their laws to control the activities of non-governmental and civil society organisations; the Carnegie Endowment for International Peace referred to this development as a virus-like spread of new laws under which international aid agencies and their partners are vilified, harassed or closed down (Sherwood 2015; Carothers and Brechermacher 2014).[33] Sovereignty was back. In 2016, Rajapaksa's successor, President Sirisena, would continue on this path when he stated in an Al Jazeera interview: 'We definitely do not need outsiders' (Al Jazeera 2016).

CHAPTER 5

Majoritarianism or divide and rule

It is only if the main Sinhale race survives like a giant tree that the other ethnic, religious, communal, cultural and linguistic groups can live in its shade, without being submissive but all in a state of assimilation. (Ven. Madille Pagnaloka Thera)[1]

Barely a week after the end of the war was declared on 19 May 2009, a UK national newspaper ran a piece under their world news section headed 'Tamils driven out of homes by ethnic cleansing', citing accounts from Trincomalee of Tamil civilians being driven out of north-eastern areas by pro-government militias, killings, kidnappings and the simultaneous encouragement of 'members of the Sinhalese majority in the south to relocate to the north' (Nelson 2009). Sources included an international aid worker and a Western human rights advocate, who used the phrase 'ethnic cleansing' to refer to a demographic push in the East that looked to be repeated in the North, particularly in the wake of war destruction and what was named a climate of terror and impunity. A key message of the article was the observation that with changes to demography, the majority Tamils would soon become a minority in the region. Three years later a report issued by The Social Architects (2012) noted that nearly 100 village names in the North, East and hill country had been changed from Tamil to Sinhalese ones. For the cinema-going public in the South, Sinhala films such as *Matha* and *Ini Avan* brought to the screen a visual drama playing out Buddhist centrality in the triumph of good over evil, a reference to the last phase of the war (Karunanayake 2014). August 2012 saw the loan from India of sacred Kapilavastu relics that received massive press coverage when sent on a display tour across the country. The President was depicted as walking barefoot carrying the relics (which are designated status symbols of a head of state) from their delivery by air across the tarmac to the VIP airport lounge, where around 100 senior monks chanted *pirith*, the Sinhala word for protection from all directions (Radhakrishnan 2012).[2]

Rajapaksa would assert Sri Lankan national interest and international policies through claims to Buddhist references and values. He maximised Sinhalese Buddhist majoritarianism to consolidate, divide and rule the polity.[3] This chapter will examine the force of Buddhist nationalist majoritarianism and how it was galvanised in accordance with political objectives, along with 'divide and rule' measures experienced in the decade after the war. It will include the rise of the BBS and the mass construction or reinvention of 'cultural heritage' in the North and the East, both parts of an instrumental project to build the unitary state in one image. The two themes are interrelated. Following military victory, the centrality of the official state religion was increasingly visible, at the expense of other long-standing faiths. Beginning in 2010, there were reports of both Muslim and Hindu sites being targeted in the North. On entry to the rebuilt Jaffna Library, long the repository of sacred Hindu and Tamil cultural texts until it was destroyed and burned during the conflict, the first welcoming object was now an enormous golden Buddha. On 14 September 2011, an estimated 100 monks led the mob destruction of a Muslim site in Ampara district, claiming that it was wrongly placed on land that had belonged to Sinhalese Buddhists for over 2,000 years. Police were present during the attack. An annual Hindu festival at the Munneswaran temple in Puttalam was disrupted in August 2011 with a resulting furore over animal sacrifice, as this is against Buddhist teaching. With the Department of Archaeology now coming under the Ministry of Defence, numerous 're'-constructions of Buddhist shrines were under way in the North and East of the country. The following year saw the destruction of the mosque and eviction of families at Anuradhapura, allegedly with the involvement of Buddhist monks. In April 2012, the

Sri Lankan government ordered a mosque to relocate when Buddhist monks in Dambulla threatened to demolish it. Minority Rights Group International (2012) expressed concern over reports that 'up to 2000 Sinhala Buddhists, including members of the clergy, protested outside and attacked the mosque.'

It is noteworthy that the thrust of these events was bold and well reported internationally, at the very time when Sri Lanka was due to take on both the hosting of the Commonwealth Heads of Government meeting (CHOGM) and the role of chair for the Commonwealth of Nations. Concern over rising levels of religious violence and attacks against places of worship was brought to the attention of the President by the UN Special Rapporteur on Freedom of Religion or Belief in May 2012. The Commonwealth Charter was adopted and announced by all Commonwealth member states in March 2013; this was the first time in its sixty-four-year history that the Commonwealth set out its core values in a single, unified document text agreed by all Commonwealth heads of government (including Rajapaksa). Principles in the charter included freedom of expression (also enshrined in Article 14 of the Sri Lankan constitution) and tolerance, respect and understanding for multiple identities.[4]

In fact, as illustrated above, the climate under this presidency was already severely tainted by repressive policies and constraints on expression. In his 2006 speech to the nation, in which he equated opposition to government policies with support for terrorism, the President had an interesting choice of words:

> I ask this of all political parties, all media, and all people's organizations. You decide whether you should be with a handful of terrorists or with the common man who is in the majority. You clearly must choose between these two sides.[5]

Considering majoritarianism

With its island-based Sinhalese population in the numerical majority, and the national minority Tamils having wide group affinity in the wider South Asia region (particularly Tamil Nadu), Sri Lanka has long offered an example of double asymmetries in power relations – contexts in which, from one frame of reference, the perceived balance of power is tilted in favour of one particular group over another. However, from another perspective, the perceived balance of power is reversed. This situation, popularly known as an issue of 'double minorities', means that each group can justifiably feel outnumbered by some other group, depending on the geographical frame of reference. The Sinhalese are a majority on the island but a minority globally. The Tamils are a minority in-country and a majority internationally. Case studies (as in Northern Ireland or Israel) indicate that the perception of being outnumbered can arouse not only concerns with social identity but also feelings of vulnerability to danger (Schaller and Abeysinghe 2006).[6] When observing meetings with the Executive between 2009 and 2012, the author frequently heard expressed the belief that Sinhalese status as a world minority made it difficult to counter global Tamil propaganda; 'with tens of millions of Tamils worldwide, the Sinhala voice is easily drowned out'.

The subject of majoritarianism is found within democratic political theory; as a facet of electoral democracies requiring management constitutionally; and through legislation assuring minority groups of their rights and access to the benefits of living in a particular society. Historically, the word carries with it the politics of entitlement but not always domination: a mixed picture that can interpret 5,000 years of Indian history, for example, as a multiplicity of faiths, languages and cultural practice, but must also factor in the violent spin-offs of new states such as Pakistan and Bangladesh as a result of critical impasses in identity and power relations. When Sri Lankan majoritarianism is viewed through a political science lens, some argue that the colonial imposition of a Westminster-style parliament 'incentivised' the creation of extreme Sinhala politics and thereby a reaction through Tamil radicalisation (Luengo-Cabrere 2012). Others call for its reinstatement in order to ensure fair governance in the country, believing it a better system for a country in which diverse peoples may all call themselves Sri Lankans while living and celebrating difference (CPA 2016a). The Institute for Democracy and Electoral Assistance's 2007 report on democracy in South Asia observed the problematic 'rise of a majoritarian ethic' in Sri Lanka (IDEA 2007; Sethi 2008).

Moreover, majoritarianism may be seen as fluid and replicable, like the proverbial peeling of the onion model, in that looking beyond (and within) the frame of Sinhala majoritarian politics it is possible to discern on a sub-regional level the LTTE leadership replicating violent majority claims through the mass expulsion of the Muslim population in 1990 from the North, when over 70,000 were ordered to leave with little notice. Speaking in 2015, Foreign Minister Mangala referenced this upheaval and historic injustice:

> The racism and majoritarianism undergirding the LTTE's expulsion of Muslims from the North is not something isolated to the Tamil community. It prevails to this day among all communities in our society. Just as the LTTE was unable to accept a multi-ethnic North, extremists in the South are unable to celebrate our country's diversity – much the less accept that Tamils, Muslims, Burghers and Malays are as much a part of Sri Lanka as the Sinhalese.
>
> Especially since the end of the war, which should have ushered introspection, magnanimity and healing, majoritarianism in the South raised its ugly head. The government indulged in an orgy of triumphalism based on equating Sri Lanka's identity with the Sinhala-Buddhist community, and relegated the minority communities to the place of unwanted guests. (Mangala 2015)

Technical measures to redress the democratic deficit were central to the brief interlude of ceasefire and negotiation, with consideration and debate on political forms such as consociationalism, power sharing, devolution frameworks and federal models. Ironically, Rajapaksa came to power after a heated 2005 election campaign in which he and his opposite number, Ranil Wickremesinghe, scrambled to woo minority votes. Rajapaksa declared his commitment to searching for an honourable peace but rejected the LTTE claim of being a legitimate representative of the Tamil people, as well as notions of any northern homeland, the Norwegian outline of an interim self-government authority for the North, and the post-tsunami operation management structure, in that these would grant the LTTE official recognition. He stated that the much violated ceasefire terms needed to be renegotiated, each plank of the platform carefully designed to appeal to the JVP and the JHU (in accordance with personally negotiated electoral agreements). Pitted against Ranil's pro-Norwegian profile, in a sense the electoral race became almost a referendum on the failed, flawed international brokerage. With a boycott on voting announced in the Tamil North, the very population for whom the agreement might have brought benefits did not vote. Even so, the result was close. Rajapaksa polled 4,887,152 votes at 50.29 per cent, while Wickremesinghe brought in 48.43 per cent with 4,706,366 votes.

Rajapaksa had signalled that international and thus neo-colonial interference was designed to denigrate the purity of Buddhist values. By consistently rendering the LTTE as purely terrorist and not political in nature, he convinced many that only his leadership would bring salvation. In the words of one political commentator, he had a twin strategy: adopt the maxim of divide and rule for the opposition and tell the people that only Rajapaksa in office would see the Tigers vanquished militarily (*The Nation* 2008). The two main opposition parties, the UNP and the JVP, were depicted by 2008 as 'split right down the middle and ... busy wallowing in their internal squabbles instead of challenging the government' (ibid.). Beyond numerical demography, theory on democratic accommodation and Machiavellian political machinations, Rajapaksa and his inner circles would build on and inflate a deep, personalised core of Sinhala Buddhist identity as a means of consolidating power: ethno-nationalism as exclusion. A 2012 study on the teaching of history on the island described a tenth-grade history text issued nationally which stated that the 'history of Sri Lanka begins after the arrival of Prince Vijaya (considered the first Sinhalese to arrive ...) with 700 followers. They were the first Aryans to come to Sri Lanka'; the researcher commented that, while the *Mahavamsa* is unreliable as a source, it is often referenced as history itself (Gray 2012).[7]

Majoritarianism in the near neighbourhood

David Rampton's (2011; 2016) scholarly examinations of deep-seated collective religious identity note regional connectivity and past fluidity in expressions of faith and identity: for example, both precolonial and early colonial Burma and Sri Lanka saw widespread examples of different religious, linguistic and other identities co-habiting in multiple ways.

> For instance, in pre-colonial and early colonial Sri Lanka, Tamil *Nayakkar* monarchs governed Kandy, the Kandyan Convention acknowledging British sovereignty was signed by 'Sinhala' chiefs in Tamil script, whilst anthropological sources indicate a residual legacy of bilingualism amongst fishing communities in the Western littoral and a syncretic history of Sinhalisation of Tamil groups and Tamilisation of Sinhala groups. In pre-colonial Burma, the situation was also similar.[8] (Rampton 2016: 16)

In Rampton's view, international and global forces in both contexts have been seen as a threat to the sovereign, unitary form of the state and to territorial integrity, with Sinhala and Burman Buddhist nationalists mobilising to reinforce these contours of the Buddhist nation-state. Writing in 2012, William McGowan observed the challenge to Aung San Suu Kyi's political rise from a chauvinistic element of Theravada Buddhist culture 'which encourages a sense of racial and religious superiority among majority Burman Buddhists at the expense of ethnic and religious minorities' (McGowan 2012).[9] He and others used the term 'Burmanization' when looking at internal power and territorial claims. Vatthana Pholsena (2014) writes in a similar vein concerning majoritarian group identities in Vietnam, Thailand, Laos and Cambodia, citing the Kinh, Thai, Lao and Khmer experience of the 'pursuit of homogenization'. A residual undercurrent – if not an overt expression – of grievance in many of Indonesia's far-flung islands relates to the expansive predominance of the majority Javanese population. This was a factor in the Acehnese civil war, with demands for self-determination including language rights and resource and revenue governance fuelling an armed struggle for years prior to a negotiated agreement. Indeed, Benedict Anderson's pivotal work *Imagined Communities: Reflections on the origin and spread of nationalism* (1983) was strongly influenced by, but not limited to, his years in Southeast Asia. In India, the May 2014 elections saw the Hindu nationalist movement BJP swept to power with a promise of *'acche din'* or 'good days', only to be defeated resoundingly nine months later in the nationally important elections in Delhi by a combination of young voters and the urban poor. The promise of good days may have been seen by them as not extending to everyone equally, but rather to a few at the proverbial upper levels of society. Majoritarianism, then, sits dangerously close to ethnocratic hierarchy in terms of application and effect.

Globalised religious militancy in the twenty-first century is a subject in its own right, one that has been examined elsewhere and is deserving of further serious inquiry. Mikael Gravers (2015)[10] points to the co-option of Buddhist monks by the generals in Myanmar as a nationalist strategy to build legitimacy for military rule; this took expression in the slogan 'One race, one language and one religion'. He also stresses the role of charismatic leadership in partnership with political elites for mobilising popular feeling, as occurred in the anti-Muslim riots that erupted in Rakhine State when a mob of young Buddhists attacked the Rohingya Muslim minority. Subsequently, some 140,000 people were displaced and over 200 killed. While it was reported that Myanmar's 947 Buddhist organisation and Sri Lanka's BBS (described below) signed a pact in 2014, it is beyond the scope of this book to interpret this beyond localised synergies and expedient, mutual cooperation (Perera 2014).

Rise of the Bodu Bala Sena

It was ironic that at a time when social media was a factor in the (then) sweep of the 'Arab Spring' and youth were taking to Arab streets in the name of reform, freedom of expression and human rights, social media in urban Sri Lanka was being used for radical hate campaigns and BBS recruitment. Consider the following quotation from a leading monk:

We faced a total blackout from local media. But we are lucky to have the new social media, the Face Book, e-mail and the Internet. Hundreds of thousands of younger people are listening to us and are with us.

BBS has begun an ideological struggle. We left the Jataka Pota in the temple library and postponed our meditating towards Nirvana (this is Engaged Buddhism now spreading in the West). We created a fertile soil for the rejuvenation of our nation and it is time for dialog or debate. (Fuller 2014)

With an incremental rise in attacks on Muslim and Christian communities between 2012 and 2014, and following violent clashes in the southern towns of Aluthgama and Beruwala, there were even clerical complaints that Facebook had blocked BBS accounts, the user stating that he had simply created another one (Liyanawatte 2014; *The Sunday Times* 2014c). The BBS held its first formal national convention in Colombo in 2012, calling for, among other things, preferential treatment in university admissions for Buddhists and the use of monks to teach history in schools. It was behind a high-profile campaign against halal meat certification and has been blamed for violent attacks on Muslim communities, including in neighbourhoods in the South. In early 2013, supporters of the BBS stormed a hotel alleging that its 'Buddha Bar' was sacrilegious, which resulted in two arrests of hotel managers (not of the attackers). It is understood that, after a meeting between the President, government ministers and the BBS on 27 January 2013, a statement was issued urging them not to be in conflict with other religious communities, but that this went out only in English, hardly the language used by the majority of supporters (Minority Rights Group International 2013). Defence Secretary Gotabaya Rajapaksa was guest of honour at the opening of a Buddhist Brigade training school, referring to the monks as those who 'protect our country, religion and race' (Stathern 2013).[11] As attacks escalated and deadly riots spread, concern also rose over the official interpretation of them. Ameer Faaiz (2014) wrote that, in the dominant narrative, 'nebulous and unnamed Muslim extremists are to blame. Following widespread condemnation of the violence, both at home and internationally,

Buddhist extremist groups and political parties represented in the ruling alliance were quick to shift the blame to unseen Muslim extremists.' His article points to the disturbing manipulation and omission of facts in statements made to the international community as well as to the Sri Lankan public.[12]

Message from M. Mahuruf, CEO of the Sri Lankan Secretariat for Muslims, circulated by email on 8 April 2013

Despite Sri Lanka's ethnic, cultural and religious diversity, the current predicament of growing religious intolerance springs from the rhetoric that this intolerance is necessary to protect the rights, values and the identity of the majority. This mindset has spread due to the efforts of the Bodu Bala Sena (BBS) and other groups, influencing their actions and the actions of individuals is such that there has been a wave of several alarming developments across Sri Lanka.

Through press conferences, television air-time and recently, a mass rally attended by 15,000 in Maharagama; Muslims' dress, mosques and the halal label are being vilified. There have been racist posters and handbills in public places, harassment of persons in Muslim dress, death threats directed at Muslim businessmen, desecration of mosques and Muslim businesses, and various public insults towards Muslim beliefs. The government is yet to call a halt to the group's activities.

According to the information gathered by the SFM the hostility against Muslims recorded 21 incidents in January. By March this went up to 54 notified incidents. While more incidents (23) were recorded in the Colombo district, reports are indicative that the phenomenon has now escalated across the districts of Kurunegala (14) and Kandy (10) as well. The BBS and the Sinhala Ravaya are orchestrating their activities through the use of poster campaigns (13 incidents), demonstrations (12) and leaflets (11). In addition, the ordinary majority are also being incited against Muslims through the use of obscene and vituperative messages via social and mainstream media. Anti-Muslim public rallies, processions including a call to boycott all Muslim business (16) establishments and targeting attacks on same have created a tense situation. The Muslim women's dress code also appears to have riled the majority.

This anti-Muslim sentiment in Sri Lanka did not spring up overnight; it has been simmering over a few years due to a few factors; global Islamic reformism effect on the Muslim communities' dress/social habits and reformists' emphasis on piety limited Muslims' everyday relationships with other ethnic groups [and] contributed to the isolation of Sri Lankan Muslims. Also, there is little information available in the public domain about Muslims in Sri Lanka, minimal reference to Muslims in the media generally and now, it is mostly derogatory. There is an urgent need to:

- institutionalize greater interaction between communities
- provide better information regarding local Muslims and Islam across the world
- engage in effective media relations

Ameen Izzadeen (2013a) reported how at dusk on Friday 12 April 2013 a small group of concerned citizens convened for a candlelight vigil outside a state-owned building that was the headquarters of the BBS. Their message was that the BBS and its hard-line monks were tarnishing the image of Buddhism and violating its precepts such as compassion and non-violence. Within an hour the police had broken up the peaceful vigil and had dragged a few of the more outspoken protestors to a police vehicle, as BBS office staff photographed the crowd. Responses to this included postings from members of the social media group 'Buddhists Questioning Bodu Bala Sena', claiming that the police action once again proved that the BBS must have state support and patronage. A petition calling on Rajapaksa to stop anti-Muslim agitation appeared on Facebook. SLMC leader and Minister of Justice Rauff Hakeem requested that the President convene a cabinet meeting to discuss the unrest and civil disturbance in the country. Hakeem also brought together other Muslim parliamentarians including Senior Minister A. H. M. Fowzie and Ministers Rishard Bathiutheen and A. L. M. Athaullah to speak about concerns for the security of minority communities. The Minister of National Language and Social Integration, Vasudeva Nanayakara, also criticised the police for being lax and called for a ban on extremist groups, including the BBS, Ravana Balaya and Sinhala Ravaya. These developments were documented by Gulbin Sultana, who also expressed the following view:

> The current hate campaign should not be seen as only a Muslim vs Budhdhist [sic] tension. It seems part of a larger strategy of establishing Budhdhist supremacy over the minority communities. After the end of the conflict in 2009 with the LTTE, expansion of Budhdhism all over the country has been visible. Numerous Buddhist Viharas are being constructed in the north and east by razing existing Hindu temples. For example, Kanniya Shivan temple in Trincomalee and the Murugan temple in Illangaithurai Muhathuwaram. A group of Buddhist monks also attacked the Foursquare Gospel Church in Kalutara in 2011. In Ambalangoda, the Assembly of God church was attacked in February 2012. A pastor in Kalutara was also attacked and a house belonging to a Christian was vandalized by Buddhist monks alleging that the church was engaged in conversions. (Sultana 2013)

Alongside the BBS, other groups promoting extremist views in Sri Lanka, such as the Sinhala Ravaya and the Hela Bodu Powura, purport to be the protectors of Sinhala Buddhism, which they claim is being threatened by Muslim and Christian religious minorities. In June 2014, a moderate Buddhist monk who had spoken out against the BBS was found unconscious and badly beaten outside Colombo (BBC News 2014). But a month later, the new Chief Justice, Mohan Peiris, was able to proclaim the Buddhist philosophical origin of human rights.[13] His speech was intriguing in its claims that Sri Lanka does not need teaching about human rights, but could in fact teach the rest of the world because human rights originate with the teaching of the Lord Buddha. An argument thus comes full circle, from a rejection of human rights by the GoSL to the ownership of their origin as being inherently Sri Lankan, except that for Sri Lankan one should read Buddhist Sinhala.

Cultural domination and majoritarian hegemony

As late as November 2015 (post-Rajapaksa presidency), the Sri Lankan navy was reported to have celebrated the laying of a foundation stone for a new Buddha statue to be built in Nainativu, also officially announcing a change of name for the island from the Tamil 'Nainathivu' to the Sinhala 'Nagadepa'.[14] In the Trincomalee district at Illangai Muhathuwaram, the long-established Ganesh temple was done away with and a Buddhist temple was built in its place, with the area renamed Lanka Patuna. 'It was,' in the words of an interviewee, 'like being slapped in the face.' These were recent examples of ethno-nationalist or majoritarian elite production of 'heritage', the erosion of people's dignity and the imposition of cultural messages as domination, relating the political to the way in which identity is made manifest in personal and social terms. How do you reconcile the need for 'closure' on the fate of loved ones, the need to remember and come to terms with past and present in order to build a future – the need for recovery of both self and group identity – with simultaneous symbolic engineering and signals of state majoritarian intent? The production of a new overlay of Buddhist Sinhalese symbolism in post-war Sri Lanka is also intrinsically linked to the effects of prolonged militarisation, land ownership, land loss and land use:

> In Periya Ullai (in Ampara) women complained that even to enter their own fields they are required to sign in and out with the military and certain areas that belong to the community have been barred under the claim of finding archaeological 'treasures'. Women used to guard their fields at night; however, now due to military presence this is no longer viable. Many women's livelihoods in this area have been agriculture and collecting and selling firewood. All these activities have been banned by military men.[15] (Women's Action Network 2013a)

The aftermath of war brought with it a marked degree of control over religious observance in the North and East, including interference with the ceremonies and rituals of Muslim, Hindu and Christian faiths: this included priests being told not to use candles or have processions, the removals of kovils, and the takeover of land that was in fact a Muslim graveyard. In a comprehensive study published in 2013, the Centre for Policy Alternatives noted concern raised by all minorities over the 'Sinhalisation' of several areas, particularly in the North and the East, through the construction of Buddhist statues, shrines and religious symbols (CPA 2013). It was observed that militarisation meant that churches, kovils and mosques were occupied in Jaffna, Mannar, Mullaitivu, Kilinochchi and Trincomalee, and that at least four mosques were under military occupation at that time – in Mannar and Trincomalee districts. The following observations of conditions under which the population was living in the North was made the following year:

> Land grabbing aside, the military is involved in the economy – from growing vegetables to running boutiques and hotels and restaurants and in effect taking land as well as jobs from civilians. They tell school children the language in which they should sing the national anthem and most recently one of their ranks pronounced on what constitutes 'acceptable' mourning. (Saravanamuttu 2014)

The notion of 'national heritage' is a modern phenomenon, a contemporary creation (Tunbridge and Ashworth 1996: 30), and observers recognise that there has been a fast increasing obsession with heritage in recent times. Heritage on a macro level is connected to the state-building project, developing over the last few centuries through emergent methods of archaeology, design, historical constructions and memorialisation (Aldridge 1989). Heritage is used to demonstrate how a nation has developed, how far it has evolved through art techniques and technical abilities. This in turn means that archaeology, history and art are used to show how long a nation has occupied an area of land and has created a community and 'a sense of national belonging among the entire population'

(Carman 1996: 79). The close proximity of Buddhist stupas, Hindu temples, Muslim mosques and Christian churches in Colombo would at one time testify to the nature of a shared island legacy, a South Asian example of the syncretic and the vernacular, which at its best could well inform Western societies about coexistence and pluralism.

Heritage is thus neither a 'naturally occurring phenomenon, nor is it universal ... it is in fact a socio-cultural construction, born at a specific moment in history' (Prats 2009). Construction is individual to each society and to the selective politics of that society: what matters enough to be kept, venerated, even showcased for outsiders through education, tourism and international attention. This involves choosing elements of the past for the needs and purposes of the present. Heritage making entails complex exchanges between multiple interest groups in processes to determine which aspects of the past are to be identified, preserved and managed as heritage, as well as the meanings to be assigned to them. Cultural heritage is also disputed, and it changes its meaning and interpretation over time as different social groups develop new or opposing views of the past, conflicting meanings and interpretations, and uses change or even overlap in a single heritage tradition, object or site (Dewasiri 2013).[16] This in turn influences the experience and legitimation of collective identities: for example, heritage tour guides at Kandarodai refer to site stupas only as evidence of Buddhism in the North, not as evidence of Buddhism historically among Tamils. In the words of one commentator: 'The neglect of syncretism in the practices of Buddhism and Hinduism renders these practices monolithic, ahistorical, and unchanging, making them the exclusive monopoly of one race or linguistic group' (Fernando 2015).

There is currently acute global concern about peoples being displaced and their sites deliberately obliterated in war zones, where identity claims are used to subordinate and destroy.[17] The wave of destruction of architectural and literary heritage – from Timbuktu to Afghanistan, Libya to Pakistan, Iraq and Syria – has even been labelled 'culture wars', a sad indictment of damage and loss (Bevan 2014).[18] Heritage also has 'intangible' forms: that is, language, poetry and song, the belief systems of groups that have been passed down over time. This weaving together of meanings and identity makes culture into a target and a means of wiping out or destroying a people or the sources of allegiance and sustenance for particular communities. Along with armed conflict, it is reasonable to say that, in a sense, Sri Lanka is also experiencing a type of culture war; it may not be visible to citizens in the South, but it is in their interest to understand it, as it will accompany the body politic through these next years of transition or non-transition.

Personal and collective grief have their own cultural norms and outlets. The destruction of a small localised religious shrine is one thing that sends a message that both the object and the belief are not worthy. The denial of ritual performance or gathering to grieve is another, and both are an assault on people's dignity. For the devout Hindu, the observance of Maleham can take place only when death is confirmed and there is acknowledgment that body and soul have separated. For persons of any faith, the unknown fate of missing loved ones compounds anguish and uncertainty, creating a void in understanding. A Centre for Policy Alternatives consultation and documentation of 'accounts by war-impacted persons' from Kilinochchi, Mullaitivu, Jaffna, Vavuniya, Trincomalee, Batticaloa, Musselli, Akkaraipattu, Puttalam and the coastal areas of the North and East highlighted the key concern: 'Psycho-social issues remain unaddressed' (CPA 2015).[19] Two aspects of this theme are identified: 1) most war-impacted people, particularly women, were highly emotional when relating their problems, which was indicative of their poor psychological status; and 2) war-impacted people are unable to bring closure to the loss of loved ones who went missing or were arrested or abducted due to inaction by the authorities in conducting investigations.

It should be noted that the treatment of grieving and its symbolic form in the North carry a contested and fraught history. From 1995, LTTE graveyards (known as *tuyilam illam* or 'resting places') were destroyed by the Sri Lankan military in an attempt to remove any physical signs of insurgence that would inspire others to be similarly militant. But these actions also 'punish' and deeply offend civilians, for whom the fallen were brothers, sisters, parents or friends. So the location of the 51st Division's military headquarters on an LTTE cemetery was perceived by the local population as aimed at reminding them of their defeat in the civil war in May 2009. 'This is a monument that adds humiliations to hurt,' a Tamil teacher was quoted as saying in a news item which suggested that respect for the dead is an important way of reaching out to a defeated people and an important step for reconciliation (Ramachandran 2011). After 2009, there were human rights groups from the South who discreetly assisted village women in improvised mourning rituals: for example, in placing unmarked stones by particular trees in remembrance of loved ones. Households sought solace in private with traditional music and stories in Jaffna. This was despite the ban on 'soft' or psycho-social services (as NGO projects), which has left 'many a potential beneficiary bereft and insecure' (WAN and CHRD 2012).[20] But even after LLRC recommendations called for the facilitation of people's attendance at religious ceremonies without hindrance, attempts to observe Maaveerar Naal (Heroes' Day) and Karthiaai (Karthikai) and the lighting of lamps at full moon at the end of the Festival of Light were disrupted by the military in the North, with measures described in an editorial by Groundviews (2012) as 'The death of freedom of assembly, expression and religion in the North of Sri Lanka'.

Eventually, main road signs in the North and East would appear in three languages (Sinhala, Tamil and English) but even in 2016 the language of administration was Sinhala. At a personal and social level, the imposition of Sinhala on signs and in documents and forms, the denial of mourning ceremonies, the ban on memorials, and the removal of religious symbols were further compounded by the very relationship between occupier and occupied. The need to request permission for social gatherings is a reminder of authority and control. Moreover, the positioning of 'civil affairs' and all decision making within military command lent it a curious similarity to colonisation, or at least it seemed so to the post-war visitor from outside. Magnanimous in their claims, military officers were quick to say that they were doing 'what was best for the people'. Problems loomed in the sense of insecurity, particularly among women, despite such a proportionally high presence of armed soldiers; in the nature of the ruling exercise when presented for wider public consumption or reporting: and in the emphasis on the army's philanthropic initiatives and the implied charitable impulse that could mean that the population was expected to show servility and gratitude. 'This is demonstrated by phrases – such as, "grateful beneficiaries", "charitable deed", "this act of benevolence by the security forces have [sic] brought great joy to the children" – used by both military officials and the MOD in speaking or writing about these activities': a juxtaposition called 'Charity and gratitude vs. rights and dignity' by one observer (Satkunanathan 2013). Doubtless many survivors have retained their resilience and integrity, against great odds exacerbated by wider spatial cultural reconstruction. Hundreds came forward to give testimony when the LLRC hearings were held, in spite of problems concerning their reception and translation. Thousands provided written submissions. Others have undertaken protests or demonstrations, including travelling by the busload to try to protest in Colombo in advance of the CHOGM meeting in November 2013. Whole families from Mannar, Vavuniya, Mullaitivu, Kilinochchi and Jaffna attempted travel to Colombo for the Samagi Human Rights Festival, also known as the Alternative Peoples Forum, to highlight Commonwealth values. Buses were stopped by the military and turned back. When groups from Mannar decided to hold a demonstration near Madhu church, and when families from further north staged a demonstration at Vavuniya, these gatherings were also disrupted (*Colombo Telegraph* 2013).

Spatial penetration and war tourism

Under the post-war Rajapaksa administration, the process of Sinhalisation intensified, with government-led efforts that systematically replaced Tamil culture and history with victory monuments dedicated to Sinhalese hegemony and Buddhist religion. This included the erection of Sinhala billboards, streets newly renamed in Sinhala, multiple monuments to Sinhala war heroes, war museums, and the construction of Buddhist temples. Spatial penetration has also been promoted through the encouragement of 'war tourism' and pilgrimage, neither of which recognise or include local experience or voices (Mittal 2015; J Stewart 2014). From the conception and construction of nine commemorative monumental stupas, one in each province, to the thirty-odd Buddha statues erected along the A9 highway between 2009 and 2012, physical imprints have altered space and structure in the name of victory since the end of the war.

War tourism in Sri Lanka fosters heritage sites that engender strong emotions among some visitors because soldiers and civilians were killed nearby, as at the Elephant Pass memorial. James Stewart (2014) notes the Sinhala signs and chooses his words carefully when he observes that 'unlike conventional so-called atrocity heritage sites, there is an effort in Sri Lanka to cover up or paper over certain aspects of the atrocities conducted in these areas. At the very least, there is a tendency to emphasize the Sinhalese victory.' He also points to a problematic aspect of this tourist infrastructure – 'its tendency to diminish and even cancel out the significance of the Tamil struggle for ethnic parity'.[21] Large-scale war monuments to victory alone serve politicised processes of remembering how the victors represent their victory, rather than providing any understanding of the history of the conflict, the reasons behind the struggles of the aggrieved, or ways to move into the future. In his acclaimed 2014 book *This Divided Island*, Samanth Subramanian chooses to conclude his post-war travel saga by describing a visit to the war museum near the now infamous Nandikadal Lagoon, near Puthukkudiyiruppu. Once a site where 350,000 desperate people were trapped at the end of the war, the target of relentless shelling by enemy armies, there is now a shiny information centre regaled with posters showing how the war was won:

> The text on the posters was all in Sinhalese: so was the headline running across the top of the wall, reading 'The Way of the victorious Vanni operation'. So was the text in another exhibit, of photographs of arms and vehicles captured from the Tigers. This was a museum where Sinhalese people were encouraged to come and revel in, and to own, a Sinhalese victory. (Subramanian 2014: 316)

Spatial penetration, then, has far-reaching consequences for the mental landscape as well as for the physical one. Monuments to victory abound, but nowhere is there recognition or honouring of suffering and loss. There are also Sinhala heritage tourist routes for pilgrims, often organised in the name of the Buddhist kingdom. Pilgrims take a well-worn path from Tellippalai to Keerimalai, to the Buddhist temple in Tiruvannamalai in Maathakal and then to Nagadeepa. They can see sacred sites, hear the old and revered stories, oblivious to any tensions among the local populations and military due to the problematic appropriation of large tracts of land for archaeological excavation purposes and the construction of new Buddhist temples. This reinforces a particular view of the heritage of the island in its entirety. The pilgrims will not see memorials at the sites of mass graves, or remnants of hidden detention centres. For those civilians in the South whose experience of the war and its end was different to that of Tamils in the North and East, there is little understanding of any different lived experience.

There is also a political economy aspect of majoritarian reach, as indicated above in the mention of land appropriation and use, the profits generated by touring parties and a new tourism industry. Of particular concern in the North is the fishing industry.

The Australian Government Refugee Review Tribunal reported a large number of claims in 2012 (continuing into 2013) that ethnic Tamils were being targeted, subject to serious discrimination and harmed due to their employment as fishermen. Common associated claims included the following: Tamil fishermen were subject to onerous permit requirements, from which Sinhalese fishermen are exempt; Tamil fishermen were restricted from fishing in lucrative 'security zones', unlike Sinhalese fishermen; the government, with the assistance of the Sri Lankan navy, was attempting to Sinhalise the fishing industry in the North as part of a broader Sinhalisation project; and there was an imputation that Tamil fishermen were pro-LTTE, and therefore subject to arbitrary searches, demands for bribes, arbitrary restrictions, and violence.

> Fishing in Tamil-dominated regions of Sri Lanka is a sensitive issue. Prior to the civil war, northern Sri Lanka produced over half of the country's total annual catch. At the height of the war in 2006, fishing in the north collapsed, contributing to less than

5 per cent of the national catch. A 2012 report for the Secure Livelihoods Research Consortium states that the resuscitation of this industry is central to post-war reconstruction in Tamil-dominated regions. While there are signs that the fishing industry is recovering, there is a perception among Sri Lankan Tamils that post-war reconstruction of the industry is primarily benefitting ethnic Sinhalese.

Furthermore, Tamils believe that they are being discriminated against by Sri Lankan authorities and Sinhalese fishermen are operating outside of the fishing cooperative societies system that has operated in the north since the 1950s. Grievances by Tamil fishermen are part of a wider anxiety regarding the perceived 'Sinhalisation' of the north following the defeat of the LTTE in 2009 (MRT and RRT 2013: 22).[22]

Division within the Commonwealth

Sri Lanka has been a member of the Commonwealth since 1948, when it joined as the Dominion of Ceylon. As such, it officially subscribes to the 1991 Harare Declaration and the Latimer House Principles endorsed at Abuja in 2003, which outline Commonwealth values. These include commitment to the rule of law, separation of powers between government departments, the independency of the judiciary and the principle of accountability. With its human rights record during and after the war and its treatment of the judiciary, including the impeachment of the Chief Justice, Sri Lanka's suitability for chairing the 2013 CHOGM was challenged by many. While Commonwealth countries took a stand over apartheid, objected to severe electoral violence in Zimbabwe, and have suspended members following the overthrow of democratically elected governments, as in Pakistan and Fiji, they resisted repeated internal calls to have a Commissioner for Human Rights. Secretary-General Kamalesh Sharma consistently supported Colombo, in spite of divided opinion among members and public calls to shift the meeting (Cowell 2013). An open letter from seven NGOs, including the Commonwealth Human Rights Initiative, reminded him of the Commonwealth Ministerial Action Group (CMAG) agreement to address all serious or persistent violations of the organisation's stated values (CIVICUS et al. 2012).

When the CHOGM was finally held between 15 and 17 November 2013 in Colombo, it had the lowest attendance recorded at the event to date: twenty-seven of fifty-three heads of government attended. Prime ministers from Mauritius, India and Canada declined to attend. David Cameron made a point of visiting Jaffna in a high-profile bid to acknowledge concerns over land and disappearances in the North. There was private, anecdotal speculation about whether US officials had briefed him or had gained a tacit understanding that he would make use of the Commonwealth opportunity to publicly signal a stronger move towards putting pressure on the GoSL for accountability. Women who travelled from as far as Mullaitivu to protest about the lack of action on their missing loved ones made their point, and were beaten by the police upon the Prime Minister's departure; unrepentant, they were still at work advocating for answers three years later.[23] Subsequently, in an unprecedented statement, China spoke out on human rights, with Foreign Ministry spokesman Qin Gang stating that 'what is important is that the relevant country should make efforts to protect and promote human rights while other countries in the world should provide constructive assistance' (*Daily Mirror* 2013). His statement came in support of calls at the CHOGM by India, Britain and others for Sri Lanka to address allegations of human rights abuses. Indeed, Cameron had stated publicly that the UK would push for an international probe into alleged war crimes (Izzadeen 2013b).[24]

Subsequently, political commentator Tisaranee Gunasekara pointed out that the 'Rajapaksas used minority-phobia as a political tool to distract the attention of Sinhala-Buddhists from growing economic ills'. Organisations such as the BBS, she says, 'were used by the then ruling family to addle Sinhala-Buddhist minds with fear and hate and to threaten the minorities into subservience' (Gunasekara quoted in Ramachandran 2016).[25] Following the ascendancy of the new government under President Sirisena, there arose a new and visible majoritarian nationalist campaign featuring posters and bumper stickers – the '*Sinha le*' campaign – which she

The view of the CHOGM

Malcolm Rodgers, Head of the London Office of the Commonwealth Human Rights Initiative from 2013 to 2014

The Commonwealth's credibility was already on the ropes. An Eminent Persons Report calling for reforms in the area of human rights, democracy and the rule of law among member states was buried at the previous CHOGM in Perth, Western Australia, in 2011. Commonwealth Secretary-General Kamalesh Sharma was branded a stooge of the Sri Lankan regime by Canadian Special Envoy Hugh Segal, as he refused to bow to widespread pressure to shift the 2013 summit to a less controversial host nation.

For the first time in 40 years the Head of the Commonwealth, the UK's Queen Elizabeth II, was not present. Of the 53 Commonwealth members only 27 heads of state attended. The leaders of Canada, Mauritius, and India, all with substantial Tamil populations, were absent. Tamil diaspora groups and humans rights organisation urged Mr Cameron to boycott the summit or change the venue. Mr Cameron controversially chose to attend, warning he would shine an international spotlight on Sri Lanka and its war record.

Just minutes after CHOGM's opening ceremony in the capital Colombo, Mr Cameron flew to Jaffna, where protestors, clutching photos of their missing loved ones, took to the streets as Mr Cameron toured the city. Women broke through the police cordon and hurled themselves at Mr Cameron's motorcade. At a resettlement camp refugees told him of the pain they endured during the 37-year conflict and the four-year military occupation since the war ended in 2009. He was the first world leader to visit Jaffna since independence in 1947.

Mr Cameron came back to Colombo with fire in his belly. At a fractious meeting he told President Rajapaksa that the Sri

Lankan government had to go further and faster on human rights and reconciliation and that the issue of accountability for the civilian war dead was not going to go away. Leaving CHOGM ahead of the gala dinner and the concluding sessions, the British Prime Minister issued a very public ultimatum.

'Let me be very clear, if an investigation is not completed by March, then I will use our position on the UN Human Rights Council to work with the UN Human Rights Commission and call for a full, credible and independent international inquiry.' Diplomatic relations were in free fall. It's not often you publicly accuse your host of war crimes on a state visit.

The CHOGM summit was meant to focus on poverty reduction and climate change but the massive global media coverage that ensued was dominated by the war crimes allegations. 'Is there anyone who has a question not about human rights?' asked a harassed Commonwealth official as a visibly angered President Rajapaksa ploughed through the final press conference.

describes as another Rajapaksa 'initiative', a 'freak show with a similar purpose – incite minority phobia among Sinhala-Buddhists and use that as a pathway for the Rajapaksas to regain lost power' (ibid.). The intimidating slogan *'Sinha le'* – literally, 'lion's blood' in Sinhala, the language of the majority of Sri Lankans – triggered fear among the island's Muslims and reflected a residual mentality with the potential to block both political reform and measures for accountability.

CHAPTER 6

Home-grown solutions and the quest for accountability

> Justice is ultimately connected with the way people's lives go, and not merely with the nature of the institutions surrounding them. (Amartya Sen)[1]

As explored in the early sections of this book, two models of post-war recovery were prominent following the defeat of the LTTE: the Sri Lankan government's Singapore model, which regarded reconciliation as synonymous with reconstruction, development and the restoration of stability; and the TNA defining reconciliation as devolution of political power to the people of the former conflict areas. And yet over the course of the next five years, dominant national discourse shifted to questions of accountability and constitutional reform. The backdrop was public concern regarding the economy, corruption and social indicators, including a growing southern-based campaign for good governance[2] and the shock electoral defeat of Mahinda Rajapaksa in January 2015 (BBC News 2015) and again in the August parliamentary election of the same year (Al Jazeera 2015). In the North and East, the critical unfinished business of land ownership, dislocation, missing persons and military occupation continued to frustrate many. Incoming President Sirisena was at pains to endorse the mantra of a home-grown solution, just as his Prime Minister Wickremesinghe made a point of endorsing the unitary state.

This chapter will question how the two models diverged, creating a space in which the question of accountability took root and held in a way that added to pressure for change within the country. For some Sri Lankans this meant accountability for personal livelihoods, the cost of living, corruption and increasing national debt. For others it was keenly highlighted in relation to human rights abuses, war crimes and a need for transitional justice processes to help all communities recover, to end impunity and to create conditions for non-repetition. As will be seen below, failure to deliver on a political solution was not related to a lack of internal proposals or mechanisms. The chapter will consider how convoluted the notion of 'home-grown' became in meaning and practice; growing disillusionment with the Rajapaksa government in terms of economic policies and creeping authoritarianism; paradoxical outcomes of the LLRC itself; and the rise of effective transnational human rights cooperation and lobbying organisations that found the Human Rights Council in Geneva a viable platform for a high-visibility sanction of the GoSL.

Meanings of home-grown: missed opportunities and new openings

In a speech to parliament at the end of October 2014, the leader of the TNA, the Hon. Rajavarothiam Sampanthan MP, outlined key moments since the end of the war regarding a political solution to address those as yet unresolved issues that had fuelled it. He recalled the visit of Ban Ki-moon to Sri Lanka in May 2009 and the joint statement issued by the UN Secretary-General and President Rajapaksa. He noted the work and recommendations of the APRC and the President's Multi-ethnic Experts Committee, which had produced a majority report outlining solutions to the national question (Jeyaraj 2011).[3] Subsequently, the TNA had attempted to enter into dialogue with the government between January 2011 and January 2012, but talks had broken down when government delegates failed to show on 17, 18 and 19 January 2012, and an impasse developed over TNA participation in yet another new parliamentary select committee (PSC) due to the barring from its agenda of any discussion of the devolution of police and land powers. In his concern over this and over the treatment of the thirteenth amendment, he had turned to India (Sampanthan 2014).

In invoking the UN, the 2006 majority report to the GoSL, attempts at bilateral dialogue, the stumbling block of the PSC with its self-limiting remit, and the role of India, Sampanthan's words reveal how enmeshed and broadly networked any notion of 'home-grown' solutions had become. An editorial opinion on the developing dilemma was voiced in 2013:

> The problem with a 'home-grown solution' since the conclusion of 'Eelam War IV' is that the Government has not said anything yet about in whose home such a solution would have to grow, or would be grown. The TNA was clear that it was to be in its backyard, and nowhere else. The war-shocked Sri Lankan Tamil Diaspora wanted it grown to their satisfaction, but by the international community. By the time the government decided that Parliament was where a solution should be sown, grown and harvested, the TNA had decided on the 'global garden'. (Sathiya Moorthy 2013)

Strictly speaking, this may not have been quite accurate insofar as the TNA felt it could not accept what were seen as unfair terms for the PSC. Conditions for planting, growing and harvesting via parliament were not sufficient. Meanwhile, it was other problematic national issues that were growing, rather than solutions.

Disappointing development

The rush to make Sri Lanka the 'Wonder of Asia' attracted a variety of potential investors. By 2014 there were growing protests over strategic enterprise planning by the government for gaming as part of tourism development, so that foreign cooperation would ensure that Sri Lanka took its place alongside Las Vegas or Macau in the list of world gambling establishments. The Casino Crisis, which was deemed the first major revolt within the Rajapaksa regime (*The Sunday Times* 2014b), resulted from the strong protests against gaming by Buddhist clergy being disregarded. For the Buddhist prelates, these plans were unethical and led to moral degradation. For many citizens they smacked of corporate gain and double standards in the enforcement and following of regulations. With multimillion-dollar deals in the offing, the Maha Sangha (the Buddhist clergy) found its objections ignored, and the JHU voted for the first time against the government. Subsequently, incoming President Maithripala Sirisena would pledge to tackle corruption through a special commission investigating public works, looking particularly at Chinese-funded infrastructure projects, the awarding of non-bid contracts and the payment of inflated prices with kickbacks for officials. Complaints had mounted, for example regarding the four-lane Colombo–Katunayake Expressway, which was 'found to be the most expensive highway ever built in terms of cost each kilometre', with the government paying SLR 1.8 billion per kilometre for the 26 kilometres linking the capital to Bandaranaike International Airport:

> Comparing it to another Chinese project, a 50km highway in Kenya that had only cost Rs. 972m per km, Mangala Samaraweera, an United National Party (UNP) MP, told reporters: 'Clearly someone or other has earned Rs 1bn per km on the Katunayake Expressway'.
>
> The $1.4bn Colombo Port City project also came under heavy criticism with regard to alleged financial misappropriations in the deal, after another UNP MP, Harsha De Silva, revealed one of project's major investors – the China Communications Construction Company (CCCC) – had been blacklisted by the World Bank due to corruption charges.[4] (Buchanan 2015)

It was not long before objections were also raised about the high cost of relaying rail track from Palai to Kankesanthurai; at more than $4 million per kilometre, this was nearly double the cost elsewhere for similar work in-country done with local labour. Concerns grew over the growth in the jobless total as China brought in its own workers, estimated at 25,000 by mid-2010, which in turn led to labour unrest (Policy Research Group 2010).[5] The government was said to be shocked when thousands of workers went on strike in four of the twelve special trade zones for five days in mid-2011, supported by the JVP, in reaction to proposals on pension reform.

When it emerged that four workers had been shot by the police and one had died of his wounds, Buddhist monks took to the streets in a march to Temple Trees in Colombo objecting to police violence. The proposed changes to the pension system were withdrawn (Sirilal 2011). Under the terms of the $2.6 billion IMF deal, the GoSL was meant to trim the public sector wage bill. There was, however, an increasing public feeling that targets for the cuts should be higher up in the public service: that is, on the governing ladder. Workers themselves were stretched, with rising prices and no sign of a peace dividend in terms of better standards of living. In that first year after the ending of the war, government nurses also went on strike, given that Rajapaksa's 2005 campaign pledge to raise public sector wages had not been delivered (Reuters 2010). Instead of any expected peace dividend, prices were going up and some wages were going down. Teachers were required to undergo military-style training that would instil discipline and nationalism, and the education sector objected to this. Within weeks of the CHOGM delegates leaving Colombo, an estimated 2,000 union workers were marching in street demonstrations; by mid-2015 worker strikes across twenty-three regional plantation companies were costing an estimated SLR 120 million daily, according to the Plantation Association (Wettasinghe 2015).

The aim here is not to attempt an exhaustive analysis of either the post-war economy or labour relations within the country, but rather to observe that large-scale infrastructure projects were not always relevant to the lives of many Sri Lankans, unless they drove big cars, flew planes or planned to dock a massive tanker at Hambantota (which saw only minimal dockings in its first years of operation, a shadow of its projected glory, suffering in comparison with the natural harbour offerings of Trinco or Galle). The new highway connecting the airport to Colombo was open in time for the CHOGM; taxi drivers would point it out with pride but only certain passengers could afford the toll fee. A growing form of critical dissent highlighted the limitations of emphasising megaproject development with little consideration for social implications. The Friday Forum consistently wrote to the government and published press releases on issues relating to social justice and economic development. Concerns included mass evictions in Colombo and the displacement of low-income families without the promised compensation or adequate rehousing; reports of police brutality from across the country; the need for a viable fund that would allow the Tamil diaspora to invest in the recovery of the North; outlines for a political solution to the national question; questions on government appointments (for example to the national Human Rights Commission); and the budget and macro-economic trends. With regard to evictions in Colombo:

> We agree that city planning and urban development is essential in the national interest. We would also point out that any form of development, particularly that which causes adverse social impacts, must be carried out according to the rule of law and with due regard to principles of equality and social justice. Such development must be implemented in the context of the Constitutional provisions regarding the right to equality under Article 12, the freedom to choose one's place of residence under Article 14(h) and the freedom to engage in any lawful occupation under Article 14(g). The State is also committed to upholding international human rights standards including the right to livelihood, personal security and shelter.[6]

Studies such as Sumith Chaaminda's (2012) *Fishing in Turbulent Waters* scrutinised infrastructure development in the North and the East, calling into question prevailing assumptions about reconciliation through development, with particular emphasis on the fishing industry. Here was a voice pointing out that development is also a discourse in power and control, with the priorities of communities varying from those of the authorities.[7] Given the lack of linkage between the two and the ensuing alienation, and given the growing structural inequalities between North and South, the study concluded that the current development strategy had served to both reinforce and reproduce existing social hierarchies, power relations and suppression among people in the war-affected areas.

The paradox of the LLRC

There were not many avenues for stories from war-affected areas to reach southern audiences. Government restrictions and censorship applied to both the Sinhala and Tamil press. A tangible southern sense of victimhood may have blunted or numbed curiosity about victims in the North. In addition, there was what Amal Jayasinghe describes as 'a degree of xenophobia' among the local media, particularly in hard-line nationalist outlets. Jayasinghe observes that when the press found it difficult to report directly on controversial stories, it would often reproduce foreign news so that the blame could be shifted if the authorities took exception (Jayasinghe 2015). That said, *The Island* reported on LLRC sessions in Mannar, quoting a Centre for Human Rights report that over 1,000 people had given evidence on 8–9 January 2011. They also listed key recommendations from the hearings, and noted problems regarding poor capacity and lack of translation (*The Island* 2011).[8] Tamil reports of LLRC proceedings via Groundviews circulated online and were later published in English on the official LLRC archive website (Groundviews 2010a, 2010b). Groundviews had earlier reported an almost complete 2010 media blackout in Sinhala and English, and that the majority of people in Kilinochchi and Mullaitivu had no advance knowledge of the LLRC's visit to the region. A few individuals who had written with requests to appear were contacted; others who heard of impending hearings spent several days trying to find out details of where and when they were to take place:

> Requests made to several government officials for information about the Commission's visit either elicited no response or the people were informed they could not attend the sessions. With much difficulty, a large number of women found out where the hearings were being held and turned up in large numbers. It transpired that most of those living in the areas the Commission was visiting were women who had suffered injuries in the war and whose husbands, fathers and sons had either been killed or were in detention or 'rehabilitation' camps. Although the merits of engaging with the LLRC can be debated, according to

activists in the area, many women felt that being able to speak about the hardships and losses they had experienced was in and of itself a relief. As has been reported in the Tamil media the LLRC was clearly unprepared to cope with the number of women who turned up and therefore requested the women to make written submissions. (Groundviews 2010c)

In the words of one external report based on transcripts made publicly available, 'almost despite itself, the LLRC's proceedings brought out serious allegations of human rights abuses by various armed groups and government forces' (Amnesty International 2011: 19). The women of Kilinochchi and Mullaitivu in particular flocked to have their say, in numbers that the LLRC was clearly unprepared for. Limited administrative support was in place, particularly for translation, and commissioners did not always appear to be sincere in their willingness to listen to or recognise the witnesses coming forward. In other words, many women felt that they were not being heard by the very mechanism that was meant to listen to them. And yet they still came, with passionate stories and detailed accounts of family members being killed or taken away by the LTTE and Sri Lankan military alike. There were widespread reports of men present who appeared to be intelligence agents taking photographs of the sessions. Clearly deeply upset and emotional when telling their personal stories, many of those testifying were also at risk in that witness protection was simply non-existent. Not only did they testify, however, but over five years later many of them were still vocal in their questioning about the missing and the lost. They had filled out form after form for relevant, ever-changing administrative requirements. Moreover, their personal stories were reaching an audience outside Sri Lanka. Women interviewed in Kilinochchi and Mullaitivu in early 2016 were still adamant in their desire for information and resolution, many of them citing the LLRC as the first time they had spoken out.

So we have a paradox, framed eloquently by de Mel when she asks why the LLRC attracted hundreds of witnesses from within Sri Lanka and approximately 5,000 written submissions when its very legitimacy was questioned by both international and local actors (de Mel 2013). Working with this question in her own inquiry and in conversation with women who testified from Batticaloa, she suggests that the LLRC, while impartial and incomplete, did acknowledge women as victim-survivors and also provided a forum for voicing information that could form the basis for future case investigations, compensation, possible prosecutions and the recording of a narrative at variance with the official one. Moreover, while LLRC conclusions were mothballed soon after release, it can be observed that certain recommendations – such as the right to information and a call for credible investigations into allegations of excesses in military behaviour (as shown in the Channel 4 video) – had reached the public domain and would stay there for debate and deliberation. For initiatives meant to demonstrate home-grown capability, however, both the report and LLRC action plan, published in English long before any translations were made available, had anomalies. Jehan Perera observed that the action plan had no preamble or background to help citizens understand why it had been issued or why it would matter to the country: in short, it was not user-friendly for the general public:

> It therefore comes across as a technical document in the form of a table with terminology that will not be familiar to most people. Terms such as 'key performance indicators', which forms a central feature of the action plan, are not in common usage within the generality of the Sri Lankan population. These are terms that are used especially by members of the international donor community who wish to assess the impact of the projects that they fund and also by those who seek to obtain their goodwill. This suggests that the action plan needs further evolution if it is to become a people-friendly document and one that is accessible to the people in both the Sinhala and Tamil languages. (Perera 2012)

In Perera's assessment, the government evidently was less interested in meeting the challenges of political transformation within Sri Lanka than in meeting the challenge of the international community in Geneva. This is in keeping with Gowing's view that the

LLRC was part of domestically driven transitional justice initiatives in Sri Lanka that largely followed a performative logic which served to consolidate and legitimise the regime in the context of external pressure for accountability from the international community; it was intended to signal progress to the international community in ways that would foreclose the possibility of addressing accountability issues. In this view, transitional justice must be understood not as a universalist project, but rather as a set of political contests in which discourse and practice are instrumentalised for disciplinary power, producing the subjects and subjectivities that best serve the interests of the state, particularly in terms of consolidating authority internally as well as possible legitimacy in the eyes of the international community (Gowing 2013: 11). For understanding the motivations behind the inception of the LLRC, such an interpretation has validity. But time proved that the performance was lacking, consolidating neither the authority nor the legitimacy of the Rajapaksa government. Domestic critics both fearlessly denounced flaws in the process and persistently asked for recommendations to be acted upon. Conceived in part to forestall interference from the UN, the LLRC report was presented to external governments and scrutinised by the UN Panel of Experts. The panel stated unequivocally that the LLRC did not satisfy standards of independence and impartiality and that domestic mechanisms were not in place for implementation. Its conclusions did not mince words, deeming the LLRC to be deeply flawed and not satisfactory to fulfil the joint commitment of the President of Sri Lanka and the Secretary-General to accountability (UN 2011a). There followed a request by the Canadian government through a draft resolution at the eighteenth regular Human Rights Council session of September 2011. The draft asked that the report of the LLRC be submitted for discussion at a council plenary the following March (2012). Canada later dropped the formal draft, but the USA took a lead at the March session by introducing a resolution calling on the GoSL to implement the recommendations of the LLRC; to initiate credible, independent action for justice, accountability, equity and reconciliation; and to outline a comprehensive action plan. The text encouraged the UNHRC and relevant mandate holders of special procedures (see below) to provide advice and technical assistance, arguing that the international community had waited almost three years for action by Sri Lankan authorities but nothing had happened.

Growing momentum

Transnational activism, advocacy and pressure had kept Sri Lanka's unfinished business of both alleged war crimes and the national question in world headlines during this time. To mark the first anniversary of the war in 2010, Amnesty International, the ICG and Human Rights Watch joined forces to campaign for an international investigation, with an Amnesty global action receiving more than 13,000 signatures for an online petition to Secretary-General Ban Ki-moon. Many of those signing were themselves Sri Lankan (Becker 2013).[9] The ICG gave considerable focus to Sri Lanka, with research and documentation culminating in its own report on war crimes in Sri Lanka, followed by a high level of press coverage and international advocacy (ICG 2010a). The Irish Forum for Peace in Sri Lanka and the International Human Rights Association Bremen began planning in June 2009 for a response to what they saw as mass violations and war crimes, concluding in two sessions of the Permanent People's Tribunal, in Dublin (2009) and Bremen (2014). The Dublin findings were to be echoed in numerous settings over the years to come: 1) that the Sri Lankan government and its military are guilty of war crimes; 2) that the Sri Lankan government and its military are guilty of crimes against humanity; 3) that the charge of genocide requires further investigation; and 4) that the international community, particularly the UK and USA, share responsibility for the breakdown of the peace process (Irish Forum for Peace in Sri Lanka 2009; International Human Rights Association 2010).

Non-governmental initiatives and official spokespersons also demonstrated concern for post-war Sri Lanka; among them were The Elders, the International Working Group on Sri Lanka, the Global Leadership Forum, Amnesty International, Human Rights Watch and Forum Asia advocacy initiatives, the Sri Lanka

Campaign for Peace and Justice, with Edward Mortimer as Chair, and the Non-official Group of Friends of Sri Lanka, headed by Ambassador Richard Armitage. South African delegations to the government encouraged dialogue with the TNA and hosted discreet tripartite meetings between the government, the TNA and diaspora representation (*Tamil Guardian* 2014). Japanese peace groups and activists were included in a special briefing on Sri Lanka hosted by the National Diet in early October 2009. Special Envoy Yasashi Akashi would later publicly encourage the GoSL to investigate allegations and cooperate with the UNHRC. In India, Tamil Nadu Chief Minister Jayalalitha Jayeram had accused the GoSL of war crimes during the final military operations against the LTTE; thousands of students and Tamil political party activists mobilised for demonstrations that Delhi found difficult to ignore (Thalpawila 2014). Hundreds of students demonstrated in Chennai with demands that India support the US resolution at the UNHRC. In what developed into 'a massive upsurge of students against alleged human rights abuses in Sri Lanka', the Tamil Nadu government closed down 525 engineering colleges and attempted to counter a state-wide strike called by the Tamil Eelam Supporters Organisation (TESO) (*The Times of India* 2013; Daniel 2013).[10] A German human rights institution, the European Center for Constitutional and Human Rights (ECCHR), sent a dossier documenting alleged Sri Lankan war crimes to the German Federal Foreign Office in early 2011, referencing in particular the 57th Division, which had been under the command of Major General Jagath Dias (acting Deputy Ambassador to Germany). Likewise, Swiss NGOs including TRIAL, the Swiss Association against Impunity, filed a criminal complaint against Dias, who was recalled to Sri Lanka on 14 September 2011 (TRIAL 2011). The Australian Human Rights Law Centre ran seminars on the crisis of impunity. While the official government position vacillated somewhat and immigration (including boat people from Sri Lanka's North) was a contested subject, at one point members of the Australian public used Melbourne cricket ground for high-profile demonstrations over the end of the war and the Tamil genocide (*Tamil Guardian* 2012).

The Geneva Process

The special procedures mechanism of the Human Rights Council mandates designated independent human rights experts to report and advise on human rights from a thematic or country-specific perspective. Special procedures are central to UN human rights systems and cover all human rights: civil, cultural, economic, political and social. Sri Lankan legal experts and activists had contributed to the refining and more robust establishment of special procedures when a UN review was under way in 2007. At that time, a petition signed by more than 12,000 individuals was presented to the President of the UNHRC in Geneva, calling on the council to maintain and strengthen the special procedures. Signed by victims of human rights violations, by defenders and lawyers, legal experts, parliamentarians, and NGOs from all over the world, the petition was delivered formally at an event that included an address via video from Sunila Abeysekera, Executive Director of INFORM Sri Lanka. That same year the Secretary-General of the International Commission of Jurists (ICJ) had met with President Rajapaksa to express serious concern about what he called a grave human rights situation in Sri Lanka, including new patterns of enforced disappearances and targeted killings of civilians as well as the shrinking space for civil society. Indeed, in the wake of the breakdown of the ceasefire agreement two years previously, some 900 people had been detained following searches in five mainly Tamil districts of Colombo, with the police and army carrying out door-to-door searches. The ICJ was also concerned that there be new and impartial investigations into the 2006 killings of seventeen ACF aid workers in Muttur and the killings of five young men in Trincomalee, with prosecutions of those responsible. The ICJ Secretary-General also called for the establishment of an international human rights field operation to help deter and prevent human rights violations on all sides. A side event on 'The human rights situation in Sri Lanka' was organised at the sixth session of the Human Rights Council by the ICJ and Human Rights Watch, on 17 September 2007. Sri Lankan representatives from human rights organisations joined with Amnesty International and the ICJ, and the GoSL was given time to reply.

The use of UN mechanisms thus had a solid track record and ownership among Sri Lankans. Precedents were in place for civilians and government to enter into dialogue and exchange views on human rights using such mechanisms. Members of the legal profession and advocates for civil and human rights forged working relationships across international networks. Partnerships formed that lobbied frantically in the last days of the war on protection issues, with sister organisations such as the International Working Group on Sri Lanka (earlier the NGO Forum), Amnesty International and Human Rights Watch in crisis mode from January 2009 (Human Rights Watch 2009). The Security Council was lobbied; delegations pleaded with US government agencies to intervene. Subsequent shock following the White Flag incident, the killing of the estimated 40,000 trapped in the Vanni, and the ethos of a victor's justice plus a genuine risk to Sri Lankan human rights activists in their own country led to a bruising reappraisal. The role of internal actors had always been to the fore. Now, in the immediate aftermath, many of them were 'too bruised to lobby' and a baton was passed initially to colleagues, on behalf of the dead and the victims.

As human rights advocacy shifted from stopping the slaughter, to issues of accountability for war crimes, and as the GoSL did not make good on its promises of promoting reconciliation and addressing Tamil grievances, the UNHRC came to be the focus for putting pressure on the Rajapaksa regime, through a resolution at one of the annual meetings of the UN Human Rights Council. (Miriam Young, Director at US Counsel on Sri Lanka)

Why the UNHRC? Based in Geneva, there is a context of international cooperation for peace and human rights. Sri Lankan activists regained their voice with strong cooperation forged between the International Working Group, Amnesty, Human Rights Watch and the ICG to lobby in Geneva and Brussels as well, issuing statements and briefings to the European Parliament, talking with Brussels-based diplomats about options on conditionality that led to the revoking of the special trade concession of GSP plus. At the EU delegation headquarters in Colombo, meanwhile, human rights defenders were welcomed and supported. Within the UN system not only is the UNHRC mandated to deal with human rights, but structurally it is accessible to individuals and civil society, through written and oral statements, side events and bilateral meetings with state representatives. There is no privileged veto power; rather, there is an open voting procedure in place.

It was possible for national and international NGOs to use complaint mechanisms with particular mandate holders in the special procedures system, and they prepared comprehensive briefings for diplomatic missions and the press. They also provided wider networking through information given to treaty bodies such as the Committee against Torture (CAT), the Committee on Economic, Social and Cultural Rights (CESCR) and the Committee on the Elimination of Discrimination against Women (CEDAW). They provided credible evidence and persuasion to influence the stance of states such as Benin, Cameroon, India, Libya, Mauritius, Nigeria and Uruguay to vote in favour of the March 2012 resolution; and Angola, Botswana, Burkina Faso, Djibouti, Jordan, Kyrgyzstan, Malaysia and Senegal to abstain (Rathgeber 2013). The UNHRC adopted Resolution 19/2 in 2012, and again, through 2013's Resolution 22/1, called on Sri Lanka to take credible steps to ensure accountability for alleged war crimes and human rights violations during the final stages of the war with the LTTE. The USA sponsored the resolution with the forty-seven members of the UNHRC; twenty-four countries voted for the resolution and fifteen against it in 2012. Another resolution against Sri Lanka was passed in the twenty-second session in March 2013, calling on the GoSL to conduct credible investigations. Twenty-four countries voted for the resolution and thirteen against it, with India among those voting for the resolution. Then came the pivotal 2014 resolution of March 2014 on 'Promoting reconciliation, accountability and human rights in Sri Lanka', through which the UN High Commissioner for Human Rights was requested to undertake a comprehensive investigation into alleged serious violations and abuses and related crimes committed by both the GoSL and the LTTE during the time period covered by the LLRC, 'and to establish the facts and circumstances of such alleged violations and of the crimes perpetrated with a view to avoiding impunity and ensuring accountability, with assistance from relevant experts and special procedures mandate holders' (OHCHR 2015a). In the words of one of the individuals who had worked for exactly this resolution: 'One of our greatest allies was the Sri Lankan government itself, with its 77 member delegation, bullying tactics, intimidation and departure from UN decorum. It was style over substance, and did not go down well.' A member of the diplomatic community privately confided his concern about 'hubris, no offering of good will and triumphalist overdrive since the end of the war'.[11]

The GoSL had protested a month earlier about unwarranted interference in the internal affairs of a sovereign state. A report by INFORM (2014), the Colombo-based Human Rights Documentation Centre, gave a vivid picture of reactive measures taken internally by government and security services in the three months leading up to the resolution, through repression of expressions of dissent; reprisals and intimidation of a Minister of Justice and a leader of the SLMC for cooperating with the UN High Commissioner for Human Rights; the disruption and closure of seminars and events; the continuing repression of journalists; and the arrests of three human rights defenders in the North while the UNHRC was in session. Excavation of a mass grave discovered near Mannar was stopped, some eighty bodies having been recovered.

Acting on this resolution meant the establishment of the OHCHR Investigation on Sri Lanka, the OISL. Its eventual comprehensive report, which covered alleged human rights violations by both the GoSL and the LTTE, began with an overview of context including the observations set out below.

Challenges and constraints: the Government of Sri Lanka

Extract from the OISL report of 16 September 2015, p. 10

1. The greatest obstacle to OISL work was the absence of cooperation and undermining of the investigation by the former Government. From the outset, it stated its

'categorical rejection' of the Human Rights Council-mandated investigation. It continued to reject repeated invitations to cooperate from the United Nations High Commissioner for Human Rights. In July 2014, the Permanent Representative of Sri Lanka to the United Nations in Geneva refused to meet with OISL coordinator and later with one of its experts, Dame Silvia Cartwright. The High Commissioner nevertheless met with the Foreign Minister in New York in September 2014. The Government also failed to respond formally to a letter sent by OHCHR on 4 December (appended) requesting detailed information.

2. Instead, the Government at all times sought to undermine the investigation by calling into question its objectivity, professionalism and integrity. Between 4 November and 2 December 2014, the Government issued several press statements, called three meetings with Colombo-based diplomats, and issued two demarches through the United Nations Resident Coordinator in Colombo, accusing OHCHR of a series of 'grave inconsistencies and contradictions which call into question the honesty, integrity and appalling levels of unprofessionalism of the OHCHR.' These allegations centred on procedural issues, particularly the deadline OISL had given for submissions.

3. On 7 November 2014, the High Commissioner for Human Rights issued a press statement urging the Government to 'focus on the substantive issues under investigation instead of obscuring them by the constant questioning of procedures'. The High Commissioner also rejected accusations of having been linked to the alleged fraudulent gathering of statements and payment of money for information. Following a meeting with the High Commissioner, the Permanent Representative of Sri Lanka in Geneva, in a letter dated 15 December 2014, reiterated the Government's position of non-cooperation.

For others within Sri Lanka, proceedings had additional significance. As a platform for victim statements and civil society submissions it was seen by some to become a symbolic memorial. But the challenge remained of translating statements into action at home. In David Whaley's[12] words:

> For most members of the Council the handling of Sri Lanka by the HRC was seen as a rare success story. It was welcomed as a case in which country-specific action in the face of serious violations of human rights – and alleged war crimes and crimes against humanity committed by all sides (GoSL, LTTE and government-aligned para-militaries) – had been initiated, against the odds, and sustained over a sufficient period of time to embarrass a regime that showed little willingness to address the root causes of conflict or lay the basis for reconciliation.
>
> This had been done in a manner that avoided direct confrontation or interference. The approach was based on the assumption that the ordinary citizens of Sri Lanka – victims of state violence and HR violations, members of national and religious minority communities, and dissenting voices in the majority community – would not accept the steady erosion of the country's traditions of democratic governance, the shift towards pariah status in the international community and the refusal to restore dignity to the Sri Lankan Tamil community. By providing a space for Sri Lankan dissenters – domestic civil society and the large diaspora community alike – the HRC conveyed the essential message that someone was listening, observing, monitoring developments in the island.

Whaley's professional background and knowledge of the UN system and actors gave him credible institutional insights and political analysis, and he gifted his time working alongside Sri Lankan and international activists in both making a case and advocating for an international investigation, arguing in part that the state was not capable of investigating itself. Arguments based on legality, substance and morality were put forward, and for many of those involved it was also personal insofar as many had experienced loss and intimidation or had had colleagues or family disappear, be detained or defamed. There was increasing evidence that those Sri Lankan citizens and human rights defenders who communicated with the UNHRC were doing so at great risk of reprisals, smear campaigns, custodial torture or enforced disappearance. Fred Carver of the Sri Lanka Campaign documented internal repression from March to May 2014 in detail, noting the Rajapaksa government's use of state media to name and denounce individuals who testified at Geneva proceedings; the arrest in the North of Jeyakumari Balendran, a Tamil mother and activist (on charges that she was harbouring a suspected terrorist), who had been present when Cameron visited and whose daughter had personally given a garland to UN High Commissioner for Human Rights Navi Pillay on her arrival; and the arrests of human rights defender Ruki Fernando and Father P. Mahesan. In the latter case, he observed the handling of the media, the eventual release of the two men, and the subsequent gagging orders on them; they could not leave the country, their phones and computers had to be handed in, and they were subject to recurrent physical intimidation, part of a long-standing pattern in the response to dissent. Carver suggests that the cumulative effect was a chilling one:

> There were numerous reasons for this: the natural effect of exhaustion following a gruelling release campaign, the spirit-sapping effect of the sheer brazenness of the Sri Lankan Government in making such a move (and the message this sent about the level of impunity they believe they enjoyed), and most influentially the uncertainty as to whether further campaigning or reporting on the issue would exacerbate the situation and goad the Sri Lankan Government into re-arresting the pair. (Carver 2014)

In response to international criticism, the government accelerated some of the very behaviours being criticised.

Normative battles

In the popular press and media of Sri Lanka, the fight between Rajapaksa and Geneva was presented as an epic battle. The President was presented as a champion of a small island pitted against conspiring international agendas with the neo-imperial intent of dominating a sovereign people. On the occasion of the GoSL carrying its own Geneva resolution in 2009, an editorial in the *Sunday Leader* proclaimed a moment of victory and 'one of the most extraordinary diplomatic coups in history' (Wijewardene 2009).[13] Here was that victory being taken away; a carefully constructed edifice being dismantled. It was construed as a new battle. Commentators such as Bandarage were arguing already in 2009 that transnational human rights activism could be used by dominant world powers to advance global political and economic hegemony; that there was an agenda through human rights promotion for the US government, the World Bank and INGOs to export neoliberal economic policies (Bandarage 2009: 204). It is true that purveyors of global governance theory in part point to an expansion of neoliberal capitalism, a crisis of accumulation and systems of economic domination and control: rulers and the ruled. It is true that there has been uneven application of stated values such as human rights, and that this has called into question the normative stance of nations such as the US or the UK and challenges the UN, which itself now makes use of private contractors. But, on the other hand, there remains an active aspiration to systems of law and legitimacy that will challenge injustice and impunity, including wider double standards. International humanitarian law, the laws of war and obligations to refrain from crimes against humanity are designed to moderate and govern behaviours so as to protect non-combatants. Moreover, Article 28 of the Universal Declaration of Human Rights states that: 'Everyone is entitled to a social and international order in which the rights and freedoms set forth in this Declaration can be fully realized' (UN n.d.).

Paper delivered at the plenary session 'Does law's global pretensions offer hope to the world?', Law and Society Association, Seattle, 28–30 May 2015

Kishali Pinto-Jayawardena, Sri Lankan lawyer, columnist and author

So in what way has global human rights norms helped us domestically? Our basic concept behind the theory of change has been formulated within the framework of Article 2 of the International Covenant on Civil and Political Rights (ICCPR). Article 2 obligates the state parties to ensure an effective remedy for violations of human rights. For this purpose, it obligates the governments to take legislative, judicial and administrative measures to ensure an effective remedy. Most commentators on Article 2 concentrate on legislative changes, such as, for example, the criminalization of acts which amount to improper use of force and violence – the criminalization of torture, forced disappearances, sexual abuse, and the like.

However, what is often ignored is the obligation of the state to take judicial and administrative measures to ensure an effective remedy. A holistic view of change from the law and order approach to the rule of law approach for the elimination of improper use of force and violence requires legislative, judicial and administrative measures. In short, the legislation must be in terms of the normative framework of the rule of law. The judicial framework should also be within such a normative framework, and the government should also ensure that administrative measures, such as budgetary provisions that enable the proper functioning of the judicial process through ensuring the necessary resources, both by way of personnel and other technical resources, are also within such a framework. Issues such as the training of the security officers and their internal discipline could be satisfactorily addressed only within a legal system which is constructed on the basis of such a normative framework.

The obligation of the state to take measures for effective remedy has been sorely lacking but much sought after in Sri Lanka. Given the legacy of 'dirty war' in the country, decades of abductions, targeted killings and the practice of 'taking no prisoners' in combat, how could any agenda for human rights receive traction? National figures have fought for decades for fundamental rights, freedom from torture and freedom of expression. Partnerships also formed: for example, as early as November 1995 the NGO Forum on Sri Lanka organised a seminar and discussion on the human rights situation in-country, attended by twenty-one international delegates and some sixty representatives of local organisations. National press coverage branded it pro-LTTE and protests followed. Peace Brigades International had to escort Tamil participants out of Colombo (Peace Brigades International 1995).[14] At the time, there was no stated government opposition to such a meeting and relevant permissions had been granted. INFORM received threatening phone calls and members of the Sri Lanka Free Media Group were attacked on the street. The UN Working Group on Enforced and Involuntary Disappearances reported in 1999 on its findings in Sri Lanka, calling on paramilitary organisations to close their detention centres; the then UN Human Rights Commission stated that the Sri Lankan government had not implemented any of its nine recommendations to prevent enforced disappearances or to bring the country up to internationally accepted standards of human rights (Jansz 2000).[15]

In August 2003, the *Journal of Humanitarian Assistance* reported on a consultative workshop on 'Unarmed monitoring and human rights field presence: civilian protection and conflict prevention' which examined the SLMM as one of its case studies. Concern was expressed over the mission's limited mandate and on particular human rights issues that were not included. Among these were the use of child soldiers, freedom of movement (beyond specific measures for LTTE members), freedom of expression and the press, and guarantees that the displaced could return to their homes and economic activity. Subsequently, Ian Martin conducted a fact-finding mission in Sri Lanka during which he encountered a strong belief 'that attention now to human rights issues was entirely supportive of the peace process, and that any early tolerance of human rights abuses would threaten the process' (Martin 2003). He reported several practical recommendations for technical assistance from UN agency or Commonwealth sources and stated that the Prime Minister had regarded these as acceptable possibilities.[16] The previous March, Martin had travelled to Kilinochchi to conduct training sessions for LTTE judges on human rights, also meeting with key political advisers including Anton Balasingham. His recommendations were overruled not by national but by UN decisions. It was an opportunity lost, and in retrospect a costly one.

Rajapaksa's strident opposition to hearing anything but the discourse of victory over his ending of the war with the LTTE, in spite of Geneva proceedings that took due note of LTTE transgressions as well, proved a normative battlefield which intertwined with a loss of confidence at home. Having literally given Colombo land to China for the Port Authority project, and having overseen corporate contracts with international investors of all backgrounds who fully embraced fairly rampant forms of capitalism, his protests and claim to moral authority waned. In a curious vein of self-fulfilling prophecy, he even accused Geneva of seeking his downfall, of having an agenda of regime change.

Major turning points

After a new government came to power, Sri Lanka under President Sirisena accepted the OISL report and co-sponsored a new UNHRC resolution in October 2015. It was a major turning point, a swift sea change that many human rights activists would have hardly thought possible. The new President stated that a domestic process (in keeping with Geneva's wording on 'credible domestic mechanism') would be initiated in June 2015. An Office of National Unity and Reconciliation (ONUR) was established and across the country the 'four pillars of transitional justice – truth, justice, reparations and non-recurrence of violence' entered the national lexicon. In the words of Bhavani Fonseka (2015):

The resolution setting up the OISL came about in the absence of any genuine steps by the Rajapaksa Government to live up to its own promises and pledges to investigate. It is also a testament to the calls by victims and survivors for truth and justice and who bravely provided testimony of past and ongoing violations.

It is in this context that the UNHRC must not fail the victims and survivors of Sri Lanka ... It is also fundamental that Sri Lanka continues to be on the agenda of the UNHRC with continued support by the international community including the OHCHR and other human rights mechanisms. Although the Sirisena Government has indicated an interest to engage, this alone should not dilute the stand taken by the international community to investigate past violations and support Sri Lanka in terms of initiatives at addressing truth, justice and reconciliation. There are several areas that require attention before Sri Lanka can initiate domestic investigations including legal and policy reform. This includes reforming the Commission of Inquiry Act and introducing legislation for victim and witness protection. Capacity building is also needed including providing trainings to judges, lawyers, court staff, investigators and forensic scientists among others.

In the flurry of ensuing activity, accountability questions were relegated to newly formed administrative streams, with justice issues and, in particular, the missing coming under the ONUR. In parallel, and under the Foreign Minister Mangala Samaraweera, a Consultation Task Force was established to work on formulating mechanisms for accountability, truth and reconciliation. An outreach process for submissions and consultation was intended to allow public participation amid calls for victim-centred measures. Figures 6.1 and 6.2 present contrasting pictures and impressions of the new organisational frameworks (which drew heavily from civil society leaders for their composition), with Figure 6.1 being drawn by a woman leader who had long worked inside the national circuit, and Figure 6.2 being posted by the UK Sri Lanka Campaign. Both are valid representations, each in its own way illustrating international connections. For many inside Sri Lanka the notion

Figure 6.1 The road to reconcile in Sri Lanka (February 2016)

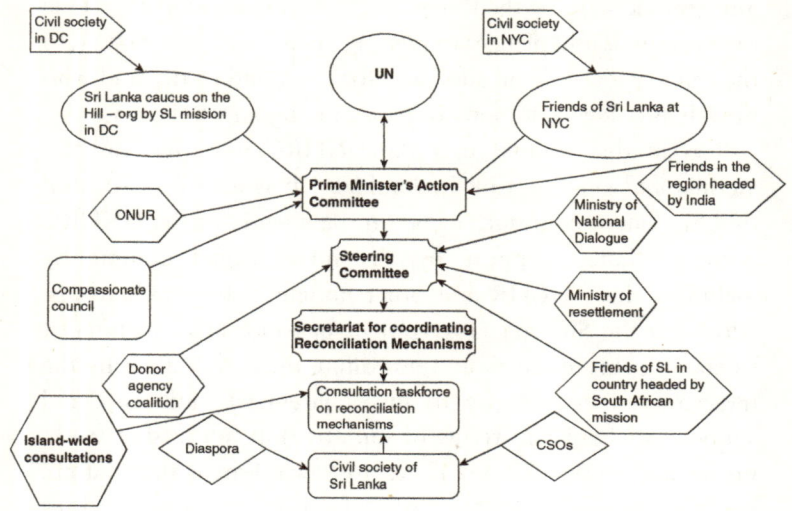

of reconciliation coming under the Ministry for Foreign Affairs must have been significant; were measures being undertaken for Geneva, or because of Geneva? Getting national buy-in was a major challenge, particularly in the South where Rajapaksa still commanded a network of loyal supporters and nationalist forces were far from curbed. The new government reassured the public that Sri Lanka could look after its own; in particular, the GoSL did not need foreign help for a hybrid judicial process and the army should not be tainted with allegations of war crimes.[17] At the same time, a constitutional reform process began; this was located within the parliament but also invited submissions, with new hopes that a political solution could be structured this way (Sri Lanka Brief 2016).

In the North and East, to some degree people could speak more freely, although surveillance remained. The military, while still present in the same numbers, was somewhat less visible. For some Tamils, the UNHRC resolution had disappointed in that it was co-sponsored by a state government that they still felt could not be trusted:

Figure 6.2 Mapping transitional justice mechanisms in Sri Lanka (February 2016)

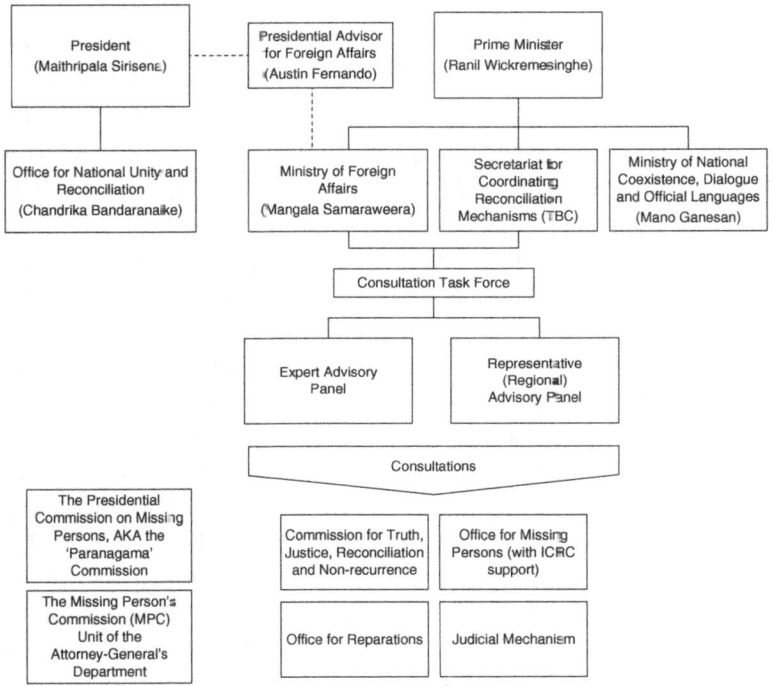

By accepting the primary responsibility of GoSL and other Sri Lankan institutions for implementation, the HRC, despite the findings of the OISL and the recommendations of the UN High Commissioner, had yet again failed to honour its responsibilities towards victims of state violence; it had missed an opportunity to address structural barriers to reconciliation and a political settlement; it had allowed improvements in democratic governance in the south and the transformation of political, economic and security relationships with the 'western world' to triumph over human rights concerns. For some, the whole HRC process had resulted in a process that they could not support and the failure of which would be a necessary prelude to more robust international action.[18]

What was meant by structural barriers? Early 2016 fact finding in the North and East revealed representative priority concerns of: 1) the failure to lift the Prevention of Terrorism Act; 2) continual military occupation, including their economic and cultural privilege; 3) lack of resolution for those with missing family members; 4) continual surveillance by TID and Criminal Investigation Department (CID) security agents, although people acknowledged that their general freedom to speak out and discuss openly had improved; 5) the failure of authorities to release political prisoners, although this had been promised again and again; and 6) unresolved land issues. The subtext remained the need for a political solution. By then, a Chief Minister for the Northern Provincial Council was in place who had not hesitated to use the word 'genocide' when addressing Colombo on the subject of the Tamil people. This meant difficulties for the TNA in its quest for participation in the political process. With these issues still seething, there were even civil society and activist voices asking whether the US sponsorship of the UNHRC resolutions had been dedicated to 'regime change', and how and whether the US would come through or deliver on accountability for human rights violations. Rajapaksa had not delivered on home-grown solutions, but it remained to be seen whether the new government would be any better.

CHAPTER 7

Small state in a large system

Sri Lanka does not exist on a separate planet; the world is more integrated than ever before; if we do not take note of how the world is changing – and I have little confidence that the people of our Island will – we are in for a rough ride. Still I guess 'it is a far, far, better thing' to go to our end with our eyes open than deluded by nationalism and religiosity. (Kumar David)

Sri Lanka's dance with global governance

Sri Lanka's dance with global governance – that is, the choreographed steps taken by state apparatus to move in relation to liberal norms and global institutions – took striking forms in the Rajapaksa decade. The regime found willing partners at times, with the state and the President going solo on other occasions. Consider the 2006 official UNESCO event to present the World Press Freedom Prize in Colombo. President Mahinda Rajapaksa participated in the award celebration, held mere months after the killing of Tamil reporter Subramaniyam Sugitharajah by unidentified gunmen following his publication of evidence disproving the government's version of events regarding the death of five students in Trincomalee (who became known as the Trinco Five).[1] The recent comprehensive study *Embattled Media* (Crawley et al. 2015: 7) states that Sri Lankan journalists had never faced such serious challenges as during the last phase of the civil war; sixteen journalists, Tamil and Sinhalese, were assassinated between 2004 and 2009. In response to the 2008 Universal Periodic Review, the GoSL pledged improvements in human rights and then took three years to commission and write a national plan, which was made available in English to diplomatic missions in December 2011, with no tangible or immediate action.

The LLRC, as we have seen, was set up in response to the UN Panel of Experts report, and concluded that, apart from a few isolated cases, security forces had not targeted civilians at the end of the war. External Affairs Minister G. L. Peiris was dispatched to Washington DC to personally show the report to Secretary of State Clinton, along with a (then rumoured) plan for implementation to demonstrate good will.[2] When High Commissioner Navi Pillay arrived in Colombo in August 2013, Rajapaksa made a show of leaving for Belarus, with state media primed – for example, the *Daily News* branded the UNHRC an 'anti-Lankan catspaw' – and the President quoted as condemning the practice of using human rights against countries such as Sri Lanka and Belarus.[3] Although the President did eventually meet with her, Gotabaya weighed in subsequently to say that she had been unduly influenced by overseas LTTE.[4]

Mahinda Rajapaksa came to power in 2005 with a narrow majority in an election boycotted by the TNA and the LTTE.[5] He inherited not so much a fractured peace process as a ceasefire already in tatters. In the speech given at his swearing-in ceremony he stated that his election showed that the majority of people did not want the country divided, and that this common national aspiration was the basis on which he would work for a new peace process. 'War,' said Rajapaksa, 'is not my method.' He was also clear about locating Sri Lanka on the world map:

> We are Asians. Asia has made a great contribution to the world. I would work in close cooperation with our Asian friends, protecting Asian value systems to make our country strong. I will follow a progressive foreign policy that suits our country.[6]

We have seen that Rajapaksa was not signalling a departure so much as a return to identifying with non-alignment, which had a well-established precedent[7] on the island, and as such his remarks will have resonated for many in the population. The emphasis in his speech on not dividing the country was at the same time a clear signal that Tamil Eelam as an independent homeland would not be countenanced. For some years, the lexicon of Sri Lanka's fight with the LTTE had already been devoted to counter-terrorism rather than war. Consider the 2001 statement by then Foreign Minister Lakshman Kadirgamar, himself subsequently assassinated in Colombo by an LTTE operative:

> There can be no questions that terror in all its manifestation must be fought relentlessly and globally. Gone are the days when a country affected by terror as my country has been for decades, can be told by the international community: we are sorry about what's happening in your land but there is nothing we can do to help because we have no laws to combat terror.[8]

Kurtz and Jaganathan (2016: 94) note that the Rajapaksa government rhetoric skilfully combined counter-terrorism with protection and non-aligned references, which resulted in severely restricting the effectiveness of political pressure, particularly from the UN, Europe and the United States. Nonetheless, the military defeat of the LTTE, virtual occupation of the North and a recovery vision and development model offered by Rajapaksa to the Sri Lankan people (that they would become both prosperous and the 'Wonder of Asia') were followed by an increase in international measures condemning both the end of the war and the failure of the peace.

This chapter will summarise findings on Sri Lanka in relation to the three questions set out at the beginning of the book: 1) What was the trajectory of the Rajapaksa government, in winning the war against the LTTE and seeking to establish a renewed unitary state?; 2) How did the government deal with international actors and norms, as well as internal opposition to the nature of the military defeat and the illiberal measures chosen for post-war recovery?; and 3) What mitigating circumstances and conditions intrinsic to 'global governance' have had an impact on Sri Lankan politics and society? It will then examine Sri Lanka's relationships in a broader international system and look for any wider learning, both political and normative. This considers Sri Lanka's small-state dilemma from several standpoints, beginning with the cross-currents of managing the interests and presence of India and China. While the GoSL was frequently presented as 'playing off' these rising power affiliations, politically and economically there were also conflicted management challenges in the post-war period. The notion of both 'Eastphalia' and 'Southphalia' will be referenced, against the backdrop of an altogether changing international system that has both geo-political and normative shifts. Sri Lanka's systemic culture of impunity and the quest for accountability are examined in the context of domestic initiatives, the UN system and emergent understandings of civilian protection. Lastly, Sri Lanka's choreographed interactions with global governance under the Rajapaksas will be contrasted with more recent developments. There remains an acute need for resolution of the national question.

A zero-sum trajectory

To provide the basis for all-out war to destroy the LTTE, the Rajapaksa government first had to effectively undermine and challenge both the legitimacy and the competency of international intervention, and with it liberal claims of conflict resolution. As already noted, Rajapaksa then turned military victory into a triumph of defeating international terrorism.[9] But he went further in seemingly extending the label of terrorist to all Tamils through the air-brushing and denial of Tamil political grievances and their historical place in the Sri Lankan social contract. Features of the political structure and culture were used to maximum advantage: the executive presidency, the role of the political Buddhism, majoritarian myth and superiority, political patronage, and the reassertion of the military in an occupation and civil administration role. This meant increasing loans from China and non-Western sources while stepping up the repression of domestic critics and civil opposition. With its post-war policy of military triumphalism, the fast-forwarding of economic and infrastructure development, the overriding of even the most basic of thirteenth amendment implementation as reform, and the official denial that Sri Lanka had minorities, much less a minority question, the Rajapaksa regime consolidated power and sought to reposition Sri Lanka on the international stage. It was a zero-sum approach.

Writing a year after the military defeat of the LTTE, David Lewis (2010: 647) suggested three factors that had allowed Rajapaksa to develop the powerful discourse needed for his tactics: 1) the flawed design of the peace process allowed for manipulation of the opposition and mobilisation of a strong constituency in favour of war; 2) the leadership benefited from shifts in global power, taking advantage of the increased influence of China but also of the shift in norms relating to sovereignty and internal conflict; and 3) it made full use of Western rhetoric on 'the war on terror' to seem not only acceptable but also congruent with wider trends towards counter-insurgency. As observed in Chapter 4, the very word 'peace' became unacceptable and was associated with pro-LTTE sentiment. While carefully packaged as facilitation, the Norwegian good intentions came to appear as something more akin to power brokering between two main parties, a process Lewis deems 'remarkably illiberal in both design and execution'. There was concern among Tamil dissidents that the LTTE had become a privileged actor with its own capacity to oppress, whereas a broader peace process might have kept intact ideas of political autonomy, inclusion and human rights. This viewpoint was courageously documented by the University Teachers for Human Rights (Jaffna),[10] by civil society analysts such as Paikiasothy Saravanamuttu (2006) and Sumanasiri Liyanage (2004), and in feminist critiques, such as that of Nimanthi Perera-Rajasingham (2008: 144), whose words are quoted below:

> While I in no way wish to underestimate the importance of two-party negotiations, it is possible, as suggested by Liyanage, for civil society not to focus exclusively on resolution, but to question the practices of both parties involved and change the very terms of their dialogue.[11]

This proved untenable in wider circles. Rajapaksa effectively further polarised what was already a fragile national discourse on whether peace with the LTTE was possible, suggesting that Western states had gone too far in conferring state-like legitimacy on the LTTE, and using national media to weave a toxic narrative on the hypocrisy of the West that soft-pedalled on LTTE terrorists while simultaneously waging its own war on terror in Afghanistan, Pakistan and Iraq (Harris 2010).

Concerning Chinese assistance, the northern neighbour indeed filled a gap when the US ended direct military aid in 2007 because of Rajapaksa's deteriorating human rights record (Popham 2010). As noted already, Chinese military aid was in place from the 1990s. Now it was increased to nearly $1 billion, with sophisticated weaponry including a free gift of six F7 fighter jets to the Sri Lankan air force.[12] Pakistan and Israel also increased supplies.[13] Interestingly, in 2007 the UK's annual sum of debt relief to Sri Lanka was cut in half because of concerns over human rights abuses, while arms exports to the country continued (Phillips 2009). The 2009 Stockholm International Peace Research Institute study on arms transfers notes other suppliers and the importance of a steady availability at short notice of ammunition from Pakistan as a major factor in the heightened government offensive of 2008 (Wezeman et al. 2009: 317). It is the conclusion of the authors that the ready availability of arms imports to Sri Lanka 'were enough to make the government confident that it could abandon an internationally brokered ceasefire and opt instead for a military solution' (ibid.: 320).

Dealing with international actors and norms and internal opposition

Defiant in its victory and adamant of its just nature, the Rajapaksa government saw itself as having defeated both its internal enemy and unwanted interference from abroad. 'No Foreign Power could switch things on or off in Sri Lanka as they pleased. The epicentre of the conflict always remained firmly in Sri Lanka,' stated the introduction to the book on Gotabaya's war (Chandraprema 2012: 10). Permanent Representative to the UN Kohona was adamant and consistent in his message that sovereignty must be respected and that the UN must support governments of states, for they had the remit for civilian protection.[14] This book has demonstrated how the GoSL utilised public relations firms for self-promotion under Rajapaksa; they employed consciously named 'anti-hegemonic diplomacy' in the UN, Geneva and New York, and strove for continual reactive image management. Northern Provincial Council elections were held partly due to intense pressure from India, Japan and the US (ICG 2013) and seemed to be timed in step with news management in advance of the CHOGM. In the build-up to the Geneva vote the following year, a diplomatic offensive saw ministers assigned to canvass UNHRC members:

Dinesh Gunawardena has been assigned to travel to Brazil, A. H. M. Fowzie to Kuwait and Dilan Perera to the Philippines. Minister Nimal Siripala de Silva was in Pakistan and later joined Minister Peiris for a visit to New Delhi where Peiris addressed diplomats of UNHRC member countries which do not have a resident mission in Colombo …
The UPFA's line of campaign became clear when President Rajapaksa took part in events in the Kalutara District on Friday. He said countries in the west were in a conspiracy to deny to Sri Lanka the hard-won victory against Tiger guerrillas. He vowed that he would not give in to such moves. That strong assertion reflected a hard line approach domestically though internationally emissaries are pleading Sri Lanka's case. That dichotomy reflects what the UPFA Government is today. (*The Sunday Times* 2014a)

Those same international emissaries also advanced the case that Tamil diaspora communities were threats in themselves. One way of attempting to deal with the diaspora was through South African good offices,[15] initially through secret meetings meant to solve the triangulation of the GoSL, the TNA and the diaspora through 'dialogue'. The Sri Lankan press had a field day when presenting awkward prospects such as meeting overseas with the Global Tamil Forum, presenting this as a climb-down from the official position (Kurukulasuriya 2012).

Meanwhile, the hard-line approach to domestic critics was relentless. According to evidence gathered by the International Truth and Justice Project (ITJP 2015), 100 'white van' abductions took place between 2009 and 2015, and a list of forty-one sites of detention were documented where torture was conducted. The

OISL would report similarly, also drawing on submissions from Sri Lankans who could approach Geneva direct. In late 2014, an individual was arrested in Colombo for reportedly distributing fake submission forms to garner false evidence, a factor used by the government to discredit the OHCHR (which, in its own later report, would categorically deny having solicited or accepted false forms) (OHCHR 2015a: 9). Along with discrediting Geneva, the message of 'international conspiracy' as a response to external deliberations on human rights in Sri Lanka was a continual refrain. UN agency workers and international NGOs were required to act under the remit of the Department of Defence, and international standards were not observed in post-war recovery operations. When the repression of domestic critics and offensive external tactics of denial faltered, when Sirisena achieved his electoral defeat of Rajapaksa and notional free speech felt safer than before, then domestic repression and deception were also named in the public media. As Rajapaksa garnered his former support base to demonstrate against the new government, Nimalka Fernando's spirited writing referencing his former 'vampire state' hit the press.[16] When the former President went public to make known his opinion of the OISL report (*Colombo Telegraph* 2015), he was refuted categorically in an article naming and explaining 'five lies' in his statement. (Rambukwella 2015).

Mitigating circumstances

The dichotomy of West versus the rest has not necessarily played out in practice over the Sri Lankan crisis. It was Costa Rica, Mexico and Austria, as non-permanent UN Security Council members at the time, who tried to get Sri Lanka on the formal agenda of the Security Council in early 2009. While the Security Council never passed a resolution on Sri Lanka, it issued a statement calling on the GoSL to fully cooperate with the UN, ICRC and other humanitarian agencies to provide humanitarian relief to displaced persons in the war zone.[17] There were trade-offs, as China, Libya and Vietnam agreed to this only after compromise over an official report on Israel's actions in Gaza (which the US had not wanted). Condemning LTTE action as well, the statement came in the wake of thousands of deaths in the Vanni, already reported by UN spokesman Gordon Weiss as a bloodbath (Leopold 2009). With no UN action forthcoming, there remained a residual motivation – whether due to conscience or professional standards among staff within the system – to press for the Secretary-General's subsequent visit to Colombo and the creation of a Panel of Experts. The book by Weiss (2012) had a major impact in challenging the official GoSL narrative, as did the severely incriminating Channel 4 documentary *No Fire Zone*. Considering the reactions of national governments, it is noteworthy that, as of May 2015, India, Nepal and Malaysia banned the film (Dayal 2015). Mauritius registered concern on Sri Lankan human rights and went on to boycott the CHOGM in Colombo.[18] The point here is quite simply that the issue of how the war ended did not go away, in spite of investment in public relations, media messaging and high-level defence seminars run in Colombo. But Kurtz and Jaganathan (2016: 103) highlight the degree to which UN diplomacy was itself public rhetoric, with loaded references to the responsibility to protect that were counterproductive in the extreme. They quote an insight from the Permanent Representative to the UN in Geneva at the time, Dayan Jayatilleka:

> If not for these external factors acting as accelerants, the war could/would probably have taken another month to finish, with greater circumspection. The international pressures were too strong for the Sri Lankan state to ignore but too weak to stop the state's military campaign, just as Sri Lanka was too weak to simply ignore the mounting pressures but too strong to be cowed by them. We had to outrun the pressures by accelerating the military offensive and closing the endgame as soon as possible.

The fraught dynamics, the mass killings of that final 'endgame', further embittered an already alienated Tamil diaspora, leading to a stand-off and to many of them criticising the GoSL over its war crimes, while the GoSL countered through accusations of diaspora support to terrorism. There was a similar disjuncture in that the dominant (initially US-led) discourse on the war against terrorism contrasted with the fact that later it was an American resolution that was decisive at the UNHRC. In contrast to the narrow membership and heavy formality of the UN Security Council, the Human Rights Council has forty-seven members elected by the General Assembly for terms of up to two consecutive three-year commitments, holds three regular sessions a year, and can call special sessions to respond to thematic and country concerns. The allocation of seats is along regional lines, with growing importance also given to other global organisations such as NAM, the OIC, the EU and the Western European and Other Group that transcend regional blocks and affinities. As noted, the OIC used its good offices to visit Colombo and speak on behalf of Muslim victims of BBS violence. Moreover, there are now 168 parties to the International Covenant on Civil and Political Rights[19] and we have seen that the covenant is actively utilised by informed Sri Lankans. Coordinated UNHRC lobbying for the censure of Sri Lanka gained momentum through concerted transnational human rights work, often assisted by the lobbying initiatives of Tamil diaspora groups in Canada, Australia, Norway, Switzerland and the US. This combination of UN system legitimacy and the connectivity of people, from victims to advocates to delegates, proved to be the strongest mitigating factor in checking the post-war behaviour of the Sri Lankan state. It proved dynamic and potent, with procedures that could be accessed and used by many.

When the EU suspended Sri Lanka's GSP plus in 2010, it was due to its failure to comply with conditions regarding the implementation of three key conventions: the International Covenant on Civil and Political Rights (ICCPR), the Convention against Torture (CAT) and the Convention on the Rights of the Child (CRC).[20] Officials in Brussels at the time were careful to state clearly that the agreement was suspended due to stipulated contractual conditions and routine review, and not as a sanction due to allegations of war crimes. The principled decision based on an official agreed undertaking with the government was highly publicised in Colombo as a signal of Western disaffection. It was seized on by opposition voices. As for the IFIs, there remain questions on conditionality and influence, particularly with regard to the IMF and World Bank. The former came through with a loan after the military victory, while other donors such as the

ADB and the World Bank reduced funding to Sri Lanka. Multilateral aid fell from $502 million in 2006 to $356 in 2007 (Goodhand et al. 2011: 47), but the GoSL balanced this out with other bilateral agreements, in particular easy borrowing from China:

> By 2008 in the context of an economic crisis and growing (albeit inconsistent) western pressure, the government needed to find new allies in order to fund the war, provide diplomatic cover and subsequently to provide the policy space to consolidate the post-war political order. The combination of western pressure regarding the conduct of the 'war for peace' and specifically human rights violations, and the willingness of eastern states including India and China to provide military and financial support for the war, whilst in the main remaining publicly silent on civilian casualties, accentuated the GoSL's tilt to the east. Geo-strategic rents were maximized by exploiting strategic competition between India and China. (ibid.: 7)

Ultimately, financial management, foreign direct investment and economic crisis would loom despite the tilt to the East. International lobbying, transnational human rights work and the US decision to sponsor the critical resolution at the UNHRC, alongside domestic economic mismanagement, proved instrumental in undermining the certainty of Rajapaksa's position. The questions of international and internal accountability had clearly converged by 2014, following five years of triumphalist showcasing of the Sri Lankan model.

Small state, large system

The Rajapaksa position was bound up with the much vaunted success of the Sri Lankan model.

Initially courting the generals from Myanmar for the model's replication in fighting insurgency, Colombo watched as the Thein Sein administration from 2011 chose instead to spearhead a return to international engagement, civilian rule and reforms, including amnesty for most political prisoners, some relaxation in censorship laws and the establishment of a National Human Rights Council.

Aung San Suu Kyi's political party, long supported by the US and EU, agreed to compete in electoral processes that led to an eventual role in government. Meanwhile, Myanmar was managing to look both East and West, continuing operations with the Chinese for the development of a 2,400 kilometre oil pipeline to run to Kunming in Yunnan Province, bypassing the Malacca Strait. The pipeline ran through two of the country's contested regions – Rakhine and Shan States (both with semi-autonomous armies) – and there were promises of money for local schools and development, plus royalties to central government.[21] In Sri Lanka, the government persisted in presenting the West and the Geneva Process as sources of unwarranted interference, and broadcast its LLRC report as a means of courting favour in the Commonwealth. The China factor was still a key element in government confidence and was promoted as being intrinsic to state credibility.[22]

The issue of Chinese power was raised in Canada during the build-up to the 2013 CHOGM meeting, when there was controversy over the Harper government's decision to boycott the event. Critics argued that there were double standards at work, specifically citing Canada's far more diplomatic and friendly posture towards China in spite of human rights concerns regarding Tibet. This argument maintained that Sri Lanka's relative lack of diplomatic and economic leverage internationally enabled the Canadian government to adopt a stern policy regarding the not-so-influential island while turning a blind eye to identical concerns in decisively influential China (Weerawardhana 2013a: 15). Although such allegations miss the context and specific ethos of Commonwealth membership and stated values, they point to the power differentials in the international system and the fact that the regional big players of China and India overshadow Sri Lankan policies.[23] China faces ongoing internal ethno-nationalist challenges in Tibet and Xinjiang, while India jealously guards against external interventions in Kashmir, Manipur and Nagaland, where its Armed Forces Special Powers rule may be compared with Sri Lanka's Prevention of Terrorism Act (Pethiyagoda 2013). Sri Lanka's small-state dilemma can be examined from several standpoints, beginning with the cross-currents of managing the interests and presence of India and

China. While the GoSL was frequently presented as 'playing off' these rising power affiliations, politically and economically there were also problems in simultaneously courting Delhi and Beijing. Prior to the liberal peace-making project undertaken through Norwegian facilitation, the global war on terror and the Co-Chairs experiment, Sri Lankan governments had enjoyed Western favour. Weerawardhana contrasts reactions to the defeat of the LTTE with historical precedents in diplomatic circles, citing, for example, how in spite of the anti-Tamil pogrom in 1983, the notorious Black July and deaths of Tamil citizens at the hands of both mobs and security services, President Jayawardene was never an unwelcome guest at the White House or at No. 10 Downing Street. In a Cold War world order, Jayawardene was a head of state with a distinctly pro-Western profile, a factor 'that prevented the West from taking a critical stance on Sri Lanka, despite UN HRC allegations that were as intense as they are at present' (Weerawardhana 2014). In his view, Sri Lanka's scope of action is constrained as a small state in the South Asian region, at the intersection of India's southerly neighbourhood and what is frequently referred to as China's 'string of pearls' strategy in the Indian Ocean:

> Western powers prioritise their relations with emerging superpowers. Given the substantive trade and strategic interests, Western governments are not in a position to be overtly critical of human rights and accountability issues of emerging superpowers. Cases such as Sri Lanka provide excellent opportunities to engage in liberal internationalist critiques on accountability, human rights and the rule of law, which in the case of Sri Lanka, is further facilitated by Colombo's lack of a clear strategy on the ethno-national question and problems in managing foreign policy apparatus. (ibid.)

The US Senate Committee on Foreign Relations (2009) report, *Sri Lanka: Recharting US strategy after the war*, refers to the 'string of pearls' thesis, the 'Great Game' of geo-political control in the Indian Ocean and American strategic interest in Sri Lanka. Balancing geo-political pressures is inherent in the legacy of Sri Lankan diplomacy.

The Rubber–Rice Pact of 1952 is particularly interesting in relation to US structural power and how it underpinned later conceptualisations of global governance. During the Korean War, the US released rubber from its stockpiles, bringing down market prices worldwide, and it subsequently refused to continue paying Sri Lanka what had been negotiated as a fair price. China agreed to buy rubber from Sri Lanka at a premium price and to supply rice at considerably less than the market price. At that time, the US was also embargoing rubber sales to China (due to the PRC's support to North Korea); they withdrew development aid to Sri Lanka for several years as a punitive measure (De Alwis 2010). Gifting from China to Sri Lanka has long been visible on the landscape: the Supreme Court Complex, the Central Telecommunications Exchange, the Bandaranaike Memorial International Conference Hall and the new Performing Arts Theatre, to name just a few examples.[24]

On the subject of India's jealous guarding of its preferential first big neighbour status (Behuria 2011) in relation to Sri Lanka, Malathi De Alwis reminds us that historically Delhi has taken measures to block US interests in Sri Lanka, just as it has been concerned more recently to maintain its role as a counterweight to rising Chinese involvement. He suggests a re-examination of the 1987 Indo-Lanka Agreement, signed after the Indian-facilitated ceasefire between the GoSL and the LTTE. Several clauses are aimed at reducing US encroachment, such as Sri Lanka agreeing to review arrangements with foreign broadcasting organisations to ensure that they are not used for military or intelligence purposes (i.e. Voice of America had just set up transmission services); and the stipulation that ports such as Trincomalee will not be 'available for military use by any country in a manner which is prejudicial to India's interests' (De Alwis 2010: 441 citing Jegananthan), referencing the US acquisition of an oil tank farm in Trinco. By the time Rajapaksa came to power, there was a weariness with the big neighbour, possibly on a par with antipathy to broader international interference. We have examined Mahinda's appeal to populist folk memory, to the glorious precolonial past and to Sinhala majoritarianism. Observers have remarked that this brought with it an additional ethos, an invisible competition for influence between the so-called anglicised elite, the neo-colonial residuals suspected of links with foreign interests, and the more grounded native, traditionalist and nationalist representatives who had a more genuine entitlement to leadership (Behuria 2011: 743). This would explain in part the cool response to India's proposed economic partnership agreement. As a small state, Sri Lanka was asserting independence in relation to historical ties:

> MR [Mahinda Rajapaksa] emerged as perhaps the only Sri Lankan leader who managed to achieve some strategic autonomy in conducting his country's foreign policy vis-à-vis India. (Behuria and Sultana 2013: 84)

But it came at a cost. In 2012, Sarath Amunugaman, Minister of International Monetary Cooperation, submitted a document to parliament which indicated that foreign debt in excess of $15 billion had been incurred by Sri Lanka, with China owed $4.9 billion including interest payments for loans worth $2.96 billion and the ADB a further $3.35 billion for loans incurred since 1997 (Reuters 2012). Looming questions on infrastructure and transportation contracts and losses (as outlined in Chapter 6) threatened the credibility of both government and the family in power. Subsequently, in 2015, central government debt came in at a staggering 76 per cent of GDP; 6 per cent of GDP was fiscal deficit, while general government interest payments accounted for 33.3 per cent of government revenues.[25] Keeping up with figures and indicators is a challenge in itself, but in mid-2016 the severity of the crisis was summed up in this way:

> The country is currently in $58.3 billion deep to foreign financiers, and 95% of all government revenue is currently going towards paying back its loans. This means that out of every hundred dollars the government brings in only $4.60 is going towards essentials like education and public services. (Shepard 2016)[26]

Maithripala Sirisena campaigned on a platform of reducing Chinese interference, using strong language which hinted that the island would become a virtual colony of the Asian giant if trends continued.[27] Now his government needed all channels open to Beijing for debt management and to sell off national projects to keep the country afloat. As the small state is also now part of the Chinese New Maritime Silk Road[28] enterprise as well, Deputy Minister Liu Jianchao paid an early visit to the new administration to smooth things over. The following year, in an address to the Regional Centre for Strategic Studies in Colombo, the Chinese Ambassador to Sri Lanka went much further, advising that UNHRC-suggested reconciliation measures should not create new conflicts, stating that it would be ill-advised to put reconciliation before development and observing that policies should not change 'with a regime change'.[29]

Reshaping global governance norms

In his use of the phrase 'regime change', Ambassador Yi Xianliang may have been referring simply to a change in government, or it may have been a telling reference to the much publicised term used when the US under President Bush and the UK under Prime Minister Tony Blair deliberately set out to remove the long-established leader of Iraq. With the war on terror setting new examples of legitimate behaviour or double standards, the apparent spectre of Western hegemonic assault on Iraq rapidly made the international intervention mode of the 1990s suspect. There arose a dichotomy between the Sri Lankan rejection of outside interference and a permissive international acceptance of internal counter-terrorism discourse and method, an environment that was slow to change as the fully fledged assault on both the LTTE and civilians escalated. The pincer effect from 21 January 2009 resulted in 300,000 civilians crowding into the so-called 'no fire zone' within the LTTE-held areas of the Vanni, an area several kilometres north of Mullaitivu and approximately 7 kilometres from the LTTE's southern and western lines of defence. This meant that sustained heavy bombardment and counter-fire created an ever shrinking area into which both rebels and civilians were constrained. The latter were captive between the fighting forces, held as human shields by the LTTE and seen as the enemy by the military.[30] This was watched in real time from world capitals.

The responsibility to protect (R2P), so objected to in principle (as expressed by G. L. Peiris), failed to operate in practice.

It was also in 2009 that the UN Secretary-General issued his first implementation report on R2P, further establishing the three foundational pillars: first, that primary responsibility for the protection of a state's civilians lies with the state itself; second, that when needed the international community can be called upon to help build the capacity of the state to do this; and third, that should all else fail there can be a response including, but not limited to, military intervention.[31] The latter issue has been divisive, coming to a head with the controversial NATO-led R2P-justified intervention in Libya in 2011. Subsequently, Brazil launched a corollary concept of 'responsibility with protection' (RwP) and China promoted 'responsible protection.'[32] As rising powers, the BRICS have generally supported R2P but have looked for moderation, careful for it not to become a doctrinal licence for Western-only policies. Thus Beijing supported several UN Security Council resolutions on Syria, including those mandating the UN Observer Mission, the destruction of Syria's chemical weapons, and most recently a humanitarian aid access plan.[33] Alden and Large (2015) trace the Chinese stance and behaviour from non-intervention to selective proactive intervention in some African conflicts such as Sudan and South Sudan. The global governance norm of R2P is being reshaped and rearticulated as a principle. Russia took its own action in Syria, and in practice the efficacy and legitimacy of UN operations have been put severely to the test, as in the crisis in South Sudan[34] and the spiralling violence central to over five years of civil war in Syria. In Syria, the siege of Madaya brought comparisons with Sri Lanka, with critics claiming that the UN was aware of starvation conditions in the town, under siege from government forces, but was hesitant to raise the matter directly with the Syrian regime because of fraught relations with officials in Damascus. This is compared with systemic failings identified in the Petrie Report on the handling of the final days of Sri Lanka's civil war (Chulov and Shaheen 2016).

When this was put to UNHCR officials in an interview, they pointed out that popular expectations for international agencies are often unrealistic. High-level political action can only come from the Secretary-General's office in conjunction with the Security Council. Agencies confront realities on the ground that must always be seen in context and in relation to the state itself. Sri Lanka had allowed open relief centres in the 1990s, with UNHCR assistance and monitors provided with safety gained through 'verbal understandings from both the government and the LTTE to abstain from military operations in these areas' (Orchard 2014: 69). Small zones, such as the 400 acre Madhu site, hosted thousands of refugees of different religious backgrounds, although security was not always continuous for the affected populations. Madhu was shut down by the GoSL in 1999, and the military routinely removed people from other centres who were then subjected to disappearances and torture (ibid.). But the 'understandings' were in operation until the 2002 ceasefire agreement, when large IDP returns led to the closure of centres.

The international norm of protection in delivery and realisation depends very much on the state in question. In the 1990s there was a more widespread concept of safe areas, when ideas of neutrality and consent were still operational, when the idea of a non-combatant existed and governments were not targeting their own populations. In Colombia, for example, in a different war, a law was adopted in 1997 to enshrine the rights of the victims of forced displacement to protection from the state, economic assistance, and long-term solutions.[35] Under Law 387, as it was known, the UNHCR and ICRC were able to provide 'software' for IDP: access to justice, family reunions, and decisions on community needs that were described as 'creating governance' among the affected populations.[36] They were also able to train some 11,000 members of the army in human rights and law.

This book has observed how an opportunity was lost at a time when the GoSL was more receptive to a human rights platform. Whether it would have altered the state's view of civilian protection or LTTE positions and actions is, of course, another question. But in the words of one UNHCR representative:

We need to de-mystify the concept of protection. Counter-insurgency does not do it. This is talking a different language, and there is a dialectic of protection. Thirty years ago we talked about not replacing the state. But you cannot build the state without the basics of assistance and access to rights. It is not stabilization, but law enforcement that is wanted. We must shift the discourse.

This sentiment is echoed by many in post-Rajapaksa Sri Lanka. Occupation of the North is a means of stabilisation, not of development. The law is not applied evenly or fairly, and yet the rule of law applied with fairness and justice is a possibility that would create conditions for a different kind of development and a different experience of society. The same concern is increasingly expressed on the international level, in that access to humanitarian space has long been under threat as an ideal sphere of action. Marcos Ferreiro examines this in a study of the trend for military aid to be embedded in counter-insurgency, and for stabilisation to be prioritised in ways that alienate populations (Ferreiro 2012). Peter Gill (2016) cites an American general who would not call the 2014 US bombing of Kobani in Syria (to stop it falling to the Islamic State) a strategic target, preferring to say that they were striking 'for humanitarian purposes', much as Putin described military action in Ukraine and Crimea as a humanitarian mission. Responding to a Russian/Syrian plan for 'safe corridors' (so evocative of the GoSL's 'no fire zones' in 2009) for Aleppo citizens in 2016, UN Special Envoy for Syria Staffan de Mistura spoke out, saying that the UN should take charge of any humanitarian corridors created in the divided city. Internal documents, meanwhile, revealed fraught deliberations within the UN on whether and how to play an effective role, even in achieving effective access to provide relief and aid to civilians (Shaheen 2016b).

In this sense, we do well to see Sri Lanka as a microcosm for broader learnings – even as a mirror for other regional contemporary dangers of associating whole populations with counter-terror and militarised policies. Moreover, the case study indicates that all-out war does not destroy aspirations based on long-held historical grievance; that occupation does not foster loyalty; and that the creation of gross insecurity on the ground will not guarantee national security in more general terms. Security is not a commodity to be found at gunpoint, nor an abstract patriotic promise when people are trying to feed their families.

Queries for a new era

For some four decades the Sri Lankan state fostered an almost constant state of emergency, with special powers displacing the criminal justice system and undermining state accountability. We have seen how immunity provisions were also enacted in the 1978 constitution during the strengthening of the executive presidency. On taking office, President Sirisena worked to pass a nineteenth amendment to cut back on further powers secured under Rajapaksa. Such was the symbolic power of this act that the Global Tamil Forum sent a congratulatory note to the President and to Prime Minister Ranil Wickremesinghe for adopting the nineteenth amendment to the Sri Lankan Constitution. Asanga Welikala (2015a: 95–6), constitutional lawyer and expert, writes of how, in South Asia, constitutional modernity was brought in through colonial power, and this in turn has substantially influenced the ideas about the state, the nation and nationalism that developed in the modern era:

> While anti-colonial sentiments pervasively influenced post-colonial nation-building, the path-dependent trajectory of the post-colonial state had been set by the autocratic colonial state. Thus the flipside of Sri Lanka's deceptively tranquil transition to independence was that, effectively, the colonial state continued unchanged, albeit with new owners and managers putting the old state to new authoritarian uses ...

Postcolonial Sri Lanka experienced state capture by the majoritarian Sinhala-Buddhist ethos and interests, 'triggering a sub-state national challenge from the Tamils, which remains constitutionally unresolved to this day' (ibid.). Contextual factors are crucial, and Welikala goes beyond the Eastphalia thesis to understand the fierce grip on sovereignty in Sri Lanka, which he characterises as Southphalia. He maintains that the Southphalian state is not post-sovereign, post-national, post-modern or post-anything – except postcolonial. He sees the European situation as representing a historically contingent experience that does not hold true in other regions of the world. He also contrasts India with Sri Lanka, and acknowledges an uneven but in some ways impressive track record for the former in managing a type of pluralism, while noting ongoing exceptions such as Kashmir. Welikala advocates and works practically for constitutional 'plurinational' reform, which could become a transformative reality for Sri Lankan society were attitudes and policies to change (Welikala 2015b). There is potential to address the national question through constitutional change in Sri Lanka, over time. Many query how momentum and consultative processes on transitional justice will relate to or interact with constitutional reform in the wake of the Geneva Process. This will depend on whether a new constitution can become a social contract under which citizens may hold those in power to account. The new government in its first eighteen months addressed some key legacy issues from the Rajapaksa era, changing Victory Day to Remembrance Day (minus military parade) and allowing the national anthem to be sung in two languages. But there are stories of ex-cadres in the North being made to sing in Sinhala by less enthusiastic members of the military. Sirisena backtracked on the UNHRC commitment to international assistance for and participation in transitional justice processes, while still frustrated Tamil communities in the North continue to demand that land, political prisoners and occupation be addressed.

As an operating mechanism of global governance, the Geneva Process matters in that it addresses systemic impunity and the need to aim for improved compliance and above all non-recurrence of human rights violations. Civil society is divided in the post-Rajapaksa era between those who are participating wholeheartedly in the new government's reform initiatives, and those who state unequivocally that regime change is not structural change, much less 'democratic transition',[37] and who do not want to be co-opted by what they see as an unreconstructed state. A film made by Sherine Xavier in 2014 entitled *The Scars of Tomorrow: Muttrupulliyaa*[38] follows the lives of four Tamil characters affected by the end of the war, one of whom observes that 'The past never seems to stay in the past'. The filming, which began in Chennai, was interrupted when it resumed in Sri Lanka due to the arrest of crew members and the confiscation of equipment. Old patterns of intimidation remain. Indeed, on 2 June 2016, a meeting was held of some eighty civil society actors and other civilians in Ampara, to discuss ways of conducting their own transitional justice discussions and consultations as an alternative track to the official government approach. On 4 June, the organisers were visited by CID using the same familiar repressive and threatening behaviour. At the time of writing, Jeyakumari Balendran, mentioned earlier for her protests to demand information about missing family members and arrested with her daughter, is still required to report regularly to the police and cannot travel out of the district or the country.[39]

A record 193 states were represented at the June 2016 session of the UNHRC in Geneva, with the UK, US and EU holding firm on the need for evidence of resolution implementation from Sri Lanka. However, the majority of Western European and other states seemed convinced that the GoSL was doing as much as possible against the odds and despite the risks involved, and that the transformation of the relationship between Sri Lanka and the UN through the UNHRC was a sign of both radical change in Colombo and commitment to full implementation of agreements reached through Council Resolution 30/1. There were indications that supporters from the global South had already moved on – pleased with their contribution to the most effective country-specific action in the (short) history of the Council and impressed by the seeming democratic transition. There was a sense that Resolution 30/1 was a significant achievement in itself, possibly due to the GoSL/US/UK agreement that took advantage of a favourable mood in the Council, a mood that is now changing. The issue now is that, globally, human rights are under threat. Concerns have been expressed over the human rights situation in no fewer than forty-nine country situations. These include China, Russia and the USA, and cover eleven European countries, eight Arab states, thirteen African states, five Latin American countries plus the US, and eleven Asian states (of which Sri Lanka and Myanmar were the last – and the least pressing).[40]

For many in Sri Lankan civil society, the real arena was now in-country. Others expressed incredulity that more pressure was not forthcoming from Geneva and Western capitals. Was this a case of revolving doors, in which a new government that made different noises and appeared compliant could get away with a continuation of the same structural flaws in the social contract, the same chasm between liberal cosmopolitan claims and patriotic or religious nationalism? How could a state be in charge of judging itself, with the military still in place, an overarching ethos of victory, and divided party politics, with Rajapaksa still in the wings ready to accuse the government of selling out? With regard to war crimes, is it possible to think long term, of extra-territoriality and universal jurisdiction, as in the case of General Pinochet?[41]

There remain calls for international participation in judicial proceedings: to oversee fair investigations and prosecutions, to fight for the rights of victims to truth and justice, to break what has been called a domestic culture of commissions (CPA 2016a). Counter-claims at national political level suggest that this is a slight or insult to war heroes. Yet it could be handled differently if there were the political will to do so. Within the broader UN system, there remains the potential to be more effective in local-level change, as shown by a July 2016 conference hosted by the UN's World Tourism Organization in Pasikudah, a village severely affected by tsunami and war. Conference materials were prepared in Sinhala and English in a Tamil-speaking area, but here was an opportunity to utilise and recognise Tamil, just as there was an option to actually engage with local people who otherwise were an abstract 'community relations' theme in the programme. The international level can reach out to the local if there is the awareness to do so, or it can alienate further. In the region, trends include a clampdown on journalists (later lifted) and full curfew in Kashmir imposed by India (Sridharan 2016a), and, in Malaysia, a sedition law dating from colonial times updated to control journalists, silence critics and censor voices in Sabah and Sarawak calling for secession from the federation; in this context, Sri Lanka could present its new Right to Information Act as a model and could lead the way in seeing that it delivers. Given the deep social divisions and legacy of acute violence in the country, work on missing persons is crucial and capable of touching many individual lives, while finding ways of dealing with the past to forge some kind of shared historical narrative will be the challenge of a generation and will call into play political but also social, educational and creative processes. To end occupation, there is the massive challenge of downsizing and retraining the security forces. The obstacles are many and the burden of expectations is high. It can be difficult to see long-term outcomes and reform, given the short terms of politics and elected office. Will actors in the international community retain appropriate connections and levels of assistance or lose the plot, moving attention to challenges elsewhere? Gill observes that in contrast to the 1990s, with the emergence of R2P thinking, there is now an era of Western disengagement and defensiveness. But in spite of the legacy of war and the Rajapaksa decade of denial and concerted repression, there are still Sri Lankans who strive for the rule of just law, equality before the law, and human, economic and cultural rights. Or, in the words of one young Sri Lankan: 'It is all very well to say the era of liberal peacebuilding is over, but don't deny it to me as part of hope for my own future.'

In fact Sri Lanka's island positioning, at a geopolitical crossroads with its ancient history of co-existence and religious plurality and claim of distinct identity and independent action, gives the potential advantage for a transformational shift from negative to positive peace. There are growing points in national activity since the joint sponsored resolution. Strong leadership could point to a different future and the need for dealing with the past in order to prevent future atrocities. Just as Kenneth Bush observed over a decade ago, there is still no indigenised widely held understanding of reconciliation. This could change. A unifying concept of reconciliation needs to be promoted in both the national languages. Work is needed for reparations including the restitution of land or meaningful compensation for the same; memorialisation which allows recognition of multiple sufferings; and effective delivery by the Office for Missing Persons. The efforts of civil society activists and newly formed mechanisms require complementary action from proactive political leadership through clear messages and vision, as per an early campaign slogan 'peace and recovery of all, by all, and for all', initially associated with the Sirisena government's platform.

Sherine Xavier has queried whether the Geneva resolution was a 'means to an end or an end to a means': that is, was the resolution a means to regime change, or was it meant to break with the impunity of the past in order to achieve genuine structural change and political reform now? In reference to the co-sponsoring of the resolution by the US and the GoSL, another question is simply the following, with regard to 2009 and 2014: Have we been betrayed again?[42] As the post-Rajapaksa government continues to mend fences with international neighbours, manage its debt and its relations with China, resume active cooperation with India and accept new invitations (the G7, the Twelfth World Islamic Economic Forum), there remains a great deal of internal unfinished business. 'The government will be able to resolve the Geneva issue due to its principles on good governance,' stated Development Strategies and International Trade Minister Malik Samarawickrama in a media briefing in mid-2016. 'We rejected the accusation [that] our security forces are responsible for the deaths of 40,000 Tamil civilians during the war. The President had discussions with G7 leaders and other officials. We hope that we would be able to resolve the Geneva human rights issue amicably.'[43] Here is a familiar tone of pushing back, a reassurance that the national house is in order. Dealing with the past and building a new future is a challenge for Sri Lankans. It remains to be seen whether appropriate external mechanisms and incentives will be found to encourage internal reform that will grant rights to Tamil and Muslim communities who have long struggled and waited for them. Some suggest 'leverage' in the use of zero-tolerance policies on sexual violence and torture as a condition before over 3,000 new Sri Lankan UN peacekeepers can be taken on and deployed. Others may seek to assist with redress for war crimes and crimes against humanity, sometimes with help from the experience of other states such as Chile or Argentina. At any rate, within a changing landscape of global governance, and with multiple steps, the dance will go on.[44]

NOTES

Introduction

1 Ranil Wickremesinghe (UNP) had served previously as Prime Minister (1993–94 and 2001–04). He was dismissed by President Chandrika Kumuratunga for lack of consultation (not keeping her informed about the peace process) and for allegedly being too lenient with the LTTE during six rounds of peace talks. The reference to atrocity during the final offensive against the LTTE refers to the now widely accepted figure of 40,000 civilians killed (Haviland 2015). See also the executive summary of the Secretary-General's Panel of Experts for a documented record of the 2009 killing of civilians by widespread shelling, the shelling of hospitals, the denial of humanitarian assistance, and extensive human rights violations in and outside the conflict zone. The report also recognises severe crimes committed by the LTTE (UN 2010).
2 The JVP is the Marxist-Leninist communist party of Sri Lanka. It undertook two armed uprisings before entering democratic politics through participation in electoral politics from 1989, first contesting nationally in 1994. The JVP had used a specific form of guerrilla warfare using killings to undermine the state, shooting officials, civil servants, police and also left-wing activists and trade union leaders who opposed their methods (Uyangoda 2005: v). The JVP unleashed its second campaign of violence in August 1987, soon after the Indo-Lanka Accord, taking the position that the Indian peacekeeping presence in the north-east was an affront to national pride.
3 The 1983 'Black July' anti-Tamil riots or pogrom sent thousands fleeing the country, and others into allegiance with armed resistance via a guerrilla group that called itself the Tamil Tigers. Many of the former became a new diaspora that funded and supported the latter. Launched in 1976 under the leadership of Velupillai Prabhakaran to fight for self-determination of the Tamil people, the LTTE pioneered the use of suicide bombers (including female bombers); killed a head of state (the incumbent President Premadasa); engaged in 'attack as spectacle' through such acts as the exploding of oil storage complexes, attacks on the Sri Lankan navy, and the destruction of twenty-five aircraft at the national airport; drove bomb-laden vehicles into landmark sites such as the Central Bank in Colombo and the revered Temple of the Tooth complex in Kandy; assassinated dozens of public figures and civil servants; and created a mini-state and a vast international network of finance, armaments acquisition and fundraising. They took to the sea and even to the air, garnering a reputation for invincibility in an era pre-dating the '9/11' branding of terror.

4 Known and recorded death squads or killer groups referred to in popular parlance have included the PRA (People's Revolutionary Army), Gonussa (Scorpion), Katussa (Chameleon) and Bassa (Owl) (Haviland 2012).
5 The definition offered by the Commission is of interest: 'Governance is the sum of many ways individuals and institutions, public and private, manage their common affairs. It is a continuing process through which conflicting or diverse interests may be accommodated and co-operative action taken. It includes formal institutions and regimes empowered to enforce compliance, as well as informal arrangements that people and institutions either have agreed to or perceive to be in their interest' (GDRC 1995).
6 Sri Lankan society, by contrast, predates the Westphalian system by some 2,000 years, with the pre-modern state founded in the third century BC by Devanampiya Tissa at Anuradhapura. This lasted until the Kandyan Kingdom was ceded to the British Crown by treaty in 1815 (Welikala 2015d: 503). Sri Lanka is unique in its linguistic heterogeneity, having eight languages spread throughout this multilingual, multiracial and multi-religion country. The diverse ethnic composition includes Sinhalese, Indian Tamils, Sri Lankan Tamils, Sri Lankan Muslims and unspecified other groups in a population of some 20 million. During the course of history, four language families developed: Indo-European, Tibeto-Chinese, Austric and Dravidian, each represented by different ethnic groups. Currently, Sinhala and Tamil are the main languages, with English remaining the second language. English is commonly used in government and is spoken competently by about 10 per cent of the population (see Wickramasuriya 2005).
7 Unipolarity as a term in international politics means a distribution of power in which there is one state with most of the cultural, economic and military influence: for example, the United States in the immediate aftermath of the implosion of the former Soviet Union. Unipolarity could also be called a hegemony or hyper-power.
8 'The core modernizing assumption, that history brings secularism, a sense of oneself as an individual human rights holder, and the erosion of collective beliefs and loyalties, is fracturing alongside the Western power that sustained it' (Hopgood 2013: 166).
9 The President of Médecins Sans Frontières, Dr Joanne Liu, stated in early 2016 that: 'What the Geneva convention and international humanitarian law brought to conflict was to mitigate war on civilians, and by not respecting that we are going backwards a hundred years. It is barbarian times.' Her comments were in reference to a surge in deadly attacks on health facilities in Syria and throughout conflict zones in the Middle East in particular. Her key concern was how a myopic focus on war against terrorism distorts approaches to conflict mitigation. See Shaheen (2016a) 'Head of Médecins Sans Frontières warns of return to "barbarian times"'.
10 Mark Duffield has previously written on the securitisation of international assistance, through public–private contractual networks linking donor governments, militaries, private companies and NGOs to govern populations at a distance, in outlying areas he called the borderlands (Duffield 2001: 308–20).

11 Soares de Oliveira's (2011: 308) study is particularly useful in that he invited further comparative analysis of illiberal peacebuilding, suggesting the following list of recurrent characteristics (some of which would apply to Sri Lanka, some not): 1) military victory or hegemonic post-war oversight; 2) hegemonic election-running, designed to earn international support yet not representing a danger to the regime; 3) secretive formal or informal structures for running the reconstruction process; 4) reconstruction opportunities distributed among insiders and the promotion of an oligarchic capitalism; 5) constitutional change to extend presidential powers and strengthen the status quo; 6) penetration or co-optation of civil society organisations (especially professional organisations) and the media; 7) acceptance of the situation by Western donors who carry on business as usual while deploying a vulgarised version of the 'transition paradigm' to explain illiberal practices; 8) a high-modernist vision and technocratic mindset, with much public expenditure on infrastructure and heavy borrowing; 9) a general amnesty, no 'justice and reconciliation', or else clearly manipulated victor's justice; and 10) a peace dividend that favours the powerful, while poverty reduction is not a priority.

12 Basil Rajapaksa, brother of the President who was Minister of Economic Development and an official senior presidential adviser, was quoted in 2010 as having had an exchange with Samantha Power, Special Assistant to US President Barack Obama on Multilateral Affairs and Human Rights, in which he asked her: 'Do you want to know our frank opinion about the US?' When she indicated in the affirmative he stated his view that: 'The US Government is a little jealous about Sri Lanka. We are a small country but we have achieved what the US has not been able to.' This was a reference to the military defeat of Tiger guerrillas while the US was still fighting insurgencies in Iraq and Afghanistan. See 'Lanka defies UN, EU, US', *The Sunday Times*, 7 June 2010, www.sundaytimes.lk/100627/Columns/political.html (accessed 20 April 2016).

13 See Ojeleye (2013: 92) and 'Nigeria's post-civil war reconciliation' at www.igbofocus.co.uk/The_Biafra/NIGERIA-S_POST-CIVIL_WAR_RECON/nigeria-s_post-civil_war_reconciliation.html (accessed 4 March 2015). For historical examples of conciliation in victory, ranging from the American Civil War to the ancient times of 18th-century BC Hammurabi, and the wisdom of Umar ibn al-Khattab in 638 AD, see Foreman (2015).

14 See 'Transnational government of Tamil Eelam's parliament dissolved for next election', *Colombo Telegraph*, 26 October 2013, www.colombotelegraph.com/index.php/transnational-government-of-tamil-eelams-parliament-dissolved-for-next-election/ (accessed 2 February 2015).

15 See 'Statement by Sri Lanka: 12th session of the Intergovernmental Working Group on the Effective Implementation of the Durban Declaration and Programme of Action, 7 April 2014' at www.ohchr.org/Documents/Issues/Racism/IWG/session12/SriLanka.docx (accessed 6 March 2015).

16 See UN Human Rights Council, 'Report of the Working Group on Enforced or Involuntary Disappearances', A/HRC/4/41, 25 January 2007; Human Rights Watch (2008) *Recurring Nightmare*.

17 In another view, '[v]iolence it appears contagious. It is like a horrible epidemic. The insurrection changed the mindset of many people, alas

negatively, both in the authority and those who almost naturally opposed it, on both sides of the ethnic divide. The reasons for the distinction are not easy to figure. The insurrection opened the flood gates. Sri Lanka never could become the same' (Fernando 2013).

18 Translations of the ancient Pali chronicle the *Mahavamsa* suggest links between the Sinhala race and Tamils early in the history of Ceylon, with the Buddhist chronicle even suggesting that the first king of the Sinhala had a Tamil wife. There is evidence that in 177 BC two Tamil kings usurped power at Anuradhapura and ruled for twenty-two years, to be followed ten years later by another who held power for a much longer period. Note the now classic translation by Wilhelm Geiger (1912).

19 See interviews by Nirgunan Tiruchelvam, featuring Dr Neelan Tiruchelvam, at www.youtube.com/watch?v=dmDHMdFyERg (accessed 6 August 2015); Keenan, A., 'A new Sri Lanka', Crisis Group website, 18 May 2015, http://blog.crisisgroup.org/asia/2015/05/18/a-new-sri-lanka/ (accessed 21 May 2016).

Chapter 1

1 World press coverage of the 12 and 13 May shelling of the Mullivaikkal hospital (killing around 100 people according to doctors), allegedly by government forces, brought widespread concern and condemnation, in light of customary law reflecting Article 19 of the Fourth Geneva Convention, which states that hospitals shall not lose their protections under international humanitarian law 'unless they are used to commit, outside their humanitarian duties, acts harmful to the enemy'. The hospital was abandoned due to continued shelling, leaving behind about 400 badly wounded patients.

2 Satellite images released by the US State Department showed changes in the civilian 'safe zone' in northern Sri Lanka, the heart of the conflict between the Tamil Tigers and the Sri Lankan forces: an almost empty beach in February 2009, then an April 2009 image showing the same site where an estimated 100,000 refugees were camped after fleeing the fighting. There was evidence that some 25,000 tents were packed into a coastal strip of about eight square miles. Thousands of civilians had fled the area over the previous few days: 'Sri Lanka: satellite imagery of a safe zone', BBC News, 24 April 2009, http://news.bbc.co.uk/1/hi/world/south_asia/8016965.stm. See also 'Updated analysis report (19 April 2009): satellite-detected damages and IDP shelter movement in CSZ Mullattivu district, Sri Lanka', 26 April 2009, www.warwithoutwitness.com/images/stories/PDF/UNOSAT_Report_Damage_IDP_analysis_19April2009_v6.pdf.

3 For a definitive account of the final days of war, see Weiss (2012) *The Cage*.

4 F. R. Satyapalan, '"Act responsibly or be chased out," Gota tells BBC and envoys', *Sunday Island*, 1 February 2009, p. 1; 'Bishops appeal to government and LTTE to review their styles of combat', ibid., p. 3. For depictions of the humanitarian dilemmas at the end of the war, see Harrison (2012) *Still Counting the Dead* and Weiss (2012) *The Cage*. The former head of UNHCR relief operations between 1989 and 1992 wrote a hard-hitting personal account of his experiences both in-country and with UN

management systems in Geneva, in which he stated somewhat prophetically in 2007: 'With the current deadly drift of events in the northeast, the situation in Sri Lanka will soon put the integrity of the United Nations commitment and the soundness of its operational protection structures to the most stringent of tests – on which the international community cannot afford to let the UN fail' (Clarance (2007) *Ethnic Warfare in Sri Lanka and the UN Crisis*, p. 275).

5 The notion of global 'norms' may be understood as 'collective understandings of the proper behaviour of actors', implying notions of how states 'ought' to – or indeed might – behave in light of customary and international law and treaty agreements. In this sense, norms function as a means towards collective legitimation of action, at least in theory. For a discussion on international norms and their application, see Wheeler (2000) *Saving Strangers*, pp. 4–11 and Legro (1997) 'Which norms matter?', p. 31.

6 The Secretary-General's Panel of Experts (UN 2011a) was composed of Marzuki Darusman (Indonesia) as Chair, Yasmin Sooka (South Africa) and Steven Ratner (United States). It was tasked with investigating and advising on any alleged violations of international human rights and humanitarian law during conduct at the end of the war in Sri Lanka. Never recognised as official by the GoSL (who called it the Darusman Report), it attracted great interest and publicity internationally. See, for example, 'Sri Lanka: UN says army shelling killed civilians', BBC News, 26 April 2011, www.bbc.co.uk/news/world-south-asia-13190576. This account states: '"Tens of thousands lost their lives from January to May 2009, many of whom died anonymously in the carnage of the final few days," said the panel, which was headed by a former Indonesian attorney general.'

7 Protests, demonstrations and public fasting had been ongoing for the previous two months or more across the world: in Canada, throughout Tamil Nadu, in Australia – particularly Sydney and Melbourne – in New York, Oslo, Paris, Amsterdam and the UK. See 'Diaspora Tamils protest, fast in increasing numbers; call for ceasefire', *Tamil Guardian*, 14 April 2009, www.tamilguardian.com/article.asp?articleid=2281 (accessed 1 June 2012).

8 Even at the height of the war against the Tamil Tigers in May 2009, India was aware that it would not be prudent to expect Rajapaksa to keep his promise on '13th plus'. A WikiLeaks cable revealed that the US sought a bigger role in pushing a political solution for Tamils but was kept at bay by India. According to the cable, then Foreign Secretary Shivshankar Menon told the US Embassy Chargé d'Affaires Peter Burleigh on 15 May 2009 that the Sri Lankan government had reassured India that 'the government would focus on the implementation of the 13th Amendment Plus as soon as possible, but Menon was skeptical' (207268: confidential, 15 May 2009; see Senadhira 2013).

9 Election results indicated that Rajapaksa had drawn on a support base in Sinhalese majority districts, with a showing of 57.88 per cent of countryside votes. Fonseka brought in a respectable 40.15 per cent with backing from most Tamil and Muslim parties, providing evidence of support for his platform despite his wartime conduct. It also indicated a failure to address or respond to 'the Tamil community's deep alienation from the UPFA regime' (Uyangoda 2011b: 132).

10 Interviews, Colombo, September 2009. It is estimated that between 2009 and 2014 some 16 per cent of Sri Lankan imports originated from China, whereas Sri Lanka's own exports to China remained stagnant at 1.2 per cent of its total exports. Sri Lanka's total exports to India, however, rose from 1 to 6 per cent of its total exports during the same period.
11 Abeyratne cites a youth unemployment rate in 1973 of 65.5 per cent and notes the mobilising factor of exclusion and blocked aspirations that coincided with liberalisation from 1977 onward. See Sirimal Abeyratne (2002) 'Economic roots of political conflict: the case of Sri Lanka', https://taxpolicy.crawford.anu.edu.au/acde/asarc/pdf/papers/2002/WP2002_03.pdf. See also Little and Hettige (2014) *Globalization, Employment and Education in Sri Lanka*, which notes that, while the seeds of conflict predated economic reform, the process of liberalisation both sharpened inequalities and created new ones, for both Sinhalese and Tamil youth. For an examination of how both the JVP and the LTTE have been the products of the failures of the socio-economic and political development of Sri Lanka, see Samaranayake (2008) *Political Violence in Sri Lanka 1971–1987*, p. 282.
12 While the shared experience of discrimination led some Muslim youth early on to join the struggle of 'the Tamil-speaking people' in the North and East, Muslim support soon fell off as militancy was increasingly defined in narrower Tamil nationalist terms. By the mid- to late 1980s, tensions between Tamils and Muslims in the North and East were running high amid LTTE attempts to extort Muslim businesses and frequent clashes, with the security forces reportedly backing Muslims in some incidents. As mutual distrust grew, the Tigers launched a campaign of ethnic cleansing in 1990 (ICG 2011a: 9).
13 Rwanda under President Kagame also sought to take Singapore's best practices into their post-genocide recovery process, drawing on Singaporean experts to help the Rwandan government reform its social security provisions and strengthen both the public and private sector workforce. The Singapore Cooperation Enterprise, a state body that focuses on public sector cooperation and exporting Singapore's model of economic and governmental development, agreed in 2008 to help Rwanda develop its public sector capacity through a memorandum of understanding signed with the Rwandan Strategy and Policy Unit. See 'The city-state releases Africa's potential with skillful aid and trade', *Africa Confidential* 1(8), 6 November 2008. Abstract available at: www.africa-confidential.com/article-preview/id/10114/The_wealthy_autocratic_model. Hewage argues that Sri Lanka and Rwanda each elicit a sense of victimhood upon which their respective foreign policies have been built. In the case of Sri Lanka, its foreign policy has largely been based on the fact that it is victimised by the constant threat of terrorism, while Rwanda invokes its experience of genocide. Therefore, it is argued that both countries adopt a foreign policy agenda based on victimhood: hence the introduction of 'victimism' into the theoretical deliberations of foreign policy analysis. See Hewage (2014) 'Victim politics and post-conflict foreign policy in Rwanda and Sri Lanka'.
14 Quotation from Nimal Siripala de Silva.

15 W. Jayamaha (Mahawewa), 'Singapore is role model for Sri Lanka to fight bribery and corruption', letter to the editor, *The Sunday Times*, 11 April 2010.

16 Paikiasothy Saravanamuttu (2010) wrote: 'Peace without unity, unity without reconciliation, and reconciliation without accountability – these are the dilemmas that both the regime and society will have to bridge if Sri Lanka is to fully grasp the historic opportunity presented by the end of the war. Only then can Sri Lanka transform from a post-war environment to a post-conflict period of growth and reconciliation.'

17 Stuart J. Kaufman takes this definition in turn from Bar-Tal and Bennink (2004) 'The nature of reconciliation as an outcome and as a process'. Another definition would be: 'Reconciliation is a societal process that involves mutual acknowledgment of past suffering and the changing of destructive attitudes and behavior into constructive relationships toward sustainable peace' (Brounéus (2003) *Reconciliation*).

18 During the final phase of the war, it is thought that thousands of LTTE combatants surrendered to the military and were kept in high-security holding centres, to be investigated and vetted by multiple divisions of the security establishment – the Military Intelligence Unit, Criminal Investigation Unit, Terrorist Investigation Unit and so forth – before they were moved to detention centres called Protective Accommodation Rehabilitation Centres (PARCs) in Jaffna, Polonnaruwa and Vavuniya. Part of their intended rehabilitation revolved around a questionnaire including 150 questions; this was later obtained by the human rights NGO The Social Architects. The Social Architects analysed the questions, finding them to be leading, 'invasive', poorly worded and confusing. The questionnaire was loaded with personal queries and tasks of assessing statements such as 'Those who elect Tamil members of parliament are LTTE supporters' or 'Those who do not follow Tamil Tigers will be punished', with no clarity whether this meant during the war or afterwards, or in the future. See http://groundviews.org/2012/06/24/post-war-sri-lankas-thought-police-the-rehabilitation-of-ex-combatants-and-the-denigration-of-tamil-identity-part-two/. After filling out the questionnaire, former cadres would be eligible for release, receiving an identity card from the International Organization for Migration stating that the individual had been rehabilitated.

19 PowerPoint performance attended by author; interviews, Colombo and Jaffna, September 2010.

20 The study and the quoted comment refer to Sri Lankan society in all its diversity and need. The following personal notes from a 2010 visit by the author to Jaffna may also be of interest:

> We heard the phrase 'one country, two nations' repeatedly. We did not hear claims to a homeland or stated interest in war crime prosecutions ... rather the fears are that civil liberties continue to be under assault and identity denied. 'Why?' (for example) do NGO affairs come under the Ministry of Defence; 'Why?' is there virtually nothing for rehabilitation in the 2011 budget? 'Why' do current development discussions continue to exclude local representation, while planning procedures are perceived as a corrupt mockery? Concern over land

and colonisation were expressed. The new budget allows for a grant of 100,000 rupees to every soldier who has a third child – given that the vast majority of the army is Sinhalese this sends a message of demographic incentive ... Thirty per cent of the Jaffna peninsula is currently high security zoned; covering areas where fourteen villages once existed and arable land languishes. A disturbing contradiction has emerged in which the police are now unarmed, but local armed militias and unidentified criminal elements create insecurity among the people. Moreover, a nostalgia for the 'old days' is expressed: i.e. an era when the LTTE (however heavy handed with critics or platform) provided a type of rule of law under which the vulnerable felt secure and domestic/petty crime was dealt with. In a Tamil-speaking community the police and army are still Sinhalese-speaking.

21 Laksiri Fernando, 'Three years on, reconciliation is getting too late', *Colombo Telegraph*, 18 May 2012, quoted in Keerawella (2013: 13).

Chapter 2

1 Under the Rajapaksa government, the Urban Development Authority and the Land Reclamation and Development Board were taken over by the Defence Ministry, controlled by Gotabaya Rajapaksa, one of the President's brothers. A first stage for urban renewal was the removal of more than 135,000 poor families from Colombo City. Thousands of families have been evicted from Slave Island, Dematagoda, Appalwatta and Ibbawatta during the past six years. The Defence Ministry mobilised the security forces to intimidate anyone opposing the evictions. Most of those evicted have not been provided with permanent homes. See V. Peiris 'Sri Lanka: evicted Colombo shanty dwellers face desperate situation', World Socialist Web Site, 9 May 2015, www.wsws.org/en/articles/2015/05/09/evic-m09.html. For an articulate critique of accelerated inequality and the use of the military to both clear people from land and then build on it, see S. Wijesiriwardena, 'Keep off the grass', Groundviews, 8 May 2014, http://groundviews.org/2014/05/08/keep-off-the-grass/. For an insight into how the navy took on park management, see J. de Silva, 'Now navy moves to supervise Viharamadevi Park', *The Island*, 8 May 2011, www.island.lk/index.php?page_cat=article-details&page=article-details&code_title=24930.

2 Guruparan points out, however, that the 'parliamentary versus presidential' debate constructs a neat dichotomy between parliamentary and presidential forms of government that does not necessarily exist in practice. He cites comparative studies documenting a trend in 'modern media democracies' towards the personalisation of politics, almost regardless of formal governance system. It is wise to consider how important a variable the intersection of personality and political system will always be (see Poguntke and Webb (2005) *The Presidentialisation of Politics*). At the same time, his work references Sri Lankan colonial history, and the way in which the executive committee system brought in by the Donoughmore Constitution was viewed by minority Tamils, Muslims, Up Country Tamils Burghers

and Europeans as a means that would bolster their relatively weak political positioning in the constitutional reform processes. The next transitional stage resulted in the Soulbury Constitution, which, when drafted, included a minority rights protection clause. Ceylon became a dominion, and the clause would not prevent ensuing legislation against minority interests being passed by the independent Ceylonese parliament. The 1972 Constitution made a total break with the British Crown, Section 1 declaring a free, sovereign and independent republic. With it came Section 2 and the declaration of the unitary state, meaning that from inception there would be problems with introducing any idea of semi-federal reform. (The phrase Up Country Tamils has been used for some time to refer to those Tamil workers brought in by, or descended from, those brought in from India by the British to work on plantations in the hill country. See 'Upcountry Tamils are Sri Lankans', *Ceylon Today*, 3 March 2016, www.ceylontoday.lk/89-121069-news-detail-upcountry-tamils-are-sri-lankans.html.)

3 Mahinda Rajapaksa v. Kudahetti 1002 SLR 223. The case was dismissed after lengthy consideration. Transcript available at www1.umn.edu/humanrts/research/srilanka/caselaw/Arrest/Mahinda_Rajapakshe_v_Kudahetti_&_Others.htm. For comment on the contrast between freedom of expression and NGO roles that contrasts the 1990s with the Rajapaksa period, see also L. Dias, 'Relevance of freedom of association in 1992 and today: Ratawawi Peramuna and its players', Groundviews, 27 July 2014, http://groundviews.org/2014/07/27/relevance-of-freedom-of-association-in-1992-and-today-ratawawi-peramuna-and-its-players/ (accessed 19 June 2015).

4 Note: it is said that the young Mahinda Rajapaksa once walked from Colombo to Kataragama calling for the abolition of the executive presidency.

5 The term 'republic' most generally means a system of government that derives its power from the people rather than from other foundations such as heredity or divine right. 'It is impossible to establish a perpetual republic,' wrote Niccolò Machiavelli in *The Discourses* (1517), 'because in a thousand unforeseen ways its ruin may be accomplished.' Machiavelli explains at the start of the third book of *The Discourses* that all worldly things have a limit to their life, and that 'in the process of time [a state's] goodness is corrupted, [and] unless something intervenes to lead it back to the mark, it of necessity kills that body'. See Z. J. Witlich, 'Necessity as virtue in the thought of Machiavelli', http://as.tufts.edu/politicalscience/sites/all/themes/asbase/assets/documents/research/necessity.pdf. This occurs because, after ten years at most, men begin to corrupt, 'to behave with greater danger and more tumult, to transgress the laws, and to do so in a manner that makes it unsafe to punish them'. The return to the beginnings of a republic comes either by extrinsic accident or internal prudence, and the preferred Machiavellian option ought to be clear: 'either good orders or good men must produce the effect' (*Discourses* III.1.1–6, pp. 209–12).

6 See also Uyangoda (2011b) 'Travails of state reform in the context of protracted civil war in Sri Lanka'. Both Uyangoda and Yiftachel are cited in Welikala (2015c) 'Constitutional from and reform in postwar Sri Lanka'.

7 This quote is taken from the final draft paper, 'Constitutional form and reform in postwar Sri Lanka' (Welikala 2015c).
8 *Daily Mirror*, 8 October 1971, cited in Edrisinha and Selvakkumaran (1990) 'Constitutional change in Sri Lanka since independence', pp. 79, 95. Quoted by Jayampathy Wickramaratne, 'The executive presidency: a left perspective', in Welikala (2015d).
9 Gunasekara's article quotes an astrological prediction from the state-owned publication *Silumina* of 7 May: 'President Mahinda Rajapaksa and the Rajapaksas will rule this country for a long time ... The Rajapaksas will become beloved leaders of this country ... The next chapter in Sri Lanka is reserved for the Rajapaksas ...'. See T. Gunasekara, 'Rajapaksa governance', *Sunday Leader*, 24 May 2010, www.thesundayleader.lk/2010/05/23/rajapaksa-governance/ (accessed 6 March 2014).
10 See also 'The 18th amendment to the constitution: process and substance', Groundviews, 2 September 2010, http://groundviews.org/2010/09/02/the-18th-amendment-to-the-constitution-process-and-substance/.
11 The new *Jana Sabha* system of government looks set to gut the powers of local-level state structures in Sri Lanka, strengthening the hands of the Colombo regime.
12 'The Centre for Policy Alternatives (CPA) is concerned about the tabling of the "Divineguma Bill" in Parliament which if enacted will have serious implications for democracy, devolution and good governance in Sri Lanka. CPA and its Executive Director filed a Petition today in the Supreme Court (SC SD 3/2012) challenging the constitutionality of the Bill': 'Divineguma Bill challenged in Supreme Court', *Colombo Telegraph*, 17 August 2012, www.colombotelegraph.com/index.php/divineguma-bill-challenged-in-supreme-court/. Others who challenged the bill included an employee of the Samurdhi Authority, the JVP. See 'JVP, CPA see monstrosity in Divineguma bill', *The Sunday Times*, 26 August 2012, www.sundaytimes.lk/120826/news/jvp-cpa-see-monstrosity-in-divineguma-bill-10110.html (accessed September 2012).
13 The Karuna faction's formal name is Tamil Makkal Viduthalai Pulikal (TMVP), which means 'Liberation Tigers of the Tamil People' in Tamil. This name was an attempt to sap legitimacy from the LTTE by taking the 'Liberation Tigers' part of its name. In less than one year after Karuna's return to Sri Lanka, the TMVP had become the most powerful paramilitary organisation in the country. It began in 2004 when Karuna broke away from the LTTE, taking about 4,000 Tiger cadres with him. After the LTTE struck back, inflicting serious losses, then President Chandrika Kumaratunga helped Karuna escape to the Indian state of Tamil Nadu, where he remained until July 2006. He remained active in managing his cadres even while living abroad. Since returning to Sri Lanka, Karuna has used strong-arm tactics to establish a powerful paramilitary group that operates under government protection. See WikiLeaks release of 18 May 2007, communication from Robert O. Blake (then US Ambassador), https://wikileaks.org/plusd/cables/07COLOMBO728_a.html (accessed 5 June 2015).
14 See ICG (2012b) 'Sri Lanka's North II: rebuilding under the military', pp. ii–iii. To quote the executive summary of this report: 'The government

208 | Notes to Chapter 2

points to the many new roads, rapid economic growth and numerous new infrastructure projects as signs of a post-war "northern spring". For most of the more than 430,000 people who have returned to their lands and villages over the past two years, however, there has been little benefit.'

15 With specific reference to conflict-affected North Mannar, Mullaitivu, and Kilinochchi districts.
16 For an accessible window on caste dynamics in Sri Lanka, see P. Perera, 'Caste and exclusion in Sinhala Buddhism', *Colombo Telegraph*, 7 March 2013, www.colombotelegraph.com/index.php/caste-and-exclusion-in-sinhala-buddhism/.

> The caste talk is getting embarrassing. Caste is never spoken about in the open in Sri Lanka but is always present. There is no caste census or reservation. It is never mentioned in newspapers except in the marriage classifieds. But it most certainly determines who we marry, who we vote for and in which Buddhist temple we worship. In this essay I would like to highlight an alternate glimpse of hierarchy, caste and exclusion in Sri Lankan Buddhism ...
>
> At the apex, one has the Govigama or agriculturalist land owning castes who account for roughly 50% of the Sinhalese population. All Sri Lankan Presidents and Prime Ministers with the exception of Ranasinghe Premadasa, belonged to this caste. Many had Anglican Christian antecedents like Bandaranaike, the founder of the ruling Sri Lanka Freedom Party ...
>
> Just below are the Karava or fishermen caste who dominate the maritime districts. The Karava account for roughly 10% of the Sinhala population. The Karava challenged Govigama power in the two Sinhala youth revolts of 1971 and 1987 led by the Janatha Vimukti Peramuna (JVP) ... The JVP appealed to the dispossessed and poor. While it did not articulate its ideology in terms of caste, its caste base was exclusively non Govigama.

The article observes that General Fonseka was also non-Govigama, and that the Karava trend for conversion was to Roman Catholicism.

17 For additional discussion of the problems of the electoral commission, see Transparency International (2010) *The Governance Report 2010*, Chapter 4. For a detailed breakdown of the electoral districts and system, see https://en.wikipedia.org/wiki/Electoral_districts_of_Sri_Lanka#Jaffna_seats_controversy.
18 See Part 1, section 1.1 at www.preventionweb.net/files/28587_local governmentpolicy.pdf.
19 Sri Lanka has a model to offer the world, but not the 'anti-terrorism' model President Mahinda Rajapaksa's administration is assiduously peddling. Rather, this is a model of political marketing, an 'all you need to know' crash course in building innocuous façades to hide insalubrious realities. The old saying suggests that all the people cannot be fooled all the time, but, as the Rajapaksas have proved, fooling all of the people some of the time and some of the people all of the time can more than suffice (Gunasekara 2011).
20 Email from Faaiz Ameer, 4 August 2013.

21 S. Kadri, 'At the CHOGM', *London Review of Books* 35(22), 21 November 2013, www.lrb.co.uk/v35/n22/sadakat-kadri/at-the-chogm (accessed 20 August 2015).

22 The following January (2015), on the electoral defeat of Rajapaksa, it would be observed that if there were a central plank to the common opposition platform in the presidential election, it was about what to do with the executive presidential system in general and the eighteenth amendment in particular, in view of the crisis of democratic governance created by the insidious authoritarianism and pervasive corruption of the Rajapaksa regime. See A. Welikala, 'The executive presidency and the Sri Lankan state: myths and realities', Groundviews, 20 January 2015, http://groundviews.org/2015/01/20/the-executive-presidency-and-the-sri-lankan-state-myths-and-realities/. See also E. Buchanan, 'Sri Lanka's new government to investigate Mahinda Rajapaksa corruption allegations', *International Business Times*, 16 January 2015, www.ibtimes.co.uk/sri-lankas-new-government-investigate-mahinda-rajapaksa-corruption-allegations-1483812 (both accessed 20 January 2015).

Chapter 3

1 India had, of course, interfered, with its own ill-fated peacekeeping attempt following the 1987 Accord; Sri Lanka was clearly perceived as a self-evident part of the Indian sphere of influence, culturally and geo-politically. China, while steering clear of political public statements, began an educational 'bridge' through its Confucian institutes and educational exchanges and cooperation as early as 1979; this was not unlike the approach of the British Council. See Rajapaksje (2016) 'Building goodwill through soft power' and 'Confucius Institute at the University of Kelaniya' at http://english.hanban.org/confuciousinstitutes/node_10738.htm.

2 Attempts at mediating a ceasefire have been mentioned above. There were also controversial overtures concerning the mass evacuation of civilians from the conflict zone. Credible reports from Colombo in March 2009 indicated that the US Pacific Command (PACOM) was planning to lead an evacuation of nearly 200,000 Tamil civilians trapped in the war-torn northern region of Sri Lanka. External Tamil activists urged that such plans be stopped as they 'would only serve to exacerbate the crisis for these civilians and support ethnic cleansing in this region. Instead of an evacuation, the "safe zones" these civilians are currently in should be strengthened, with full access for aid workers, journalists and human rights monitors.' See 'U.S. Tamil group urges Pacific Command not to abet Colombo's war on Tamils', TamilNet, 3 March 2009, www.tamilnet.com/art.html?catid=13&artid=28575. Note: US Marines had delivered aid in the aftermath of the 2004 tsunami, an action that was highly controversial and sensitive in the region.

3 High Commissioner Pillay suffered vitriolic abuse in the national press in Sri Lanka and elsewhere, being accused of bias in that her background was Indian Tamil while her nationality was South African. She spoke of this in an interview given after she finally gained access to Sri Lanka for an official mission in 2013, saying that she was highly offended by comments in the Sri

Lankan media accusing her of bias because of her ethnicity. 'Some media, ministers, bloggers and various propagandists in Sri Lanka have, for several years now, on the basis of my Indian Tamil heritage, described me as a tool of the LTTE (Liberation Tigers of Tamil Eelam). They have claimed I was in their pay, the "Tamil Tigress in the UN". This is not only wildly incorrect, it is deeply offensive,' said Pillay. In the same vein, she added: 'The LTTE was a murderous organisation that committed numerous crimes and destroyed many lives ... those in the diaspora who continue to revere the memory of the LTTE must recognise that there should be no place for the glorification of such a ruthless organisation.' Journalist Kalinga Seneviratne noted that these comments had not stopped the Sri Lankan media and the blogosphere continuing their attacks on the perceived bias of both the UNHRC and its head for allegedly overstepping their mandate to attack the Sri Lankan government from its own soil. See C. Haviland, 'Sri Lankan foreign minister denounces UN Rights Chief', BBC News, 1 June 2010, www.bbc.co.uk/news/10204507 (accessed 10 February 2012).

4 The Indian Prime Minister Manmohan Singh raised the question of a political settlement granting Sri Lanka's Tamils more autonomy. 'India is caught in a strategic quandary regarding Sri Lanka,' said Iskander Rehman at Delhi's Institute for Defence Studies and Analysis. 'Its sizeable Tamil population means that it feels a natural sense of solidarity with the Tamil civilian population but it knows that if it criticises the government too harshly it may risk losing even more strategic space to the Chinese.' See 'India's deals with Sri Lanka heighten stakes in "Great Game" with Beijing', *The Guardian*, 9 June 2010, www.theguardian.com/world/2010/jun/09/sri-lanka-india-china-great-game (accessed 27 March 2015).

5
> In her cable to Washington, Butenis seeks to explain why there is so little momentum towards the formation of a 'truth and reconciliation' commission, or any other form of accountability. Most Tamil Tiger commanders, also under suspicion for war crimes such as the use of civilians as human shields, had been killed at the end of the war. President Rajapaksa had meanwhile fought an election campaign promising to resist any international efforts to prosecute 'war heroes' in the nation's army. Not only was the Colombo government not interested in investigating itself, but Tamils in Sri Lanka unlike those abroad were also nervous about the issue as it might make them targets for reprisals. (Borger 2015)

Butenis wrote: 'While they wanted to keep the issue alive for possible future action, Tamil leaders with whom we spoke in Colombo, Jaffna and elsewhere said now was not time and that pushing hard on the issue would make them "vulnerable".' See 'Sri Lanka war-crimes accountability: the Tamil perspective', 15 January 2010, https://wikileaks.org/plusd/cables/10COLOMBO32_a.html (accessed 12 September 2016).

6 See www.channel4.com/news/sri-lanka-execution-video-evidence-of-war-crimes.

7 In the words of one civil servant in Colombo on hearing this news: 'Small states need big hitters in the international game. Israel has the US, Zimbabwe

has South Africa. We need our ancient neighbour to go to bat for us, not against us.' Conversation with author, Colombo, December 2010.
8 Photograph of sign taken by author, September 2012.
9 'The wise give up the idea of victory and defeat', public statement by the Friday Forum, 11 April 2012, received by email.
10 Prageeth Ekneligoda was a journalist and cartoonist who commented on democracy, human rights, and the need for free expression. He was also a father and a husband, and his wife Sandya lodged complaints with the police and National Human Rights Commission, later filing a habeas corpus case in the Court of Appeal. She campaigned tirelessly for an investigation and the return of her husband, writing personally to the President and his wife, standing outside parliament and reaching out to other families of disappeared people. Eventually she also appealed to the UN, which led to her being invited to give testimony in Geneva.
11 Personal observations of international human rights experts present and Sri Lankan observers.
12 Spokesperson for the UN High Commissioner for Human Rights Rupert Colville quoting Miss Pillay said that during this Human Rights Council session, there has been an unprecedented and totally unacceptable level of threats, harassment and intimidation directed at Sri Lankan activists who had travelled to Geneva to engage in the debate, including by members of the 71-member official Sri Lankan government delegation. ('Navi Pillay warns Sri Lanka', *Daily Mirror*, 23 March 2012, www.dailymirror.lk/17609/tech)
13 See the discussion on this phrase as part of a 'long tradition of political obfuscation' at www.globalpolicy.org/qhumanitarianq-intervention.html (accessed 20 July 2015)
14 Author interview with G. L. Peiris, then Minister of Export Development and International Trade, 3 February 2009, Colombo. (He was appointed Minister for External Affairs in 2010.)
15 '"Lies Agreed Upon" to be screened at UN', *Sunday Observer*, 4 September 2011, www.sundayobserver.lk/2011/09/04/new14.asp (accessed 3 June 2015).
16 See, for example, 'Sri Lanka probe "clears military"', BBC News, 14 July 2009, http://news.bbc.co.uk/2/hi/south_asia/8149728.stm (accessed 3 March 2015). Sri Lanka's national human rights panel cleared the army of the 2006 killing of seventeen people working for the French charity Action Against Hunger. The head of the inquiry commission said he had been unable to find out who was to blame 'because he ran out of funds'. The bodies of the Action Against Hunger workers were found in the northeastern town of Muttur. Truce monitors blamed security forces, who denied the charge. Heavy fighting had been going on in the area between troops and Tamil rebels fighting for an independent state. Fifteen of the bodies were found lying down and shot at close range on 7 August 2006, in a case that caused an international outcry. Two other bodies were found later. The aid staff – all but one ethnic Tamils – were working on tsunami relief projects in the area.

17 See 'Local intelligence breaks LTTE's Malaysia network', Ceylon Today, 1 June 2014, www.mea.gov.lk/index.php/en/news-from-other-media/4714-local-intelligence-breaks-lttes-malaysia-network- (accessed 2 April 2015). Note: Yasmin Sooka's respected work *An Unfinished War: Torture and sexual violence in Sri Lanka 2009–2014. A documentation of post-war atrocities* documented surveillance operations and the monitoring of both Tamils in the island and members of the Tamil diaspora in their country of residence, those involved in protests or activism and those Tamils merely visiting Sri Lanka. Data was collected for a database maintained by the authorities, making Tamils vulnerable to the above crimes being committed against them if they returned to Sri Lanka. It also stated that research on human face detection is reportedly under way within the Department of Statistics and Computer Science at the University of Colombo. 'From a witness protection point of view, there are reasonable grounds to believe that Sri Lanka intelligence is using highly sophisticated facial recognition software to identify protesters from abroad if they return home.' See www.barhumanrights.org.uk/unfinished-war-torture-and-sexual-violence-sri-lanka-2009-2014 (accessed 25 March 2016).

18 The speaker was chairman of the Bharatiya Janata Party (BJP) Committee for Strategic Action, Dr Subramanian Swamy, at an international seminar in Colombo in August 2014. See 'Dealing with devolution', *The Hindu*, 23 September 2014, www.thehindu.com/opinion/lead/dealing-with-devolution-in-sri-lanka/article6435956.ece (accessed 4 April 2016).

19 See 'Civil lawsuit filed against Major General Shavendra Silva', BBC Sinhala, 24 September 2011, www.bbc.com/sinhala/news/story/2011/09/110924_lawsuit.shtml (accessed 28 March 2016).

20 See 'Sri Lanka president receives US court summons', BBC News, 19 June 2011, www.bbc.co.uk/news/world-south-asia-13826803 (accessed 28 March 2016).

21 See 'Spy cables reveal Sri Lanka hyped up Tamil Tiger postwar threat', Aljazeera America, 4 March 2015, http://america.aljazeera.com/articles/2015/3/4/spy-cables-reveal-sri-lanka-knew-truth-about-ltte-threat.html (accessed 4 April 2016).

22 See 'OHCHR investigation on Sri Lanka', www.ohchr.org/EN/HRBodies/HRC/Pages/OISL.aspx (accessed 2 May 2015).

23 See 'Being punished for ending terrorism: Rajapaksa on UN Resolution', Amarasara News, 23 March 2014, www.amarasara.info/wordpress1/?m=201403&paged=6.

24 See 'Names of the first lot of Sri Lankan war criminals & genocidaires released by Transnational Government of Tamil Eelam', 18 May 2014, www.einpresswire.com/article/205438728/names-of-the-first-lot-of-sri-lankan-war-criminals-genocidaires-released-by-transnational-government-of-tamil-eelam (accessed 5 August 2014). Names included previous and current presidents, officials and former military persons.

Chapter 4

1 The extract comes from the poem '1958 ... '71 ... '77 ... '81 ... '83', available in Gunatilleke (2015) *Confronting the Complexity of Loss*, p. 35.

For a profile of the poet, see 'Literary legacies: Jean Arasanayagam', Sunday Observer, 20 April 2008, www.sundayobserver.lk/2008/04/20/imp17.asp.

2 For the response of Transparency International Sri Lanka to the parliamentary report concerning adverse references, see www.tisrilanka.org/?p=376 (accessed 5 January 2015).

3 It was support of lobbying for 'responsibility to protect' (R2P) in Sri Lanka that cost International Centre for Ethnic Studies (ICES) Head Rama Mani her Sri Lankan visa for 'security reasons', leading to her being forced to leave the country. See 'Govt. cancels Dr. Rama Mani's visa', *The Sunday Times*, 3 February 2008, www.sundaytimes.lk/080203/News/newsoo24.html. See also R. Abeywardena, 'Berghof chief asked to leave', *The Sunday Times*, 30 December 2007, www.sundaytimes.lk/071230/News/newsoo01.html.

4 Bob Rae, Canadian politician and former Head of the Forum of Federations (who had been an adviser on federal models during the peace negotiations), arrived with a full visa in June 2009 and was denied entry to Sri Lanka and sent back the following day. Rohan Edrisinha wrote in the *Journal of Not-for-Profit Law* in May 2010:

> One of the striking features of the report of the select committee was that it seemed to lack appreciation of the scope of freedom of association and speech and expression in a democratic society. The committee was critical of NGOs that advocated federalism on the basis that the President had been elected in November 2005 on a platform that promised to preserve the unitary character of the Constitution, and that the NGOs were acting in a manner "contradictory to the mandate given by the people of the country." Furthermore, many NGOs working in conflict affected areas were censured for engaging in activities prejudicial to national security. (Edrisinha 2010)

5 Apart from the political ramifications explored by Mampilly, subsequent evaluations of immense aid flows during the post-tsunami period 'highlight the negative effects that too much money managed in a poorly coordinated manner can have, creating poor targeting, uneven standards of assistance and corruption. For example some post-tsunami assistance provides substantially higher housing support than the programmes offered by the ADB, EU and World Bank, and this has created increased tension' (Chapman et al. 2009: 32). Note: There was concern that the LTTE responded to tsunami aid flows by shifting its governance strategy away from a degree of cooperation with the government to a strategy dependent on aid flows from abroad. This shift affected conflict dynamics by furthering unilateral claims and inspiring anger in Colombo, thus bringing about an altered dynamic that further veered away from negotiated settlement towards a more violent outcome.

6 There was a sense that the LTTE had used tsunami aid to political ends, which led to anger in government circles. Also, perceptions that much tsunami assistance was wasted resulted in acute disappointment and further damaged the reputation of relief and development agencies in the eyes of local stakeholders.

7 Perera quotes Dr V. Suresh on the problem of funding, which has 'monetised human rights action' in both India and Sri Lanka. Perera's concern is the

absence of a pluralistic, secular, open mindset in the deep South, and the failure to understand Tamil and human rights activism, which maintains the status quo of division.

8 See the IIGEP's public statement of 6 March 2008 at www.hrw.org/sites/default/files/related_material/IIGEP%20public%20statement.pdf (accessed 2 July 2016).

9 For more on 'Do No Harm', spearheaded by Mary Anderson, see www.conflictsensitivity.org/do-no-harm-local-capacities-for-peace-project/; http://cdacollaborative.org/publication/do-no-harm-how-aid-can-support-peace-or-war/.

10 For a subsequent critique of neoliberal 'empire in denial' and of extreme professional norms and excesses, see Chandler (2006) and Easterly (2014). Burke and Mulakala (2011) observe that Sri Lanka has never been strongly aid-dependent. But top-down development approaches popular in the 1970s favoured support to a strong central government and overrode localised opinions or feelings, as is often cited with regard to the Mahaweli Basin development scheme, which caused upheaval and resentment among affected minorities. This shifted in the late 1980s, with a new emphasis on governance reform and liberalised economic policies.

11 'The institutional framework in place for the promotion and protection of human rights has fundamental capacity problems' (UNDP 2012: 14). See also Keenan (2007) 'The trouble with evenhandedness' and Korf (2006) 'Dining with devils?'

12 Following the 2002 ceasefire, most projects immediately adopted a post-conflict approach, where the assumption was that the war-affected areas would begin to need recovery and that a peace dividend would underpin the transition from a ceasefire to a peace agreement. The largest projects sprang from the joint needs assessment in 2003, and the multilateral strategy that emerged in 2004 sought to coordinate the transition process from conflict to peace through five thematic areas (Chapman et al. 2009: 22).

13 Walton is helpful in qualifying the term 'civil society'. He states that international actors supporting peace in Sri Lanka tended to utilise a normative view of civil society as a realm capable of building trust and cooperation, promoting and protecting rights and democracy and restraining an unruly state. This focus on the democratising potential of civil society has obscured a more influential set of organisations capable of mobilising without reference to liberal democratic goals. He chooses to use a broader meaning: an arena of uncoerced collective action around shared interests, purposes and values, citing the LSE Centre for Civil Society's 'What is Civil Society' (see www.lse.ac.uk/collections/CCS/what_is_civil_society.htm).

14 Quoting Niland (2014a), the government's subsequent Consultative Committee on Humanitarian Assistance (CCHA) established in 2006:

> was widely seen as an Orwellian structure that served as an instrument of Colombo's propaganda in a sophisticated campaign to intimidate and emasculate the relief community. Colombo used visa and travel permits, the threat of expulsion from the country, character

assassination and allegations of pro-Tiger sympathies to coerce and control the relief system ... Threats to staff safety, particularly national staff, were a valid concern. In August 2006, 17 *Action Contre la Faim* (ACF) local staff were murdered in an execution style killing in their agency compound shortly after the SLA retook Muttur in the Eastern Province. The aid community protested the killing of their colleagues, but did not seize the potential watershed moment to renegotiate the space and parameters of humanitarian action.

15 This article was originally read as dated 30 December 2010 at www.defence.lk/new.asp?fname=20081004_03, but by mid-2016 this URL was no longer available. However, an earlier version with the same title dated 3 October 2008 could be accessed via the *Asian Tribune* on 20 September 2016 at www.asiantribune.com/node/13504.

16 See also www.rethinkfragility.com and the opening 'Prologue' for the Sri Lankan experience and the impact this had on the author.

17 Kenneth Bush (1961–2016) was a prominent practitioner and scholar specialising in post-war recovery whose work pioneered the research and evaluation method and analysis in relation to conflict dynamics, ethics and power relations. He worked with a broad spectrum of policy, development and humanitarian organisations, and also held positions such as Research Director of the International Conflict Research Institute at the University of Ulster (Northern Ireland), founding professor of the Conflict Studies Programme of St Paul University (Ottawa, Canada), Executive Director at the Post-war Reconstruction and Development Unit of the University of York (UK) and latterly Senior Lecturer in the School of Government and International Affairs at Durham University's Global Security Institute.

18 Interview with David Whaley, 19 August 2015.

19 In compromise it was agreed that the Sri Lankan Human Rights Commission would take on the monitoring role. In the wake of subsequent GoSL military tactics this had little effect.

20 In fact, there were multiple national military missions to provide an immediate response to the tsunami emergency, with Austria, Belgium, Canada, Greece, India, Italy and Pakistan also deploying troops to deal with the devastation caused by the natural disaster and for the delivery of relief supplies.

21

PACOM launching an evacuation of Tamil civilians supports the Sri Lankan government's campaign of ethnic cleansing of this region. Tamils have been under attack by the Sri Lankan government since last September; evacuating them from Vanni and delivering them to the Sri Lankan government is equivalent to being an accomplice to genocide. As American citizens, we implore you to put an immediate stop to PACOM plans to evacuate these civilians. We do not want their blood on our hands. Instead of an evacuation, we urge the U.S. government to expand the 'safe zone' these civilians are in, and strengthen their security by allowing aid workers, journalists and human rights monitors full access to the region. We also ask the U.S. government to

pressure the Sri Lankan government to accept a ceasefire to provide respite to these besieged civilians. (TamilNet 2009)
22. A full exposition of the Norwegian story regarding their experience as a third party was published in 2015. *To End a Civil War: Norway's peace engagement with Sri Lanka* was written by Mark Salter in close cooperation with Eric Solheim and Vidar Helgeson. For details and a film record of their book launch in London, see www.soas.ac.uk/south-asia-institute/events/28oct2015-to-end-a-civil-war-norways-peace-engagement-with-sri-lanka.html (accessed 9 January 2016).
23. *Rights Up Front* serves as a plan of action to meet such goals. Outlined within the document are six specific points that can make a 'qualitative difference in the way the UN system meets its responsibilities':

   1. Integrating human rights into the lifecycle of all staff, so that they all understand what the UN's mandates and commitments to human rights mean for their respective department, agency, fund or programme.
   2. Adopting an 'Article 99 attitude' in order to tell member states what they need to hear. The UN will engage more proactively and strategically with member states, including through, as Deputy-Secretary-General Eliasson suggested, providing horizon-scanning briefings to the Security Council.
   3. Ensuring coherent strategies of action on the ground and leveraging the UN system's capacities.
   4. At headquarters, adopting a 'whole-of-UN' approach to engagement with member states and with teams on the ground, and to do so well before a crisis strikes to enable early action.
   5. Achieving greater impact in the UN's human rights protection work.
   6. Developing a more robust system for gathering and analysing information on serious violations of human rights and humanitarian law in order to support such activities.

24. See www.responsibilitytoprotect.org/index.php/crises/crisis-in-sri-lanka and Niland (2014b) *Inhumanity and Humanitarian Action*. One very personal report that received wide informal circulation was Julian Vigo's 'Independent Report on Sri Lanka and United Nations Human Rights Violations', *Sri Lanka Guardian*, 11 April 2012, www.srilankaguardian.org/2012/04/independent-report-on-sri-lanka-and-un.html (accessed 2 January 2016).
25. Sri Lanka and Iran have an historic economic partnership. Iran sells crude oil cheaply to Sri Lanka and Sri Lanka buys its arms and armaments from Iran. Iran funds many Sri Lankan energy development projects, from hydroelectric power to oil refineries. Iran's investments in Sri Lanka were tallied in 2008 at approximately US$450 million. Iran is also the largest lender and aid donor to Sri Lanka. It provided loans to Sri Lanka for the purchase of military equipment during the Sri Lankan Civil War and also trained Sri Lankan military personnel. Sri Lanka was the first Asian country which Iranian President Mahmoud Ahmadinejad visited when he assumed office. (Walker (2011) 'Sri Lanka and Iran')

26 Japan was the highest donor in the OECD list, with $388 million of its funding included in OECD budget lines. See statistics at www.oecd.org/dac/stats/LKA.gif.
27 This observation refers to the bitter contestation between armed groups vying for the role of key leading representative of the Tamil cause. In targeted killings, the People's Liberation Organisation of Tamil Eelam (PLOTE) killed 280 Tamil Elam Liberation Organisation (TELO) cadres in 1986, and forced the Eelam Revolutionary Organisation of Students (EROS) to the sidelines and others to the Eastern Province.
28 Third High Level Forum on Aid Effectiveness, 'Accra Agenda for Action', 4 September 2008, www.undp.org/mdtf/docs/Accra-Agenda-for-Action.pdf. For both the Paris Declaration and the Accra Agenda for Action, see OECD (n.d.).
29 The IFRC's code of conduct is available at www.ifrc.org/publicat/conduct/code. See also www.icrc.org/eng/assets/files/publications/icrc-002-1067.pdf (accessed 2 January 2016).
30 For the 20 October 2009 presentation of the findings of the 'OECD DAC Evaluation of Donor Activities in Support of Conflict-Sensitive Development and Conflict Prevention and Peacebuilding in Sri Lanka', see www.oecd.org/countries/srilanka/ (accessed 10 January 2016).
31 A paper dedicated to the 'OECD at 50 and beyond' (available at www.oecd.org/about/) articulates the informing principles of the OECD:

> Today, we are focused on helping governments around the world to: Restore confidence in markets and the institutions that make them function; Re-establish healthy public finances as a basis for future sustainable economic growth; Foster and support new sources of growth through innovation, environmentally friendly 'green growth' strategies and the development of emerging economies; Ensure that people of all ages can develop the skills to work productively and satisfyingly in the jobs of tomorrow.

> The conflicted and uneven effects of economic liberalisation are well documented for Sri Lanka. Ameresekere (2011) amassed and analysed primary sources documenting how resources were plundered throughout the 1980s and early 2000s; formal policies 'at the behest of the International Monetary Fund (IMF), the World Bank and the Asian Development Bank, set the stage for widespread corruption and allowed an unprecedented illicit transfer of public wealth into privileged and private hands'. He examines the privatisation and outright sale of the facilities of the Port of Colombo, the national insurance company and prized tea plantations, ministries entering supply contracts with private banks, construction agreements with foreign firms, corruption and theft. His study also documents public interest litigation fighting economic crime, fraud and corruption.

32 Dibbert (2014) reflected that the shrinking space for NGOs could be viewed as a microcosm of broader trends on the island, in which freedom of association and movement were increasingly curtailed.
33 In India, a women's organisation working on gender and human rights in cooperation with Oxfam was visited in Chennai by government agents

asking for registration information; the Ford Foundation in Delhi was put under pressure until it felt obliged to freeze its funding. See 'Ford Foundation freezes funding to India as Modi sarkar clamps down on NGOs', Firstpost, 14 July 2015, www.firstpost.com/blogs/life-blogs/ford-foundation-freezes-funding-india-modi-govt-clamps-ngos-2342146.html.

Chapter 5

1 Cited in Doole (2016) 'Advent of "Sinha-le" movement reawakening the racial monster'.
2 Note: Post-war Sri Lanka has also seen the prolonged and heightened use of political Buddhism as a mobilising force to assert a type of control, in the name of protecting Sri Lankan Buddhists. Sinhala political Buddhism has been a feature of internal violence and civil war dynamics, warranting attention from analysts and observers for some years (see, for example, DeVotta (2007) 'Sinhalese Buddhist nationalist ideology').
3 There was a bold narrative, a 'new genealogy for the Ruling Family. According to this ... the Rajapaksas are direct descendants of Dutugemunu – the Hero-king of Sinhala-Buddhism – and the Family of King Suddhodana, the Buddha's father' (Gunasekara 2014b). Note: The invocation of so-called Buddhist sayings and quotations in political speeches and parliamentary debate warrants careful scrutiny: for example, cultural sayings are not to be confused with religious references. Women's groups in Sri Lanka expressed concern over the renewed currency given to 'familial ideology' and the assumed central role of the mother in every family unit, as expressed in both the *Mahinda Chintana* and earlier in the President's 2005 election manifesto, both implying that empowering women meant giving them the power to raise children for the good of society. Similarly, in strained parliamentary debates over domestic violence, the old proverb 'violence in the home is only until the rice is cooked' is invoked in opposition to modern 'Western influence' for clear legislation. See Kodikara (2012) *Only Until the Rice is Cooked?* Kodikara provides an old proverb from English culture too, perhaps to demonstrate that social values can change: 'A woman, a dog, and a walnut tree, the more you beat them the better they be' (ibid.: 20).
4 See the full Commonwealth Charter at http://thecommonwealth.org/our-charter (accessed 2 March 2016).
5 Address to the nation, 6 December 2006, available at www.priu.gov.lk/news_update/Current_Affairs/ca200612/20061207address_to_the_nation.htm. Also quoted in Human Rights Watch's 'Return to war' at www.hrw.org/reports/2007/srilanka0807/8.htm.
6 Note: Sinhala culture and literature that evolved and developed within Sri Lanka were solidified by Buddhism. It became the source and secret of unity through history, which is why these key areas continue to be a target for annihilation by the Christian West and its local stooges. There are only 14.8 million Sinhalese-speaking Sinhala and thus both the ethnic group and its language must be protected. All other cultures and languages in Sri Lanka originated from other countries. It was the Sinhalese who built Sri Lanka's civilisation (Waduge 2013).

Notes to Chapter 5 | 219

7 Gray concludes: 'Currently, the Sinhalese-dominated centralised education system has created a non-plural concept of history that is isolating minority populations' (2012: 8).
8 See also Walton and Hayward (2014) *Contesting Buddhist Narratives*.
9 McGowan's comments came just after a mass exodus of some 90,000 Rohingya who had fled persecution by crossing into Bangladesh.
10 In the words of Gravers:

> The chronicle tells the story of the Buddhist king Dutthagāminī who – after a long war against the evil (Tamil) King Elāra – evicted the Tamils in the second century BC. Dutthagāminī's story is used as if it was factual history. It describes Dutthagāminī as a dhammarāja, a righteous king according to Buddhism, who fights demons and protects Buddhism through a holy war. The legend reads as an allegory of Māra's attack on the Buddha before his enlightenment. The evil tempter Māra and his army were wiped out when the Earth Goddess wrung her wet hair and the ensuing flood swept away the army of evil, i.e., the ultimate defence of the Buddha and dhamma (the doctrine). Deegalle (2003), a Sinhala monk, explained that Dutthagāminī showed remorse after killing his enemy and gave Elāra the last honours. Dutthagāminī was comforted by monks who said that it was no worse to kill 'evil unbelievers' than to kill animals. Thus, the Mahāvamsa can be interpreted as a dispensation of the non-violence principle which states that killing of all sentient beings produces demerit and contradicts mettā ('loving kindness'). (Gravers (2015) 'Anti-Muslim Buddhist nationalism in Burma and Sri Lanka', p. 17)

See also Deegalle (2003) 'Is violence justified in Theravāda Buddhism?'
11 Stathern also refers to militant actions by Buddhists in other settings and times, for example among the Samurai in Japan, in anti-colonial struggle, and in contemporary Burma/Myanmar. He reminds us that in terms of doctrinal principles and precepts, it is possible to compare the difference between Christian teachings and the wars conducted by nations who would call themselves Christian.
12 See also Deen (2014) 'UN chief urges Sri Lanka to protect Muslims under attack'.
13 See the complete speech of 14 July 2014 featuring the Chief Justice at www.youtube.com/watch?v=VFcYFY8XpFohttps://www.youtube.com/watch?v=VFcYFY8XpFo (accessed 14 July 2014).
14 See reporting and separate posted news items at www.tamilguardian.com/article.asp?articleid=16418 (accessed 9 July 2015).
15 Another example would be the case of women in Ashraf Nagar, Ampara district, who filed a fundamental rights case in the Supreme Court over land requisitioned by the military, seeking restoration or adequate compensation. Response from the military included blocking off water supplies to the petitioners, preventing relatives from visiting them, and the blasting of Buddhist prayers through a loudspeaker all day in front of the home of a Muslim petitioner (Women's Action Network 2013b).

16 Dewasiri suggests that: 'It was as a reaction to the growing strength of the Traditional Tamil Homeland ideology that the Sinhala-Buddhists developed the notion of the "Sinhala-Buddhist Heritage of the North and the East"' (Dewasiri 2013: 2). He also explores the 'archaeologising of the North and East' with particular reference to pilgrimage-cum-tourism by Sinhala-Buddhists from the South.
17 For example, see Rose-Greenland and Müge Göçek (2014) 'Cultural heritage and violence in the Middle East'.
18 For additional background study, see During (2011) *Cultural Heritage and Identity Politics*.
19 Problems also identified included the missing and high levels of sexual violence and harassment experienced among women survivors in the North and East.
20 See also the section on p. 6 that deals with cultural rights (WAN and CHRD 2012).
21 See also Hyndman and Amarasingam (2014) '"Touring terrorism"'.
22 Commercial fishing in northern Sri Lanka was not an exclusively Tamil enterprise before the war:

> in some districts approximately 20 per cent of fishing licences were held by Sinhalese fishermen. There were also a number of fishermen from the Sri Lankan Muslim community. However, during the war, both Muslim and Sinhalese fishermen were expelled from the north by the LTTE. Since the defeat of the LTTE, a number of Sinhalese fishermen have returned to the north and northeast. (MRT and RRT (2013) 'Sri Lanka: treatment of opposition groups, citizens and persons with certain LTTE links', p. 22)

> The Migration Review Tribunal and Refugee Review Tribunal draw on ICG reports, including 'Sri Lanka's North II: rebuilding under the military' (ICG 2012b). The Australian Refugee Review Tribunal's (RRT's) 2012 paper was released amid concerns about a rising number of Sri Lankan 'boat people' seeking refuge in Australia. See 'More people boarding boats to Australia', IRIN, 12 July 2012, www.irinnews.org/report/95855/sri-lanka-more-people-boarding-boats-australia (accessed 27 February 2016). It needs to be said that the rumour network in both Jaffna and Colombo in 2012 claimed (informal) military complicity in selling boat passage to Australia to young unemployed Tamil males, but this is anecdotal in nature.

23 Personal conversations with women gathering at Kumulumunai Puspampal village near Mullaitivu, February 2016.
24 Ameen Izzadeen, deputy editor of *The Sunday Times*, stated in an editorial printed by Aljazeera that Britain had put Sri Lanka on notice:

> Either launch an independent domestic probe on alleged war crimes before March, or face an international inquiry. In March 2014, the UN Human Rights Council will hear a report from UN Human Rights Chief Navi Pillay on the progress Sri Lanka has made in addressing war crime charges. A bad report is likely to pave the way for the United States, Britain, Canada and other Western powers to move for an international inquiry.

25 See also 'Sri Lanka's pluralist ethnic fabric under threat as anti-Muslim drive gains pace', UK Tamil News, 21 January 2016, www.uktamilnews.com/?p=19295 (accessed 12 March 2016).

Chapter 6

1 Quote taken from Sen (2009) *The Idea of Justice*, p. x.
2 Citizens' movements for good governance were a major driving force in propelling the common candidate Maithripala Sirisena to electoral victory over Rajapaksa, under a banner of 'Yahapalanaya' (righteous government). For an influential and substantial work that provides documentation and evidence for such demands, see Visalingam (2011). For a wry overview of how patterns can repeat themselves when people are in power, see 'A year of yahapalanaya' (*The Sunday Times* 2015).
3 The report was far-sighted in its recommendations, among them: 1) Sri Lanka would not be defined as unitary or federal; 2) every constituent people would have the right to internal self-determination; 3) a comprehensive bill of rights would be included in the constitution; 4) power would be devolved to the provinces with provincial government and legislatures; 5) four options were given for consideration on a merger of North and East; and 6) there would be parity of status for the Sinhala and Tamil languages. Crucially, the report also recommended devolved police and land powers to provincial level. In Jeyaraj's (2012) view, the report had accomplished valid work: 'This is a home-grown solution recommended by the multi-ethnic Panel of Experts appointed by the President.' But it had not been acted upon.
4 For general information on the economy and the election that saw Rajapaksa's demise, see Rajapaksa (2014) 'A fault in his stars?'
5 For some whose own employment was not threatened by this development, there was concern about the importing of Chinese convicts, whether on ethical or personal security grounds (Soysa 2010).
6 Friday Forum press release, 20 May 2011, sent by email to author.
7 Chaaminda draws on Escobar (1995) for her analysis.
8 The Bishop of Mannar reported 146,679 missing persons in a submission, and was later investigated and interviewed by the CID (*Colombo Telegraph* 2010).
9 Conversation with Yolanda Foster, London, 27 January 2016. See a full account in Becker (2013) *Campaigning for Justice*. Human rights group advocacy had seen success, notably through Human Rights Watch and the assistance of US Senator Patrick Leahy in the commissioning of a senate report on Sri Lanka produced by the State Department's Office of War Crimes.
10 Alongside domestic considerations of the politics in Tamil Nadu, informal conversations in 2013 with Delhi insiders suggested that the impeachment of the Chief Justice in Sri Lanka was a bridge too far for many in the Indian government, and that similar 2008 actions in Pakistan may have contributed to the derailing of talks on Kashmir and Jammu. The Pakistan case is documented at www.ibanet.org/Article/Detail.aspx?ArticleUid=D931C72B-D13C-4557-AE96-7337C9375666 (accessed 2 March 2016).

11 Sri Lanka Brief reported the previous month that, for the American public, a lengthy pro-Sri Lanka advert was shown on national television, assuring transatlantic audiences that all was well on the island. A 28-minute video, 'Sri Lanka: Reconciling and Rebuilding', appeared as paid programming on the US network NBC from the Thompson Advisory Group, a Washington-based advocacy and strategy group hired by the Central Bank of Sri Lanka 'at a whopping cost of US$ 66,600 (Rs. 8,337,600) per month' (Bastians 2014). For more on this and on the diplomatic offensive launched by the government, see 'Pillorying Pillay', *The Sunday Times*, 8 September 2013, www.sundaytimes.lk/130908/editorial/pillorying-pillay-61387.html.

12 Private document outlining the Sri Lanka situation analysis, received by email from D. Whaley on 9 March 2016.

13 Wijewardene's article (2009) includes the following interesting extension in thought:

> That the Rajapaksas' diplomacy was able to thwart the machinations of the most powerful nations on earth is something that not just Sri Lankans but people across the developing world can be proud of. Few if any small third world nations have stood up to the West as successfully as the Rajapaksa regime did at the Human Rights Council. Of course many will argue that the atrocities and human rights violations committed in the last days of the war were sufficiently extreme that a UN sponsored investigation was justified. However for most Sri Lankans a UN sponsored investigation would have been an unwelcome and unacceptable intrusion in the nation's sovereignty.

14 The NGO Forum was incorporated as the International Working Group on Sri Lanka in 1996.

15 Jansz (2000), quoted in Punyasena (2003) 'The façade of accountability' and Jayawardene (2000) 'Torture amidst the New Year crackers', describing the letter from the UN Special Rapporteur on Torture to the Sri Lankan President dated 15 November 1999.

16

> There are a number of ways in which international human rights monitors could be associated with current or envisaged arrangements, beyond the SLMM. An official body, including the proposed parliamentary committee or the National Human Rights Commission, could invite such assistance, which could then be provided through an intergovernmental organization of which Sri Lanka is a member – the United Nations or the Commonwealth. In view of the reluctance of previous Sri Lankan governments to invite any expanded UN role, I asked about the acceptability of – for example – technical advice on human rights monitoring through the Office of the High Commissioner for Human Rights (OHCHR) and/or the use of UN Volunteers as human rights monitors. (UNVs have played such a role effectively elsewhere, and are already deployed in the work of UNICEF and UNHCR in Sri Lanka.) This was explicitly regarded as an acceptable possibility by the Prime Minister, who referred to the very different attitude of his government to the role of the UN, indicated by his request to the Secretary-General to send a UN needs

assessment mission to Sri Lanka. (Martin (2003) 'Unarmed monitoring and human rights field presence')

17 President Sirisena said that while the UN report released in September 2015 had pointed to army involvement in war crimes, the report had failed to mention names. He said it was important to determine whether such crimes actually took place. He said: 'If the Sri Lankan Army is alleged for such crimes, our concern should be to free them from those allegations. If anyone has committed a crime, there's no doubt that they should be punished. However it is wrong to make the entire army guilty for what happened.' The president also dismissed reports from the advocacy group Freedom from Torture that people in detention were still being tortured. (Ameen (2016) 'Sri Lanka President wants "internal" crimes court')

For an alternative view on the need for international assistance on accountability in Sri Lanka, see Fonseka and Ganesnathasan (2016) *Hybrid vs. Domestic*.

18 Private document outlining the Sri Lanka situation analysis, received by email from D. Whaley on 9 March 2016.

Chapter 7

1 See 'Director General of UNESCO visits the Democratic Socialist Republic of Sri Lanka 2-4 May 2006', http://portal.unesco.org/en/ev.php-URL_ID=32868&URL_DO=DO_TOPIC&URL_SECTION=201.html (accessed 24 May 2016).
2 'GL-Clinton deal on LLRC implementation revealed', *The Sunday Leader*, 24 June 2012, www.thesundayleader.lk/2012/06/24/gl-clinton-deal-on-llrc-implementation-revealed/ (accessed 4 May 2016).
3 'Sri Lanka slams UN rights body', AFP Reuters, 28 August 2013, www.thesundaily.my/news/808985 (accessed 16 May 2016). The response from HC Pillay was calm and clear; Sri Lanka had been one of the states assisting in formulating the framework of human rights under which she was mandated to do her work.
4 'Gotabhaya Rajapaksa criticises Navi Pillay visit', *The Hindu*, 3 September 2013, www.thehindu.com/news/international/south-asia/gotabhaya-rajapaksa-criticises-navi-pillay-visit/article5089460.ece?utm_source=InternalRef&utm_medium=relatedNews&utm_campaign=RelatedNews (accessed 27 May 2016).
5 Well-founded speculation continues on whether money changed hands to prevent a Tamil turnout which in all probability would have supported his opponent, Ranil Wickremesinghe. For an account of WikiLeaks cables indicating a multimillion-dollar payoff to the Tigers, see U. Kurukulasuriya, 'Rajapaksa - Tiger deal on WikiLeaks and political analysis', *Colombo Telegraph*, 7 April 2012, www.colombotelegraph.com/index.php/rajapaksa-tiger-deal-on-wikileaks-and-political-analysis/ (accessed 15 December 2014). See also D. B. S. Jeyaraj, 'LTTE-enforced boycott lost Ranil the presidency in 2005', *Daily Mirror*, 24 October 2014,

www.dailymirror.lk/55085/ltte-enforced-boycott-lost-ranil-the-presidency-in-2005; N. Kannangara, 'Rajapaksa – LTTE deal in 2005 back in the limelight', *The Sunday Leader*, 6 December 2015, www.thesundayleader.lk/2015/12/06/rajapaksa-ltte-deal-in-2005-back-in-the-limelight/ (all accessed 26 May 2016).

6 Speech of 19 November 2005. Available at www.priu.gov.lk/execpres/speeches/2005/20051119president_rajapaksa_at_swearing_ceremony.html (accessed 25 May 2016).

7 The post-independence stance was radically altered when the 'pro-West' UNP government came to power in 1977, opening up the country to Bretton Woods-style economic liberalisation and the encroachment of new bilateral and multilateral donors as well as foreign investment. With these new connections and the exodus of thousands of Tamils in the wake of the 1983 pogrom, processes of militarisation and internationalisation accelerated (Raheem and Loganathan 2005: 9). The tension between the name 'Socialist Republic' and the actions of liberalising political elites has been a continual theme in Sri Lankan history and politics.

8 Address by the Honourable Lakshman Kadirgamar, at the Fifty-Sixth Session of the United Nations General Assembly, New York, Tuesday 13 November 2001. Quoted in *In Search of Peace: Selected speeches and interviews by the late Foreign Minister Lakshman Kadirgamar*. Colombo: Department of Government Printing, pp. 187–9. See also A. Roberts (2012) *Democracy, Sovereignty and Terror*.

9 See the graphic description of enemy, tactics and assault in Chandraprema (2012) *Gota's War*, which takes as its starting point the notion that foreigners had got it wrong and offers Gotabaya Rajapaksa's story to set the record straight: 'Without Mahinda there would have been no decision to wage war. Without Gotabhaya, no victory' (ibid.: 13).

10 See their documents, particularly Special Report No. 20 (April 2006) on 'Terrorism, counterterrorism and the challenges to human rights advocacy', at www.uthr.org/specialreport.htm. See also Special Report No. 30 (2009), 'Let them speak', which includes the following observation on the dilemma of many Tamils in the North:

> Thus even during the peace process the active section of the LTTE concentrated on furthering their control over the Tamils, conscripting children, training suicide cadres and killing opponents. Many experienced cadres on the other hand left the organisation after going through the punishment, got married and started raising families. The same applied to officers who wanted to live as officers in peacetime, raising children, sending them for an English education and university, ensuring good career prospects.

11 Part of the thrust of this argument was frustration over the forcible recruitment of child soldiers by the LTTE, which received little sanction by intermediaries after the ceasefire. See 'Sri Lanka: Tamil Tigers forcibly recruit child soldiers', Human Rights Watch, 11 November 2004, www.hrw.org/news/2004/11/11/sri-lanka-tamil-tigers-forcibly-recruit-child-soldiers (accessed 14 May 2016). UNICEF worked to urge the children's release and the end of the practice. See 'UNICEF urges Tamil Tigers to

stop recruiting child soldiers in Sri Lanka', UN News Centre, 22 January 2004, www.un.org/apps/news/story.asp?NewsID=9533&Cr=child&Cr1= soldiers#.Vo22Br4YO4E (accessed 30 May 2016). There is also a Tamil view that LTTE elite leaders were somehow corrupted or spoiled by the so-called peace process, taken out of context and removed somewhat from their dedication to revolutionary zeal. This demoralised or tainted what had been a genuine, well-founded struggle.

12 'How Beijing won Sri Lanka's civil war', *The Independent*, 22 May 2010, www.independent.co.uk/news/world/asia/how-beijing-won-sri-lankas-civil-war-1980492.html (accessed 25 November 2015).

13 For documentation on arms transfers to Sri Lanka leading up to the final offensive, see Wezeman et al. (2009) 'International arms transfers'. They note that between mid-2002 and mid-2007 Sri Lanka took delivery of some $140 million worth of military equipment from China. Israel, Ukraine and Pakistan were also substantial suppliers, with Pakistan receiving a 2008 supply deal worth $25 million.

14

There is a need to recognise the fundamental role of the State in civilian protection. In the first instance, the role of governments in civilian protection should be respected as it is their primary responsibility to protect their own citizens. The UN and the humanitarian agencies must support and assist governments and in doing so be sensitive to ground realities, including respect for the sovereignty of States. ('President confident of coming through', *The Nation*, www.nation. lk/2011/05/15/politics.htm (accessed 3 May 2016))

15 Ivor Jenkins, a former South African minister, was made a consultant to the government. The Swiss also supported South African initiatives to promote conciliatory meetings and consideration of a Truth and Reconciliation Commission (TRC) for Sri Lanka. Privately, some Sri Lankans held the view that you could not replicate the South African TRC model in Sri Lanka, not least because 'Sri Lanka is a shame culture and not a guilt culture'.

16 N. Fernando, 'The battle for the kingdom he lost', *Colombo Telegraph*, 23 April 2015, www.colombotelegraph.com/index.php/the-battle-for-the-kingdom-he-lost/. A sample from this article:

We want a better system of governance, peace and reconciliation to be established, to put an end to abuse of power and corruption. The rape of mother Lanka including her daughters have gone unpunished. These criminals have to be brought before the courts of the people. Justice and accountability for all have to be established. The future of our country rests upon building a new vision and activism based on a new leadership able to end the 'rogue regime' culture that still lives within the cracks and corners of the Sri Lankan State. We cannot afford the dark ages of Sri Lankan politics to return back and remain silently for the return of the Vampires.

17 The official statement was issued by the UN Security Council on 13 May 2009 as SC/9659, 'Security Council press statement on Sri Lanka'.

18 'Mauritius PM to boycott Sri Lanka Commonwealth meet', *The Times of India*, 13 November 2013, http://timesofindia.indiatimes.com/world/

south-asia/Mauritius-PM-to-boycott-Sri-Lanka-Commonwealth-meet/articleshow/25669609.cms (accessed 4 June 2016).

19 See United Nations Treaty Collection data at https://treaties.un.org/pages/ViewDetails.aspx?src=TREATY&mtdsg_no=IV-4&chapter=4&clang=_en.

20 'GSP plus: Lanka has a long way to go, 27 conventions', Sri Lanka Brief, 14 May 2016, http://srilankabrief.org/2016/05/gsp-plus-lanka-has-a-long-way-to-go-27-conventions (accessed 5 June 2016).

21 The ambitious project was completed successfully in 2015. See 'New China–Myanmar oil pipeline bypasses Malacca trap', *The Hindu*, 30 January 2015, www.thehindu.com/news/international/world/new-chinamyanmar-oil-pipeline-bypasses-malacca-trap/article6839352.ece; 'With oil and gas pipelines, China takes a shortcut through Myanmar', Forbes Asia, 9 February 2015, www.forbes.com/sites/ericrmeyer/2015/02/09/oil-and-gas-china-takes-a-shortcut/#78c4ac4d2d40 (accessed 20 May 2016).

22 'China urges international community not to complicate Sri Lanka issue' Xinhua, 30 April 2011, http://news.xinhuanet.com/english2010/china/2011-04/30/c_13853179.htm (accessed 2 May 2016). According to one estimate, Chinese government lending increased in the decade from 2002 fifty-fold to $490 million in 2012, compared with $211 million from Western countries and lending agencies. See A. Ondaatjie, 'Growing China ties let Sri Lanka rebuff U.S. war inquiry push', Bloomberg, 6 March 2014, www.bloomberg.com/news/articles/2014-03-06/growing-china-ties-let-sri-lanka-rebuff-u-s-war-inquiry-push (accessed 2 March 2015).

23 It is noteworthy that in May 2016 Prime Minister Justin Trudeau issued a statement on the seventh anniversary of the end of the war in Sri Lanka, which included the following comment:

> Tamil-Canadians are an integral part of our country and have overcome much adversity. I extend my deepest sympathy and support to Canadians of Tamil descent.
>
> I am encouraged that the Sri Lankan government is committed to working with the United Nations Human Rights Council and the international community towards seeking accountability in their country. A robust accountability mechanism must enlist the confidence of the victims of this war, through the meaningful engagement of foreign and Commonwealth investigators, prosecutors, and judges. Canada will continue to engage the international community in investigating and addressing serious violations of international law in Sri Lanka and around the world. We stand willing to assist the government of Sri Lanka in fulfilling this commitment. (http://pm.gc.ca/eng/news/2016/05/18/statement-prime-minister-canada-seventh-anniversary-end-war-sri-lanka)

The Trudeau statement is a reminder of how important Tamil diaspora lobbying has been in highlighting human rights abuses at the UNHRC. Diaspora activism as a political force was instrumental in the eventual enactment of (ongoing) reform in Myanmar, and India turned a blind eye to both Burmese dissidents and Nepali opposition groups (during Nepal's civil war) in Delhi so long as they operated lawfully and under the radar. China has long objected to the visibility of the Tibetan diaspora in India under the leadership of the Dalai Lama. There is a Uyghur American Association that has lobbied the US government on human rights concerns in China, and a Kashmiri group in the UK that lobbies on behalf of Kashmir for changes in the policy of India. Diasporas form networks of influence, regardless of whether they come from small states or big powers

24 De Alwis mentions a joke circulating in Colombo which recalls that several centuries ago the King of Kotte elicited the help of the Dutch to get rid of the Portuguese and ended up having the Dutch occupying parts of his kingdom. The new King of Kotte – i.e. President Mahinda Rajapaksa – elicited the help of the Indians and the Chinese to get rid of the LTTE and now these two countries have annexed the entire island: the Chinese have taken the South and the northern half has gone to the Indians. While there is no clear or finite division of northern and southern spheres, or 'spoils', the story highlights Sri Lanka's vulnerable positioning vis-à-vis global and regional power.

25 Moody's, 'The Asia-Pacific debt heat map', which was shared for research by a registered user via email. Registered users may access this at www.moodys.com/research/Moodys-Credit-impact-from-environmental-issues-varies-widely-across-sectors--PR_339980.

26 At time of writing, Sri Lanka was also undergoing or emerging from turmoil in the Central Bank and a major bond-selling scandal. Shepard references Ekanayake (2016) for his work on macro-economic analysis and growing crisis:

> The overall size of the Sri Lankan economy is about US$75 billion in terms of GDP estimation while the volume of public debt has reached $81.2 billion or almost 100 per cent of GDP at the end of 2015. Out of the total debt, foreign debt burden is around $49.2 billion or absorbing almost 34 per cent of export earnings for annual foreign debt repayment while total debt repayment is equalled to the government annual revenue in 2015. During the last regime, borrowing from foreign capital markets at exorbitant rates of interest and shorter repayment periods resulted in extra debt burden while utilising those funds lavishly for White-Elephant-Type projects.

27 'The land the white man took by means of military strength is now being obtained by foreigners paying ransom to a handful of persons ... If this trend continues our country would become a colony and we would become slaves.' This quote is from Sirisena's election manifesto and is quoted in Pearson (2015) 'Why Sri Lanka's election matters for China'.

28 Otherwise known as 'One Belt One Road' information. See www.xinhuanet.com/english/special/silkroad/ (accessed 2 May 2016). For a map and an analysis of the historical context of what has been called the greatest economic diplomacy since the Marshall Plan in Europe following World War Two, see C. Clover and L. Hornby, 'China's great game: road to a new empire', *Financial Times*, 12 October 2015, www.ft.com/cms/s/2/6e098274-587a-11e5-a28b-5022683cd644.html#axzz4Au8MlY7d (accessed 7 June 2016).

29 'Ensure UNHRC proposals won't create new conflicts: China', *Daily Mirror*, 7 June 2016, www.dailymirror.lk/110577/Ensure-UNHRC-proposals-

won-t-create-new-conflicts-China-#sthash.zpcZrog9.Gvqb3Lma.dpuf (accessed 7 June 2016).

> Chinese Ambassador in Sri Lanka, Yi Xianliang yesterday had advised Lankan leaders to see that the reconciliation mechanisms suggested by the UNHRC do not create new conflicts, the Indian News Express said ...
> 'It would be ill advised to put reconciliation before development because it is only all round equitable development which will prevent social, political and economic conflicts,' he said ...
> The envoy said that mutual antagonism in South Asia will be mitigated if China, India and Pakistan form an economic alliance and co-opt Lanka and other South Asian nations. Lanka and India should sign the Economic and Technical Cooperation Agreement (ETCA).

30

> The government's strategy to win the war (and indeed its strategy from mid-2008) was to coral the LTTE and the Tamil population of the north into an ever smaller area. As the LTTE's remaining territory around Mullaitivu and Puthukkudiyiruppu continued to shrink as a result of further SLA advances, the Sri Lankan government declared a limited ceasefire from 1–3 February 2009 to allow civilians to cross out of the war zone and into government-held territory. The LTTE ignored this declaration, however, using the pause to launch a counterattack and restricting the number of civilians allowed to leave its territory sometimes by shooting those who tried to escape (the LTTE's use of civilians as 'human shields' ...). A number of motives underlay the desire of the LTTE to keep Tamil civilians in the conflict zone. Firstly, the LTTE wanted to maintain the outward appearance of a Tamil Eelam state with a territory and a population. Secondly, the presence of civilians in the conflict zone provided a buffer against the SLA. Thirdly, and relatedly, the LTTE calculated that the Sri Lankan military would continue to advance without regard for civilian casualties, and that this would prompt the international community to push for a ceasefire which would allow the LTTE time to regroup. (Richards (2014) 'An institutional history of the Liberation Tigers of Tamil Eelam (LTTE)', p. 64)

31 'Implementing the responsibility to protect: report of the Secretary-General', 12 January 2009, www.un.org/en/ga/search/view_doc.asp?symbol=A/63/677 (accessed 4 June 2016).

32 R. Zongze, 'Responsible protection: building a safer world', China Institute of International Studies, 15 June 2012, www.ciis.org.cn/english/2012-06/15/content_5090912.htm. The following view was expressed from Delhi:

> China had been strictly adhering to its policy of non-interference in internal affairs of other countries. This has enabled it to consistently support Sri Lanka in the UNHRC over the war crimes allegations. As opposed to this India's support had been hesitant and subject to internal pressures from Tamil Nadu. This has created a mental bias in Sri Lanka in favour of China. In the long term, increase in China's role in Sri Lanka's trade and diplomacy could affect India's strategic prospects

well beyond Sri Lanka in the IOR. (R. Hariharan, *Sri Lanka Guardian*, 4 August 2014, www.srilankaguardian.org/2014/08/india-china-and-sri-lanka-uneasy.html (accessed 2 February 2016))

33 O. Stuenkel, 'Responsible protection: Chinese norm entrepreneurship?', Post-Western World, 24 January 2015, www.postwesternworld.com/2015/01/24/responsible-protection-entrepreneurship/ (accessed 4 June 2016).

34 The UN Mission in South Sudan took steps to protect some 65,000 civilians near Bor in 2014, opening its own compounds to take in those who had fled but meeting opposition from government troops and militia fighters. See D. Smith, 'South Sudan soldiers "try to force entry into UN base sheltering civilians"', *The Guardian*, 20 January 2014, www.theguardian.com/world/2014/jan/20/south-sudan-soldiers-united-nations-compound-shelter-civilians (accessed 10 May 2016).

35 Law 387, as it is known, was adopted on 18 July 1997. It remains one of the world's most advanced pieces of legislation in this domain. See M.-H. Verney, 'Challenges remain in implementation of landmark Colombian law', UNHCR, 18 July 2007, www.unhcr.org/news/latest/2007/7/469e2c3b4/challenges-remain-implementation-landmark-colombian-law.html (accessed 28 May 2016).

36 Interview with two high-ranking UNHCR officials (with extensive field experience) based in Geneva, 9 May 2016. The UNHCR undertook its own system-wide review, contributing to the Inter-Agency Standing Committee on the Centrality of Protection in Humanitarian Action, and applying new thinking on access to rights and innovation in response, for example in the Central African Republic.

37 The 9 June 2016 hearings were held in Washington on Sri Lanka's democratic transition. See https://democrats-foreignaffairs.house.gov/legislation/hearings/sri-lanka-s-democratic-transition-new-era-us-sri-lanka-relationship. The US government had already initiated a special partnership programme with the GoSL as well as military assistance and new offers of aid.

38 'Art through the lens of war: Muttrupulliyaa ...?', International Policy Digest, 17 September 2014, http://intpolicydigest.org/2014/09/17/art-lens-muttrupulliyaa/ (accessed 12 June 2016).

39 T. Paramsothy, 'Ritual & recovery in post-conflict Sri Lanka', *Colombo Telegraph*, 20 March 2015, www.colombotelegraph.com/index.php/ritual-recovery-in-post-conflict-sri-lanka/ (accessed 22 May 2016).

40 Credit for these observations goes in full to David Whaley, who was present at the Geneva proceedings in June 2016 and shared his record of them by email.

41 General Augusto Pinochet led a seventeen-year regime in Chile that was responsible for mass human rights violations. He was indicted in Spain in 1998 and subsequently arrested in London. He died before being convicted but had over 300 criminal charges levelled against him.

42 The Human Rights Council resolution of 2014 arose following non-compliance with 2013 UNHRC requests to Sri Lanka, but it lacked teeth or full sanctions, calling instead for a full investigation into allegations of human rights violations and war crimes committed at the end of the war. In light of the change of government in Colombo, an unusual step was taken

by the High Commissioner to delay for six months the presentation of the ensuing report in 2015. See 'Zeid requests "one time only" deferral of key report on Sri Lanka conflict', OHCHR, 16 February 2015, www.ohchr.org/EN/NewsEvents/Pages/DisplayNews.aspx?NewsID=15574 (accessed 2 August 2016). See also Oakland Institute (2016).

43 'Good governance will solve Geneva issue', *Daily News*, 1 June 2016, www.dailynews.lk/?q=2016/06/01/political/83381 (accessed 10 June 2016).

44 Both the nature of the dance and the need for continual international interest are expressed by Nirmanusan Balasundaram thus:

> Critics have noted that Sri Lanka has held the belief that prolonging this issue, through engaging in a process of time and space buying, will eventually lead to the eradication of the justice and accountability issue from the international agenda ... Sri Lanka's president said in an interview that 'nations which had distanced themselves and the UN are now friendly with us. The loud cries of war crimes allegations have receded. The loud cries for setting up War Crimes Tribunal to probe the allegation have ceased too.' His comments serve as a clear indication of the absence of political will by the Sri Lankan government. ('Sri Lanka wants the world to forget about justice for war victims. Please don't', *The Guardian*, 27 June 2016, www.theguardian.com/commentisfree/2016/jun/27/sri-lanka-wants-the-world-to-forget-about-justice-for-war-victims-please-dont (accessed 2 August 2016))

BIBLIOGRAPHY

Abdelal, R. and Krotz, U. (2014) 'Disjoining partners: Europe and the American imperium' in Pauly, L. W. and Jefferson, B. W. (eds) *Power in a Complex Global System*. Abingdon: Routledge.
ADB (2003) 'Sri Lanka civil society: an overview'. Civil Society Brief. Mandaluyong City, Philippines: Asian Development Bank (ADB). Available at www.adb.org/publications/civil-society-briefs-sri-lanka (accessed 5 December 2016).
Aftenposten (2011) '06.05.2009: Sri Lanka President discusses humanitarian assistance with co-chair ambassadors'. Aftenposten [online], updated 12 October 2011. Available at www.aftenposten.no/spesial/wikileaksdokumenter/06052009-SRI-LANKA-PRESIDENT-DISCUSSES-HUMANITARIAN-ASSISTANCE-WITH-CO-CHAIR-AMBASSADORS-5118526.html (accessed 3 November 2015).
Agence France-Presse (2005) 'US marines end Sri Lanka tsunami mission, foreign troops set to leave'. Relief Web [online], 10 February. Available at http://reliefweb.int/report/sri-lanka/us-marines-end-sri-lanka-tsunami-mission-foreign-troops-set-leave (accessed 3 March 2015).
Al Jazeera (2010) 'Profile: Mahinda Rajapaksa'. Al Jazeera, 19 November. Available at www.aljazeera.com/focus/2010/01/20101281759855487.html (accessed 3 October 2012).
Al Jazeera (2015) 'Sri Lanka's PM defeats ex-president in elections'. Al Jazeera [online], 19 August. Available at www.aljazeera.com/news/2015/08/sri-lanka-elections-150818133605788.html (accessed 28 March 2016).
Al Jazeera (2016) 'Sri Lankan president: no allegations of war crimes'. Al Jazeera [online], 29 January. Available at www.aljazeera.com/programmes/talktojazeera/2016/01/sri-lankan-president-allegations-war-crimes-160128150748006.html (accessed 20 February 2016).
Alden, C. and Large, D. (2015) 'On becoming a norms maker: Chinese foreign policy, norms evolution and the challenges of security in Africa'. *The China Quarterly* 221: 123–42.
Aldridge, D. (1989) 'How the ship of interpretation was blown off course in the tempest: some philosophical thoughts' in Uzzell, D. (ed.) *Heritage Interpretation. Vol. 1: The natural and built environment*. London: Belhaven, pp. 77–8.
Ameen, A. (2016) 'Sri Lanka President wants "internal" crimes court'. BBC News [online], 21 January. Available at www.bbc.co.uk/news/world-asia-35376719 (accessed 4 May 2016).
Ameresekere, N. S. (2011) *Fiscal Mismanagement: Lack of public accountability. Case Study Sri Lanka: A country under the purview of IMF, World Bank and ADB*. Milton Keynes: Author House.

Amnesty International (2010) 'Sri Lanka: end witch hunt against the media and NGOs'. Amnesty International, 10 March. Available at www.amnesty.org/en/press-releases/2010/03/sri-lanka-end-witch-hunt-against-media-and-ngos/ (accessed 10 January 2016).

Amnesty International (2011) *When Will They Get Justice? Failures of Sri Lanka's Lessons Learned and Reconciliation Commission*. London: Amnesty International. Available at www.amnesty.org/en/documents/ASA37/008/2011/en/ (accessed 7 January 2014).

Anderson, B. (1983) *Imagined Communities: Reflections on the Origin and Spread of Nationalism*. London: Verso.

Anketell, N. and Welikala, A. (2013) 'A systemic crisis in context: the impeachment of the Chief Justice, the independence of the judiciary and the rule of law in Sri Lanka'. Policy Brief. Colombo: Centre for Policy Alternatives, p. 23.

Appadurai, A. (ed.) (2001) *Globalization*. Durham, NC: Duke University Press.

Asian Human Rights Commission (2007) 'Sri Lanka: ICJ concerned about grave human rights situation and effectiveness of criminal justice system'. Asian Human Rights Commission [online], 15 June. Available at www.humanrights.asia/news/forwarded-news/AHRC-FP-009-2007 (accessed 2 March 2015).

Asian Tribune (2009) 'As China adheres to non-interference it supported Sri Lanka in the multilateral fora'. *Asian Tribune*, 7 July. Available at http://asiantribune.com/node/21646 (accessed 2 July 2015).

Asian Tribune (2010) 'No nation on earth can wish Sri Lanka's Tamil community more good fortune than Sri Lanka itself – President Mahinda in the UN'. *Asian Tribune*, 24 September. Available at www.asiantribune.com/news/2010/09/24/no-nation-earth-can-wish-sri-lanka%E2%80%99s-tamil-community-more-good-fortune-sri-lanka-its (accessed 10 January 2014).

Bandarage, A. (2009) *The Separatist Conflict in Sri Lanka: Terrorism, ethnicity, political economy*. Abingdon: Routledge.

Bar-Tal, D. and Bennink, G. H. (2004) 'The nature of reconciliation as an outcome and as a process' in Bar-Siman-Tov, Y. (ed.) *From Conflict Resolution to Reconciliation*. Oxford: Oxford University Press.

Barta, P. (2014) 'In Sri Lanka's post-tsunami rise China is key'. *The Wall Street Journal*, 18 December. Available at www.wsj.com/articles/in-sri-lankas-post-tsunami-rise-china-is-key-1418938382 (accessed 2 July 2015).

Bastian, S. (2013) 'The political economy of post-war Sri Lanka'. ICES Research Paper 7. Colombo: International Centre for Ethnic Studies (ICES).

Bastians, D. (2014) 'Sri Lanka: the road from Geneva'. Sri Lanka Brief [online], 6 February. Available at http://srilankabrief.org/2014/02/sri-lanka-the-road-from-geneva/ (accessed 3 June 2015).

BBC News (2014) 'Sri Lanka moderate monk critical of anti-Muslim violence beaten'. BBC News [online], 19 June. Available at www.bbc.co.uk/news/world-asia-27918343 (accessed 19 January 2016).

BBC News (2015) 'Sri Lanka's Rajapaksa suffers shock election defeat'. BBC News [online], 15 January. Available at www.bbc.co.uk/news/world-asia-30738671 (accessed 28 March 2016).

Becker, J. (2013) *Campaigning for Justice: Human rights and advocacy in practice*. Stanford, CA: Stanford University Press.
Behuria, A. K. (2011) 'Rajapaksa's Sri Lanka: time to move beyond complacency'. *Strategic Analysis* 35(5): 739–44.
Behuria, A. and Sultana, G. (2013) 'MR's India policy: engage and countervail'. *Strategic Analysis* 37(1): 84–100.
Bevan, R. (2014) 'Culture wars: tracking the destruction of Middle East monuments'. *Evening Standard* [online], 27 August. Available at www.standard.co.uk/news/world/culture-wars-tracking-the-destruction-of-middle-east-monuments-9693006.html (accessed January 16 2015).
Bhadrakumar, M. K. (2009) 'Sri Lanka wards off Western bullying'. *Asia Times* [online], 27 May. Available at www.atimes.com/atimes/South_Asia/KE27Dfo1.html (accessed 19 June 2015).
Bhikkhu, T. (1999) 'The customs of the noble ones'. [Online.] Available at www.accesstoinsight.org/lib/authors/thanissaro/customs.html (accessed 20 January 2015).
Biziouras, N. (2014) *The Political Economy of Ethnic Conflict in Sri Lanka*. Abingdon: Routledge.
Borger, J. (2010) 'WikiLeaks cables: "Sri Lankan President responsible for massacre of Tamils"'. *The Guardian*, 4 December. Available at www.theguardian.com/world/2010/dec/01/wikileaks-sri-lanka-mahinda-rajapaksa (accessed 4 December 2010).
Brounéus, K. (2003) *Reconciliation: Theory and practice for development cooperation*. Stockholm: Swedish International Development Cooperation Agency.
Buchanan, E. (2015) 'Sri Lanka's new government to investigate Mahinda Rajapaksa corruption allegations'. *International Business Times*, January 16. Available at www.ibtimes.co.uk/sri-lankas-new-government-investigate-mahinda-rajapaksa-corruption-allegations-1483812 (accessed 2 February 2016).
Burke, A. and Mulakala, A. (2005) *Donors and Peacebuilding: Part of the Sri Lanka strategic conflict assessment 2005*. Washington, DC: World Bank, p. 26. Available at http://documents.worldbank.org/curated/en/2005/01/14551123/donors-peacebuilding-part-sri-lanka-strategic-conflict-assessment-2005-2000-2005 (accessed 20 February 2015).
Burke, A. and Mulakala, A. (2011) 'An insider's view of donor support' in Goodhand, J., Spencer, J. and Korf, B. (eds) *Conflict and Peacebuilding in Sri Lanka: Caught in the peace trap?* Abingdon: Routledge, pp. 150–67.
Bush, K. (1998) '1998 Peace and Conflict Impact Assessment (PCIA)'. Berlin: Berghof Foundation. Available at www.berghof-foundation.org/fileadmin/.../dialogue1_bush.pdf (accessed 12 January 2015).
Bush, K. (2003a) *The Intra-Group Dimensions of Ethnic Conflict in Sri Lanka*. Basingstoke and New York: Palgrave.
Bush, K. (2003b) 'PCIA five years on: the commodification of an idea'. Berlin: Berghof Foundation. Available at www.berghof-foundation.org/fileadmin/redaktion/Publications/Handbook/Dialogue_Chapters/dialogue1_bush.pdf (accessed 10 October 2015).
Buthpitiya, V. (2013) 'Reconciling rights, responsibilities and disjunctures: an assessment of Sri Lanka as post war development hub'. Colombo: Law

& Society Trust. Available at www.lawandsocietytrust.org/PDF/resource/srilanka_post_war.pdf (accessed 14 May 2015).

Carman, J. (1996) *Valuing Ancient Things: Archaeology and law*. London Leicester University Press.

Carothers, T. and Brechenmacher, S. (2014) *Closing Space: Democracy and human rights support under fire*. Washington, DC: Carnegie Endowment for International Peace. Available at http://carnegieendowment.org/2014/02/20/closing-space-democracy-and-human-rights-support-under-fire (accessed 2 March 2015).

Carver, F. (2014) 'The Sri Lankan Government is crushing dissent'. International Policy Digest [online], 9 August. Available at http://intpolicydigest.org/2014/08/09/the-sri-lankan-government-is-crushing-dissent/ (accessed 17 March 2016).

Chaaminda, S. (2012) 'Fishing in turbulent waters'. ICES Working Paper. Colombo: International Centre for Ethnic Studies (ICES).

Chan, L.-H. (2011) *China Engages Global Health Governance: Responsible stakeholder or system-transformer?* London: Palgrave Macmillan.

Chandler, D. (2006) *Empire in Denial: The politics of statebuilding*. London: Pluto Press.

Chandraprema, C. A. (2012) *Gota's War: The crushing of Tamil Tiger terrorism in Sri Lanka*. Colombo: Ranjan Wijeratne Foundation.

Chapman, N., Duncan, D., Timberman, D. and Abeygunawardana, K. (2009) *Evaluation of Donor-supported Activities in Conflict Sensitive Development and Conflict Prevention and Peacebuilding in Sri Lanka: Main evaluation report*. Paris: Organisation for Economic Co-operation and Development. Available at www.oecd.org/countries/srilanka/44138006.pdf (accessed 14 July 2015).

Chulov, M. and Shaheen, K. (2016) 'Crisis exposes UN's failure to provide aid'. *The Guardian*, 4 February.

CIVICUS, Commonwealth Human Rights Initiative, FORUM-Asia, Human Rights Law Centre of Australia, Human Rights Watch, Sri Lanka Campaign for Peace and Justice and United Nations Association of the UK (2012) 'Open letter to the Commonwealth Secretary-General'. 21 September. Available at www.civicus.org/images/Open_Letter_to_the_Commonwealth_Secretary_General__21_09_2012.pdf (accessed 24 February 2016).

Clarance, W. (2007) *Ethnic Warfare in Sri Lanka and the UN Crisis*. London and Colombo: Pluto Press and Vijitha Yapa Publications.

Cochrane, F., Duffy, R. and Selby, J. (eds) (2003) *Global Governance, Conflict and Resistance*. Basingstoke: Palgrave Macmillan.

Colman, P. (2010) 'Sri Lanka and the 18th Amendment'. *Le Monde Diplomatique*, 10 September. Available at http://mondediplo.com/blogs/sri-lanka-and-the-18th-amendment (accessed 23 November 2014).

Colombo Telegraph (2010) 'Mannar bishop questioned by Sri Lankan CID on "disappearances"'. *Colombo Telegraph* [online], 10 May. Available at www.colombotelegraph.com/index.php/mannar-bishop-questioned-by-sri-lankan-cid-on-disappearances/ (accessed 10 May 2016).

Colombo Telegraph (2012) 'Expose: full text of Sharma's buried report: impeachment violated Commonwealth principles, sowed seeds of anarchy'.

Bibliography | 235

Colombo Telegraph [online], 9 September. Available at www.colombotelegraph. com/index.php/expose-full-text-of-sharmas-buried-report-impeachment-violated-cwealth-principles-sowed-seeds-of-anarchy/ (accessed October 2013).

Colombo Telegraph (2013) 'Sri Lanka blocks freedom of movement during CHOGM'. *Colombo Telegraph* [online], 13 November. Available at www.colombotelegraph.com/index.php/sri-lanka-blocks-freedom-of-movement-during-chogm/ (accessed 5 December 2013).

Colombo Telegraph (2014a) 'Rajapaksa's daily cost to taxpayer a staggering Rs 23.4 million: Sobitha Thera'. *Colombo Telegraph* [online], 29 August. Available at www.colombotelegraph.com/index.php/rajapaksas-daily-cost-to-taxpayer-a-staggering-rs-23-4-million-sobitha-thera/ (accessed 12 March 2015).

Colombo Telegraph (2014b) 'OIC questions govt. over its links with BBS'. *Colombo Telegraph* [online], 21 June. Available at www.colombotelegraph. com/index.php/oic-questions-govt-over-its-links-with-bbs/ (accessed 3 February 2015).

Colombo Telegraph (2015) 'Reject the UN war crimes report: Mahinda Rajapaksa tells govt.' *Colombo Telegraph* [online], 22 September. Available at www.colombotelegraph.com/index.php/reject-the-un-war-crimes-report-mahinda-rajapaksa-tells-govt/ (accessed 4 May 2016).

Colombo Telegraph (2016) 'Rajapaksa sentenced Sri Lanka into a 10 trillion debt trap: PM Wickremesinghe'. *Colombo Telegraph* [online], 9 March. Available at www.colombotelegraph.com/index.php/rajapaksa-sentenced-sri-lanka-into-a-10-trillion-debt-trap-pm-wickremesinghe/.

Cowell, F. (2013) 'Commonwealth hamstrung to fight abuse in Sri Lanka'. The Conversation [online], 15 November. Available at http://theconversation. com/commonwealth-hamstrung-to-fight-abuse-in-sri-lanka-20192 (accessed 15 January 2016).

CPA (2009) 'Civil society fact finding report to Vavuniya', September 2008, cited in *A Profile of Human Rights Issues in the Vanni and Vavuniya*. Colombo: Centre for Policy Alternatives (CPA). Available at http://cpalanka. org/wp-content/uploads/2009/3/Vanni_Report.pdf (accessed 2 May 2015).

CPA (2013) 'Attacks on places of religious worship in post-war Sri Lanka'. Colombo: Centre for Policy Alternatives (CPA). Available at www.cpalanka. org/attacks-on-places-of-religious-worship-in-post-war-sri-lanka/ (accessed 5 March 2015).

CPA (2015) 'Reconciliation and ways forward'. Colombo: Centre for Policy Alternatives (CPA).

CPA (2016a) 'Preliminary submission by the Centre for Policy Alternatives (CPA) to the Public Representation Commission'. Colombo: Centre for Policy Alternatives (CPA). Available at www.cpalanka.org/wp-content/uploads/2016/01/CPA-Submission-to-the-PRC-Final.pdf (accessed 2 March 2016).

CPA (2016b) *Hybrid vs. Domestic: Myths, realities and options for transitional justice in Sri Lanka*. Colombo: Centre for Policy Alternatives (CPA). Available at www.cpalanka.org/wp-content/uploads/2016/01/Hybrid-vs.-Domestic-Myths-Realities-and-Options-for-Transitional-Justice-in-Sri-Lanka.pdf.

Crawford, A. (2009) 'Sri Lanka: 12 killed at hospital'. Sky News, 2 February. Available at http://news.sky.com/story/667068/packed-sri-lanka-hospital-shelled (accessed 22 January 2014).

Crawley, W., Page, D. and Pinto-Jayawardena, K. (2015) *Embattled Media: Democracy, governance and reform in Sri Lanka*. New Delhi: Sage Publications.

Daily Mirror (2012) 'Navi Pillay warns Sri Lanka'. *Daily Mirror* [online], 23 March. Available at www.dailymirror.lk/17609/tech (accessed 5 February 2016).

Daily Mirror (2013) 'China asks SL to protect and promote human rights'. *Daily Mirror* [online], 18 November. Available at www.dailymirror.lk/38914/china-asks-sl-to-protect-and-promote-human-rights#sthash.PpxdTsmo.dpuf (accessed 2 March 2016).

Daily Mirror (2014) 'Pakistan must learn from LTTE's defeat – Pakistan officer'. *Daily Mirror* [online], 13 July. Available at www.dailymirror.lk/49644/pakistan-must-learn-from-lttes-defeat-pakistan-officer#sthash.3StdK8AZ.dpuf (accessed 13 August 2014).

Daniel, S. (2013) 'Hundreds of students arrested in Chennai for anti-Lanka protests'. NDTV [online], 18 March. Available at www.ndtv.com/india-news/hundreds-of-students-arrested-in-chennai-for-anti-lanka-protests-516551 (accessed 25 March 2015).

Dayal, S. (2015) 'Atrocities in the frame'. openDemocracy [online], 11 May. Available at www.opendemocracy.net/samir-dayal/atrocities-in-frame (accessed 4 June 2016).

De Alwis, M. (2010) 'The China factor in post-war Sri Lanka'. *Inter-Asia Cultural Studies* 11(3): 434–46. Available at http://dx.doi.org/10.1080/14649373.2010.484201.

de Mel, N. (2013) 'The promise of the LLRC: women's testimony and justice in post-war Sri Lanka'. ICES Research Paper 4. Colombo: International Centre for Ethnic Studies (ICES).

de Silva, J. (2005) *Globalisation, Terror and the Shaming of a Nation: Constructing local masculinities in a Sri Lankan village*. Bloomington, IN: Trafford Publishing.

Deegalle, M. (2003) 'Is violence justified in Theravāda Buddhism?' *The Ecumenical Review* 55(2): 122–31.

Deen, T. (2014) 'UN chief urges Sri Lanka to protect Muslims under attack'. Inter Press Service News Agency [online], 3 July. Available at www.ipsnews.net/2014/07/u-n-chief-urges-sri-lanka-to-protect-muslims-under-attack/ (accessed 10 August 2015).

Demmers, J. (2012) *Theories of Violent Conflict*. Abingdon: Routledge.

Department of National Planning (2010) *Sri Lanka: The emerging Wonder of Asia. Mahinda Chintana – vision for the future*. Colombo: Development of National Planning and Ministry of Finance and Planning. Available at www.adb.org/sites/default/files/linked-documents/cps-sri-2012-2016-oth-01.pdf (accessed 15 February 2014).

DeVotta, N. (2007) 'Sinhalese Buddhist nationalist ideology: implications for politics and conflict resolution'. Policy Studies Paper 40. Washington, DC: East-West Centre. Available at www.eastwestcenter.org/publications/

sinhalese-buddhist-nationalist-ideology-implications-politics-and-conflict-resolution-s (accessed 10 August 2015).
DeVotta, N. (2013) 'Sri Lanka's ongoing shift to authoritarianism under Rajapaksa and his cronies'. *Colombo Telegraph*, 23 February. Available at www.colombotelegraph.com/index.php/sri-lankas-ongoing-shift-to-authoritarianism-under-rajapaksa-and-his-cronies/ (accessed 1 March 2014).
DeVotta, N. (2015) 'Sri Lanka: from counter-terrorism to soft authoritarianism' in Jarvis, L. and Lister, M. (eds) *Critical Perspectives on Counter-terrorism*. Abingdon: Routledge, pp. 210–30.
Dewasiri, N. R. (2013) '"History" after the war: historical consciousness in the collective Sinhala-Buddhist psyche in post-war Sri Lanka'. ICES Research Paper 9. Colombo: International Centre for Ethnic Studies (ICES).
Dibbert, T. (2014) 'Sri Lanka's NGO clampdown'. The South Asia Channel, FP Group [online], 25 July. Available at http://foreignpolicy.com/2014/07/25/sri-lankas-ngo-clampdown/ (accessed 20 September 2015).
Dingwerth, K. and Pattberg, P. (2006) 'Global governance as a perspective on world politics'. *Global Governance: A Review of Multilateralism and International Organizations* 12(3): 195.
Doole, C. (2016) 'Advent of "Sinha-le" movement reawakening the racial monster'. Sri Lanka Brief [online], 14 January. Available at http://srilankabrief.org/2016/01/advent-of-sinha-le-movement-reawakening-the-racial-monster/ (accessed 15 September 2015).
Duffield, M. (2001) 'Governing the borderlands: decoding the power of aid'. *Disasters* 25(4): 308–20.
Duffield, M. (2014 [2001]) *Global Governance and the New Wars*. London: Zed Books.
During, R. (ed.) (2011) *Cultural Heritage and Identity Politics*. n.p.: Silk Road Research Foundation. Available at https://slkrd.files.wordpress.com/2011/09/978-94-6173-076-3-cultural-e1.pdf (accessed 16 January 2015).
Easterly, W. (2014) *The Tyranny of Experts: Economists, dictators, and the forgotten rights of the poor*. New York: Basic Books.
Edrisinha, R. (2010) 'Sri Lanka'. *International Journal of Not-for-Profit Law* 12(3): 35–40. Available at www.icnl.org/research/journal/vol12iss3/special_5.htm (accessed 2 January 2015).
Edrisinha, R. and Selvakkumaran, N. (1990) 'Constitutional change in Sri Lanka since independence'. *Sri Lanka Journal of Social Sciences* 13(1&2): 79–103.
Ekanayake, P. (2016) 'Sri Lanka is on the door-step of a public debt-driven economic crisis'. *The Sunday Times*, 20 March. Available at www.sundaytimes.lk/160320/business-times/sri-lanka-is-on-the-door-step-of-a-public-debt-driven-economic-crisis-186653.html.
Escobar, A. (1995) *Encountering Development: The making and unmaking of the Third World*. Princeton, NJ: Princeton University Press.
EU (2013) 'Declaration by the High Representative, Catherine Ashton, on behalf of the EU on the impeachment of Sri Lankan Chief Justice'. European Union (EU), 13 January. Available at www.consilium.europa.eu/uedocs/cms_Data/docs/pressdata/en/cfsp/134837.pdf (accessed 24 August 2015).

Faaiz, A. M. (2014) 'Stop blaming the victims'. *Colombo Telegraph* [online], 5 July. Available at www.colombotelegraph.com/index.php/stop-blaming-the-victims/ (accessed 4 September 2015).

Fernandez, M. (2013) 'Sri Lanka: a tale of two chief justices'. Al Jazeera [online], 18 January. Available at www.aljazeera.com/indepth/features/2013/01/2013 117122157590337.html (accessed 16 July 2015).

Fernando, J. (2015) 'Heritage & nationalism: a bane of Sri Lanka'. *Colombo Telegraph* [online], 30 March. Available at www.colombotelegraph.com/index.php/heritage-nationalism-a-bane-of-sri-lanka/ (accessed 10 September 2015).

Fernando, L. (2013) 'April 1971 JVP uprising: not to make the same mistake again'. *The Island* [online], 12 April. Available at www.island.lk/index.php?page_cat=article-details&page=article-details&code_title=76058 (accessed 22 January 2015).

Ferreiro, M. (2012) 'Blurring of lines in complex emergencies: consequences for the humanitarian community'. *The Journal of Humanitarian Assistance*, 24 December. Available at http://sites.tufts.edu/jha/archives/1625 (accessed 15 March 2016).

Fidler, D. P., Kim, S. W. and Ganguly, S. (2009) 'Eastphalia rising?: Asian influence and the fate of human security'. *Articles by Maurer Faculty*. Paper 114. Available at www.repository.law.indiana.edu/facpub/114.

Firstpost.com (2013) 'Chinese makes its presence felt at CHOGM summit in Sri Lanka'. Firstpost.com [online], 17 November. Available at www.firstpost.com/world/chinese-makes-its-presence-felt-at-chogm-summit-in-sri-lanka-1235057.html (accessed 1 April 2015).

Fonseka, B. (2015) 'Exploring international and domestic modalities for truth and justice in Sri Lanka'. Groundviews [online], 9 February. Available at http://groundviews.org/2015/02/09/exploring-international-and-domestic-modalities-for-truth-and-justice-in-sri-lanka/ (accessed 15 May 2015).

Fonseka, B. and Ganeshathasan, L. (2016) *Hybrid vs. Domestic: Myths, realities and options for transitional justice in Sri Lanka*. Colombo: Centre for Policy Alternatives. Available at www.cpalanka.org/wp-content/uploads/2016/01/Hybrid-vs.-Domestic-Myths-Realities-and-Options-for-Transitional-Justice-in-Sri-Lanka.pdf (accessed 2 February 2016).

Foreman, A. (2015) 'Mercy in victory is as ancient as war'. *The Wall Street Journal* [online], 2 April. Available at www.wsj.com/articles/mercy-in-victory-is-as-ancient-as-war-1427985451 (accessed 2 August 2015).

Foucault, M. (1991) 'Governmentality' in Burchell, G., Gordon, C. and Miller, P. (eds) *The Foucault Effect*. London: Harvester Wheatsheaf.

Frerks, G. and Van Leeuwn, M. (2000) *The Netherlands and Sri Lanka: Dutch policies and intervention with regard to the conflict in Sri Lanka*. The Hague: Netherlands Institute of International Relations 'Clingendael'. Available at www.clingendael.nl/sites/default/files/20000000_cru_paper_frerks.pdf (accessed 5 July 2016).

Fuller, P. (2014) 'Speech by the Ven. Galagoda Atte Gnanasara Thero of the BBS'. Paul Fuller: Buddhist Studies [blog], 4 October. Available at drpaulfuller.wordpress.com/2014/10/04/speech-by-ven-galagoda-atte-gnanasara-thero-of-the-bbs/ (accessed 2 March 2016).

Furedi, F. (1994) 'The moral rehabilitation of imperialism' in *The New Ideology of Imperialism*. London: Pluto Press.
Gamage, D. (2015) 'Sri Lanka buying US congressmen'. *Asian Tribune* [online], 6 March. Available at www.asiantribune.com/node/86522 (accessed 2 August 2015).
Ganeshathasan, L. and Mendis, M. (2015) 'Policy brief: devolution in the Northern Province September 2013–February 2015'. Colombo: Centre for Policy Alternatives.
GDRC (1995) *Our Global Neighborhood: The Report of the Commission on Global Governance*. Kobe: Global Development Research Center (GDRC). Available at www.gdrc.org/u-gov/global-neighbourhood/ (accessed 10 July 2015).
Geiger, W. (1912) *Mahavamsa: The Great Chronicle of Ceylon*. London: Pali Text Society, Oxford University Press. Available at http://what-buddhasaid. net/library/pdfs/mahavamsa.geiger.pdf (accessed 2 February 2015).
Gill, P. (2016) *Today We Drop Bombs, Tomorrow We Build Bridges: How foreign aid became a casualty of war*. London: Zed Books.
Glatz, A.-K. (2014) 'Almost five years of peace but tens of thousands of war-displaced still without solution'. Internal Displacement Monitoring Centre [online], 4 February. Available at www.internal-displacement.org/south-and-south-east-asia/sri-lanka/2014/almost-five-years-of-peace-but-tens-of-thousands-of-war-displaced-still-without-solution/ (accessed 15 January 2015).
Global Peace Support (2006) 'Sri Lanka: the following of a Lee Kwan Yew model aggravated the Sri Lankan ethnic crisis'. Global Peace Support, 25 July. Available at www.globalpeacesupport.com/globalpeacesupport.com/post/2011/07/06/SRI-LANKA-The-following-of-a-Lee-Kwan-Yew-model-aggravated-the-Sri-Lankan-e280a6e280a6.aspx (accessed September 2011).
Godbole, A. (2015) 'Did the Chinese model of growth defeat Rajapaksa?' Institute for Defence Studies and Analyses [online], 12 January. Available at www.idsa.in/idsacomments/DidtheChineseModelofGrowthDefeatRajapaksa _AvinashGodbole_120115.html (accessed 4 November 2015).
Goodhand, J. (2010) 'Stabilizing a victor's peace: humanitarian action and reconstruction in East Sri Lanka'. *Disasters* 34(S3): S342–67. Available at www.researchgate.net/publication/46818471_%27Stabilising_a_victor%27s_ peace_Humanitarian_action_and_reconstruction_in_east_Sri_Lanka%27.
Goodhand, J., Rampton, D., Venugopal, R. and de Mel, N. (2011) 'Sri Lanka strategic policy assessment 2011'. Available at http://personal.lse.ac.uk/ venugopr/Sri%20Lanka%20Strategic%20Policy%20Assessment%202011. pdf (accessed 2 April 2016).
Gowing, R. (2013) 'War by other means: an analysis of the contested terrain of transitional justice under the "Victor's Peace" in Sri Lanka'. LSE Working Paper 13-138. London: Development Studies Institute, London School of Economics and Political Science (LSE).
Gowrinathan, N. and Mampilly, Z. (2009) 'Aid and access in Sri Lanka'. *Humanitarian Exchange* No. 43. London: Overseas Development Institute (ODI).
Gravers, M. (2015) 'Anti-Muslim Buddhist nationalism in Burma and Sri Lanka: religious violence and globalized imaginaries of endangered identities'. *Contemporary Buddhism* 16(1): 1–27.

Gray, N. (2012) 'Written by the victors: the teaching of Sri Lankan history' in *Beyond the Wall*. Colombo: Home for Human Rights.

Groundviews (2010a) 'Media reports – Tamil – Killinochchi – Mullaitivu sessions'. LLRC Archives [online], 19 September. Available at www.llrcarchive.org/2010/09/newspaper-reports-killinochchi-and-mullaitivu-sessions/ (accessed 2 May 2013).

Groundviews (2010b) 'Translation of Tamil newspaper reports on the Lessons Learnt and Reconciliation Commission hearings held in Killinochchi and Mullaitivu'. Groundviews [online], 19 September. Available at http://groundviews.org/2010/09/23/translation-of-tamil-newspaper-reports-on-the-lessons-learnt-reconciliation-commission-hearings-held-in-killinochchi-and-mullaitivu/ (accessed 4 April 2016).

Groundviews (2010c) '"Learning lessons" from those affected by war: does the Lessons Learnt and Reconciliation Commission really listen?' Groundviews [online], 24 September. Available at http://groundviews.org/2010/09/24/%E2%80%98learning-lessons%E2%80%99-from-those-affected-by-war-does-the-lessons-learnt-and-reconciliation-commission-really-listen/ (accessed 2 September 2014).

Groundviews (2012) 'The death of freedom of assembly, expression and religion in the North of Sri Lanka'. Groundviews [online], 1 December. Available at http://groundviews.org/2012/12/01/the-death-of-freedom-of-assembly-expression-and-religion-in-the-north-of-sri-lanka/ (accessed 7 May 2013).

Gunasekara, T. (2010) 'Rajapaksa governance'. *Sunday Leader*, 24 May. Available at www.thesundayleader.lk/2010/05/23/rajapaksa-governance/ (accessed 6 March 2014).

Gunasekara, T. (2011) 'Rajapaksa devolution'. *Himal Southasian* [online], July. Available at http://old.himalmag.com/component/content/article/4548-rajapakse-devolution.html (accessed 1 December 2011).

Gunasekara, T. (2014a) 'War, peace and the manufacturing of Rajapaksa myths'. Groundviews [online], 28 May. Available at http://groundviews.org/2014/05/28/war-peace-and-the-manufacturing-of-rajapaksa-myths/ (accessed 2 April 2015).

Gunasekara, T. (2014b) 'Buddhism, Sinhala-Buddhism, and Rajapaksa-Buddhism'. *Sri Lankan Guardian* [online], 10 April. Available at www.srilankaguardian.org/2014/04/buddhism-sinhala-buddhism-and-rajapaksa.html (accessed 10 July 2015).

Gunatilleke, G. (2015) *Confronting the Complexity of Loss: Perspectives on truth, memory & justice in Sri Lanka*. Colombo: Law & Society Trust. Available at http://lawandsocietytrust.org/content_images/publications/documents/truth%20memory%20%20justice_final%20-%20a5.pdf.

Gunawardena, D. (2015) 'Contradictions of the Sri Lankan state'. *Economic and Political Weekly* 1(9): 56.

Guruparan, K. (2015a) 'Flawed expectations: the executive presidency, resolving the national question and Tamils' in Welikala, A. (ed.) *Reforming Sri Lankan Presidentialism: Provenance, problems and prospects*. Colombo: Centre for Policy Alternatives.

Guruparan, K. (2015b) 'Why Sirisena's victory is not a victory for Sri Lanka's Tamils'. *The Caravan* [online], 13 January. Available at www.

caravanmagazine.in/vantage/why-sirisenas-victory-not-victory-sri-lankas-tamils (accessed 25 January 2015).
Haniffa, A. (2009) 'US shelves evacuation of Tamils caught in LTTE areas'. Rediff India Abroad [online], 12 March. Available at www.rediff.com/news/2009/mar/12us-shelves-evacuation-plan-for-tamils-from-ltte-areas-inlanka.htm (accessed 15 December 2015).
Harmer, C. (2014) 'Book review: *Global Governance and the New Wars* by Mark Duffield'. Available at http://blogs.lse.ac.uk/lsereviewofbooks/2014/04/15/book-review-global-governance-and-the-new-wars-mark-duffield/ (accessed 15 December 2015).
Harris, E. J. (2005) 'Detachment and compassion in early Buddhism'. Available at www.accesstoinsight.org/lib/authors/harris/bl141.html (accessed 20 January 2015).
Harris, S. (2005) 'Sri Lanka: aid effectiveness – a scoping of development partner perceptions for DFID-SEA'. Revised Draft. London: Department for International Development. Available at http://webarchive.nationalarchives.gov.uk/+/http://www.dfid.gov.uk/mdg/aid-effectiveness/newsletters/srilanka-report.pdf (accessed 2 August 2014).
Harris, S. (2010) 'Humanitarianism in Sri Lanka: lessons learned?' Briefing Paper. Medford, MA: Feinstein International Center, Tufts University. Available at http://fic.tufts.edu/assets/Sri-Lanka-Briefing-Paper.pdf (accessed 27 May 2016).
Harrison, F. (2012) *Still Counting the Dead: Survivors of Sri Lanka's hidden war*. London: Portobello Books.
Harrison, F. (2013) 'Who is Mahinda Rajapaksa? Hero or war criminal? Sri Lankan leader stands accused'. *Independent*, 14 November. Available at www.independent.co.uk/news/world/asia/hero-or-war-criminal-sri-lankan-leader-mahinda-rajapaksa-under-pressure-8940591.html (accessed 22 June 2016).
Haviland, C. (2010) 'Sri Lankan foreign minister denounces UN Rights Chief'. BBC News [online], 1 June. Available at www.bbc.co.uk/news/10204507 (accessed 10 February 2012).
Haviland, C. (2012) 'Sri Lanka's sinister white van abductions'. BBC News [online], 14 March. Available at www.bbc.com/news/world-asia-17356575 (accessed 2 February 2016).
Haviland, C. (2015) 'UN Human Rights Council urges Sri Lanka war crimes court'. BBC News [online], 16 September. Available at www.bbc.co.uk/news/world-asia-34266471 (accessed 4 September 2015).
Hewage, K. (2014) 'Victim politics and post-conflict foreign policy in Rwanda and Sri Lanka'. Available at www.e-ir.info/2014/07/24/victim-politics-and-post-conflict-foreign-policy-in-rwanda-and-sri-lanka/ (accessed 7 July 2015).
Hofferberth, M. (2015) 'Mapping the meanings of global governance: a conceptual reconstruction of a floating signifier'. *Millennium: Journal of International Studies* 43(2): 598–617.
Höglund, K. and Orjuela, C. (2012) 'Hybrid peace governance and illiberal peacebuilding in Sri Lanka'. *Global Governance* 18(1): 89–104.
Holt, S. (2011) *Aid, Peacebuilding and the Resurgence of War: Buying time in Sri Lanka*. London: Palgrave Macmillan.

Hopgood, S. (2013) *The Endtimes of Human Rights*. Ithaca, NY: Cornell University Press.

Human Rights Watch (2008) *Recurring Nightmare: State responsibility for 'disappearances' and abductions in Sri Lanka*. New York: Human Rights Watch.

Human Rights Watch (2009) 'War on the displaced: Sri Lankan army and LTTE abuses against civilians in the Vanni'. HRW [online], 19 February. Available at www.hrw.org/report/2009/02/19/war-displaced/sri-lankan-army-and-ltte-abuses-against-civilians-vanni (accessed 12 February 2016).

Human Rights Watch (2012) 'UN Rights Council: Sri Lanka vote a strong message for justice'. HRW [online], 22 March. Available at www.hrw.org/news/2012/03/22/un-rights-council-sri-lanka-vote-strong-message-justice (accessed 7 July 2014).

Hyndman, J. (2009) 'Siting conflict and peace in post-tsunami Sri Lanka and Aceh, Indonesia'. *Norsk Geografisk Tidsskrift / Norwegian Journal of Geography* 63: 89–96.

Hyndman, J. and Amarasingam, A. (2014) '"Touring terrorism": landscapes of memory in post-war Sri Lanka'. *Geography Compass* 8(8): 560–75.

ICG (2010a) War Crimes in Sri Lanka'. *Asia Report 191*. Brussels: International Crisis Group. Available at www.crisisgroup.org/asia/south-asia/sri-lanka/war-crimes-sri-lanka (accessed 2 May 2015).

ICG (2010b) 'The Sri Lankan Tamil diaspora after the LTTE'. Asia Report 186. Brussels: International Crisis Group. Available at www.crisisgroup.org/~/media/Files/asia/south-asia/sri-lanka/186%20The%20Sri%20Lankan%20Tamil%20Diaspora%20after%20the%20LTTE.pdf (accessed 4 April 2016).

ICG (2010c) 'Sri Lanka: deciphering the constitutional coup'. International Crisis Group (ICG) [podcast], 4 October. Available at www.crisisgroup.org/~/media/MP3/podcast-sri-lanka-ak-oct.ashx (accessed 2 April 2015).

ICG (2010d) 'Sri Lanka: a bitter peace'. Asia Briefing 99. Brussels: International Crisis Group (ICG). Available at www.crisisgroup.org/en/regions/asia/south-asia/sri-lanka/B099-sri-lanka-a-bitter-peace.aspx (accessed 2 November 2014).

ICG (2011a) 'Reconciliation in Sri Lanka: harder than ever'. Asia Report 209. Brussels: International Crisis Group (ICG).

ICG (2011b) 'Ministry of Defence propaganda film "Lies Agreed Upon" misses the point'. 17 September. Available at: www.colombotelegraph.com/index.php/ministry-of-defence-propaganda-film-lies-agreed-upon-misses-the-point/ (accessed 1 February 2012).

ICG (2012a) 'Sri Lanka's North I: the denial of minority rights'. Brussel: International Crisis Group (ICG), pp. 9–16. Available at www.crisisgroup.org/~/media/Files/asia/south-asia/sri-lanka/219-sri-lankas-north-i-the-denial-of-minority-rights (accessed 7 July 2014).

ICG (2012b) 'Sri Lanka's North II: rebuilding under the military'. Asia Report 220. Brussel: International Crisis Group (ICG). Available at www.iccnow.org/documents/ICG-sri-lankas-north-ii-rebuilding-under-the-military.pdf.

ICG (2013) 'Sri Lanka's Potemkin peace'. Asia Report 253. Brussels: International Crisis Group (ICG). Available at www.crisisgroup.org/en/regions/asia/south-asia/sri-lanka/253-sri-lanka-s-potemkin-peace-democracy-under-fire.aspx (accessed 2 November 2015).

ICJ (2012) *Authority without Accountability: The crisis of impunity in Sri Lanka*. Geneva: International Commission of Jurists (ICJ). Available at www.refworld.org/pdfid/50ac365b2.pdf (accessed 28 May 2015).

ICRC (2012) 'Case study: conflict in the Vanni'. Geneva: International Committee of the Red Cross (ICRC). Available at www.icrc.org/casebook/doc/case-study/sri-lanka-conflict-vanni-case-study.htm; www.un.org/News/dh/infocus/Sri_Lanka/FOE_Report_Full.pdf (accessed 4 March 2015).

IDEA (2007) 'State of democracy in South Asia'. Institute for Democracy and Electoral Assistance (IDEA) [online], 6 February. Available at www.idea.int/asia_pacific/sod_south_asia.cfm (accessed 3 January 2015).

IDMC (2009) 'Sri Lanka: civilians displaced by conflict facing severe humanitarian crisis'. Internal Displacement Monitoring Centre (IDMC), Norwegian Refugee Council, 1 May. Available at www.internal-displacement.org/assets/library/Asia/Sri-Lanka/pdf/SriLanka-Overview-May09.pdf (accessed 7 July 2014).

INCORE (2005) 'INCORE study visit to Sri Lanka 8th–16th October 2005'. Londonderry: INCORE, University of Ulster. Available at www.incore.ulst.ac.uk/policy/lilp/Octo5Report.pdf (accessed 3 February 2015).

INFORM (2014) *Repression of Dissent in Sri Lanka*. Colombo: INFORM Human Rights Documentation Centre. Available at www.dgvn.de/fileadmin/user_upload/menschenr_durchsetzen/bilder/News/Repression_of_Dissent_in_Sri_Lanka_-_Jan-March_2014_-_English_28Apr2014_.pdf (accessed 12 March 2016).

International Human Rights Association (2010) 'People's Tribunal on Sri Lanka: its inception and its goals'. PT Sri Lanka [online], 28 March. Available at www.pptsrilanka.org (accessed 20 March 2016).

International IDEA (2008) 'State of democracy in Southeast Asia: Sri Lanka'. Available at www.idea.int/sod/worldwide/upload/Sri-Lanka-_Summary-1-EXECUTIVE-SUMMARY_SP.pdf (accessed 13 August 2015).

IPS (2010) 'Q&A: Sri Lanka remains defiant of U.N. chief'. Inter Press Service News Agency [online], 19 March. Available at www.ipsnews.net/2010/03/qa-sri-lanka-remains-defiant-of-un-chief/.

Irish Forum for Peace in Sri Lanka (2009) 'Dublin Tribunal finds against Sri Lanka on charges of war crimes'. Press Release, 18 January. Available at www.ifpsl.org/index.php?option=com_content&task=blogsection&id=5&Itemid=28 (accessed 2 February 2015).

ITJP (2015) *A Still Unfinished War: Sri Lanka's survivors of torture and sexual violence 2009–2015*. International Truth and Justice Project Sri Lanka. Available at www.itjpsl.com/wp-content/uploads/2015/07/Stop-Torture-Report.pdf (accessed 2 March 2016).

Izzadeen, A. (2013a) 'OPED: anti-Muslim hate campaign intensifies in Sri Lanka'. Inter Press Service News Agency [online], 6 May. Available at www.ipsnews.net/2013/05/oped-anti-muslim-hate-campaign-intensifies-in-sri-lanka/ (accessed 5 May 2014).

Izzadeen, A. (2013b) 'Rights, realism and duplicity: the two faces of Rajapaksa'. Al Jazeera [online], 25 November. Available at www.aljazeera.com/indepth/opinion/2013/11/rights-realism-duplicity-two-faces-rajapaksa-20131119121229668197.html (accessed 5 March 2015).

Jabbar, Z. (2014) 'President can be another Mahasen if only he listens to reason'. *The Island* [online], 12 November. Available at www.island.lk/index.php?page_cat=article-details&page=article-details&code_title=114045 (accessed 3 October 2015).

Jansz, F. (2000) 'UNHCR says all unofficial places of detention must be dissolved'. *The Lanka Academic* [online], 28 April. Available at www.lacnet.org/the_academic/archive/2000/2000_04_27 (accessed 5 September 2014).

Jayasekera, S. A. (2011) 'Pinch of dictatorship is good for Sri Lanka'. *Daily Mirror* [online], 5 July. Available at http://print.dailymirror.lk/news/49121.html (accessed 18 February 2015).

Jayasinghe, A. (2015) 'Journalism on the front line' in Crawley, W., Page, D. and Pinto-Jayawardena, K. (eds) *Embattled Media: Democracy, governance and reform in Sri Lanka*. New Delhi: Sage Publications.

Jayatilleka, D. (2015) 'Sri Lanka's counter-hegemonic coalition & the distortion of diplomatic history'. *Colombo Telegraph* [online], 3 April. Available at www.colombotelegraph.com/index.php/sri-lankas-counter-hegemonic-coalition-the-distortion-of-diplomatic-history/ (accessed 4 August 2015).

Jayawardene, K. P. (2000) 'Torture amidst the New Year crackers'. *The Sunday Times* (Colombo), 16 April.

Jayawickrama, N. (2015) 'The judiciary under the 1978 constitution' in Welikala, A. (ed.) *Reforming Sri Lankan Presidentialism: Provenance, problems and prospects*. Colombo: Centre for Policy Alternatives.

Jeyaraj, D. (2010) 'The language controversy over Sri Lankan national anthem'. [Blog], 17 December. Available at http://dbsjeyaraj.com/dbsj/archives/1871 (accessed 14 July 2014).

Jeyaraj, D. B. S. (2011) 'Remembering the APRC expert panel "majority" report'. [Blog], 19 December. Available at http://dbsjeyaraj.com/dbsj/archives/3311 (accessed 10 March 2016).

Jeyaraj, D. B. S. (2012) 'Eric Solheim reveals how LTTE leadership rejected plan to save lives of cadres and civilians in final phase of war'. [Blog], 14 October. Available at http://dbsjeyaraj.com/dbsj/archives/11643 (accessed 3 September 2015).

Kaleck, W. (2015) 'Double standards: international law and the West. Brussels: Torkel Opsahl Academic EPublisher. Available at http://fichl.us5.list-manage.com/track/click?u=e2f902f28b8d5cc80761dee44&id=ed4992baf2&e=bec2a91298.

Kalyvas, S. N. (2006) *The Logic of Violence in Civil War*. Cambridge: Cambridge University Press.

Karunanayake, D. P. (2014) 'Militant Buddhism and post-war Sri Lankan cinematic memory work'. *South Asian Review* 35(3): 79–94.

Kaufman, S. J. (2006) 'Escaping the symbolic politics trap: reconciliation initiatives and conflict resolution in ethnic wars'. *Journal of Peace Research* 43(2): 201–18.

Keenan, A. (2007) 'The trouble with evenhandedness: on the politics of human rights and peace advocacy in Sri Lanka' in Feher, M. (ed.) *Nongovernmental Politics*. New York: Zone Books.

Keerawella, G. (2013) 'Post-war Sri Lanka: is peace a hostage of military victory?' ICES Research Paper 8. Colombo: International Centre for Ethnic Studies (ICES).

Kelegama, S. (2014) 'China–Sri Lanka economic relations: an overview'. *China Report* 50(2): 131–49. Available at www.ips.lk/staff/ed/publications_ed/international/china_srilanka_economic/china_sl_economics.pdf.

Kelegama, S. and de Mel, D. (2007) 'Country study prepared for the project Southern Perspectives on Reform of the International Development Architecture: Sri Lanka'. Colombo: Institute of Policy Studies of Sri Lanka and North–South Institute. Available at www.nsi-ins.ca/content/download/southern_persp_srilanka.pdf (accessed 3 February 2016).

Kelegama, T. (2013) 'The UN Internal Review Panel and Sri Lanka's urgent need for accountability'. Delhi: Institute for Defence Studies and Analysis. Available at www.idsa..n/issuebrief/TheUNInternalReviewPanelReportandSriLankasAccountability_tkelegama_090113 (accessed 12 July 2014).

Kleinfeld, M. (2003) 'Strategic troping in Sri Lanka: September Eleventh and the consolidation of political position'. *Geopolitics* 8(3): 105–26.

Kodikara, C. (2012) *Only Until the Rice is Cooked? The Domestic Violence Act, familial ideology and cultural narratives in Sri Lanka*. ICES Working Paper 1. Colombo: International Centre for Ethnic Studies (ICES).

Kohona, P. (2009) 'Interview with the *Daily Mirror*'. 20 August. Quoted by Kaleck, W. (2015) 'Double standards: international law and the West'. Brussels: Torkel Opsahl Academic EPublisher. Available at http://fichl.us5.list-manage.com/track/click?u=e2f902f28b8d5cc80761dee44&id=ed4992baf2&e=bec2a91298 (accessed 2 October 2014).

Korf, B. (2006) 'Dining with devils? Ethnographic enquiries into the conflict-development nexus in Sri Lanka'. *Oxford Development Studies* 34(1): 47–64.

Kretzmer, D. (2009) 'Rethinking the application of IHL in non-international armed conflicts'. *Israel Law Review* 42: 8–45.

Krishna, S. (1996) 'Producing Sri Lanka: J. R. Jayewardene and postcolonial identity'. *Alternatives: Global, Local, Political* 21(3): 303–20.

Kumarage, C. (2014) 'Rajapaksa's regime deception and international obligations'. *Colombo Telegraph* [online], 1 July. Available at www.colombotelegraph.com/index.php/rajapaksa-regimes-deceptions-and-sri-lankas-international-obligations/ (accessed 3 November 2015).

Kurtz, G. and Jaganathan, M. M. (2016) 'Protection in peril: counterterrorism discourse and international engagement in Sri Lanka in 2009'. *Global Society* 30(1): 94–112.

Kurukulasuriya, L. (2012) 'Sri Lanka takes a beating in SA – and not just in cricket'. *Sunday Times*, 15 January. Available at www.sundaytimes.lk/120115/Columns/Lasandak.html (accessed 15 February 2016).

Lall, A. (2014) 'Post-war development in Northern Sri Lanka: why some people are unable to return to their lands'. Secure Livelihoods Research Consortium (SLRC) [online], 12 February. Available at www.securelivelihoods.org/blogpost/52/-Post-war-development-in-Northern-Sri-Lanka-why-some-people-are-unable-to-return-to-their-lands (accessed 19 January 2015).

Lamy, P. (2015) 'The past, present and future of global governance'. Global Policy [online], 10 April. Available at www.globalpolicyjournal.com/blog/10/04/2015/past-present-and-future-global-governance (accessed 15 June 2015).

Law and Society Trust (2014) 'Big picture: putting the mega development ambitions of Sri Lanka in context'. The Island [online], 13 August. Available at www.island.lk/index.php?page_cat=article-details&page=article-details&code_title=108420 (accessed 7 July 2015).

Legro, J. W. (1997) 'Which norms matter? Revisiting the "failure" of internationalism'. International Organization 51(1): 31–63.

Leopold, E. (2009) 'Sri Lanka: UN Security Council makes its first move'. The Huffington Post [online], 13 May. Available at www.huffingtonpost.com/evelyn-leopold/sri-lanka-un-security-cou_b_203259.html (accessed 2 May 2016).

Lewis, D. (2010) 'The failure of a liberal peace: Sri Lanka's counterinsurgency in global perspective'. Conflict, Security & Development 10(5): 647–71.

Little, A. and Hettige, S. T. (2014) Globalization, Employment and Education in Sri Lanka: Opportunity and division. Abingdon: Routledge.

Liyanage, D. (2013) 'Folklore and contemporary mass media: an assessment with special reference to Sri Lanka'. Social Sciences and Humanities Review 1(1): 231–48. Available at www.hss.ruh.ac.lk/ejournal/publications/volume01/folklore%20_massmedia.pdf (accessed 22 June 2015).

Liyanage, S. (2004) 'Resumption of talks: is it so crucial?' Daily News [online], 30 October. Available at http://archives.dailynews.lk/2004/10/30/fea01.html.

Liyanawatte, D. (2014) 'Sri Lankan hardline Buddhists say Facebook accounts blocked after violence'. Reuters [online], 27 June. Available at http://uk.reuters.com/article/uk-sri-lanka-violence-facebook-idUKKBN0F213W20140627 (accessed 10 May 2015).

Lo Schiavo, L. (2014) 'Governance, civil society, governmentality. The "Foucauldian moment" in the globalization debate: theoretical perspectives'. International Journal of the Humanities and Social Science 4(13): 181–97. Available at www.ijhssnet.com/journals/Vol_4_No_13_November_2014/21.pdf (accessed 2 December 2015).

Luengo-Cabrere, J. (2012) 'Democracy and civil war in Sri Lanka'. Research Paper. Partnership for Research in International Affairs and Development (PRIAD) (PRIAD). Available at www.priad.org/wp-content/uploads/2013/04/Democracy-and-Civil-War-in-Sri-Lanka2.pdf (accessed 17 April 2014).

Lunstead, J. (2007) The United States' Role in Sri Lanka's Peace Process 2002–2006. Colombo: Asia Foundation.

Machiavelli, N. (1996) Discourses on Livy. Trans. H. C. Mansfield and N. Tarcov. Chicago: University of Chicago Press.

Mampilly, Z. (2009) 'A marriage of inconvenience: tsunami aid and the unraveling of the LTTE and the GoSL's complex dependency'. Civil Wars 11(3): 302–20.

Mangala, S. (2015) 'Speech for the commemoration of the 25th anniversary of the Muslims of the Northern Province'. Lanka-e-News [online], 30 October. Available at http://lankaenews.com/news/890/en (accessed 2 February 2015).

Martin, I. (2003) 'Unarmed monitoring and human rights field presence: civilian protection and conflict prevention'. Journal of Humanitarian Assistance

[online], 1 August. Available at https://sites.tufts.edu/jha/archives/61 (accessed 26 February 2016).
McGowan, W. (2012) 'Aung San Suu Kyi's Buddhist problem'. Foreign Policy [online], 17 September. Available at http://foreignpolicy.com/2012/09/17/aung-san-suu-kyis-buddhism-problem/ (accessed 3 July 2015).
Mckenzie, R. (2014) 'Sri Lankan elections: choice between a dictatorial executive presidency and an inclusive democracy'. EP Today [online], 18 December. Available at http://eptoday.com/sri-lankan-elections-choice-dictatorial-executive-presidency-inclusive-democracy/ (accessed 3 December 2015).
Meyer, E. (2015) 'Sri Lanka's China dilemma'. Forbes, 23 February. Available at www.forbes.com/sites/ericrmeyer/#271ab02076b0.
Ministry of Defence Sri Lanka (2011) Humanitarian Operation: Factual Analysis July 2006-May 2009. Colombo: Ministry of Defence. Available at www.defence.lk/news/20110801_Conf.pdf (accessed 2 June 2015).
Ministry of Defence Sri Lanka (2014) 'A changing US role and the numbers game'. Colombo: Ministry of Defence. Available at www.defence.lk/new.asp?fname=srilanka_war_on_terror_revisited_20140124_08 (accessed 2 February 2015).
Minority Rights Group International (2012) 'MRG concerned about the attack and relocation of a mosque in Sri Lanka, calls on Sri Lankan government to take immediate action to protect religious freedoms'. Press Release, 26 April 2012. Available at www.minorityrights.org/11324/minorities-in-the-news/mrg-concerned-about-the-attack-and-relocation-of-a-mosque-in-sri-lanka-calls-on-sri-lankan-government-to-take-immediate-action-to-protect-religious-freedoms (accessed 24 January 2016).
Minority Rights Group International (2013) 'Islamophobia and attacks on Muslims in Sri Lanka'. London: Minority Rights Group International. Available at http://minorityrights.org/publications/islamophobia-and-attacks-on-muslims-in-sri-lanka-march-2013/ (accessed 10 September 2015).
Mittal, A. (2015) The Long Shadow of War: The struggle for justice in postwar Sri Lanka. Oakland, CA: The Oakland Institute. Available at www.oaklandinstitute.org/sites/oaklandinstitute.org/files/OI_The_Long_Shadow_of_War_o.pdf (accessed 4 February 2016).
Montlake, S. (2009) 'How "US war on terror" emboldened Sri Lanka's'. The Christian Science Monitor [online], 6 March. Available at www.csmonitor.com/World/Asia-South-Central/2009/0306/p01s04-wosc.html (accessed 2 February 2015).
MRT and RRT (2013) 'Sri Lanka: treatment of opposition groups, citizens and persons with certain LTTE links'. Issue Paper. Canberra: Australian Government, Migration Review Tribunal (MRT) and Refugee Review Tribunal (RRT). Available at www.refworld.org/pdfid/5=f62c1a4.pdf (accessed 10 January 2016).
Nadarajah, S. and Rampton, D. (2015) 'The limits of hybridity and the crisis of liberal peace'. Review of International Studies 41(1); 49-72.
Nadarajah, S. and Vimalarajah, L. (2008) The Politics of Transformation: The LTTE and the 2002-2006 peace process in Sri Lanka. Berlin: Berghof Research Centre.

Nandy, S. (2015) 'The UN at 70: a 60 year journey with Sri Lanka'. Inter Press Service News Agency [online], 18 May. Available at www.ipsnews. net/2015/05/the-u-n-at-70-a-60-year-journey-with-sri-lanka/ (accessed 22 May 2015).

Natarajan, S. (2012) 'Media freedom in post war Sri Lanka and its impact on the reconciliation process'. Oxford: Reuters Institute for the Study of Journalism, University of Oxford.

Nayar, K. P. (2009) 'US taps Elhi on Lanka foray – Washington to sound out Menon on evacuation mission'. *The Telegraph* (India), 8 March. Available at www.telegraphindia.com/1090308/jsp/frontpage/story_10642588.jsp (accessed 3 June 2015).

Nelson, D. (2009) 'Tamils driven out of homes by "ethnic cleansing"'. *The Daily Telegraph*, 26 May.

Newman, P. (2012) 'LLRC confirms need for an impartial international enquiry'. *The Weekend Leader* [online], 5 January. Available at www.theweekendleader.com/Causes/906/lankan-lie.html#sthash.om74x659.dpuf (accessed 2 June 2015).

Niland, N. (2014a) 'Sri Lanka: unrestricted warfare and limited protective humanitarian action' in 'Policy debate: humanitarian protection in the midst of civil war: lessons from Sri Lanka'. *International Development Policy/ Revue internationale de politique de developpement*, Articles and Debate 5.2. Geneva: The Graduate Institute.

Niland, N. (2014b) *Inhumanity and Humanitarian Action: Protection failures in Sri Lanka*. Somerville, MA: Feinstein International Center, Tufts University. Available at http://fic.tufts.edu/assets/Inhumanity-and-Humanitarian-Action_9-15-2014.pdf.

Niland, N., Holmes, J. and Bradley, M. (2014) 'Policy debate: humanitarian protection in the midst of civil war: lessons from Sri Lanka'. *International Development Policy/Revue internationale de politique de developpement*, Articles and Debate 5.2. Geneva: The Graduate Institute.

Oakland Institute (2016) *Waiting to Return Home: Continued plight of the IDPs in post-war Sri Lanka*. Oakland, CA: The Oakland Institute. Available at www.jdslanka.org/images/documents/displacement_land_issues/waiting_to_return_oakland_institute.pdf (accessed 4 May 2016).

Oberst, R. C. (2010) 'Country report: Sri Lanka' in 'Countries at the crossroads 2010'. Freedom House [online], 6 April. Available at www.ecoi.net/local_link/137714/237990_en.html (accessed 20 December 2014).

OECD (n.d.) *The Paris Declaration on Aid Effectiveness and the Accra Agenda for Action*. Paris: Organisation for Economic Co-operation and Development (OECD). Available at www.oecd.org/dac/effectiveness/34428351.pdf.

OHCHR (2015a) *Report of the OHCHR Investigation into Sri Lanka (OISL)*. Geneva: Office of the United Nations High Commissioner for Human Rights (OHCHR). Available at www.ohcr.org/EN/HRBodies/HRC/RegularSessions/.../A_HRC_30_CRP_2.docx (accessed 2 March 2016).

OHCHR (2015b) 'Special procedures of the Human Rights Council'. Geneva: Office of the United Nations High Commissioner for Human Rights (OHCHR) [online]. Available at www.ohchr.org/EN/HRBodies/SP/Pages/Welcomepage.aspx (accessed 22 April 2016).

OHCHR (n.d.) 'OHCHR investigation on Sri Lanka'. Geneva: Office of the United Nations High Commissioner for Human Rights (OHCHR) [online]. Available at www.ohchr org/EN/HRBodies/HRC/Pages/OISL.aspx (accessed 4 February 2015).

Ojeleye, O. (2013) *The Politics of Post-War Demobilisation and Reintegration in Nigeria*. Farnham: Ashgate Publishing.

Ondaatjie, A. (2014) 'Growing ties let Sri Lanka rebuff US war inquiry push'. Bloomberg [online], 6 March. Available at www.bloomberg.com/news/2014-03-06/growing-china-ties-let-sri-lanka-rebuff-u-s-war-inquiry-push.html (accessed 3 August 2015.

Orchard, P. (2014) 'Revisiting humanitarian safe areas for civilian protection'. *Global Governance* 20: 55–75.

Pardesi, M. S. (2012) 'The legacy of 1969 and China's India policy'. Available at www.idsa.in/system/fies/jd 6 4_ManjeetSPardesi.pdf (accessed 10 March 2016).

Pathirana, S. (2010) 'Sri Lanka "pays PR firm £3m to boost post-war image"'. BBC News [online], 22 October. Available at www.bbc.co.uk/news/world-south-asia-11606899 (accessed 18 March 2015).

Peace Brigades International (1995) 'War, NGOs and propaganda: anti-NGO sentiments in Sri Lanka'. Peace Brigades International [online], December. Available at www.peacebrigades.org/archive/lanka/slp9503.html (accessed 14 March 2014).

Pearson, N. O. (2015) 'Why Sri Lanka's election matters for China'. *Business Week*, 6 January. Available at http://businessweek.com/news/2015-01-06/why-srilankas-election-matters-for-china (accessed 7 January 2015).

Peiris, G. H. (2005) 'A polarized vote in Sri Lanka'. *Asia Times* [online], 23 November. Available at www.atimes.com/atimes/South_Asia/GK23Dfo1.html (accessed 3 March 2016).

Perera, J. (2012) 'LLRC action plan and taking LLRC report seriously'. *Colombo Telegraph* [online], 30 July. Available at www.colombotelegraph.com/index.php/llrc-action-plan-and-taking-llrc-report-seriously/ (accessed 2 March 2015).

Perera, K. (2014) 'Paid NGO professionals, volunteer activism and Rajapaksa's advantage in South'. *Colombo Telegraph* [online]. 4 April. Available at www.colombotelegraph.com/index.php/paid-ngo-professionals-volunteer-activism-and-rajapaksas-advantage-in-south/ (accessed 28 September 2015).

Perera, M. M. (2014) 'Alliance between radical Burmese and Sri Lankan monks will "destroy true Buddhism"'. AsiaNews.it [online], October. Available at www.asianews.it/news-en/Alliance-between-radical-Burmese-and-Sri-Lankan-monks-will-destroy-true-Buddhism--32317.html (accessed 9 March 2016).

Perera-Rajasingham, N. (2008) 'The politics of the governed: maternal politics and child recruitment in the Eastern Province of Sri Lanka' in Coomaraswamy, R. and Perera-Rajasingham, N. (eds) *Constellations of Violence: Feminist interventions in South Asia*. New Delhi: Women Unlimited, pp. 121–48.

Pethiyagoda, K. (2013) 'India's approach to international intervention and the responsibility to protect'. Working Paper. Oxford Oxford Institute for Ethics, Law, and Armed Conflict. Available at www.elac.ox.ac.uk/downloads/pethiyagoda%202013.pdf.

Petrie, C. (2014) 'The challenges of UN action in situations of escalating conflict'. New World [online], 5 March. Available at www.una.org. uk/magazine/spring-2014/charles-petrie-challenges-un-action-situations-escalating-conflict (accessed 10 December 2015).

Phillips, L. (2009) 'While condemning Sri Lanka violence EU still sells arms to government'. EUobserver [online], 19 May https://euobserver.com/news/28155 (accessed 4 May 2016).

Pholsena, V. (2014) 'Ethnic minorities, the state and beyond, focus on mainland Southeast Asia'. Seatide Online Paper 1. Available at www.seatide.eu/download.php?filename=30300%201425007719.pdf (5 February 2015).

Pinto-Jayawardena, K. (2015) 'The promise and the pathos of the law in Sri Lanka'. Paper presented at the plenary sessions of the American Law and Society Association (LSA), Seattle, 28–30 May. Available at http://archive.lankanewsweb.net/features/10943-the-promise-and-the-pathos-of-the-law-in-sri-lanka-kishali-pinto-jayawardena (accessed 15 July 2015).

Poguntke, T. and Webb, P. (eds) (2005) *The Presidentialisation of Politics: A comparative study of modern democracies*. New York: Oxford University Press.

Policy Research Group (2010) 'Chinese embrace may prove too costly to Sri Lanka'. *Tamil Guardian* [online], 2 June. Available at www.tamilguardian.com/article.asp?articleid=2747 (accessed 12 July 2014).

Popham, P. (2010) 'How Beijing won Sri Lanka's civil war'. *Independent*, 22 May. Available at www.independent.co.uk/news/world/asia/how-beijing-won-sri-lankas-civil-war-1980492.html (accessed 10 November 2015).

Prats, L. (2009) 'Heritage according to scale' in Peralta, E. and Anico, M. (eds) *Heritage and Identity: Engagement and demission in the contemporary world*. New York: Routledge, pp. 76–90.

Punyasena, W. (2003) 'The façade of accountability: disappearances in Sri Lanka'. *Boston College Third World Law Journal* 23 (1) [online]. Available at http://lawdigitalcommons.bc.edu/cgi/viewcontent.cgi?article=1126&context=twlj (accessed 2 February 2015).

Quakers in the World (n.d.) 'Quakers in action: international mediation and conciliation'. Quakers in the World [online]. Available at www.quakersintheworld.org/quakers-in-action/210 (accessed 3 November 2015).

Quick, I. (2015) 'Follies in fragile states: double loop, London' quoted in Punyasena, W. (2003) 'The façade of accountability: disappearances in Sri Lanka'. *Boston College Third World Law Journal* 23(1) [online]. Available at http://lawdigitalcommons.bc.edu/cgi/viewcontent.cgi?article=1126&context=twlj (accessed 2 February 2015).

Radhakrishnan, R. K. (2012) 'Thousands offer worship to Kapilavastu relics in Sri Lanka'. *The Hindu* [online], 20 August. Available at www.thehindu.com/news/international/thousands-offer-worship-to-kapilavastu-relics-in-sri-lanka/article3794883.ece (accessed 12 September 2012).

Raheem, M. (2013) *Protracted Displacement, Urgent Solutions: Prospects for durable solutions for protracted IDPs in Sri Lanka*. Colombo: Centre for Policy Alternatives, commissioned by Norwegian Refugee Council. Available at www.scribd.com/doc/168824135/Protracted-Displacement-Urgent-Solutions-Prospects-for-Durable-Solutions-for-Protracted-IDPs-in-Sri-Lanka (accessed 3 January 2016).

Raheem, M. and Loganathan, K. (2005) 'Internationalisation of the Sri Lankan peace process'. Background Paper for Conference on International Dimensions of the Peace Process in Sri Lanka, Centre for Policy Alternatives, Colombo, 8–9 July 2005.
Rajagopalan, S. (1997) 'National integration in India, Sri Lanka and Pakistan: constitutional and elite visions'. *Nationalism and Ethnic Politics* 3(4): 1–38.
Rajapaksa, M. (2014) 'A fault in his stars?' *The Economist* [online], 29 November. Available at www.economist.com/news/asia/21635072-mahinda-rajapaksa-expected-coronation-instead-he-faces-tricky-election-fault-his-stars (accessed 4 February 2016).
Rajapaksha, K. (2013) 'A deconstruction of the Sri Lankan government's post-war economic and human development model and its ideology'. University of Peradeniya, July. Available at www.academia.edu/7149383/A_Deconstruction_of_the_Sri_Lankan_Governments_Post-war_Economic_and_Human_Development_Model_and_Its_Ideology (accessed 4 March 2015).
Rajapaksje, R. D. P. S. (2016) 'Building goodwill through soft power: an analysis of China's reputation in Sri Lanka'. *Journal of Politics and Law* 9(1): 48–54.
Rajasingham-Senanayake, D. (2011) 'Is post-war Sri Lanka following the "military business model"?' *Economic and Political Weekly* 46(14).
Ramachandran, S. (2011) 'Colombo digs grave for Tamil harmony'. *Asia Times* [online], 26 March. Available at www.atimes.com/atimes/South_Asia/MC26Df02.html (accessed 12 November 2014).
Ramachandran, S. (2016) 'Sri Lanka's pluralist ethnic fabric under threat as anti-Muslim drive gains pace'. *Asia Times* [online], 20 January. Available at http://atimes.com/2016/01/sri-lankas-pluralist-ethnic-fabric-under-threat-again-as-sinha-le-campaign-gains-pace/ (accessed 10 March 2015).
Rambukwella, N. (2015) 'Five lies in Mahinda Rajapaksa's statement on OHCHR report'. *Colombo Telegraph* [online], 26 September. Available at www.colombotelegraph.com/index.php/five-lies-in-mahinda-rajapaksas-statement-on-ohchr-report/ (accessed 27 May 2016).
Rampton, D. (2011) '"Deeper hegemony": the politics of Sinhala nationalist authenticity and the failures of power-sharing in Sri Lanka'. *Commonwealth & Comparative Politics* 49(2): 245–73.
Rampton, D. (2016) 'Social orders, state formation and conflict: Buddhist nationalism in Sri Lanka and Myanmar'. Working Paper. March. Available at www.researchgate.net/publication/297220059_Social_Orders_State_Formation_and_Conflict_Buddhist_Nationalism_in_Sri_Lanka_and_Myanmar (accessed 2 May 2016).
Ranjan, A. (1998) 'A far seeing leader of government'. In Sinhala only. *Dinamina*, 19 November.
Rasooldeen, M. D. (2013) 'OIC expresses concern over Sri Lanka's ethnic tensions'. *Arab News* [online], 20 March. Available at www.arabnews.com/news/445453 (accessed 20 August 2015).
Rathgeber, T. (2013) *Performance and Challenges of the UN Human Rights Council: An NGO's view*. Berlin: Friedrich-Ebert-Stiftung.
Ratwatte, C. (2012) 'Darusman, LLRC and Petrie: three reports on the end of war in Sri Lanka'. Colombo: Centre for Human Rights Research. Available

at www.chrsrilanka.com/Darusman,LLRC_and_Petrie_Three_Reports_on_ the_End_of_War_in_Sri_Lanka_-5-547.html (accessed 17 March 2015).

Reuters (2010) 'Sri Lanka nurses in job action as labour action grows'. AsiaOne News [online], 10 November. Available at http://news.asiaone.com/News/Latest%2BNews/Asia/Story/A1Story20101110-246670.html (accessed 3 October 2015).

Reuters (2012) 'Sri Lanka owes $15 bln on foreign borrowings since 1997'. Reuters [online], 19 July. Available at http://in.reuters.com/article/srilanka-debts-idINL4E8IJ3NK20120719 (accessed 15 August 2013).

Revise, N. (2009) 'Bitter with West, Sri Lanka turns East for cash and support'. Agence France-Presse, 3 May.

Rezwan (2013) 'Sri Lanka: reactions to the impeachment of the Chief Justice' Global Voices [online], 19 January. Available at https://globalvoicesonline.org/2013/01/19/sri-lanka-reactions-to-the-impeachment-of-the-chief-justice/ (accessed 4 August 2014).

Richards, J. (2014) 'An institutional history of the Liberation Tigers of Tamil Eelam (LTTE)'. CCDP Working Paper 10. Geneva: Centre on Conflict, Development and Peacebuilding (CCDP), Graduate Institute of International and Development Studies. Available at http://graduateinstitute.ch/files/live/sites/iheid/files/sites/ccdp/shared/Docs/Publications/CCDP-Working-Paper-10-LTTE-1.pdf (accessed 24 May 2016).

Richards, P. (1997) *Fighting for the Rain Forest: War, Youth and Resources in Sierra Leone*. Oxford: James Currey.

Roberts, A. (ed.) (2012) *Democracy, Sovereignty and Terror: Lakshman Kadirgamar on the Foundations of International Order*. London and New York: I. B. Tauris.

Roberts, M. (2012) 'Sinhalaness and its reproduction' in Welikala, A. (ed.) *The Sri Lankan Republic at Forty: Reflections on Constitutional History, Theory and Practice*. Colombo: Centre for Policy Alternatives, pp. 253–87.

Rose-Greenland, F. and Müge Göçek, F. (2014) 'Cultural heritage and violence in the Middle East'. openDemocracy [online], 4 October. Available at www.opendemocracy.net/arab-awakening/fiona-rosegreenland-fatma-müge-göçek/cultural-heritage-and-violence-in-middle-east (accessed 15 January 2015).

Saddlesmania (2009) 'LTTE leader Velupillai Prabhaakaran killed by Sri Lankan Troops'. YouTube [online video], 18 May. Available at www.youtube.com/watch?v=5Ht4ZtEk83g (accessed 6 December 2014).

Samaranayake, G. (2008) *Political Violence in Sri Lanka 1971–1987*. New Delhi: Gyan Publishing House.

Samath, F. (2009) 'Sri Lanka casts wider donor net'. *The National* [online], 18 June. Available at www.thenational.ae/news/world/south-asia/sri-lanka-casts-wider-donor-net (accessed 18 June 2009).

Sampanthan, R. (2014) 'On the Rajapaksa budget, his thinking on Tamil issues and our position on the Rajapaksa budget'. [Online], 1 November. Available at https://groups.yahoo.com/neo/groups/srilankamuslims/conversations/messages/5177 (accessed 4 May 2015).

Saparamadu, C. and Lall, A. (2014) 'Resettlement of conflict-induced IDPs in Northern Sri Lanka: political economy of state policy and practice'. SLRC Working Paper 10. London: Secure Livelihoods Research Consortium (SLRC), Centre for Poverty Analysis.

Saravanamuttu, P. (2006) 'Democratization of the peace process' in Large, J. and Sisk, T. (eds) *Democracy, Conflict and Human Security*. Stockholm: International IDEA, pp. 207–17.
Saravanamuttu, P. (2010) 'Sri Lanka embarking on troubling political trajectory'. *Jakarta Globe*, 20 August. Available at www.thejakartaglobe. com/opinion/sri-lanka-embarking-on-troubling-political-trajectory/391983 (accessed 5 December 2014).
Saravanamuttu, P. (2014) 'From post-war to post-conflict: reconciliation is pivotal'. Colombo: International Centre for Ethnic Studies. Available at www. ices.lk/wp-content/uploads/2014/02/From-Post-War-to-Post-%E2%80%93-Conflict-Reconciliation-is-Pivotal-Dr.-Paikiasothy-Saravanamuttu.pdf (accessed 2 September 2015).
Sathiya Moorthy, N. (2013) 'In whose homes are the solutions grown?' *The Sunday Leader* [online], 29 December. Available at www.thesundayleader.lk/2013/12/29/in-whose-homes-are-the-solutions-grown/ (accessed 9 March 2016).
Satkunanathan, A. (2012) "What Sri Lanka is …": acknowledging the ethnic conflict in post-war reconciliation'. openDemocracy [online], 9 March. Available at www.opendemocracy.net/opensecurity/ambika-satkunanathan/what-sri-lanka-is-acknowledging-ethnic-conflict-in-post-war-reconc (accessed 10 May 2015)
Satkunanathan, A. (2013) 'Militarisation as panacea: development and reconciliation in post-war Sri Lanka'. openDemocracy [online], 19 March. Available at www.opendemocracy.net/opensecurity/ambika-satkunanathan/militarisation-as-panacea-development-and-reconciliation-in-post-w (accessed 9 January 2015).
Schaller, M. and Abeysinghe, A. M. N. D. (2006) 'Geographical frame of reference and dangerous intergroup attitudes: a double minority study in Sri Lanka'. *Political Psychology* 27(4): 615–31.
Sen, A. (2009) *The Idea of Justice*. Cambridge, MA: Harvard University Press.
Senadhira, S. (2013) 'Sri Lanka and the 13th amendment: what is "13 plus"?' Institute of Peace and Conflict Studies [online], 11 July. Available at www. ipcs.org/article/south-asia/ipcs-debate-sri-lanka-and-the-13th-amendment-what-is-4034.html (accessed 5 December 2014).
Senguptajan, S. (2009) 'UN leads evacuation from Sri Lanka'. *The New York Times*, 29 January. Available at www.nytimes.com/2009/01/30/world/asia/30lanka.html?_r=0 (accessed 3 June 2014).
Sethi, H. (ed.) (2008) 'SoD summary: state of democracy in South Asia (Sri Lanka)'. New Delhi: SDSA Team and Oxford University Press. Available at www.idea.int/sod/worldwide/state-of-democracy-in-south-asia-sri-lanka.cfm (accessed 3 January 2015).
Shaheen, K. (2016a) 'Head of Médecins Sans Frontières warns of return to "barbarian times"'. *The Guardian*, 8 March. Available at: www.theguardian. com/world/2016/mar/07/wars-are-being-fought-as-in-barbarian-times-warns-medecins-san-frontieres-chief (accessed 10 March 2016).
Shaheen, K. (2016b) 'Syria: UN considers role in Russia's "deeply flawed" humanitarian corridors plan'. *The Guardian*, 5 August. Available at www. theguardian.com/world/2016/aug/05/syria-un-considers-role-in-russias-deeply-flawed-humanitarian-corridors-plan (accessed 1 August 2016).

Shanie (2011) 'The watchdog role of media and vigilance of civil society'. *Sri Lanka Guardian* [online]. Available at www.srilankaguardian.org/2011/03/watchdog-role-of-media-and-vigilance-of.html (accessed 1 July 2015).

Shashikumar, V. K. (2009) 'Lessons from the war in Sri Lanka'. *Indian Defence Review* 24(3) (July–September).

Shepard, W. (2016) 'China tells Sri Lanka: we want our money, not your empty airport'. Forbes [online], 31 July. Available at www.forbes.com/sites/wadeshepard/2016/07/31/china-to-sri-lanka-we-want-our-money-not-your-empty-airport/#6fa50d9e1169 (accessed 2 August 2016).

Sherwood, H. (2015) 'Human rights groups face global crackdown "not seen in a generation"'. *The Guardian* [online], 26 August. Available at www.theguardian.com/law/2015/aug/26/ngos-face-restrictions-laws-human-rights-generation (accessed 2 November 2015).

Shillong Times (2011) 'Lanka to take action against guilty in war crimes'. *Shillong Times* [online], 25 November. Available at www.theshillongtimes.com/2011/11/25/lanka-to-take-action-against-war-crimes/ (accessed 2 October 2015).

Sirilal, R. (2011) 'Sri Lanka workers strike for fifth day, more unrest feared'. Reuters [online], 2 June. Available at www.reuters.com/article/srilanka-unions-idUSL3E7H30EX20110603 (accessed 10 March 2016).

Sirimane, S. (2014) 'Lanka to be the "Wonder of Asia"'. *Sunday Observer* [online], 21 December. Available at www.sundayobserver.lk/2014/12/21/fea06.asp (accessed 9 January 2014).

Soares de Oliveira, R. S. (2011) 'Illiberal peacebuilding in Angola'. *Journal of African Studies* 49(2): 287–314.

Sooka, Y. (2014) *An Unfinished War: Torture and sexual violence in Sri Lanka 2009–2014. A documentation of post-war atrocities.* London: Bar Human Rights Committee. Available at www.barhumanrights.org.uk/unfinished-war-torture-and-sexual-violence-sri-lanka-2009-2014.

Sorbo, G., Goodhand, J. and Klem, B. (2011) *Pawns of Peace: Evaluation of Norway's peace efforts in Sri Lanka, 1997–2009.* Oslo: Norad Evaluation Department. Available at www.oecd.org/countries/srilanka/49035074.pdf (accessed 2 February 2014).

Soysa, U. (2010) 'Why does Sri Lanka need Chinese convicts?' *The Sunday Leader* [online], 18 July. Available at www.thesundayleader.lk/2010/07/18/why-does-sri-lanka-need-chinese-convicts/ (accessed 15 January 2015).

Sri Lanka Brief (2016) 'Sri Lanka constitution reform is very open, very transparent process – Dr Jayampathy Wickramaratne'. Sri Lanka Brief [online], 3 March. Available at http://srilankabrief.org/2016/03/sri-lanka-constitution-reform-this-is-a-very-open-very-transparent-process-dr-jayampathy-wickramaratne/ (accessed 5 March 2016).

Sri Lanka Liberal Democrats (2009) 'Abolishing the Executive Presidency'. 23 August. Available at http://srilanka-liberaldemocrats.blogspot.co.uk/2009/08/abolishing-executive-presidency.html (accessed 3 July 2014).

Sridharan, V. (2016a) 'Curfew continues in Kashmir but media gag lifted'. *International Business Times*, 21 July. Available at www.ibtimes.co.uk/curfew-continues-kashmir-media-gag-lifted-1571782.

Sridharan, V. (2016b) 'Pressure mounts on Modi government as curfew continues in India's Kashmir'. *International Business Times*, 8 August.

Available at www.ibtimes.co.uk/pressure-mounts-modi-government-curfew-continues-indias-kashmir-1574897 (accessed 8 August 2016).
Srinivasan, M. (2014) 'Military presence in Sri Lanka's north is worrisome: Wigneswaran'. The Hindu [online], 12 June. Available at www.thehindu.com/news/international/south-asia/military-presence-in-sri-lankas-north-is-worrisome-wigneswaran/article6108055.ece (accessed 10 July 2015).
Stathern, A. (2013) 'Why are Buddhist monks attacking Muslims?' BBC News [online], 2 May. Available at www.bbc.co.uk/news/magazine-22356306 (accessed 4 May 2015).
Stewart, J. (2014) 'After the slaughter: war tourism in modern Sri Lanka'. E-International Relations [online], 28 February. Available at www.e-ir.info/2014/02/28/after-the-slaughter-war-tourism-in-modern-sri-lanka/ (accessed 5 November 2015).
Stewart, P. (2014) 'The unruled world: the case for "good enough" global governance'. Foreign Affairs 93(1). Available at www.foreignaffairs.com/articles/2013-12-06/unruled-world (accessed 18 February 2015).
Stewart, P. and Strachern, A. (2002) Violence: Theory and ethnography. London and New York: Continuum.
Subramanian, S. (2014) This Divided Island: Stories from the Sri Lankan war. London: Atlantic Books.
Sultana, G. (2013) 'Religious tensions in Sri Lanka'. Institute for Defence Studies and Analyses [online], 22 April. Available at http://idsa.in/idsacomments/ReligiousTensionsinSriLanka_gsultana_220413 (accessed 2 May 2015).
Tambiah, S. (1992) Buddhism Betrayed? Religion, politics and violence in Sri Lanka. Chicago: Chicago University Press.
Tambiah, S. J. (1986) Sri Lanka: Ethnic fratricide and the dismantling of democracy. London: I. B. Tauris.
Tamil Guardian (2012) 'Hundreds of Australians protest against Sri Lankan cricket tour'. Tamil Guardian [online], 26 December. Available at www.tamilguardian.com/article.asp?articleid=6665 (accessed 22 April 2016).
Tamil Guardian (2014) 'Enter South Africa'. Tamil Guardian [online], 19 April. Available at www.tamilguardian.com/article.asp?articleid=10689 (accessed 2 February 2016).
Tamilnation.org (n.d.) 'Sri Lanka's laws'. Available at http://tamilnation.co/srilankalaws/72constitution.htm (accessed 3 March 2015).
TamilNet (2009) 'U.S. Tamil group urges Pacific Command not to abet Colombo's war on Tamils'. TamilNet [online], 3 March. Available at www.tamilnet.com/art.html?catid=13&artid=28575 (accessed 17 December 2015).
TGTE (2010) 'TGTE embarking on struggle with determination'. Press Release. Transnational Government of Tamil Eelam (TGTE), 17 June. Available at www.tamilnet.com/img/publish/2010/06/Tgte_E_press_release_June_2010.pdf (accessed 2 March 2016).
Thaheer, M., Peiris, P. and Pathiraja, K. (2013) Reconciliation in Sri Lanka: Voices from former war zones. Colombo: International Centre for Ethnic Studies.
Thakur, R., Job, B., Serrano, M. and Tussie, D. (2014) 'The new phase in the consolidation and expansion of global governance'. Global Governance 20(1): 1–4.

Thalpawila, O. N. (2014) 'India–Sri Lanka relations: in post civil war era in Sri Lanka'. *Research Forum: International Journal of Social Sciences* 2(1). Available at http://ijss.publicationsupport.com/docs/paper/Volume-2/Issue_1/IJSSV2I1-102.pdf (accessed 15 April 2016).

The Economist (2009) 'Where have all the people gone?' *The Economist*, 29 January. Available at www.economist.com/node/13022139 (accessed 10 January 2014).

The Economist (2010) 'Putting the raj in Rajapaksa: reconciliation takes a back seat as a band of brothers settles in'. *The Economist*, 20 May. Available at www.economist.com/node/16167748 (accessed 17 June 2015).

The Economist (2012) 'Sri Lanka and the UN: stricter standards'. *The Economist*, 1 March. Available at www.economist.com/blogs/banyan/2012/03/sri-lanka-and-un (accessed 10 May 2015).

The Hindu (2011) 'A brother out of control'. *The Hindu*, 16 August. Available at www.thehindu.com/opinion/editorial/article2359597.ece (accessed 22 March 2015).

The Hindu (2014) 'Rajapaksa asks Tamils to "forget the past"'. *The Hindu*, 18 December. Available at www.thehindu.com/news/international/south-asia/forget-the-past-rajapaksa-tells-tamils/article6704799.ece (accessed 2 February 2015).

The Island (2011) 'CHR Sri Lanka report on LLRC Mannar session: oscillation between hope and hopelessness'. *The Island* [online], 17 January. Available at www.island.lk/index.php?page_cat=article-details&page=article-details&code_title=16163 (accessed 2 March 2016).

The Nation (2008) 'Rajapaksa sticks with divide and rule policy'. *The Nation* [online], 4 May. Available at www.nation.lk/2008/05/04/mynation.htm (accessed 26 January 2016).

The Social Architects (2012) *Salt on Old Wounds: The systematic Sinhalization of Sri Lanka's North, East and Hill Country*.

The Sunday Times (2014a) 'Geneva: hard line at home, heart cry abroad'. *The Sunday Times* [online], 2 February. Available at www.sundaytimes.lk/140202/columns/geneva-hard-line-at-home-heart-cry-abroad-81854.html (accessed 27 May 2016).

The Sunday Times (2014b) 'Casino crisis: first major revolt within Rajapaksa regime'. *The Sunday Times* [online], 27 April. Available at www.sundaytimes.lk/140427/columns/casino-crisis-first-major-revolt-within-rajapaksa-regime-93805.html (accessed 24 August 2015).

The Sunday Times (2014c) 'Why Facebook disabled Minister and BBS'. *The Sunday Times* [online], 27 July. Available at www.sundaytimes.lk/140727/columns/why-facebook-disabled-minister-and-bbs-108699.html (accessed 2 February 2016).

The Sunday Times (2014d) 'US probes monitoring MP's huge deals with PR firms'. *The Sunday Times* [online], 24 August. Available at www.sundaytimes.lk/140824/columns/us-probes-monitoring-mps-huge-deals-with-pr-firms-114679.html (accessed 15 March 2015).

The Sunday Times (2015) 'A year of yahapalanaya'. *The Sunday Times* [online], 13 December. Available at www.sundaytimes.lk/151213/sunday-times-2/a-year-of-yahapalanaya-174879.html (accessed 15 February 2016).

The Times of India (2013) 'Tamil Nadu shuts engineering colleges as campus stir spreads'. *The Times of India* [online], 19 March. Available at http://timesofindia.indiatimes.com/india/Tamil-Nadu-shuts-engineering-colleges-as-campus-stir-spreads/articleshow/19055539.cms?referral=PM (accessed 20 April 2016).

transCurrents (2008) 'Rajapaksa snubs Manmohan Singh by refusing to declare ceasefire and commence negotiations'. transCurrents [online], 13 November. Available at http://transcurrents.com/tc/2008/11/post_70.html (accessed 5 February 2015).

Transparency International (2010) *The Governance Report 2010*. Colombo: Transparency International.

TRIAL (2011) 'Criminal complaint filed against Deputy Ambassador of Sri Lanka for war crimes'. TRIAL International [online], 3 August. Available at www.trialinternational.org/latest-post/criminal-complaint-filed-against-deputy-ambassador-of-sri-lanka-for-war-crimes/ (accessed 20 April 2016).

Tunbridge, J. E. and Ashworth, G. (1996) *Dissonant Heritage: Managing the past as a resource in conflict*. Chichester: John Wiley and Sons.

UN (2010) 'Executive summary of the Secretary-General's Panel of Experts on accountability in Sri Lanka'. New York: United Nations (UN). Available at www.un.org/News/dh/infocus/Sri_Lanka/POE_Report_Executive_Summary.pdf (accessed 17 March 2016).

UN (2011a) *Report of the Secretary-General's Panel of Experts on Accountability in Sri Lanka*. New York: United Nations (UN). Available at www.un.org/News/dh/infocus/Sri_Lanka/POE_Report_Full.pdf (accessed 2 March 2015).

UN (2011b) 'Report of the Secretary-General's Panel of Experts on accountability in Sri Lanka: executive summary'. New York: United Nations (UN). Available at www.un.org/News/dh/infocus/Sri_Lanka/POE_Report_Executive_Summary.pdf (accessed 5 February 2014).

UN (2012) *Report of the Secretary-General's Internal Review Panel on United Nations Action in Sri Lanka: November 2012*. New York: United Nations (UN). Available at www.un.org/News/dh/infocus/Sri_Lanka/The_Internal_Review_Panel_report_on_Sri_Lanka.pdf (accessed 22 May 2015).

UN (2014) 'Sri Lanka: Pillay alarmed by intercommunal violence, calls for end to hate speech'. United Nations (UN), Human Rights Office of the High Commissioner [online], 15 June. Available at www.ohchr.org/EN/NewsEvents/Pages/DisplayNews.aspx?NewsID=14715 (accessed 24 February 2015).

UN (n.d.) 'The Universal Declaration of Human Rights'. New York: United Nations (UN). Available at www.un.org/en/universal-declaration-human-rights/ (accessed 28 October 2015).

UNDP (2012) *Assessment of Development Results: Evaluation of UNDP contribution. Sri Lanka*. New York: United Nations Development Programme (UNDP) Evaluation Office. Available at www.oecd.org/derec/undp/srilanka.pdf.

UNHCR (1997) *Background Paper on Refugees and Asylum Seekers from Sri Lanka*. Geneva: United Nations High Commissioner for Refugees (UNHCR). Available at www.refworld.org/docid/3ae6a6470.html (accessed 6 June 2016).

UN Regional Information Centre for Western Europe (2011) 'Human rights bodies to decide on full international inquiry'. [Online]. Available at www.

unric.org/en/sri-lanka/27122-human-rights-bodies-to-decide-on-full-international-inquiry (accessed 15 May 2015).
US Senate Committee on Foreign Relations (2009) *Sri Lanka: Recharting US strategy after the war*. Washington, DC: Committee on Foreign Relations, United States Senate. Available at www.foreign.senate.gov/imo/media/doc/SRI.pdf (accessed 1 March 2016).
UTHR (J) (2008) 'Pawns of an un-heroic war'. Special Report 31. Jaffna: University Teachers for Human Rights (Jaffna) (UTHR(J)). Available at www.uthr.org/SpecialReports/spreport31.htm (accessed 21 November 2015).
Uvin, P. (1998) *Aiding Violence: The development enterprise in Rwanda*. West Hartford, CT: Kumarian Press.
Uyangoda, J. (2005) 'Preface' in Perera, V., Kodithuwakku, M. and Bandara, D. (eds) *The Pen of Granite: A Richard de Zoysa 25th year memorial*. Colombo: Pawprint Publishing.
Uyangoda, J. (2011a) 'Sri Lanka in 2010'. *Asian Survey* 51(1): 131–7.
Uyangoda, J. (2011b) 'Travails of state reform in the context of protracted civil war in Sri Lanka' in Stokke, K. and Uyangoda, J. (eds) *Liberal Peace in Question: Politics of state and market reform in Sri Lanka*. London: Anthem Press.
Uyangoda, J. (2015) 'For a fresh beginning in Sri Lanka'. *The Hindu* [online], 10 January. Available at www.thehindu.com/todays-paper/tp-opinion/for-a-fresh-beginning-in-sri-lanka/article6773474.ece (accessed 13 January 2015).
Vaughan, M. (2011) 'After Westphalia, whither the nation state, its people and its government institutions?' Paper presented at the International Studies Association Asia-Pacific Regional Conference, 29 September. Available at http://espace.library.uq.edu.au/view/UQ:266787/AfterWestphalia.pdf (accessed 10 March 2015).
Venugopal, R. (2015) 'Democracy, development and the executive presidency in Sri Lanka'. *Third World Quarterly* 36(4): 670–90. Available at http://dx.doi.org/10.1080/01436597.2015.102440 (accessed 5 January 2015).
Verité Research (2012) 'Sri Lanka: LLRC Implementation Monitor. Statistical and analytical review no. 1'. Colombo: Verité Research. Available at www.veriteresearch.org/download-pdf_spreport.cfm?pdf_id=26. [The 367-page LLRC report can be downloaded at www.defence.lk/warcrimes/lessons_learnt_and_reconciliation_commission_final_report.html.]
Vikalpa Sri Lanka (2012) 'LLRC recommendation, Geneva resolution & future of the motherland – Dr Paikiasothy Saravanamuttu'. YouTube [online video], 16 May. Available at www.youtube.com/watch?feature=player_embedded&v=h77rvACI2dY.
Vimalarajah, L. and Cheran, R. (2010) 'Empowering diasporas: the dynamics of post-war transnational Tamil politics'. Berghof Occasional Paper 31. Berlin: Berghof Foundation.
Visalingam, A. C. (2011) *Good Governance and the Rule of Law*. Colombo: Citizens Movement for Good Governance.
Volkan, V. (1997) *Blood Lines: From ethnic pride to ethnic terrorism*. Boulder, CO: Westview Press.

Waduge, S. (2013) 'National identity and Sinhale majority'. *Daily News* [online], 18 October. Available at www.dailynews.lk/?q=features/national-identity-and-sinhala-majority (accessed 5 November 2014).

Walker, L. (2011) 'Sri Lanka and Iran: the 2030 nuclear power plant and Iranian support'. Institute of Peace and Conflict Studies [online], 11 February. Available at www.ipcs.org/article/nuclear/sri-lanka-and-iran-the-2030-nuclear-power-plant-and-3331.html (accessed 10 November 2015).

Walton, M. J. and Hayward, S. (2014) *Contesting Buddhist Narratives: Democratization, nationalism and communal violence in Myanmar*. Policy Studies 71. Honolulu: East-West Center.

Walton, O. and Saravanamuttu, P. (2011) 'In the balance? Civil society and the peace process 2002–2008' in Goodhand, J., Spencer, J. and Korf, B. (eds) *Conflict and Peacebuilding in Sri Lanka: Caught in the peace trap?* Abingdon: Routledge, pp. 183–200. Available at http://eprints.bham.ac.uk/645 (accessed 21 June 2015).

WAN and CHRD (2012) 'The situation of internally displaced, resettled and relocated women in the north and east of Sri Lanka. NGO Report: 2nd universal periodic review of Sri Lanka (November 2012)'. Women's Action Network (WAN) and Centre Human Rights and Development (CHRD). Available at http://lib.ohchr.org/HRBodies/UPR/Documents/Session14/LK/JS8_UPR_LKA_S14_2012_JointSubmission8_E.pdf (accessed 12 September 2015).

Wang, H. and Rosenau, J. N. (2009) 'China and global governance'. *Asian Perspective* 33(9): 5–39.

Weaver, M. and Chamberlain, G. (2009) 'Sri Lanka declares end to war with Tamil Tigers'. *The Guardian*, 19 May. Available at www.theguardian.com/world/2009/may/18/tamil-tigers-killed-sri-lanka (accessed 15 May 2015).

Weerawardhana, C. (2013a) 'From Ottawa to Colombo: on Canada's international role at the hour of Eastphalia'. *Études canadiennes/Canadian Studies* 75: 97–127. Available at https://eccs.revues.org/275.

Weerawardhana, C. (2013b) 'Forgotten woes: Sri Lanka's neoliberal politics'. openDemocracy [online], 27 September. Available at www.opendemocracy.net/opensecurity/chaminda-weerawardhana/forgotten-woes-sri-lanka%E2%80%99s-neoliberal-politics.

Weerawardhana, C. (2014) 'Problems of success? Post-war Sri Lanka's international challenges'. Groundviews [online], 11 May. Available at http://groundviews.org/2014/05/11/problems-of-success-post-war-sri-lankas-international-challenges/ accessed 2 April 2016).

Weiss, G. (2012 [2011]) *The Cage: The fight for Sri Lanka and the last days of the Tamil Tigers*. London: Vintage and Bodley Head.

Welikala, A. (2008) 'The devolution project in Sri Lanka: towards two nations in one state?' in Edrisinha, R. and Welikala, A. (eds) *Essays in Federalism in Sri Lanka*. Colombo: Centre for Policy Alternatives, pp. 67–84.

Welikala, A. (ed.) (2012) *The Sri Lankan Republic at 40: Reflections on constitutional history, theory and practice*. Colombo: Centre for Policy Alternatives.

Welikala, A. (2015a) 'Southphalia or southfailure? National pluralism and the state in South Asia' in Tierney, S. (ed.) *Nationalism and Globalisation: New settings, new challenges*. Oxford: Hart, pp. 95–6.

Welikala, A. (2015b) 'Sri Lanka's long constitutional moment'. *The Round Table* 104(55): 551–62.
Welikala, A. (2015c) 'Constitutional from and reform in postwar Sri Lanka' in Tushnet, M. and Khosla, M. (eds) *Unstable Constitutionalism: Law and politics in Sri Lanka*. Cambridge: Cambridge University Press, pp. 320–54.
Welikala, A. (ed.) (2015d) *Reforming Sri Lankan Presidentialism: Provenance, problems and prospects*. Colombo: Centre for Policy Alternatives.
Wettasinghe, C. (2015) 'Ongoing worker strike costs RPCs heavily'. *Daily Mirror* [online], 10 July. Available at www.dailymirror.lk/79099/plantation-crisis (accessed 2 March 2016).
Wezeman, T., Bromley, M. and Wezeman, P. D. (2009) 'International arms transfers' in *SIPRI Year Book 2009: Armaments, disarmament and international security*. Stockholm: Stockholm International Peace Research Institute (SIPRI), pp. 315–20. Available at www.sipri.org/yearbook/2009/files/SIPRIYB0907.pdf (accessed 14 November 2015).
Wheeler, N. J. (2000) *Saving Strangers: Humanitarian intervention in international society*. Oxford: Oxford University Press.
Wheeler, T. (2012) *China and Conflict-affected States: Between principle and pragmatism. Sri Lanka*. London: Saferworld. Available at www.saferworld.org.uk/downloads/pubdocs/FAB%20Sri%20Lanka.pdf (accessed 15 October 2015).
Whitman, J. (2009) *The Fundamentals of Global Governance*. Basingstoke: Palgrave Macmillan.
Wickramasuriya, S. R. (2005) 'The present socio-economic-political climate in postcolonial Sri Lanka & the myth of English as a means of access to social equality'. Available at http://ro.uow.edu.au/cgi/viewcontent.cgi?article=2462&context=edupapers (accessed 10 February 2015).
Wijewardene, R. (2009) 'The known devil's advocate: in defence of Mahinda Rajapaksa'. *The Sunday Leader* [online], 6 December. Available at www.thesundayleader.lk/2009/12/06/the-known-devil%E2%80%99s-advocate-in-defence-of-mahinda-rajapaksa/ (accessed 7 September 2015).
Wijeyeratne, R. (2013) *Nation, Constitutionalism and Buddhism in Sri Lanka*. London: Routledge.
Wilson, M. (2014) 'Sri Lanka hires up in Washington amid war crimes probe'. *The Hill* [online], 23 October. Available at http://thehill.com/business-a-lobbying/lobbying-contracts/221722-sri-lanka-hires-up-in-washington-amid-war-crimes-probe (accessed 6 March 2015).
Women's Action Network (2013a) 'Militarized north-east Sri Lanka: Muslim and Tamil women systematically crushed by lawlessness and expropriation'. *Colombo Telegraph* [online], March 12. Available at www.colombotelegraph.com/index.php/day-and-night-bana-and-militarized-north-east-sri-lanka/ (accessed 20 March 2015).
Women's Action Network (2013b) 'Ashraf Nagar: the courageous struggle of peasants against the forcible land acquisition in Ampara District'. Groundviews [online], 19 January. Available at http://groundviews.org/2013/01/19/ashraf-nagar-the-courageous-struggle-of-peasants-against-the-forcible-land-acquisition-in-ampara-district/ (accessed 21 May 2015).
Yiftachel, O. (2006) *Ethnocracy: Land and identity politics in Israel/Palestine*. Philadelphia, PA: University of Pennsylvania Press.

INDEX

References to the endnotes are indicated by n preceding the page number.

51st Division, HQ built on LTTE graveyard, 137
57th Division, accused of war crimes, 157
58th Brigade, accused of war crimes, 91

A9 Highway, 35, 36
abductions, 167, 179; of Red Cross workers, 109 see also schoolboys, abduction of
Abeysekera, Sunila, 158
Accelerated Mahaweli Development Programme, 59
accountability, 37, 39, 41, 46, 58, 73–4, 91, 92, 144, 145, 146–7, 159, 169, 172, 176, 192; definition of processes of, 80; quest for, 146–72
Accra Agenda for Action, 117
Aceh, 118; civil war in, 128–9
Action Contre la Faim (ACF), 91, 108; aid workers killed, 158, n211, n215
activism, transnational, 156
Afghanistan, 20
Ahmadinejad, Mahmoud, n216
aid, international: linked to reform or peace, 119; regimes of, international, 15, 113–21
Akashi, Yasashi, 157
Aleppo, no fire zones in, 191

All Ceylon Muslim Congress (ACMC), 45
All Ceylon Tamil Congress (ACTC), 45
Alternative Peoples Forum see Samagi Human Rights Festival
Amman, Pottu, 110
Amnesty International, 14, 39, 76, 95, 156, 158, 159
Amunugaman, Sarath, 187
Anderson, Benedict, *Imagined Communities*, 129
Anderson, Mary, 100, n214
animal sacrifices, protests against, 123
Annan, Kofi, 3, 100
Appadurai, A., 18
Arasanayagam, Jean, 94
archeology, land appropriated for, 141
architectural heritage, destruction of, 136
Armitage, Richard, 157
Ashraf Nagar, women protest over land requisitions, 219
Ashton, Catherine, 58
Asian Development Bank (ADB), 97, 107, 182, n217; debt owing to, 187
assassinations, n198, n217
Association of Parents of Missing Soldiers, 44

Association of Southeast Asian Nations (ASEAN), 81
asylum applications: by Sri Lankans, 99; by Tamils, 89
Athaullah, A. L. M., 133
Aung San Suu Kyi, 128, 184
Australia, issue of immigration in, 157, n220
Australian Government Refugee Review Tribunal, 141
Austria, 180

Babakhel, Mohammad Ali, 27
Balasingham, Anton, 168
Balaya, Ravana, 133
Balendran, Jeyakumari, 194; arrest of, 164
Ban Ki-Moon, 28, 37, 70, 79, 156, 189; visit to Sri Lanka, 147
Bandara, Navarthne, 56
Bandaranaike, Sirimavo, n208
Bandaranaike International Airport: development of, 32; road link to, 149
Bandaranayake, Shirani, impeachment of, 57, 68, 87, 161
Bangladesh, 66–7, 125
Bar Association: members issued with death threats, 57; protests by, 58
Bassa killer group, n199
Bastian, Sunil, 16–17, 43
Bathiutheen, Rishard, 133
Bayart, J.-F., 17
BBC, 25
Belarus, 88, 174
Bell Pottinger Group, 83–4
Beltway company, 85
Bharatiya Janata Party (BJP) (India), 90, 129
Biafran War, 12
bilingualism, 128
Black July (1983), 98, 185, n198

Blair, Tony, 80, 188
Blake, Robert O., n207
Bodu Bala Sena (BBS), 65, 69, 123, 132; rise of, 129–34
Bosnia, Western intervention in, 80
Boutros-Ghali, Boutros, 99
Brahimi, Lakhdar, 73
Bretton Woods system, 5
BRICS countries, 6, 13, 189
Buddha, 50; seen as originator of human rights, 133–4; statues of, 123, 134, 135, 140
Buddhism, 127, 136, n219; construction of shrines and temples, 123, 134, 139; engaged, 130; establishment of holy sites, 41; expansion of, 133; monasteries as seats of learning, 32; political, 5, 10, 50, n218; precepts of, 12; privileged role of, 51, 52; stupas, 136, 140; Theravada, 12, 128; tourist routes, 141 see also Sinhalese Buddhist identity
Buddhist centrality, 122
Buddhist majoritarianism, 122–45, 192
Buddhist monks, 65, 123–4, 132, 133, 150; cooptation of, 129; protest against gaming tourism, 148–9
Burleigh, Peter, n202
Burma / Myanmar, 93, 118, 184, 194, n226; aid from, 72
Burman Buddhist identity, 128
Burmanisation, use of term, 128
Bush, George, 188
Bush, Kenneth, 105, 106, n215
Butenis, Patricia, n210

Cabraal, A.N., 83
Cameron, David, visit to Jaffna, 143, 144, 164

Canada, 155; boycott of CHOGM, 184; Tamil community in, 89
Carnegie Endowment for International Peace, 121
Cartwright, Silvia, 162
Carver, Fred, 164
Casino Crisis, 148–9
caste dynamics in Sri Lanka, n208
ceasefire, 23, 99, 100–1, 105, 114, 158, 178, n221
censorship, 152, 183
Central Bank of Sri Lanka, 85, 86, n227
Central Intelligence Agency (CIA), *World Factbook*, 30
Centre for Human Rights, 152
Centre for Peace Alternatives, 135
Centre for Policy Alternatives (CPA), 56, n207; documenting of war, 137
Ceylon Workers Congress (CWC), 45
Chaaminda, Sumith, *Fishing in Turbulent Waters*, 151
Chechnya, 11; counter-insurgency in, 20, 116
checkpoints and roadblocks, 35
child soldiers, 42, 167; recruited by LTTE, n224
China, 11, 12, 13, 23, 27, 73, 76, 81, 88, 115, 175, 180, 194, 196, n228; aid agenda of, 1–4; aid provided by, 35, 44, 149; buys rubber from Sri Lanka, 186; debt owing to, 187; diplomatic support for Sri Lanka, 82; funding provided by, 67–8; gifts to Sri Lanka, 186; imports its own workers, 149; influence of (growing, 177, 184–5; reduction of, 187–8); land given to, 168; loans from, 30, 176, 183, n226; military aid from, 178, 183; oil pipeline to, 184; 'One China' policy, 27; policy of non-interference, n228; Sri Lanka imports from, n203; statement on human rights, 143; 'string of pearls' strategy of, 185; supports UN policy on Syria, 189
China Communications Construction Company, 149
Chinese convicts, imported as labour, n221
Christianity, 133, 136, n208
Christians: attacks on, 130; rites interfered with, 135
civil society: polarisation of, 101; reduced space for, 158; use of term, n214
civilians: as casualties, 15, 108 (denial of, 93); death toll of, 196; evacuation of, 109–10; killing of, 82, 111; protection of, 20, 25, 75, 189, n229; used as human shields, 79, 188, n210, n228 *see also* safe zones for civilians
Clinton, Hillary, 74, 75
Co-Chair Group of States, 23, 185
Colombia, forced displacements in, 190
Colombo: beautification of, 47; port (development in, 31, 35, 149, 168; privatisation of, n217)
Colombo-Katunayake Expressway, costs of, 149
Colville, Rupert, n211
Commission of Inquiry Act, 169
Commission on Global Governance, 4
Committee Against Torture (CAT), 160
Committee on Economic, Social and Cultural Rights (CESCR), 160

Committee on the Elimination of Discrimination Against Women (CEDAW), 160
Common Humanitarian Action Plan (CHAP), 106
Commonwealth, 70, 184; Charter of, 67; Sri Lanka membership of, 142
Commonwealth Heads of Government Meeting (CHOGM), 64, 66–8, 124, 139, 142–5, 150, 179, 181, 184
Commonwealth Human Rights Initiative, 142
Commonwealth Law Conference, 66
Commonwealth Lawyers Association, 66
Commonwealth Legal Education Association, 66
Commonwealth Magistrates' and Judges' Association, 66
Commonwealth Ministerial Action Group, 142–3
consociationalism, 126
constitution, n221; 13th amendment, 28, 29, 65, 147, n202; 17th amendment, 56; 18th amendment, 55, 56, 59, n207; 19th amendment, 192; of 1972, 51, n206; of 1978, 31, 53, 54, 55; rights accorded under, 151; unitary nature of, 62–3 see also Donoughmore constitution and Soulbury constitution
constitutional reform, 27–9, 146
Consultation Task Force, 169
Consultative Committee on Humanitarian Assistance, 214
Convention against Torture (CAT), 182
Convention on the Rights of the Child (CRC), 182
Coomaraswamy, Radhika, 3

corruption, 33–4, 65, 68, 146, 147, 149, n206, n213; combatting of, 20, 117, n217
Costa Rica, 180
Council of the EU, 14
counter-insurgency, 11, 35, 114, 183, 190
counter-terrorism, 175, 176, 181, 188, n208; methods of, 2
Cranford Johnson Robinson PR, 84
credit for achieving peace, 100
Crimea, 191
Cuba, 73, 74, 88
cultural domination, 134–9
culture wars, 136–7
Cyclone Nargis, 118

Dalai Lama, n226
dams, building of, 59
Darusman, Marzuki, 79
David, Kumar, 173
de-mining, 36, 60, 61, 120
dead, respect for, 138
death squads, n199
debt: management of, 188, 196; sovereign, 187, n227
defence spending, 35
demilitarisation, 39, 40
Democratic People's Front (DPF), 45
Democratic Republic of Congo, 20
Democratic Republic of Korea, 88
Department for International Development (DFID), 106
Devanampiya Tissa, n199
development: central control of, 59; policy, reinvention of, 9 see also unipolar command development
development assistance, shift in emphasis, 99–103

Index | 265

devolution, 27–9, 40, 126
Dhanapala, Jayantha, 3
Dharmadasa, Visaka, 44
Dias, Jagath, 157; accused of war crimes, 91
diaspora *see* Tamil diaspora
dirigisme in economic policies, 54
disappearances, 2, 14, 34, 39, 71, 99, 104, 137, 143, 153, 164, 166, 190, n211 *see also* abductions
displaced persons, 25–6, 106
displacements, forced, 190
divide and rule, 122–45
Divinegume plan, 57
'Do No Harm', principle of, 100, n214
Doctors of the World, 97
Donoughmore constitution, n205–6
double minorities, concept of, 125
Duffield, Mark, 116, n199
Dutch Burghers, 94
Dutthagamini, n219
Dutugemunu, King, 49–50, n218

Eastern Awakening programme, 35
eastward turn of policy, 5, 183
Economic and Technical Cooperation Agreement (ETCA), 228
education, 32, 50, 187; of former LTTE cadres, 42
Eelam People's Democratic Party (EPDP), 45, 60
Eelam Revolutionary Organisation of Students (EROS), 19, 45, 217
Egypt, 73, 74
Ekneligoda, Prageeth, n211
Ekneligoda, Sandhya, 78, n211
Elder, James, 71–2
Elders, The, 156
elections, 53–4, 63, 102, n202;

boycotting of, 127, 174; for Eastern Provincial Council, 64; for Northern Provincial Council, 179; of 2009, 29; of 2010, 90; of 2015, 1, 146
Eliasson, Jan, n216
Elizabeth II, Queen, 144
Emergency Architects, 108
Ennals, Martin, 98
ethnic cleansing, n209; use of term, 122
ethnocracy, 52
European Centre for Constitutional and Human Rights, 157
European Union (EU), 23, 58, 101, 159, 182, 194; requirement of accountability, 73–4; suspends Sri Lanka's GSP status, 83, 182
evictions, in Colombo, 151
extortion, 60
extrajudicial killings, 39, 99, 104

F-7 fighters, gifted from China, 178
facial recognition software, n212
family, ideology of, n218
fear, fostering of, 72
federalism, 29, 126
Fernando, Laksiri, 44
Fernando, Nimalka, 180
Fernando, Ruki, 164
fishermen, n208
fishing industry, 151; discrimination against, 141–2, n220; obstructed by mines, 61
'Five Hubs Plus Tourism' document, 31
Fonseka, Bhavani, 168–9
Fonseka, Sarath, 29, 75, n202, n208
Ford Foundation, freezes aid to India, n218
Foreign Agents Registration Act (FARA) Unit, 84–5, 86

Forum Asia, 156
FORUT organisation, 95
Foucault, Michel, 7
Four Square Gospel Church, attack on, 133
Fowzie, A. H. M., 133, 179
free speech *see* freedom of expression
freedom from torture, 88, 167
Freedom from Torture group, n223
Freedom House, report on Sri Lanka, 96
freedom of assembly, 138
freedom of expression, 88, 124, 138, 152, 167, 180
Friday Forum, 77–8, 150
Fujimori, Alberto, 71
Furedi, Frank, 80

G20 group, 6
Geneva Conventions, 8, 26, n201; Protocols I and II, 82
Geneva Process, 158–64, 193
genocide: charges of, 156; use of term, 172
Georgia, 20
Germany, 95, 157
Ghandi, Rajiv, assassination of, 23
global governance *see* governance, global
Global Leadership Forum, 156
Global Tamil Forum (GTF), 90, 179, 192
globalisation, 18, 113; concept of, 4–5
Gonussa killer group, n199
governance: global, 173 (contested understandings of, 4–8; definition of, 115; features of, 8; in Sri Lankan context, 11–15; norms of, 113–21; norms of, reshaping of, 188–92; theory of, 165); good, 146, n221; use of term, 22
Government of Sri Lanka (GoSL), 7, 10, 12, 34, 41, 72, 82, 102, 106, 114, 175–6; hire of lobbying firms, 86; human rights violations by, 79; 'Integrity of the Judicial System' resolution, 87; non-answerability of, 88; power-sharing discussions, 105 *see also* Rajapaksa regime
governmentality, concept of, 7
Govigama caste, n208
Grama Rajya, 57
graveyards, razing of, 41
grieving: cultural norms of, 137; difficulties of, 42
Gunasekara, Tisaranee, 47, 143
Gunawardena, Dinesh, 179

Hakeem, Rauff, 132–3
halal food, criticism of, 131
Hambantota, 64; construction of airport in, 32; construction of oil refineries in, 32; port development in, 31, 35, 150; power plant in, 32
Hammurabi, n200
Harare Declaration, 142
health, indicators for, 50
Herath, Viritha, 96
heritage, uses of, 135–6
heteroglossia, 18
high security zones, 35, 37, 62
Hindu nationalism, 129
Hindu sites: targetting of, 123; razing of, 41, 133
Hinduism, 137
Hindus, rites interfered with, 135
home-grown, meaning of, 147–8
'home-grown solutions', 16, 146–72
Hua Chunying, 82

Index | 267

hubs, 37; concept of, 31–2
human rights, 81, 82, 88, 91, 101, 143, 151, 165, 185, 190; global norms of, 166; monitoring of, n222; observers, 107; seen as originating from Buddha, 133–4; transnational activism regarding, 165; under threat globally, 194; violations of, 26, 28–9, 37, 64, 71, 76, 79, 107, 113, 153, 158, 160, 161–2, 183, 193, n222; underreporting of, 111
Human Rights Council see UN Human Rights Council
Human Rights Law Centre (Australia), 157
Human Rights Watch (HRW), 39, 76, 95, 156, 158, 159
humanitarian corridors, 109, 191
humanitarian imperative, 118
humanitarian intervention, use of term, 80
Humanitarian Operation: Factual analysis report, 80
'humanitarian pause', 73–4

identity politics, instrumentalisation of, 16
Illangai Muhathuwaraman, demolition of Ganesh temple, 134
impunity, 14, 91, 92, 162, 164, 193; crisis of, 157; of presidency, 55, 192
Independent Commission to Investigate Allegations of Bribery or Corruption, 34
Independent Commissions, 55
India, 12, 23, 73, 74, 81, 125, 129, 147–8, 175, 179, 181, 193, 196, n227, n228; demonstrations in, 157; foreign policy of, 184–5, 186–7, n210; influence of, n209;

loan of Kapilavastu relics, 122–3; military aid from, 183; Tamils living in, 90, 98
Indian Peacekeeping Force, attack on Jaffna, 98
Indo-Sri Lanka Agreement, 28
Indonesia, 36, 128
infant mortality, rates of, 51
INFORM organisation, 167
infrastructure projects, 150
Ini Avan film, 122
insider-outsider dichotomy, 94
Institute for Democracy and Electoral Assistance, 125–6
Institute of Peace and Conflict Studies, 114
Inter-Agency Standing Committee on the Centrality of Protection in Humanitarian Action, n229
Internal Review Panel on United Nations Action in Sri Lanka ... (Petrie Report), 23, 189, 111–12
internally displaced persons (IDPs): relief for, 180; resettlement of, 28, 36, 60; statistics for, 120
international assistance, 97–9
International Commission of Jurists (ICJ), 58, 158
International Committee of the Red Cross (ICRC), 25, 79, 98, 109, 180, 190; required to close offices, 59
International Convention on Civil and Political Rights (ICCPR), 6, 26, 166, 182; violation of, 88
International Criminal Court (ICC), 91; Rome Statute, 82
International Crisis Group (ICG), 39, 87, 156, 159; report, 36
International Federation of the Red Cross and Red Crescent Societies (IFRC), 118

International Human Rights Association Bremen, 156
International Independent Group of Eminent Persons, 99
International Institute of Strategic Studies (IISS), 83
International Monetary Fund (IMF), 37, 103, 107, 182, n217; closes Sri Lanka office, 72–3; offers credit facility, 34, 72
International Organization for Migration (IOM), n204
International Truth and Justice Project (ITJP), 179
International Working Group on Sri Lanka, 156, 159, 167, n222
International Alert, 99
Internet, 130
internment of Tamils, 89
Investigating the Operations of Non-governmental Organisations, select committee, 95
Iran, 12; aid from, 72, 114; relations with Sri Lanka, n216
Iraq, 24–5; Western intervention in, 80, 81
Iraq Body Count, 20
Irion, Mark, 86
Irish Forum for Peace in Sri Lanka, 156
Islam, 66
Islamophobia, 68
Island at War documentary, 19
Israel, war in Gaza, 20

Jaffna Library, burning of, 105, 123
Jana Sabha, 63–4, n207
Janathā Vimukthi Peramuna (JVP), 49, 98, 102, 105, 127, 149, n203, n208; uprising of, 1–2, 14
Japan, 23, 93, 101, 179; aid from, 106, 107, 114, n217

Japan peace conference, 2
Japanese peace groups, 157
Jathika Hela Urumaya (JHU), 50, 62, 65, 102, 127
Jayasinghe, Amal, 152
Jayatilleka, Dayan, 73–4, 181
Jayawardene, J. R., 2, 30, 32, 185
Jayeram, Jayalalitha, 157
Jenkins, Ivor, n225
Journal of Humanitarian Assistance, 167
journalists: control of, 195; killings of, 173
judiciary, weakness of, 52

Kadirgamar, Lakshman, 175
Kagame, Paul, n203
Kalyvas, S. N. *The Logic of Violence in Civil War*, 17
Kandyan convention, 128
Kandyan Kingdom, 19, n199
Karava caste, n208
Karthiaai (Karthikai), 138
Karuna group, 60, n207
Kashmir, 193; curfew in, 195
Katussa killer group, n199
Keenan, Alan, 20, 89
kidnappings, 122; for ransom, 60
Kilinochchi, 24; destruction of infrastructure in, 36; women of, 153
Killing Fields documentary, 75–6
Knaul, Gabriela, 58
Kobani, US bombing of, 191
Kohona, Palitha, 11, 20, 91, 178
Kosovo, establishment of, 115
Kouchner, Bernard, 27, 74
Kumaratunga, Chandrika, 55, 105, n198, n207
Kurunegala, 64

Lall, Aftab, 61–2
land: issues of, 193; ownership of,

146; requisitioned by military, 61, n219
languages: Chinese, 154; English, 33, 40, 97, 173, 195, n199; heterogeneity of, in Sri Lanka, n199; problems of translation, 153; Sinhala, 33, 123, 145, 154, 195, n199, n218, n221 (for singing of national anthem, 135, 193; imposition of, 138, 139); Tamil, 45, 154, 195, n199, n221
Latimer House Principles, 68, 142
Law 387, n229
Leahy, Patrick, n221
Lee Kuan Yew, 30
Lessons Learned and Reconciliation Commission (LLRC), 38, 39, 41, 64, 75, 76, 91, 92, 138, 147, 174; conclusions mothballed, 154; hearings of, 139; motivations of, 155; paradox of, 152–6; report of, 184 (only published in English, 40)
Levick company, 86
Lewis, David, 177
liberalism, myopia of, 17
Liberation Tamil Tigers of Eelam (LTTE), 2, 3, 12, 13, 19, 20, 22, 24, 25, 28, 60, 78, 82, 86, 89, 92, 93, 101–2, 105, 106, 108, 110, 112, 114, 126–7, 141, 161, 167, 174, 176, 177–8, 188, 190, n198, n203, n210, n224, n225, n228; access to imprisoned members, 40; attempts to extort Muslim businesses, n203; criticism of, 180; defeat of, 9, 23, 27–8, 44, 67, 70, 73, 89, 93, 111, 116, 138, 146, 175, 177, 185, n200; destruction of administration of, 53; expulsion of Muslims, 126; graveyards destroyed by military, 137; human rights violations by, 26, 79, 87; judges, training of, 168; listed as terrorist organisation, 14, 71; makes use of tsunami aid, n213; surrender of troops, n204; surveillance of, 91; takes over Muttur, 108; use of civilians as human shields, 188, n228

Liberty International Group LLC, 85, 86
Libya, 180; aid from, 72; NATO intervention in, 189
Lies Agreed Upon documentary, 86–7
life expectancy, rates of, 51
literacy, 50; rates of, 51
literary heritage, destruction of, 136
Liu, Joanne, n199
Liu Jianchao, 188
Liu Xiaobo, 82
Liyanage, Sumanasiri, 177
Look East policy, 25
Lunstead, Jeffrey, 100

Maaveerar Naal (Heroes' Day), 138
Machiavelli, Niccolò, n206
Mack, Connie, 86
Mackay, Peter, 71–2
Madaya, siege of, 189
Madhu refugee camp, closure of, 190
Maha Sangha, 149
Mahajana Eksath Peramuna (MEP), 50
Mahavamsa, n201; as historical record, 127
Mahaweli Authority, 59–60
Mahaweli Basin development scheme, n214

Mahesan, Father P., 164
Mahinda Chintana, 31, 30, 37, 61, n218
Mahuruf, M., 131–2
Majeed, Najeeb Abdul, 44
majoritarianism *see* Buddhist majoritarianism
Malaysia, 93, 181; sedition law in, 195
Maleham, observance of, 137
Mani, Rama, 95, n213
Manik Farm, 26
Mannar, discovery of mass grave at, 161
Māra, tempter figure, n219
Martin, Ian, 167–8
Marzoof, Saleem, 34
Matha film, 122
Mauritius, boycott of CHOGM, 181
Médecins Sans Frontières (MSF), 97
Mel, N. de, 153–4
Menon, Shivshankar, n202
Mexico, 180
Miliband, David, 27, 74
military, 35, 172; as army of occupation, 36; claims to act on behalf of people, 138–9; involved in agriculture, 36, 61; involved in economy, 36, 135; seizure of land for bases, 61
Minority Rights Group International, 124
missing persons, 196, n221 *see also* disappearances
Mistura, Staffan de, 191
monuments *see* war monuments
Moro Islamic Liberation Front, 93
Mortimer, Edward, 157
mosques, desecration of, 66, 131; destruction of, at Amuradhapura, 123; ordered to relocate, 124; under military occupation, 135

mother, centrality accorded to, n218
mourning rituals, improvisation of, 138
Movement for Inter-Racial Justice and Equality (MIRJE), 97
Mullaitivu district, 24; destruction of infrastructure in, 36; women of, 153
Mullivaikkal hospital, shelling of, n201
Muralitharan, Vinayagamurthi (alias Karuna), 105
Muslim sites, targetting of, 123
Muslims, 28, 66, 145, 197, n203, n220; attacks on, 130–1, 182; dress and customs (of women, 132; vilification of, 66); expulsion of, 126; lack of protection for, 69; maltreatment of, 131–3, n219; rioting against, 129; rites interfered with, 135; Muttur, n211; NGOs pressured to quit, 108
Myanmar *see* Burma/Myanmar

Nainativu, changing of name, 134
Nanayakara, Vasudeva, 133
Nandikadal Lagoon, war museum, 140
nation-state, 8, 53 *see also* state, Westphalian model of
national anthem: to be sung in Sinhala, 33; to be sung in two languages, 193
National Human Rights Council, establishment of, 183
National Policy on Local Government, 63
Nelson Mullins company, 85
Nepal, 181
Netherlands Institute of Human Rights, 98

Index | 271

neutrality, required of agencies, 118
New Maritime Silk Road, 188
NGO Forum *see* International Working Group on Sri Lanka
No Fire Zone documentary, 154, 181
no fire zones, 20, 79, 82, 110, 188, 191
Nobel Prize, award boycott by Sri Lanka, 82
nodes of authority, 9
Non-Aligned Movement (NAM), 11, 70, 74, 182
non-alignment, 174
non-governmental organisations (NGOs), 9, 14, 23, 60, 78, 93, 95, 160, 165, n213; activities of, 97–9; become targets, 16; government's hostility towards, 96–7; involvement of seen as neo-colonial, 102–3; new encroachment of, 105–6; not permitted to hold press conferences, 120–1; ordered to quit Vanni, 108; relocate to Vavuniya, 103; required to act under remit of Department of Defence, 59, 180; staff threatened and intimidated, 95 *see also* Action Contre la Faim
non-interference, 70–93, n228; concept of, 15
Non-official Group of Friends of Sri Lanka, 157
Non-Violent Peace Force, 108
norms, global, concept of, n202
Norochcholai, power plant in, 35
North Korea, 186
Norway, 101, 105; engagement in peace-brokering, 23, 24, 49, 81, 99, 101, 110–11, 126, 177, 185, n216
nuclear power, 32

Obama, Barack, n200
Office of National Unity and Reconciliation (ONUR), 168
Office of the United Nations High Commissioner for Human Rights (OHCHR), 70, 99, 169; attempts to discredit, 180; criticism of, 162
OHCHR Investigation on Sri Lanka (OISL), 161, 171, 180; deadline for submissions, 162; report, 161–2, 168
'One Belt One Road', n227
Operation Liberation, 19
Organisation for Economic Cooperation and Development (OECD): aid from, 114; Development Assistance Committee (DAC), 119; principles of, n217
Organisation of Islamic Cooperation (OIC), 65–6, 68–9; visit to Colombo, 182
Ossetia, 20
outnumbering, perception of, 125
outside interference, rejection of, 188
outsiders, 94–121; concept of, 94 (used as blanket term, 95)
Oxfam, 109

Pakistan, 12, 74, 76, 125, n228; military supplies from, 178, n225
Panama, Western intervention in, 80
Panel of Experts, 75, n221
para-militaries, 167; war crimes of, 163
parallel structures, establishment of, 65
Paris Declaration on Aid Effectiveness, 116–17
parliamentary select committees (PSC), 147–8

parliamentary systems of government, 47
Pasikudah village, 195
Pathmanathan, Kumaran, 110–11; arrest of, 90
Patriotic Front, 57
Patten, Chris, 73
Patton Boggs LLP, 84
peace: 'hybrid', 10; promotion of, 119; use of term, 177
Peace and Conflict Impact Analysis tool, 106
Peace Brigades International (PBI), 99
peace dividend, 150; use of term, 119
'Peace Village' (Vavuniya), 42
peacebuilding: concept of, 99; illiberal, 9–10; liberal, 25, 100, 196; use of term, 119
Peiris, G. L., 75, 174, 179, n211; visit to UK, 83
Peiris, Mohan, 133
pensions, reform of, 149–50
People's Alliance Government, 24
People's Liberation Organisation of Tamil Eelam (PLOTE), 45, 115, n217
People's Revolutionary Army (PRA), n199
Perera, A. P., 84
Perera, Dilan, 179
Perera, Jehan, 154
Perera, Kusal, 97–8
Perera-Rajasingham, Nimanthi, 177
Permanent People's Tribunal, 156
Peru, 71
Petrie, Charles, 112–13
Petrie Report *see* Internal Review Panel on United Nations Action in Sri Lanka
Philippines, 93

Pillay, Navaneethan, 58, 69, 75, 78, 164, n209–10, n211, n220, n223; visit to Colombo, 174
Pinochet, Augusto, n229
Pinto-Jayawardena, Kishali, 88, 166
Plantation Association, 150
Platform for Freedom, 40
ports, development of, 31, 35, 149, 168
Post Tsunami Operational Management Structure, 102
post-conflict projects, 103, 104–5
post-war recovery, models of, 146–72
poverty, reduction of, 44, 57, 97, 106, 145
Power, Samantha, n200, 200
power sharing, 119, 126
Powura, Hela Bodu, 133
Prabhakaran, Velupillai, 25, 90, 110, 115, n198
Pradeshiya Sabhas, 63
Premadasa, R., 30, 98; death of, n198
presidency, executive, 47–69
President's Multi-ethnic Experts Committee, 147
presidential system, 47–8; calls for abolition of, 68
Presidential Task Force, 41, 60, 62, 120
Prevention of Terrorism Act, 2, 39, 172, 184
privatisation, 103, n217
proportional representation, 53–4
protection, 191; as norm of UN, 114
Protective Accommodation Rehabilitation Centres (PARC), 204
public relations campaigns of GoSL, 83–8, 178

Public Security Ordinance, 2
push back, within UN system, 71,
 73–83
Putin, Vladimir, 191

Qin Gang, 143
Quakers, training manual on
 mediation, 99
Quick, Ian, 103–4

race riots, 1, 97
Rae, Bob, n213
railways: building of, 35; Palai to
 Kankesanthurai, 149
Rajapaksa, Basil, 41, 48, 57, 60,
 87, n200
Rajapaksa, Chamal, 48; appointed
 Speaker, 56
Rajapaksa, Gotabaya, 23, 24–5,
 29, 47, 48, 92, 174, 178, n201,
 n205
Rajapaksa, Mahinda, 14, 44,
 47–69 *passim*, 92, 102, 113,
 115–16, 126, 143, 144, 145,
 158, 168, 170, 172, 179, 180,
 186, 195, n202, n207; address
 to Non-Aligned Movement,
 70; address to UN General
 Assembly, 38, 81; agrees to
 inquiry into disappearances
 and killings, 99; called by
 Ban Ki-moon, 111; claims to
 Buddhist values, 123; elected
 prime minister, 49, 105, 174;
 electoral defeat of, 1, 146,
 n209; executive presidency of,
 55–8; foreign policy of, 187;
 governing responsibilities of, 48;
 honorifics of, 50; likened to King
 Dutugemunu, 18, 49; manifesto
 aims of, 30; opposition to
 international agencies, 26, 72;
 presented as champion of a
 small island, 165; protest walk
 of, n206; summons against, 91;
 views on peace initiatives, 24;
 views on outsiders, 120; visit to
 Northern Ireland, 49
Rajapaksa regime, 3, 5, 7, 8, 12,
 14, 15, 21, 25, 37, 43, 61, 93,
 95, 114, 120, 139, 155, 159,
 169, 173, 175, 176, 178, 183,
 196, 206, n222; disillusionment
 with, 147; split in, 148; use of
 state media, 164
Rajapaksa model, 27
Rampton, David, 128
Rathnapriya, Saman, 56
Ratner, Steven, 79, n202
Ravaya, Sinhala, 133
reconciliation, 12, 15, 22, 28, 29,
 37–46, 58, 59, 71, 84, 91, 105,
 138, 155, 188; concept of, n204;
 through development, 151
recovery, competing models for,
 22–46
Red Cross, workers abducted, 109
regime change, use of term, 188
regional hub, concept of, 31–7
rehabilitation, 38
Rehman, Iskander, n210
religion, privileging of, 52
religious militancy, 129
religious observance, controls over,
 135
religious shrines, destruction of,
 137
resettlement of populations, 59,
 60, 62
responsibility to protect (R2P), 189
Richards, Paul, 17
right to information, 154
Right to Information Act, 195
roads: building of, 35, 149; to
 Bandaranaike airport, 150
Rodgers, Malcolm, 144–5

Rohingya Muslims, n219; attacks on, 129
Ropers, Norbert, 95
Rubber-Rice Pact, 186
rule of law, 185, 191, 196
Rumaraghe, Chandra, 82–3
Russia, 11, 20, 76, 116, 194
Russian Federation, 88
Rwanda, n203; genocide in, 100

Sabah, 195
safe zones for civilians, 190, n201, n215 see also no fire zones
Samagi Human Rights Festival, 139
Samaraweera, Mangala, 126, 149, 169
Samarawickrama, Malik, 196
Sampanthan, Rajavarothiam, 43, 147, 148
Sampur: power plant at, 32; special economic zone, 33
Sangha, Buddhist, 176
Saravanamuttu, Paikiasothy, 22, 37, 40, 177
Sarawak, 195
Saudi Arabia, 93
schoolboys, abduction of, 14, 17
Secretariat for Muslims (SFM), 66
Secure Livelihoods Research Consortium, 142
Securities Exchange Commission (SEC), 65
security forces, downsizing and retraining of, 196
Segal, Hugh, 144
self-determination, 115
Sen, Amartya, 146
Senanayake, Dudley, 54
sexual violence, 39, 197
Shama, Kamalesh, 142, 144
Shanie, 33
Shining Path, defeat of, 71
Silva, Harsha De, 149

Silva, Shavendra, 90–1
Silva, de, J., 17, 18
Singapore, 32; viewed as corrupt state, 33–4
Singapore model, 22, 30–1, 32, 62, 146, n203, n204; criticism of, 33
Singh, Manmohan, 25, 28, n210
Sinha le campaign, 143
Sinhala majoritarianism, 186
'Sinhala only' policy, 33
Sinhalese Buddhist identity, 127, 128, 134, 145, 192, n218; dominance of, 116
Sinhalese ethnic group, 20, 28, 52–3, 63, 122, 140; as majority population, 124; dominance of, 18
Sinhalese farmers, privileging of, 59
Sinhalese nationalism, 49, 53
Sinhalisation, 135, 141
Sirisena, Maithripala, l1, 62, 84, 93, 121, 143, 146, 149, 168, 169, 180, 192, 193, 196–7, n221, n222, n230; elected president, 20–1; election campaign of, 187–8
small states, 16, 173–97, n210; agency of, 11
Sobitha, Maduluwawe, 68
Social Architects, The, n204; report, 122
social gatherings, permissions required for, 138
social media, use of, 90; for hate campaigns, 129–30
social welfare schemes, 50–1
Solheim, Eric, 110
Somalia, Western intervention in, 80
Sooka, Yasmin, 79, n202, n212
Soulbury constitution, 51–2, n206
South Asian Association for Regional Cooperation (SAARC), 70, 74

Index | 275

South Sudan, 115, 189
Southern Expressway, 35
Southphalia, use of term, 192–3
sovereignty, 5, 115, 121, 128, 178, 192
spatial penetration, 139–42
special economic zones, 33
Sri Lanka: as Wonder of Asia, 148, 175; declared primacy of Buddhism in, 52; economic growth in, 34; in international community, 5–6; per capita income in, 30; perception of corruption in, 34; public debt of, 30; seen as development miracle, 51 see also Government of Sri Lanka (GoSL)
Sri Lanka Campaign for Peace and Justice 156–7, 164, 169
Sri Lanka Committee for Solidarity with Palestine, 48
Sri Lanka Free Media Group, members attacked, 167
Sri Lanka Monitoring Mission (SLMM), 107, 167, n222
Sri Lanka Muslim Congress (SLMC), 43, 44, 45
'Sri Lankan model', 3, 15, 27, 183
Sri Lankans in UN peacekeeping forces, 197
Standing International Forum on Ethnic Conflict, Development and Human Rights (SIFEC), 98
state: non-Westphalian models of, 19; post-colonial, 192, 193; unipolar, 58–60, 62–5; unitary, 13, 47–69; Westphalian model of, 4, 5 see also small states
state of emergency, 192
State Security Agency (South Africa), 91

statistics for conflict deaths, 18, 19, 25–6
Steve Hedges and Majority Group LLC, 84
Stockholm International Peace Research Institute (SIPRI), 178
streets, renaming of, 139
strikes, 149; in Tamil Nadu, 157; of nurses, 150
Structural Adjustment Programs, 103
Subramanian, S., *This Divided Island*, 140
Suddhodana, King, n218
Sugitharaja, Subramaniyam, 173
suicide, of small farmers, 68
suicide bombers, pioneered by LTTE, n198
Sultana, Gulbin, 133
Sunday Times, report on lobbying firms, 84–6
Supreme Court, 57, 87
Suresh, V., n213
Swamy, Subramanian, n212
Swiss Council of Eelam Tamils, 91
Swiss Foundation for Mine Action, 104
Switzerland meeting, statement of, 45–6
Syria, foreign policy decisions regarding, 189

Taiwan, 27
Tajikistan, 88
Tamil *Nayakkar* monarchs, 128
Tamil Arasu Kadchi (TAK), 45
Tamil diaspora, 86, 89–91, 125, 144, 148, 179, 181, n202, n209, n210, n226; in USA, 110; investment by, 151; lobbying by, 182; surveillance of, 90; viewed as threat, 89
Tamil Eelam, 13, 115, 174, n228

Tamil Eelam Liberation Organisation (TELO), 45, 115, n217
Tamil Eelam Supporters Oganisation (TESO), 157
Tamil Makkal Viduthalai Puhkal (TMVP), 45, 107, n207
Tamil Nadu, 98, 124, n207; strike in, 157
Tamil National Alliance (TNA), 28, 40, 43, 44, 45, 92, 146, 147, 172, 174, 179; councillors go into hiding, 43
Tamil United Liberation Front (TULF), 45, 105, 115
Tamil websites, blocking of, 91
Tamils, 28, 29, 53, 108, 115, 124, 163, 164, 170, 176, 193, 197, n203, n209–10; 1993 killings of, 2; attacks on, 19; death toll of, 185, 196; demand for self-determination, 63; evicted from homes, 122; exodus of, n224; fishermen, targeting of, 141–2; grievances of, 12 (non-acceptance of, 42); lack of voice, 41–2; memorials not permitted for, 41; pogrom against, n198; recognition for the dead and missing, 44; registration of travellers, 35–6; rights of, 22 *see also* India, Tamils in, *and* Tamil diaspora
Tamils Against Genocide, 91
teachers, required to do military-style training, 150
Temple of Tooth, Kandy, n198
Terrorism Investigation Division (TID), 90
terrorist, use of term, 14–15, 24
Thailand, 93
Thein Sein, 183
Thera, Madille Pagnaloka, 122

Thompson Advisory Group, 85, n222
Tibet, 27, 184
Timor-Leste, independence of, 115
Tiruchelvam, Neelan, n201
Tokyo Donor Conference on Reconstruction and Development of Sri Lanka, 101
torture, 166, 179, 190, 197, n223 *see also* freedom from torture
Torture Victims Protection Act (USA), 91
tourism, 32; involving gaming, 148 *see also* war tourism
transition, 22, 193
transitional justice, 155, 168, 193, 194
Transnational Government of Tamil Eelam (TGTE), 13, 46, 90, n200, n212
Transparency International, 33–4, 95
TRIAL organisation, 157
Trincomalee: killing of students in (Trinco Five), 158, 173; port development in, 186
Truth and Reconciliation Commission, promotion of, 225
truth commissions, 71
tsunami (December 2004), 96, 101, 102–3, 117, 118–19, 195; relief effort, 106–7, n211, n213, n215 (involvement of US Marines in, 110), response to, 96
Tsunami Affected Areas Program, 101
Turkey, 93

Ukraine, 191
Umar ibn al-Khattab, n200
United Nations (UN), 14, 20, 70, 92, 104, 148, 155, 165, 175, 180, 181; advisory panel,

Index | 277

proposal of, 38; assistance rejected by Sri Lankan government, 9; computer system, external surveillance of, 107; demonstrations against, 10; diplomacy of, 181; false allegations against, 107; gagging order on agencies of, 120; morale hit by killing of staff members, 113; protests against, 76; regime non-cooperation with, 15; Report of the Secretary General's Panel of Experts, 78–9; report on atrocities, 20; rescue convoy, 110; resistance to interference of, 37; *Rights Up Front* report, 113, n216; threats against staff, 109; withdraws staff from Vanni, 107–8 *see also* UN system
UN Charter, 77, 81, 82
UN Children's Fund (UNICEF), 71, 104
UN Committee on Measures to Eliminate International Terrorism, 38
UN Convention Against Corruption, 34
UN Development Programme (UNDP), 98
UN High Commissioner for Human Rights, 69, 74, 92, 161, 162, 171
UN High Commissioner for Refugees (UNHCR), 25, 98, 109, 159, 189–90, n229; census of IDPs, 120
UN Human Rights Commission, 167
UN Human Rights Council (UNHRC), 16, 24–5, 39, 40, 64, 69, 73, 74, 76, 77, 82–3, 111, 144–5, 147, 155, 156, 157, 159, 12, 163, 164, 179;

182, 185, 188, 194, n210, n222, n226; criticism of, 174; GoSL sponsored resolution debated, 73, 87; lobbying of, 179; mandate of, 160; petition presented to, 158; Resolution 19/2, 160; Resolution 22/1, 160; Resolution 25/1, 91–2; Resolution 30/1, 194; resolution of 2014, 160–1, 229; resolution of 2015, 168, 171
UN Independent Review Panel, 26, 39
UN Mission in South Sudan, n229
UN Office for Project Services (UNOPS), 72, 109
UN Panel of Experts, 26, 87, 91, 111, 155, 174, 181, n198, n202
UN Security Council, 111–12, 180, 182, 190; debate on protection of civilians, 75; lobbying of, 159
UN Special Advisory Panel, 77
UN Special Rapporteur on Freedom of Religion or Belief, 124
UN system, 5, 6, 8, 12, 71–2, 99, 110, 111, 158, 159, 160, 176, 182, 195, n202 (failures of, 16; Sri Lanka's contribution to, 2 (in peacekeeping forces, 3))
UN Universal Periodic Review, 41
UN Working Group on Enforced and Involuntary Disappearances, 14, 167
Union of Soviet Socialist Republics (USSR), 97, 99, 114
unipolar command development, 60–5
unipolarity, use of term, n199
United Bhikku Front (UBF), 65
United Kingdom (UK), 93, 156, 165, 185, 194; aid to Sri Lanka, reduction of, 178; Tamil community in, 89

United National Party (UNP), 2, 34, 43, 65, 105, 127
United People's Freedom Party (UPFA), 43, 49, 179
United States of America (USA), 13, 23, 101, 114, 156, 160, 165, 175, 179, 185, 194, n200, n216; acquisition of oil tank farm in Trinco, 186; foreign policy of, 181–2; lobbying of, 159; march on Colombo embassy of, 76; military aid from, ended, 178; resolution at Human Rights Council, 155; withdraws development aid, 186
US Marines, involvement in tsunami emergency, 110
US Pacific Command (PACOM), 110, n209, n215
US Senate Committee on Foreign Relations, report on Sri Lanka, 185–6
Universal Declaration of Human Rights, 8, 165
Universal Periodic Review, 173
University Teachers for Human Rights (Jaffna) (UTHR (J)), 108–9, 177
Uthuru Wasanthaya, 41
Uvin, Peter, *Aiding Violence*, 100
Uyghur American Association, n226–7

Vadamarachchi region, 19
Vamsa tradition of historiography, 52
Vanni, 25, 106, 107; agencies and NGOs removed from, 108, 117; assault on, 23–4; chieftaincies of, 19; civilians trapped in, 159; death toll in, 181; evacuation of civilians from, n215–16; military operations in, 26, 39, 79, 113, 140, 188
Vavuniya, 103; demonstration in, 139; insecurity in, 104
Victory Day, renamed to Remembrance Day, 193
Vieira de Mello, Sérgio, 113
Vietnam, 180
Vigo, Julian, n216
Vijaya, Prince, 127
village names, changed to Sinhalese names, 122
violence: concept of, 17; 'meaningless', 17
Voice of America, 186

Waduge, Shenali, 102–3
war crimes, 20, 29, 64, 86, 91, 92, 145, 147, 156, 159, 160, 182, n212, n220, n230; investigation of, 69, 75; issue of extra-territoriality, 195; of GoSL, 157, 160, 163, 170, 181; of LTTE, 160, 163, n210
'war for peace', 183
war monuments, erection of, 140–1
war on terror, 15, 24, 101, 177, 181, 185, 188
war tourism, 139–42
Washington Consensus, 5
Watchlist on Trafficking in Persons, 84
Weerawansa, Wimal, 77
Weiss, Gordon, *The Cage*, 75, 181
Welikala, Asanga, 192–3
Whaley, David, 107, 163, n229
White Flag incident, 159
Wickrematunge, Lasantha, funeral of, 95
Wickremesinghe, Ranil, 49, 105, 126–7, 146, 192, n198, n223
WikiLeaks, 75, 91, 113, n202, n207, n223

Wilson, Megan, 86
women: attend LLRC hearings, 152–3; beating of, n218; livelihoods of, banned by military, 134; Muslim dress code of, 132; protests of, 143 (over land requisition, n219)
Working Group on Enforced or Involuntary Disappearances, 48
World Bank, 103, 106, 107, 114, 149, 165, 182, n217; reduces funding to Sri Lanka, 183
World Food Programme (WFP), 109
World Press Freedom Prize, 173
World Tourism Organization, conference of, 195

Xavier, Sherine, 196; *The Scars of Tomorrow*, 193–4
xenophobia, of media, 152

Yang Jiechi, 27, 81
Yi Xianliang, 188, n228
Young, Miriam, 159
Young Men's Christian Association (YMCA), 96
Yugoslavia, 100